MASTERPLOTS
FIFTEEN-VOLUME
COMBINED EDITION

Volume Fifteen
U.S.A.-Zule

MASTERPLOTS

15-Volume Combined Edition
FIFTEEN HUNDRED AND TEN
Plot-Stories and Essay-Reviews
from the
WORLD'S FINE LITERATURE

Edited by
FRANK N. MAGILL

Story Editor
DAYTON KOHLER

VOLUME FIFTEEN — U.S.A.-ZULE

SALEM PRESS
INCORPORATED
NEW YORK

This work also appears under the title of
MASTERPIECES OF WORLD LITERATURE IN DIGEST FORM

U. S. A.

Type of work: Novel
Author: John Dos Passos (1896-   )
Type of plot: Social chronicle
Time of plot: 1900-1935
Locale: The United States
First published: 1930, 1932, 1936

Principal characters:
FAINY McCREARY (MAC), a labor organizer
JANEY WILLIAMS, a private secretary
JOE WILLIAMS, her brother
J. WARD MOOREHOUSE, a public relations executive
ELEANOR STODDARD, an interior decorator
CHARLEY ANDERSON, an airplane manufacturer
RICHARD ELLSWORTH SAVAGE, Moorehouse's assistant
EVELINE HUTCHINS, Eleanor Stoddard's partner
ANNE ELIZABETH TRENT (DAUGHTER), a relief worker
BEN COMPTON, a radical
MARY FRENCH, a labor worker
MARGO DOWLING, a movie star

Critique:

U. S. A. is a collective novel in the sense that it deals with a great variety of characters, each moving upon his own social level, but all presented within the limits of a single novel. The result is a complete cross-section of American life covering the political, social, and economic history of the United States from the beginning of the century to the depression-ridden, war-threatened thirties. In addition to the life stories of his people, Dos Passos employs three technical devices to make his survey more complete: the Newsreel, quotations from newspapers, speeches, popular songs; the Camera Eye, brief impressionistic sketches from the author's own life; and biographies of public figures, such as radicals, inventors, and statesmen typical of their times. No other writer has attempted a wider panoramic view of our national life. The separate titles of Dos Passos' trilogy are *The 42nd Parallel, Nineteen Nineteen,* and *The Big Money.*

The Story:

The Spanish-American War was over. Politicians with mustaches said that America was now ready to lead the world.

Mac McCreary was a printer for a fly-by-night publisher in Chicago. Later he worked his way to the West Coast. There he got work as a printer in Sacramento and married Maisie Spencer, who could never understand his radical views. They quarreled and he went to Mexico to work in the revolutionary movement there.

Janey Williams, growing up in Washington, D. C., became a stenographer. She was always ashamed when her sailor brother, Joe, showed up, and even more ashamed of him after she became secretary to J. Ward Moorehouse. Of all Moorehouse's female acquaintances, she was the only one who never became his mistress.

J. Ward Moorehouse's boyish manner and blue eyes were the secret of his success. They attracted Annabelle Strang, the wealthy nymphomaniac he later divorced. Gertrude Staple, his second wife, helped to make him a prominent public relations expert. His shrewdness made him an ideal man for government service in France during World

War I. After the war he became one of the nation's leading advertising executives.

Because Eleanor Stoddard hated the sordid environment of her childhood her delicate, arty tastes led her naturally into partnership with Eveline Hutchins in the decorating business, and eventually to New York and acquaintanceship with J. Ward Moorehouse. In Europe with the Red Cross during the war, she lived with Moorehouse. Back in New York in the twenties she used her connections in shrewd fashion and became engaged to a member of the Russian nobility.

Charley Anderson had been an aviator in the war. A successful invention and astute opportunism made him a wealthy airplane manufacturer. He married a wife who had little sympathy for his interest in mechanics. In Florida, after a plane crash, he met Margo Dowling, an actress. Charley Anderson's series of drunks ended in a grade crossing accident.

Joe Williams was a sailor who had been on the beach in Buenos Aires. In Norfolk he met Della, who urged him to give up seafaring and settle down. Unable to hold a job, he shipped out again and almost lost his life when the ship he was on was sunk by a German submarine. When Joe got his third mate's license, he and Della were married. He was ill in the East Indies, arrested in New York for not carrying a draft card, and torpedoed once more off Spain. Della was unfaithful to him. Treated coldly the few times he looked up his sister Janey, he shipped for Europe once more. One night in St. Nazaire he attacked a huge Senegalese who was dancing with a girl he knew. His skull was crushed when he was hit over the head with a bottle.

Teachers encouraged Dick Savage in his literary talents. During his teens he worked at a summer hotel and there he slept with a minister's wife who shared his taste in poetry. A government official paid his way through Harvard, where Dick cultivated his estheticism

and mild snobbery before he joined the Norton-Harjes ambulance service and went to Europe. There some of his letters about the war came to the attention of censorship officials and he was shipped back to the United States. His former sponsor got him an officer's commission and he returned to France. In Italy he met a relief worker named Anne Elizabeth Trent, who was his mistress for a time. When he returned to the United States, he became an idea man for Moorehouse's advertising agency.

Eveline Hutchins, who had a small artistic talent, became Eleanor Stoddard's partner in a decorating establishment in New York. All her life she tried to escape from boredom through sensation. Beginning with the Mexican artist who was her first lover, she had a succession of affairs. In France, where she was Eleanor's assistant in the Red Cross, she married a shy young soldier named Paul Johnson. Later she had a brief affair with Charley Anderson. Dissatisfied, she decided at last that life was too dull for endurance and died from an overdose of sleeping pills.

Anne Elizabeth Trent, known as Daughter, was the child of moderately wealthy Texans. In New York she met Webb Cruthers, a young anarchist. One day, seeing a policeman kick a woman picketer in the face, Daughter attacked him with her fists. Her night in jail disturbed her father so much that she returned to Texas and worked in Red Cross canteens. Later she went overseas. There she met Dick Savage. Pregnant, she learned he had no intention of marrying her. In Paris she went on a drunken spree with a French aviator and died with him in a plane crash.

Benny Compton was the son of Jewish immigrants. After six months in jail for making radical speeches, he worked his way west through Canada. In Seattle he and other agitators were beaten by deputies. Benny returned East. One day police broke up a meeting where he was speaking. On his twenty-third birthday Benny went to Atlanta to serve a ten-year sentence. Released after the war, he lived for a time with Mary French, a fellow traveler in the party.

Mary French spent her childhood in Trinidad, where her father, a physician, did charity work among the native miners. Mary, planning to become a social worker, spent her summers at Jane Addams' Hull House. She went to Washington as secretary to a union official, and later worked as a union organizer in New York City. There she took care of Ben Compton after his release from Atlanta. While working with the Sacco-Vanzetti Committee she fell in love with Don Stevens, a fellow party member. Summoned to Moscow with a group of party leaders, Stevens returned to New York with a wife assigned to him by the party. Mary went back to her committee work for laboring men's relief.

Margo Dowling grew up in a rundown house in Rockaway, Long Island, with her drunken father and Agnes, her father's mistress. At last Agnes left her lover and took Margo with her. In New York Agnes became the common-law wife of an actor named Frank Mandeville. One day, while drunk, Mandeville raped the girl. Margo ran off to Cuba with Tony, an effeminate Cuban guitar player, whom she later deserted. She was a cheerful companion for Charley Anderson, who gave her a check for five thousand dollars on his deathbed. In Hollywood she met Sam Margolies, a successful producer, who made a star of her.

Jobless and hungry, a young hitchhiker stood by the roadside. Overhead droned a plane in which people of the big money rode the skyways. Below the hitchhiker with empty belly thumbed cars speeding by. The haves and the have-nots—that was America in the depression thirties.

UTOPIA

Type of work: Humanistic treatise
Author: Sir Thomas More (1478-1535)
Time: Reign of Henry VII of England
Locale: Antwerp, England, Utopia
First published: 1516

> *Principal characters:*
> THOMAS MORE, the author
> PETER GILES, a citizen of Antwerp and a friend of Thomas More
> RAPHAEL HYTHLODAY, a traveler and acquaintance of Peter Giles

How to make a better world for men to live in has fascinated the minds of thinkers in every age. From Plato to the present day, a span of almost two and a half millenniums, men have been thinking and writing about what the world would be like if men could create an earthly paradise. One of the most famous pieces of such thought and writing is Sir Thomas More's *Utopia,* a work so famous in Western civilization that its title has come to be symbolic in our minds for any idealized state. Originally written in Latin, the international language of medieval and Renaissance Europe, the book was widely read, and as early as 1551 a translation into English was made by Ralph Robinson, a London goldsmith.

The book is in two parts, with the second part, curiously enough, written first, in 1515, and the introductory half written in the following year. The book begins with a narrative framework in which More tells how he traveled to Antwerp on a royal mission and there met Peter Giles, a worthy citizen of Antwerp, who in turn introduced him to Raphael Hythloday, whose name means literally in Greek "a talker of nonsense." Hythloday proved to be more than a mere mariner, for in his conversation he appeared to More to be a man of ripe wisdom and rare experience. The fictional Hythloday was supposedly a companion of Amerigo Vespucci when that worthy was supposed to have made his voyages to America. It was on one of his voyages with Vespucci that Hythloday, according to his own account, discovered the fabled land of Utopia, somewhere in the oceans near the Western hemisphere.

Actually, the first part of *Utopia* does not deal with the legendary island; in it Hythloday tells how, during the reign of King Henry VII, he visited England, conversed with Cardinal Morton, and suggested to that Churchman, who was Henry VII's chancellor, some reforms which might benefit England. Among the reforms the fictional Hythloday suggested were the abolishment of the death penalty for theft, the prevention of gambling, less dependence upon the raising of sheep for wool, the disuse of mercenary soldiers, cheaper prices for all commodities, and an end to the enclosure of the common lands for the benefit of great and wealthy landlords. Although Cardinal Morton is made to listen intently to Hythloday's suggestions, More introduces a lawyer who objects that Hythloday's reforms could not be undertaken and that they would not be deemed desirable by anyone who knew the history and customs of England.

In the first part of his *Utopia,* More is obviously pointing out some of the social and economic evils in sixteenth-century European life. More than that, he is suggesting that only an outsider can see the faults with an objective eye. The introduction of the lawyer's objections, which are cut short by Cardinal Morton, suggest also that More discerned in sixteenth-century society persons who opposed reform and who sought reasons for doing so. Part one of the *Utopia* is More's way of preparing the reader for the section in which his ideal realm is delineated.

In the second part, Hythloday expounds at length about the culture of the mythical land of Utopia, which he had visited during his travels. Hythloday describes Utopia as an island kingdom which is crescent shaped and about five hundred miles in perimeter, separated from other lands by a man-made channel constructed by its founder, the fabulous King Utopus, who saw that the Utopian experiment, if it were to succeed, must be isolated and protected from the encroachments of warlike and predatory neighbors. The island is divided into fifty-four shires, or counties, each with its own town, no town more than a day's walking journey from its neighbors. The central city, Amaurote, is the capital, the seat of the prince who is the island's nominal ruler.

The government of Utopia is relatively simple and largely vested in older men, in patriarchal fashion. Each unit of thirty families is ruled by one man chosen by election every year. Each ten groups of families elect a member of the island council. This council in turn elects the prince, who serves throughout his lifetime unless deposed because of tyranny. The council meets every three days to take up matters of consequence to the people, and no decision is made on the same day the problem is advanced, lest undue haste cause mistakes.

It is not in government alone that More introduces suggestions for reform in his *Utopia*. In this ideal state every one works, each man having a trade or craft, except the unusually talented who are selected for training and service in the academy of learning. The work day is six hours long, with the time divided equally between the morning and the afternoon. Each person spends a two-year period working as a farmer in the shire outside the city in which he resides. Since everyone works, there is more than enough food and all other commodities for the inhabitants. All goods are community-owned, with each person guarding what is given him for the benefit of the commonwealth. The tastes of the people are simple; no one, having enough for himself, desires to have more than his fellows. Even the prince of Utopia is

designated only by the symbol of a sheaf of grain, symbol of plenty. Each person is garbed in durable clothing of leather, linen, or wool. Jewelry is given to children to play with, so that everyone associates such baubles with childishness. Gold and silver are despised, being used for chamber pots, chains for slaves, and the marks of criminal conviction.

In the dialogue Sir Thomas More interjects some objections to the communal idea, but this is the only point on which he seems to have reservations; yet even on this point Hythloday's answers to his objections satisfy him.

Violence, bloodshed, and vice, says Hythloday, have been done away with in Utopia. Lest bloodshed of any kind corrupt the people, slaves are required to slaughter the cattle. Dicing and gambling are unknown. The people choose instead to labor for recreation in their gardens, improve their homes, attend humanistic lectures, enjoy music, and converse profitably with one another. The sick are provided for in spacious hospitals erected in each quarter of each city. In the event of a painful and incurable illness, the priests consult with the patient and encourage him to choose death administered painlessly by the authorities. Although no one is required to do so, everyone eats in mess halls where slaves prepare the meals under the supervision of the wives of the family group. At mealtime young and old eat together, except for children under five; and enlightening, pleasant conversation is encouraged.

The Utopian criminal is enslaved, rather than put to death, as he was in sixteenth-century England. Adultery is regarded as a crime and punished by slavery. Marriage for love is encouraged, but also prudence in selecting a mate. Males must be twenty-two and women eighteen before marriage is permitted. The welfare of the family is a state matter, since the family is the basic unit of the Utopian state. The people are anxious for the commonwealth to be rich, for the Utopians buy off their enemies and use their wealth to hire foreign mercenary soldiers; they hope in this manner to encourage potential enemies to murder one another.

The Utopians are described as a religious people who practice toleration almost unknown in Catholic Tudor England. Some are Christians; others worship God in other ways. Atheism and militant sectarianism are alike forbidden.

Two points should be made in connection with Sir Thomas More's work. One is that his borrowings from Plato and other earlier authors did not prevent him from adding much that was his own in theory and practice. The second point is that in the four and a half centuries since the writing of *Utopia* some of the author's ideas have been put into effect —unlikely as they may have appeared to his contemporaries. We may never in human society come to the Utopian ideal, but surely we are closer than men were in the sixteenth century. Perhaps some of the credit should go to Sir Thomas More.

VANESSA

Type of work: Novel
Author: Hugh Walpole (1884-1941)
Type of plot: Historical chronicle
Time of plot: Late nineteenth and early twentieth centuries·
Locale: England
First published: 1933

Principal characters:
VANESSA PARIS, daughter of Adam Paris
BENJIE, her cousin and lover
TOM, Benjie's son
SALLY, daughter of Vanessa and Benjie
ELLIS, Vanessa's husband

Critique:

Vanessa, the last novel in the Herries chronicle, brings the family to the 1930's. Like its three predecessors, Vanessa is concerned with many people and many years, and the multiplicity of characters becomes necessarily more marked and confusing. Although many readers of the novel are lost in trying to follow the fortunes of so many descendants of the earlier Herries, Walpole does accomplish very well what appears to be a chief aim —to show that the strength of the Herries family is a strength of England and that its weakness is a national defect.

The Story:

Vanessa was fifteen when her grandmother, Judith Paris, died. At the funeral Adam, her sincere but unpolished father, made a speech which was admired only by Vanessa and her mother, Margaret. Adam loved his mother well and spoke with too much sincerity. His numerous relatives would rather have heard a eulogy of the proud family of Herries.

At the funeral Vanessa noticed everyone, and her beauty made even the most distant relatives notice her. She had special interest, however, for her cousin Benjie. Already she knew she loved him. Benjie was a rascal who could not fit in well with his haughty family. He was capable of hard work and common sense for a while, but he had sporadic fits of wildness. Some of his rela-

tives believed that no good could come from Benjie's heritage. His uncle had killed his father. One grandfather had committed suicide. The other one was living out a mad dotage.

Vanessa also noticed hesitant, stiff Ellis Herries, her distant cousin. Ellis managed to remark that it was a nice day. As soon as Vanessa agreed, she ran out— to meet Benjie.

Adam did not like to have her go walking with Benjie, even though Benjie was personable. Benjie kissed Vanessa, however, and she promised to marry him when she grew up. Vanessa was so good and beautiful that Benjie had qualms about such a promise. He told her the truth about his character and his wildness, and he attacked her faith in God. But Vanessa resolved to hold fast to her promise.

In 1880 Vanessa became engaged to Benjie. Still uneasy about his unworthiness, Benjie agreed that no one should know of the engagement and that they should not meet for two years. Then if they still wanted to do so, they would be married.

In the meantime Vanessa went to London to stay with her city cousins. Dressed in fashionable clothes, lovely Vanessa soon became an admired belle. She had many proposals of marriage, the most insistent from her cousin Ellis. Ellis was good and sober, already a respected financier. But Vanessa thought only of Benjie.

Vanessa returned home to Fell House to care for her ailing father and wait for the two years to end. Then, in 1882, Fell House burned down and Adam perished in the blaze. Too distraught to think of marriage at that time, Vanessa put Benjie off. Several weeks later she went to The Fortress to stay with Elizabeth, Benjie's mother, and to await the return of her fiancé. When he did come back, Vanessa knew that something had happened.

She soon learned the story. Sometime before Benjie had become acquainted with the Halliday family and had been attracted to their daughter Marion. After Adam Paris died, he went to visit the Hallidays. Following an evening of gaiety, he went upstairs to bed. In his room he found Marion, who was waiting for him at the urging of her mother. Marion became pregnant, and she and Benjie were married. Without bitterness Vanessa wished him a happy marriage and went back to London.

At the age of twenty-six, honored as the reigning beauty of London society, Vanessa finally decided to give in to Ellis and be kind to him. So Ellis and Vanessa were married, and Vanessa became the great lady of highly fashionable Hill House.

One day, quite by accident, she saw Benjie and his son Tom at the Jubilee Celebration. She did not talk with him, but she did learn that Marion had left Benjie for another man. After struggling with her inclinations for some time, she met Benjie again and visited with him as an old friend.

Meanwhile it was becoming more and more impossible for her to live with Ellis. His mind was weakening rapidly and he had delusions of persecution. To the outward eye, however, he still was the sober financier. One night he locked himself and Vanessa in their room and announced that he intended to cut her throat and then his own. She talked him out of the notion, but she was afraid of

him from that time on.

Then Ellis brought in two elderly cousins to take charge of the house and to spy on Vanessa. As his next step he engaged an obliging doctor to interview his wife. Before Vanessa was quite aware of what was happening, she learned that she was to be confined in an asylum for the insane. In her fear and helplessness she turned to Benjie for help. At last, when both were nearing forty and without benefit of marriage, Vanessa and Benjie went away to live together.

Tom, Benjie's son, and Vanessa became great friends, and for a time she lived a happy life at The Fortress. Gradually Benjie's absences from home became less frequent, and sometimes Vanessa would accompany him on his week-long rambles. On one occasion they were caught in a storm. Much upset and exhausted, he and Vanessa found shelter in a farmhouse, and there among strangers their daughter Sally was born.

But the household at The Fortress was soon broken up. Ellis' mind gave way completely, and he could amuse himself only by playing with toys. He cried much of the time for Vanessa, until it seemed that he could not live long without her. At last Vanessa took Sally to London and vowed she would stay with Ellis until he died.

Ironically, Ellis became stronger and better, and for years Benjie could not see Vanessa. In fact, Vanessa died before Ellis. At her deathbed Benjie and Ellis met without rancor.

The rest of the numerous Herries family were all stolid, respectable people, still pillars of Victorian rectitude. Only Benjie and Sally were free and untrammeled. Sally expected to marry Arnold Young, and even became his mistress for a year. But Arnold's mother objected to the marriage. Benjie's reputation was bad, and Sally herself was illegitimate. At last Arnold married another woman.

Benjie continued his irregular life. In South Africa he had lost an arm fighting the Boers. In World War I, in spite of being over sixty years old, he served with the Russians. At the age of seventy he was still brown of skin and spare of body. Sally, too, became respectable and redeemed herself in the eyes of her relatives. At a social gathering she met a blind French veteran who was working for the League of Nations in Berlin. She married him and went to Berlin to aid the cause of international peace. From that time on she rarely saw her father or any other members of the Herries family.

Only Benjie, of all the Herries, was still unconventional. After he was seventy, he bought a caravan and with one manservant lived a gipsy life. He intended to spend his last days going to fairs and visiting farm folk. Faithfully he did his setting up exercises and took cold showers out of doors. The other Herries always said that he was truly the great-grandson of that Francis Herries who married Mirabell Starr, the gipsy—lusty old Rogue Herries of whom the family was now half ashamed, half proud.

VANITY FAIR

Type of work: Novel
Author: William Makepeace Thackeray (1811-1863)
Type of plot: Social satire
Time of plot: Early nineteenth century
Locale: England and Europe
First published: 1847-1848

Principal characters:
BECKY SHARP, an adventuress
AMELIA SEDLEY, her friend
JOSEPH SEDLEY (JOS), Amelia's brother
RAWDON CRAWLEY, Becky's husband
MISS CRAWLEY, Rawdon's wealthy aunt
OLD SIR PITT CRAWLEY, Rawdon's father
YOUNG SIR PITT CRAWLEY, Rawdon's brother
GEORGE OSBORNE, Amelia's husband
CAPTAIN WILLIAM DOBBIN, Amelia's friend

Critique:

Vanity Fair, the best known of Thackeray's works, has justly joined the ranks of the classics, for in it Thackeray has created characters as great as any in English literature. Most of his people are not good people, but then they were not intended to be. Thackeray shows that goodness often goes hand in hand with stupidity and folly, that cleverness is often knavery. A cynical story, this novel was intended to expose social hypocrisy and sham. Although Thackeray was frankly moralistic, his moral does not in any way overshadow a magnificent novel or the life-like characters he created.

The Story:

Becky Sharp and Amelia Sedley became good friends while they were students at Miss Pinkerton's School for girls. It was proof of Amelia's good, gentle nature that she took as kindly as she did to her friend, who was generally disliked by all the other girls. Amelia overlooked as much as she could the evidences of Becky's selfishness.

After the two girls had finished their education at the school, Becky accompanied her friend to her home for a short visit. There she first met Joseph Sedley, Amelia's older brother Jos, who was home on leave from military service in India. Jos was a shy man, unused

to women, and certainly to women as designing and flirtatious as Becky. His blundering and awkward manners did not appeal to many women, but Becky was happy to overlook these faults when she compared them with his wealth and social position. Amelia innocently believed that her friend had fallen in love with her brother, and she discreetly tried to further the romance.

To this end she arranged a party at Vauxhall, at which Becky and Jos, along with Amelia and her admirer, George Osborne, were present. There was a fifth member of the group, Captain Dobbin, a tall, lumbering fellow, also in service in India. He had long been in love with Amelia, but he recognized how much more suitable for her was the dashing George Osborne. But all the maneuvering of the flirtatious Becky and the amiable Amelia was not sufficient to corner Jos, who drank too much punch and believed that he had made a silly figure of himself at the party. A day or so later a letter delivered to the Sedley household announced that Jos was ill and planned to return to India as soon as possible.

Since there was no longer any reason for Becky to remain with the Sedleys, she left Amelia, after many tears and kisses, to take a position as governess to two young girls at Queen's Crawley. The head of the household was Sir Pitt Crawley, a cantankerous old man renowned for his miserliness. Lady Crawley was an apathetic soul who lived in fear of her husband's unreasonable outbursts. Deciding that she would have nothing to fear from her timid mistress, Becky spent most of her time ingratiating herself with Sir Pitt and ignoring her pupils. Becky also showed great interest in Miss Crawley, a spinster aunt of the family, who was exceedingly wealthy. Miss Crawley paid little attention to Sir Pitt and his children, but she was fond of Rawdon Crawley, a captain in the army and a son of Sir Pitt by a previous marriage. So fond was she of her dashing young nephew that she supported him through school and paid all his gambling debts with hardly a murmur.

During Becky's stay, Miss Crawley visited Sir Pitt only once, at a time when Rawdon was also present. The handsome young dragoon soon fell prey to Becky's wiles and followed her about devotedly. Becky also took care to ingratiate herself with the holder of the purse strings. Miss Crawley found Becky witty and charming, and did not attempt to disguise her opinion that the little governess was worth all the rest of the Crawley household put together. And so Becky found herself in a very enviable position. Sir Pitt was obviously interested in her, as was his handsome son. Miss Crawley insisted that Becky accompany her back to London.

Becky had been expected to return to her pupils after only a short stay with Miss Crawley. But Miss Crawley was taken ill and she refused to allow anyone but her dear Becky to nurse her. Afterward there were numerous other excuses to prevent the governess from returning to her duties. Certainly Becky was not unhappy. Rawdon Crawley was a constant caller, and a devoted suitor for Becky's hand. When the news arrived that Lady Crawley had died, no great concern was felt by anyone. But a few days later Sir Pitt himself appeared, asking to see Miss Sharp. Much to Becky's surprise, the baronet threw himself at her feet and asked her to marry him. Regretfully, she refused his offer. She was already secretly married to Rawdon Crawley.

Following this disclosure, Rawdon and his bride left for a honeymoon at Brighton. Old Miss Crawley, chagrined and angry, took to her bed, changed her will, and cut off her nephew without a shilling. Sir Pitt raved with anger.

Amelia's marriage had also precipitated a family crisis. Her romance with George had proceeded with good wishes on both sides until Mr. Sedley, through some unfortunate business deals, lost most of his money. Then George's snobbish father ordered his son to break his engagement to a penniless woman. George, whose affection for Amelia was never stable, was inclined to accept this parental command. But Captain Dobbin, who saw with distress that Amelia was breaking her heart over George, finally prevailed upon the young man to go through with the marriage, regardless of his father's wishes. When the couple arrived in Brighton for their honeymoon, they found Rawdon and Becky living there happily in penniless extravagance.

Captain Dobbin also arrived in Brighton. He had agreed to act as intercessor with Mr. Osborne. But his hopes of reconciling father and son were shattered when Mr. Osborne furiously dismissed Captain Dobbin and took immediate steps to disown George. Captain Dobbin also brought the news that the army had been ordered to Belgium. Napoleon had landed from Elba. The Hundred Days had begun.

In Brussels the two couples met again. George Osborne was infatuated with Becky. Jos Sedley, now returned from India, and Captain Dobbin were also stationed in that city, Captain Dobbin in faithful attendance upon neglected Amelia. Everyone was waiting for the next move Napoleon would make, but in the meantime the gaiety of the Duke of Wellington's forces was widespread. The Osbornes and Crawleys attended the numerous balls. Becky, especially, made an impression upon military society and her coquetry extended with equal effect from general to private. The fifteenth of June, 1815, was a famous night in Brussels, for on that evening the Duchess of Richmond gave a tremendous ball. Amelia left the party early, broken-hearted at the attentions her husband was showing Becky. Shortly after she left, the men were given orders to march to meet the enemy. Napoleon had entered Belguim, and a great battle was impending.

As Napoleon's forces approached, fear and confusion spread through Brussels, and many of the civilians fled from the city. Not so Amelia or Becky. Becky was not alarmed, and Amelia refused to leave while George was in danger. She remained in the city some days before she heard that her husband had been killed. Rawdon returned safely from the battle of Waterloo. He and Becky spent a gay and triumphant season in Paris, where Becky's beauty and wit gained her a host of admirers. Rawdon was very proud of the son she bore him.

Amelia, too, had a child. She had returned to London almost out of her mind with grief, and only after her son was born did she show any signs of rallying.

When Becky grew bored with the pleasures of Paris, the Crawleys returned to London. There they rented a large home and proceeded to live well on nothing a year. By this time Becky was a past master at this art, and so they lived on a grander scale than Rawdon's small winnings at cards would warrant. Becky had become acquainted with the nobility of England, and had made a particular impression on rich old Lord Steyne. At last all society began to talk about young Mrs. Crawley and her elderly admirer. Fortunately Rawdon heard nothing of this ballroom and coffee house gossip.

Eventually, through the efforts of Lord Steyne, Becky achieved her dearest wish, presentation at Court. Presented along with her was the wife of the new Sir Pitt Crawley. The old man had died,

and young Sir Pitt, his oldest son and Rawdon's brother, had inherited the title. Since then friendly relations had been established between the two brothers. If Rawdon realized that his brother had also fallen in love with Becky, he gave no sign, and he accepted the money his brother gave him with good grace. But more and more he felt himself shut out from the gay life that Becky enjoyed. He spent much time with his son, for he realized that the child was neglected. Once or twice he saw young George Osborne, Amelia's son.

Amelia struggled to keep her son with her, but her pitiful financial status made it difficult to support him. Her parents had grown garrulous and morose with disappointment over their reduced circumstances. At length Amelia sorrowfully agreed to let Mr. Osborne take the child and rear him as his own. Mr. Osborn still refused to recognize the woman his son had married against his wishes, however, and Amelia rarely saw the boy.

Rawdon was now deeply in debt. When he appealed to Becky for money, she told him that she had none to spare. She made no attempt to explain the jewelry and other trinkets she bought. When Rawdon was imprisoned for a debt, he wrote and asked Becky to take care of the matter. She answered that she could not get the money until the following day. But an appeal to Sir Pitt brought about Rawdon's release, and he returned to his home to find Becky entertaining Lord Steyne. Not long afterward Rawdon accepted a post abroad, never to return to his unfaithful, designing wife.

Amelia's fortunes had now improved. When Jos Sedley returned home, he established his sister and father in a more pleasant home. Mrs. Sedley having died, Jos resolved to do as much as he could to make his father's last days happy. Captain Dobbin had returned from India and confessed his love for Amelia. Although she acknowledged him as a friend, she was not yet ready to accept his love. It was Captain Dobbin who went to Mr. Osborne and gradually succeeded in reconciling him to his son's wife. When Mr. Osborne died, he left a good part of his fortune to his grandson, appointing Amelia as the boy's guardian.

Amelia, her son, Captain Dobbin, and Jos Sedley took a short trip to the continent. This visit was perhaps the happiest time in Amelia's life. Her son was with her constantly, and Captain Dobbin was a devoted attendant. Eventually his devotion was to overcome her hesitation and they were to be married.

At a small German resort they encountered Becky once more. After Rawdon left her, Becky had been unable to live down the scandal of their separation. Leaving her child with Sir Pitt and his wife, she crossed to the continent. Since then she had been living with first one considerate gentleman and then another. When she saw the prosperous Jos, she vowed not to let him escape as he had before. Amelia and Jos greeted her in a friendly manner, and only Captain Dobbin seemed to regard her with distrust. He tried to warn Jos about Becky, but Jos was a willing victim of her charms.

Becky traveled with Jos wherever he went. Although she could not get a divorce from Rawdon, Jos treated her as his wife, and in spite of Captain Dobbin's protests he took out a large insurance policy in her name. A few months later his family learned that he had died while staying with Becky at Aix-la-Chapelle. The full circumstances of his death were never established, but Becky came into a large sum of money from his insurance. She spent the rest of her life on the continent, where she assumed the role of the virtuous widow and won a reputation for benevolence and generosity.

VATHEK

Type of work: Novel
Author: William Beckford (1759-1844)
Type of plot: Romantic allegory
Time of plot: The past
Locale: Arabia
First published: 1786

Principal characters:

VATHEK, an Arabian sultan
GIAOUR, a magician and a prince of darkness
CARATHIS, Vathek's mother
EMIR FAKREDDIN, a noble prince
NOURONIHAR, his daughter
GULCHENROUZ, her betrothed

Critique:

Lovers of fantastic Arabian tales and Oriental romances will doubtless find *Vathek* more than satisfactory as a work of pure imagination. In addition, the influences of Voltaire and Chateaubriand lend deeper levels of meaning to make the book both an allegory and a work of social criticism.

The Story:

Vathek was an Arabian caliph whose reign had been marked by turbulence and unrest. A sensuous person, he had built five palaces, one devoted to the enjoyment of each of the five senses, and his particular fondness for food and women consumed much of his time. In addition to the gratification he found in the life of the senses, he tried also to master the sciences and the deep, unfathomable secrets of the world beyond. To this end he built a huge tower where he pursued his studies in astronomy and astrology. There Carathis, his mother, burnt refuse and live bodies to appease the dark powers.

One day Vathek got from a hideous, repulsive stranger some mysterious sabers bearing letters which the caliph was unable to decipher. He offered great rewards to anyone who could read them; but since the punishment for failure was also great, few accepted the offer. At last an old man appeared and read the inscriptions. But the next morning Vathek discovered that the inscriptions had changed to words of different import. From that time on the letters on the sabers changed daily.

Vathek sank into despair, unable to enjoy anything whatever. He begged the stranger to return and to explain the inscription to him, for he was sure that the letters were the key to the dark kingdom and the riches Vathek hoped to find there. The stranger, Giaour, finally reappeared. He told Vathek that only a sacrifice would put the powers in a receptive mood. On a journey with his court, Vathek managed to throw fifty young children into a chasm as victims for the bloodthirsty Giaour. Angered by his cruelty, his people began to hurl execrations at Vathek, but his guards returned him safely to his palace.

Carathis continued her own sacrifices in the tower, to the disgust and anger of the people, who more and more objected to Vathek's defiance of Mahomet and the Moslem creed. Commanded by a message written on a mysterious piece of parchment, Vathek and his court set out on a pilgrimage in search of the mountains of Istakhar where the secrets of the dark world would be revealed to him.

On the way they met the messengers of Emir Fakreddin, a deeply religious prince. For some time Vathek was Fakreddin's guest. Although he loathed the prayers and religious ceremonies observed by his host, he was attracted to Fakreddin's daughter, the lovely Nouronihar. She and her cousin, Gulchenrouz, had been betrothed for a long time and their love had the approval of the emir and his people, who were pleased by the devotion of the young people to one another.

Nouronihar so attracted Vathek that he plotted to seize her by force. Fakreddin, already scandalized by Vathek's behavior, was informed of the plot. He and his court determined to outwit Vathek by administering a drug to the young lovers. When Vathek saw them in their deathlike trance, he was convinced that they were dead. Then Nouronihar and Gulchenrouz were secretly taken to a safe retreat and looked after by Fakreddin's servants. The young people, awaking, believed that they had really died and that they were now in Paradise.

One day, however, Vathek discovered Nouronihar, who had strayed from the hidden retreat. Yielding at last to his entreaties, she became the favorite of his harem. As Vathek and his wives and followers continued their journey, Nouronihar came to share her lord's ambition; she too wished to enjoy the pleasures of that strange other world. Like Vathek, she was willing to resort to anything, even to the most unscrupulous behavior, to realize their desires.

At last, after a long journey, the couple arrived at the mountains of Istakhar and entered the secret retreat of Eblis, dread lord of darkness. There they found all the beautiful and strange wealth they had so long desired. They were given permission to roam through the palace and to enjoy its treasures as much as they wished. In the vast domed hall of the palace they saw creatures whose hearts were continually devoured by fire. A like fate, they learned, was to be theirs as well, for they had sought knowledge that no mortal should know.

In the meantime, Carathis had been summoned to the abode of Eblis. Transported upon the back of an evil monster, she came at once to the mysterious palace and was overjoyed to view its secrets at last. Then, before the eyes of Vathek and Nouronihar, her heart caught fire and a consuming flame burst forth to punish her eternally for her crimes. A moment later flames began to burn in the hearts of Vathek and Nouronihar.

But Gulchenrouz and the fifty children whom Vathek had sacrificed were saved miraculously from death and carried to an earthly paradise. For them, life was perpetual happiness. Not having sought evil, they achieved the good life.

THE VENETIAN GLASS NEPHEW

Type of work: Novel
Author: Elinor Wylie (1885-1928)
Type of plot: Fantasy
Time of plot: 1782
Locale: Italy and France
First published: 1925

Principal characters:

PETER INNOCENT BON, an unworldly cardinal
VIRGINIO, his Venetian glass nephew
ROSALBA BERNI, called Sappho the Younger, Virginio's bride
MONSIEUR DE CHASTELNEUF, the Chevalier de Langeist
ANGELO QUERINI, philosopher and scholar
COUNT CARLO GOZZI, a writer of fairy tales

Critique:

Although Elinor Wylie is best remembered as a poet, she wrote during her brief career four fantastic and ironic novels unlike anything else in the whole range of American fiction. *The Venetian Glass Nephew* is the most completely realized of her novels, reflecting the qualities of her poetic imagination and style. A subtle fable of life and art, it marches with minuet grace and precision along its fantastic course. Virginio, the man of glass, and Rosalba, his flesh-and-blood bride, are more than figures in a romance which seems on the surface as slight and fragile as its spun-glass hero. Under the brittle brilliance of this novel there is a darkly personal note of mocking irony and almost silent grief. What might have been a slight work of artifice becomes through its underlying meaning a work of limited but authentic art. M. de Chastelneuf, idealist, cynic, and charlatan, is, of course, the famous Casanova under thin disguise.

The Story:

The heart of Peter Innocent Bon, cardinal prefect of the Congregation of the Propaganda, was filled with happiness that was almost childlike in its simplicity. After thirty years he was to see his native Venice once more, for brilliant, vain Pius VI, about to visit its lagoons and golden palaces, had named the aged cardinal a member of his suite.

Peter Innocent, in 1782, was in the eighty-first year of his age. A shy, mild man, he seldom appeared in the rich vestments of his office, but went inconspicuously about Rome in the gray-brown garb of the Franciscan Friars Minor, a robe suited to the humility of a follower of St. Francis.

Only one small regret marred Peter Innocent's pleasure as he viewed again the city of his youth. Pius was traveling in state, and he and many of his suite were accompanied by their nephews. Peter Innocent had no nephews; his brother had fathered only daughters and his sisters were in holy orders. Seeing the satisfaction other churchmen found in the company of their young kinsmen, he wished that he too might have enjoyed such comfort in his old age. But prayers, fasting, and pilgrimages to holy shrines had given him no nephew of his own, and the thought of parenthood would have been as foreign to the chastity of his mind as to that of his body.

During the Venetian visit Pius treated Peter Innocent with particular graciousness and asked him to represent the pontiff at the singing of a new cantata at the Incurabili. Listening to the music, the cardinal felt that its subject, the return of Tobias, was appropriate to his own situation.

As he left the Incurabili a hand touched his shoulder. He turned to find

Alvise Luna, the famous glass blower of Murano, at his elbow. Luna, whom the cardinal had known in earlier days, complained that he had fallen upon evil times. Willing to help his old friend, and not knowing that the man was under suspicion as a sorceror, Peter Innocent went with him to his cellar workshop. There he met a masked stranger whom Luna introduced as M. de Chastelneuf, Chevalier de Langeist. Peter Innocent was amazed when the men displayed their miraculous wares, a flying golden griffin, a glass stag that walked, glass birds that sang. When they asked if they might execute a commission for some bauble he had in mind, Peter Innocent reached a sudden decision. He asked modestly if they could make him a nephew such as he had always desired.

At Luna's warning glance Chastelneuf repressed the smile and the ribald comment that rose to his lips. Solemnly he assured the cardinal that such a work of art was difficult but not impossible. If he would return in three days he could see for himself the result of their labors.

Peter Innocent went to Luna's cellar three nights later. In a chamber scented with spices and incense Chastelneuf brought to life a figure of Venetian glass that lay upon a covered bier. The cardinal's nephew stood revealed as a handsome young man of nineteen or twenty, of complexion so fair as to seem translucent, with yellow hair as fine as spun glass. He was dressed completely in white and wore a strange ring of crystal. Peter Innocent baptized him Virginio.

The cardinal, as much concerned for his nephew's mind as he was for his person and his soul, decided to send him to Altichieri, there to study under the noble Angelo Querini, who had been Voltaire's friend. On his arrival Virginio met Rosalba Berni, Querini's lovely ward. Some thought her a descendant of Francesco Berni, the poet; others whispered the name of Cardinal de Bernis. At eighteen she was a prodigy of learning and a poet known officially as Sappho

the Younger. Virginio had never seen anyone so beautiful, and Rosalba was not so engrossed in the classics as to fail to notice how handsome he was. Scholarly Querini, always indulgent toward Rosalba, gave them his blessing when they announced their desire to wed.

Meanwhile Peter Innocent had gone to consult Count Carlo Gozzi, his long-time friend and a writer of fairy tales, on matters connected with Virginio's future. He found Chastelneuf closeted with the count; the chevalier had come to discuss the match between Rosalba and Virginio. To Peter Innocent and the count he explained the reason for his interest in the girl. Years before he had loved Caterina, Rosalba's mother, but because of his attachment to another woman he had callously relinquished his innocent beloved to Cardinal de Bernis, a notorious libertine. The cardinal had loved Caterina faithfully, however, and Rosalba was the daughter of that affectionate union. After the mother's death de Bernis had been summoned to Rome. Rosalba, already famous for her beauty and learning, had become the spoiled darling of French scholars and philosophers. After Voltaire's death Querini had become her guardian.

As Chastelneuf finished his story Rosalba and Virginio appeared, having driven from Altichieri in the chevalier's carriage. Seeing their happiness and youthful high spirits, Peter Innocent and his friends decided that the wedding should take place at once.

But the marriage of Virginio and Rosalba did not end as happily as one of Count Gozzi's fairy tales. Chastelneuf had seen to it that Virginio could play the part of a tender and devoted husband, but there had been no provision for the contingencies of daily association with a hoyden such as Rosalba had suddenly become. He splintered too easily; sometimes, after a hearty embrace, Rosalba found particles of glass in her palms. Games like hide-and-seek and blindman's-buff, in which she sportively delighted, were impossible for him. Privately, she and Virginio were unhappy, and, realizing their unhappiness, Peter Innocent, Querini, Chastelneuf, and Count Gozzi were wretched as well.

At last, after Rosalba had tried to end her misery by leaping into a bonfire, Chastelneuf made a desperate suggestion. If she were willing to endure the agony of fire, she could be changed into a woman of the finest Sèvres porcelain. Rosalba agreed for Virginio's sake and because of her own love. Through winter snows she and Chastelneuf and Peter Innocent traveled to the ancient town of Sèvres, in France. While Peter Innocent, in an inn at Versailles, read aloud from the life of St. Francis, she and Chastel-

neuf went to the abandoned Dubois factory and there she was transformed into a proper bride for a Venetian glass lover.

So Virginio and Rosalba returned to Venice in the twilight of a dimming century, to live happily in a delicate, beautiful world of porcelain and Murano glass. There Pietro Longhi painted them in his old age. With fragile grace the lovers look out from the miniature he made, and reflected in the mirrors that surround them are the faces of Peter Innocent Bon, Angelo Querini, and Count Carlo Gozzi. M. de Chastelneuf is not in the antique miniature; it is believed that he had retired to Bohemia.

VENICE PRESERVED

Type of work: Drama
Author: Thomas Otway (1652-1685)
Type of plot: Tragedy of intrigue
Time of plot: The Renaissance
Locale: Venice
First presented: 1682

Principal characters:
JAFFEIR, a young Venetian, formerly Priuli's servant
PRIULI, Jaffeir's father-in-law, a senator
BELVIDERA, Priuli's daughter and Jaffeir's wife
PIERRE, friend and fellow conspirator of Jaffeir
RENAULT, another conspirator
ANTONIO, a senator

Critique:

Venice Preserved, Or, A Plot Discovered was very popular when it was written because of the numerous plots and counterplots that were rife in the 1680's in England under Charles II. It is reputed also to have been revived on the stage more often than any other non-Shakespearian tragedy, largely because of the powerful emotional appeal. The reader cannot help drawing some comparisons with Shakespeare's *Othello,* for in both plays the hero has robbed a rich and influential Italian father of a daughter. For minds more finely drawn, the emotional appeal of Jaffeir, torn as he is between his loyalty to his friend and his loyalty to his wife, is even greater than the touching final scenes between the old senator and his star-crossed daughter. In addition to the topical interest and the emotional appeal, the play has a third source of interest: the animalistic Antonio, who symbolizes the decadence of the Venetian senate.

The Story:

Jaffeir, formerly the servant of Priuli, a senator of Venice, had secretly wooed and married Belvidera, Priuli's daughter. For three years the couple lived comfortably and blissfully, despite the father's antagonism. Then Jaffeir lost his fortune. When he went to ask Priuli for aid, in the name of Belvidera, the old senator refused to help in any way, and

he swore that his ungrateful daughter and her equally ungrateful husband would have to make their way as best they could. Jaffeir, after reminding Priuli that it was he who had saved Belvidera from a shipwreck after which she had fallen in love with him, left the senator's home in a most unhappy frame of mind.

Soon afterward Jaffeir met Pierre, a friend who had given long and faithful, though unrewarded, service to Venice. Pierre, sympathizing with Jaffeir, offered him the means of getting revenge on Priuli and striking, as he put it, a blow for liberty against the bad government of the senate. Jaffeir agreed to meet Pierre that night and to become a member of the band of conspirators. When he arrived home, Jaffeir was also comforted by Belvidera, who claimed that she was rich as long as she had his love, no matter how little fortune they possessed.

Meanwhile Pierre had gone to visit Aquilina, a courtesan whom he loved. He was extremely incensed with the woman because she had given herself for money to old Antonio, a senator. Antonio's theft of his mistress made Pierre more eager than ever for revenge. He made Aquilina, who loved him, swear to extract all the information she could from Antonio and pass it on to the conspirators, who were meeting that night in Aquilina's house.

When midnight came, Jaffeir was sadly bewailing his fate on the Rialto. There

3993

Pierre met him and conducted him to the conspirators' meeting place. Because the plotters were unwilling to take Jaffeir into their number, he brought Belvidera and offered her as hostage for his honesty. The leader of the plotters, Renault, and the Spanish ambassador, who also had a hand in the plot to ruin the government, accepted her as hostage. She was to be killed if Jaffeir failed them in any way.

The next day Jaffeir's hopes for revenge and his confidence in his fellow conspirators was shaken when he learned that Renault had offered violence to Belvidera and had been driven off only by her screams. Belvidera swore that she would bear anything, if only she knew why she had been offered as a hostage. Jaffeir, seeing the predicament she was in, and thinking it only fair that she know the truth, revealed the plot to assassinate the senate and take over the city. Because the mass assassination would include her father, Belvidera, greatly shocked, tried to convince her husband that terrible wrongs would be committed against innocent people in the mass slaughter that was planned.

In the evening the conspirators met to complete plans for the uprising, which was to take place that same night. At the meeting Jaffeir was seized with revulsion for the plot and the conspirators; he slipped away from the meeting and went to Belvidera. The two started toward the chamber where the senate council was meeting. On the way they were taken prisoners by the ducal guard and escorted to the council. To the senators and the duke Jaffeir admitted his part in the plot and prevailed on their fear to gain a general amnesty for his friends in exchange for information preventing the overthrow of the government. Within a matter of minutes, the other conspirators were brought in as prisoners. They, including Pierre, were furious with Jaffeir for revealing the plot. Pierre, refusing to listen to Jaffeir, much less to forgive him, slapped Jaffeir's face.

The senators, although they had given their word that the conspirators would be permitted to live, broke their promise and sentenced the prisoners, including Pierre, to death on the wheel. Jaffeir's rage knew no bounds when he learned of that perfidy. He offered to stab Belvidera, who had been pledged as hostage for his faithfulness to the plot. When his love prevented his actually killing her, he persuaded her to go to her father and seek his aid in rescuing the conspirators, lest her own life be forfeit for their deaths. Priuli, overcome at last by his love for his daughter, agreed to help Belvidera. His promise, however, was made too late.

When Jaffeir arrived at the scene of execution, he learned that all of the conspirators except Pierre had already been killed by the public executioner. Pierre had been saved until last because he had been granted a request to speak to Jaffeir. On the scaffold Pierre apologized for slapping Jaffeir's face and asked him a boon. Jaffeir readily assented and Pierre whispered to him. He asked that Jaffeir save him from an ignominious death by stabbing him instead. Jaffeir immediately complied and then turned his dagger into his own breast. He died within seconds of his friend.

Aquilina, hoping to save Pierre's life, had gone to seek the aid of Antonio. When the senator refused to help her, she stabbed him and left him to die. In the meantime Belvidera, overcome by her fears, had become distraught in her father's house. In spite of Priuli's efforts and those of his servants, she became steadily worse. She quickly went mad, even before she knew of her husband's death by his own hand; he had told her when she saw him last that they would never meet again. Before the messenger arrived to tell of Jaffeir's death, her husband's ghost appeared before her. Shortly after the messenger came and left, the ghosts of Jaffeir and Pierre appeared briefly. Following their appearance she went into a frenzy and died. Her father, sick of the bloodshed, plotting, and violent death, begged his attendants to take him away to a lonely place where the sun never shone, so that he might mourn in solitude and darkness the loss of his daughter and her unhappy fate.

VENUS AND ADONIS

Type of work: Poem
Author: William Shakespeare (1564-1616)
Type of plot: Mythological romance
Time of plot: Remote antiquity
Locale: Ancient Greece
First published: 1593

Principal characters:
VENUS, goddess of love
ADONIS, a handsome youth loved by Venus

Critique:

Shakespeare's *Venus and Adonis* gains most of its beauty from the magnificent imagery and figurative language with which the poet adorned the ancient tale. The sources for the poem, whether they were from Ovid or more recent writers, are unimportant, as the value of Shakespeare's version lies in his additions and not in the original story. The discussion of hunting, the incident of the stallion and the jennet, and the scenes of the fox and the hare are among the beauties which Shakespeare added.

The Story:

In all the world there was no more beautiful figure, no more perfectly made creature, than young Adonis. Although his beauty was a delight to the sun and to the winds, he had no interest in love. His only joy was in hunting, in riding over the hills and fields after the deer and the fox. When Venus, the goddess of love, saw the beauty of young Adonis, she came down to earth because she was filled with love for him.

Meeting him one morning in the fields as he rode out to the hunt, she urged him to dismount, tie his horse to a tree, and talk with her. Adonis had no desire to talk to any woman, or even to the goddess, but she forced him to do as she wished. Reclining by his side, she looked at him with caressing glances and talked passionately of the wonder and glory of love. The more she talked, the more she begged him for a kind look, a kiss, the more anxious he became to leave her and go on with his hunting. But Venus was not easily repulsed, and although Adonis sought to leave she urged him to stay. She told him how even the god of war had been a willing prisoner of her charms, and she numbered all the pleasures she could offer him if he would accept her love. Blushing, Adonis finally broke from her arms and went to get his horse.

At that moment his stallion heard the call of a jennet in a field nearby. Aroused, he broke the leather thong that held him and ran to her. At first the jennet pretended to be cold to the stallion's advances, but when she perceived that Adonis was about to overtake his mount, she gave a neigh of affection and the two horses galloped away to another field. Adonis was left behind.

Dejected, he stood thinking of the hunt that he was missing because his horse had run away. Venus came up to him again and continued her pleas of love. For a while he listened to her, but in disgust he turned finally and gave her such a look of scorn that the lovesick goddess fainted and fell to the ground. Thinking that with an unkind look he had killed her, Adonis knelt beside her, rubbed her wrists, and kissed her in hope of forgiveness.

After a while Adonis rose to his feet. Venus, recovering from her swoon, asked him for one last kiss. He grudgingly consented before he turned to leave. Venus asked when she could meet him the next day. Adonis replied that he would not see her, for he was to go boar hunting. Struck with a vision, the goddess warned the youth that he would be killed by a boar if he hunted the next day, and she begged him to meet her instead. When she threw herself on the boy and carried him to the earth in her arms in a last attempt to gain his love, Adonis admonished the goddess on the difference between heavenly love and earthly lust. He left her alone and weeping.

The next morning found Venus wandering through the woods in search of Adonis. In the distance she could hear the cries of the dogs and the voices of the hunters. Frantic because of her vision of the dead Adonis, she rushed through the forest trying to follow the sounds of the hunt. When she saw a wounded and bleeding dog, the fear she felt for Adonis became almost overpowering. Suddenly she came upon Adonis lying dead, killed by the fierce wild boar he had hunted.

The grief of Venus knew no bounds. If this love were taken from her, then never again should man love happily. Where love was, there also would mistrust, fear, and grief be found.

The body of Adonis lay white and cold on the ground, his blood coloring the earth and plants about him. From this soil there grew a flower, white and purple like the blood that spotted the skin of Venus' dead love. With a broken heart Venus left earth to hide her sorrow in the dwelling place of the gods.

THE VICAR OF BULLHAMPTON

Type of work: Novel
Author: Anthony Trollope (1815-1882)
Type of plot: Domestic realism
Time of plot: Nineteenth century
Locale: England
First published: 1870

Principal characters:
FRANK FENWICK, the Vicar of Bullhampton
HARRY GILMORE, Squire of Bullhampton
JANET FENWICK, Frank's wife
MARY LOWTHER, her friend
WALTER MARRABLE, Mary's cousin
THE MARQUIS OF TROWBRIDGE, a wealthy landlord
JACOB BRATTLE, a mill owner
SAM BRATTLE, his son
CARRY BRATTLE, his daughter

Critique:

Another novel of clerical life and society, *The Vicar of Bullhampton* is noteworthy for the introduction of a prostitute as a sympathetic character. Trollope showed considerable courage in attempting to portray this type of character during the Victorian Era. Although he felt forced to apologize to his readers in his introduction, he still retained Carry Brattle as one of the chief characters of the book. The theme of this novel, as in so much of Trollope's fiction, centers about the difficulty of acquiring money and making a successful marriage.

The Story:

The town of Bullhampton was a typical English country parish. Although the Marquis of Trowbridge owned most of the land, he had no residence within ten miles of it. The rest of the land was owned by Squire Harry Gilmore, a good friend of the Vicar of Bullhampton. The squire had recently become a daily visitor at the vicarage, for the vicar's wife had a guest, Mary Lowther, with whom Squire Gilmore was much in love. But Mary could not bring herself to become engaged to the squire, because, as she told Janet Fenwick, she simply was not in love with him. Janet and the vicar tried to persuade her that her views would change for the better after marriage. In spite of their well-meant advice, Mary still would not give her consent.

One evening, as the squire left the vicarage, he saw three men loitering in the orchard. He recognized one of them as Sam Brattle, son of Jacob Brattle, the mill owner. Jacob was a crabbed, hard-working old man who had reared a large family. Most of the children had turned out well, except Sam, who consorted with low companions, and Carry, who had gone away to the city and there become a woman of the streets. No one ever spoke of the wayward daughter at the Brattle home, for she had broken her father's heart. The chief desire of Jacob's life was to have his old mill repaired, and he finally succeeded in obtaining the necessary money to finance the project from Squire Gilmore.

Because Mary could not bring herself to accept the squire and her presence disturbed him greatly, she finally left for home. She lived at Loring with her aunt, Miss Marrable, an old spinster who was much interested in Squire Gilmore's devotion to Mary.

Back in Bullhampton the vicar tried to find out if Sam Brattle had been in his orchard with the other men that night, but the most he could learn was that two men, one an ex-convict and the other a complete stranger, had been hanging around the town and that Sam was well acquainted with both of them. A few days later one of the farmers of the community was found murdered and his secret strongbox emptied of its contents. The only person who had known the location of the strongbox was a servant girl who was a good friend of Sam Brattle. Sam was arrested, to be released a short time later because the magistrate could find no real evidence against him. Nevertheless, the Marquis of Trowbridge thought he should be held in custody, and sharp words passed between the marquis and the vicar on the subject. Sam returned to the mill because the vicar stoutly defended him.

At Loring, meanwhile, Mary Lowther had fallen deeply in love with her cousin, Walter Marrable. Walter, a soldier returned from India, was trying to regain an inheritance from his father, who had cheated him out of it. If this repossession were possible, Walter would be a wealthy man and would not have to return to India to make his fortune. During their walks together, Mary was a sympathetic listener to his troubles. Soon they were in love with each other. This situation worried Mary's aunt because Walter's attempt to regain his money was not proving successful. Before the end of the month Walter and Mary were engaged.

In Bullhampton, the head constable was investigating the home of the ex-convict in an attempt to secure evidence concerning the murder. The suspect's mother and a young woman, supposedly his wife but in reality Carry Brattle, his mistress, refused to tell the constable anything. The vicar, in the meantime, had another stormy interview with the marquis, who insisted that Sam was guilty and should be put in prison. The vicar proclaimed Sam's innocence, however, for he had faith in the young man. The upshot of the matter was that the marquis threatened to write to the bishop in complaint of the vicar. At last he did so, but the bishop merely sent his letter along to the vicar, with a friendly note advising

him not to cross the marquis too often.

Love was not going smoothly at Loring. Mary Lowther, happy over her engagement to Walter, wrote to Janet and also to Squire Gilmore, telling them her news. The young squire went into a decline, and for weeks he stayed at his home and refused to see anyone. Mary's and Walter's marriage plans had to be broken off, however, when it was discovered that Colonel Marrable, Walter's father, had spent every cent of the inheritance. Walter, now penniless, was forced to apply once more for service in India.

Janet and the vicar, hearing the news, asked Mary to return for a visit in Bullhampton; they hoped, during her stay, to renew her romance with the squire. Also, the Fenwicks needed diversion at the time, for they were plagued by the erection of a new Methodist chapel across the street from the vicarage. The new chapel was the work of the Marquis of Trowbridge and the Methodist minister, both of whom disliked the vicar intensely. One of his latest offenses, in their eyes, was a visit to Carry Brattle, the fallen woman living at the ex-convict's house. The vicar had taken her from this wretched place and found a home for her with a farm family, since her father would not hear of her living at the mill.

When Mary arrived again in Bullhampton, Squire Gilmore's spirits immediately improved. He continued to woo Mary, and at last she resignedly became engaged to him. Never really in love with him, she merely attempted to play the part of being happy. But she was a bad actress.

The vicar sought legal advice on the building of the chapel so close to the vicarage. When he discovered that the land was really his, he went to interview the marquis. Although the vicar could have insisted that the chapel be torn down at once, he suggested to the marquis that it be allowed to stand for the time being, with the understanding that someday it would have to be removed. The marquis was greatly upset by the news, as was the Methodist minister.

Walter Marrable, before his departure for India, went to visit his uncle, a wealthy baronet. He was in poor health, as was his only son. When the son died, the old gentleman made his will in favor of Walter. He hoped that Walter might marry his ward, but Mary Lowther was still in Walter's heart.

Carry Brattle, through the workings of the vicar, at last returned home. Her mother and sisters joyfully welcomed her back, but her father remained stubborn. Because Carry tried everything in her power to please him, her father was finally reconciled to her. At the trial of the ex-convict for murder, Carry and Sam were summoned as witnesses. Then it was revealed that Sam had been trying to arrange for a marriage between Carry and the suspected murderer and for that reason had been with the two men before the crime was committed. Sam was cleared entirely.

When Walter's uncle died, the young man inherited his money. Mary broke her engagement with Squire Gilmore and married Walter, her real love. The squire was crushed, and in their sympathy for their good friend the vicar and his wife regretted that Mary had ever come to Bullhampton.

THE VICAR OF WAKEFIELD

Type of work: Novel
Author: Oliver Goldsmith (1728-1774)
Type of plot: Sentimental romance
Time of plot: Eighteenth century
Locale: Rural England
First published: 1766

Principal characters:

DR. PRIMROSE, the vicar of Wakefield
DEBORAH, his wife
GEORGE, the oldest son
SOPHIA, the younger daughter
OLIVIA, the older daughter
MR. BURCHELL, in reality Sir William Thornhill
SQUIRE THORNHILL, Dr. Primrose's landlord and Olivia's betrayer
ARABELLA WILMOT, betrothed to George

Critique:

Buried in the rationalism of the eighteenth century was a strain of idealism and sentimentality which is clearly expressed in *The Vicar of Wakefield*. In this novel the interplay of the ideal and the real present a simple, lovable character in his struggle to maintain his ideals. Goldsmith's material cannot be said to be original, but his wit and gentle candor are his own. For these qualities he has been loved by many readers.

The Story:

Dr. Primrose and his wife, Deborah, were blessed with five fine children, of whom the two daughters, Olivia and Sophia, were remarkable for their beauty. The Primrose family lived in a quiet rural community, where they enjoyed both wealth and good reputation. The oldest son, George, fell in love with Arabella Wilmot, daughter of a neighbor, and the two families made mutual preparations for the wedding. Before the wedding, however, Dr. Primrose and Miss Wilmot's father quarreled over the question of a man's remarrying after the death of his wife. Dr. Primrose stoutly upheld the doctrine of monogamy. Mr. Wilmot, who was about to take his fourth wife, was insulted. The rift between the two families widened when news came that Dr. Primrose's broker had run off with all his money. Mr. Wilmot broke off the wedding plans, for the vicar was now a poor man.

George departed for London to make his fortune and the rest of the family prepared to go to another part of the country, where Dr. Primrose had found a more modest living. On the way they met a man who won the admiration of Dr. Primrose by a deed of charity to a fellow traveler. The man, Mr. Burchell, rode along with them. Suddenly Sophia was thrown from her horse into a stream, from which Mr. Burchell was able to save her. The gratitude of Deborah assured Mr. Burchell of a warm welcome whenever he should choose to call on them.

Their new home was on the estate of wealthy Squire Thornhill, a young man known for his attentions to all the young ladies in the neighborhood. Deborah thought that either of her daughters would make a good match for the young squire. Soon afterward a fortunate meeting drew the squire's attention toward Olivia, and her mother's scheming made Squire Thornhill a steady caller at the Primrose home, where Olivia blushingly protested that she thought him both bold and rude. Mr. Burchell, too, called frequently, but his interest seemed to center upon Sophia, who did not deny her pleasure at his attention. Dr. Primrose, however, could not approve of Mr. Burchell, for he had lost all his fortune and seemed to live in comparative poverty that revealed indifference to his fallen condition.

Two noble ladies from the city met the Primrose family in their rustic retreat, and Sophia and Olivia became charmed by talk of city ways. When the women spoke of their need for companions in their households, Deborah immediately suggested that Olivia and Sophia be selected. The two daughters were pleased at the thought of going to the city, despite Mr. Burchell's vigorous objections. All was set for the journey, however, when Deborah received a letter stating that a secret informant had so slandered Olivia and Sophia that the city ladies would not consider them as fit companions. At first Deborah and her husband could not imagine who the slanderer could have been. When they learned that Mr. Burchell had been the informant, Dr. Primrose ordered him from the house. With no signs of remorse or shame Mr. Burchell left.

Olivia began to insist that Squire Thornhill's repeated visits meant only that he intended to marry her. Dr. Primrose, not believing that the squire really would marry Olivia, suggested to his daughter that she consider the offer of a neighboring farmer, Mr. Williams. When the squire still failed to ask for her hand, Olivia agreed to marry the young farmer and the wedding date was set. Four days before her wedding Olivia ran away. Through the help of Squire Thornhill, Dr. Primrose learned that it was Mr. Burchell who had carried the girl away.

Saddened by his daughter's indiscretion, the resolute father set out to find her and to help her. On his journey he became ill and lay in bed in an inn for three weeks. On his recovery he gave up all hope of finding Olivia and started home. On the way there he met Miss Arabella Wilmot, who inquired about George. Dr. Primrose assured her that George had not been heard from since he had left his family to go to London. Squire Thornhill, who was courting Arabella, asked about Olivia, but the father could give him no news. Fortune brought George, impoverished and in ill luck, back to his father at that time. Pitying the bad fortune of the young boy, Squire Thornhill gave him a commission in the army and sent him away. Arabella promised to wait for her former sweetheart to make his fortune and to return to her.

Dr. Primrose started for home once more. At a roadside inn he found his dear Olivia, who told him her terrible story. The villain with whom she had run away was not Mr. Burchell. It had been Squire Thornhill, who had seduced her after a mock ceremony by a false priest. Growing tired of her, the squire had left her. Dr. Primrose took the girl home with him. But bad luck had not forsaken the vicar. As he approached his house he saw it catch fire and burn to the ground. His family escaped, but all their belongings were destroyed.

Kindly neighbors helped the penniless Primroses to set up living quarters in an outbuilding on the estate. News came that Squire Thornhill intended to marry Arabella Wilmot. This report angered Dr. Primrose; then to add to his indignation Squire Thornhill came to see him and offered to find a husband for Olivia so that she could stay near the squire. Enraged at this offer, the doctor ordered him away. The squire then demanded Dr. Primrose's quarterly rent payment which, since the disaster of losing his home, the vicar could not pay.

Squire Thornhill had Dr. Primrose sent to debtors' prison. Soon after being lodged in prison, the vicar encountered his son, George, who, having learned of the squire's cruelty, had attacked him and had been sentenced to hang for attempted murder. Dr. Primrose felt that the happiness of his life was completely shattered. Next he learned that Sophia had been kidnaped.

But virtue and honesty were soon rewarded. Sophia had been rescued by Mr. Burchell, who turned out to be the squire's uncle, Sir William Thornhill. With the squire's treachery exposed, the

Primrose family was released from its misery. Arabella and George were reunited. Even Olivia was saved from shame, for she learned that the priest who had married her to the squire had been a genuine priest. Sophia married Sir William, and Arabella married George. Dr. Primrose looked forward to his old age with happiness and joy in the good fortune of his children. Even he was rewarded for his virtue. The broker who had run away with his money was apprehended, and Dr. Primrose was once again a wealthy man.

THE VICOMTE DE BRAGELONNE

Type of work: Novel
Author: Alexandre Dumas, father (1802-1870)
Type of plot: Historical romance
Time of plot: Seventeenth century
Locale: France and England
First published: 1848-1850

Principal characters:
LOUIS XIV, King of France
LOUISE DE LA VALLIÈRE, lady in waiting and mistress of the king
D'ARTAGNAN, an officer of the king's musketeers
ATHOS, the Comte de la Fère
PORTHOS, M. du Vallon
ARAMIS, M. D'Herblay and Bishop of Vannes
RAOUL, the Vicomte de Bragelonne, son of Athos
FOUQUET, Minister of Finance
COLBERT, an ambitious politician
CHARLES II, King of England

Critique:

The novels of the older Dumas have an enduring popularity for many readers, and *The Vicomte de Bragelonne,* the last of the D'Artagnan romances, is no exception. This novel has particular interest because it deals with the last adventures of that swashbuckling hero, D'Artagnan. The story itself is the characteristic Dumas type, filled with vivid action, humorous incident, and interesting characters. In reality this romance contains four different but related plots—the restoration of Charles II, the story of Louis XIV's infatuation for Louise de la Vallière, the intrigues and downfall of the ambitious Fouquet, and the perennially popular tale of the mysterious prisoner in the iron mask. These stories have, from time to time, been taken from the longer romance and printed as novels complete in themselves. As a result, some confusion has arisen over the titles and order of the D'Artagnan series.

The Story:

Louis XIV, the young king of France, en route to Spain to ask for the hand of Marie Theresa, the Spanish Infanta, stopped overnight at the castle of Blois to visit his uncle, the Duc d'Orléans. There he met for the first time Louise de la Vallière, the lovely stepdaughter of the

duchess' steward. Louise was betrothed to Raoul, the Vicomte de Bragelonne, son of the Comte de la Fère. Another arrival at Blois during the royal visit was the Stuart pretender, Charles II, who came to ask for a loan of a million livres and French aid in regaining the English throne. When Cardinal Mazarin, chief minister of King Louis, refused to lend the money, Charles then turned for assistance to the Comte de la Fère, who had been an old friend of his royal father. The comte was a former musketeer who had been known as Athos many years before, when he had performed many brave feats with his three friends, Porthos, Aramis and D'Artagnan.

Disappointed because Mazarin and the king refused to help Charles, D'Artagnan resigned his commission as lieutenant of the king's musketeers and joined his old friend, Athos, in an attempt to place Charles upon the throne of England. Planning to capture General Monk, leader of the Parliamentary army, D'Artagnan visited Planchet, a former servant who had been successful in trade. Using funds borrowed from Planchet, he recruited fourteen resolute and dependable men and sailed with them for England. In England, in the meantime, the troops of Lambert and

General Monk prepared to fight at Newcastle. While the armies waited, Athos arrived to see General Monk and get his aid in recovering a treasure left by the unfortunate Charles I in a vault in Newcastle. This treasure was to be General Monk's bribe for restoring Charles II to the throne. On the general's return from Newcastle, D'Artagnan daringly captured the Parliamentary leader and took him, concealed in a coffin, to France. Athos, who had promised General Monk to remain in England for a time, was arrested by Monk's soldiers and accused of complicity in the general's disappearance.

In France D'Artagnan took Monk to Charles and after a satisfactory interview with the pretender Monk was released and sent back to England. There Monk on his return secured the release of Athos. Monk, won over to the Stuart cause, planned for the return of Charles to England, while the pretender made like preparations in France.

When Charles became king, he made General Monk Duke of Albemarle and commander of the English armies. To Athos the grateful king gave the Order of the Golden Fleece. For his part in the restoration D'Artagnan requested only Monk's sword. After he had received it, he resold it to Charles for three hundred thousand livres. General Monk gave D'Artagnan lands in England. After paying off his men D'Artagnan went to Calais to see Planchet, whom he approached with a long face and a sad tale of failure. When Planchet showed his true loyalty to his former master, D'Artagnan had not the heart to tease the merchant any longer; he acknowledged the success of the venture and paid Planchet one hundred thousand livres in return for the funds he had advanced.

Louis XIV had been completely dominated by Cardinal Mazarin, his minister, but the death of the latter eased the king's unhappy situation. After Mazarin's death, the ambitious Fouquet, as finance minister, and Colbert, as intendant, began a race for power. Suspicious of Fou-

quet, the king sent for D'Artagnan, recommissioned him as captain of the king's musketeers, and sent him to Belle-Isle-en-Mer to secure a report on Fouquet's mysterious activities there.

At Belle-Isle D'Artagnan found his old companion in arms, Porthos, now M. du Vallon, busy with plans for fortifying the island. The former musketeer was working under the direction of Aramis, now Bishop of Vannes and also known as M. D'Herblay. D'Artagnan hurried back to Paris to the king to give him the details of the situation at Belle-Isle, but he was beaten in the race to arrive there first by the two conspirators, who reported to Fouquet the discovery of the plot to fortify the island. To prevent trouble, Fouquet at once rushed to the king and presented to him the plan for the fortifications on Belle-Isle. He explained glibly that the fortifications might be useful against the Dutch.

Athos, the Comte de la Fère, asked the king's consent to the marriage of his son Raoul, the Vicomte de Bragelonne, to Louise de la Vallière, now a maid of honor at the court. Louis refused on the grounds that Louise was not good enough for Raoul. In reality the king, a passionate lover of various ladies of the court, had, in spite of his recent marriage to Marie Theresa, fallen in love with Louise. He dispatched Raoul at once to England to be rid of him as a rival.

Aramis and Fouquet were plotting to replace the king with a man of their choice, and to this end they annually paid a large sum of money to M. de Baisemeaux, governor of the Bastille. These schemers also attached themselves to Louise de la Vallière after they realized the power she would have with the king.

Among the court plotters also were Mademoiselle de Montalais, a lady in waiting, and her lover, Malicorne, a courtier. They were interested in all court affairs, particularly in the relationship between Mademoiselle de la Vallière and the king, and they stole letters with the idea of blackmail at an opportune time.

D'Artagnan moved to an estate close to the court to watch for palace intrigues. He was particularly interested in the plans of Aramis, who was trying to become a cardinal and planning to betray the king to secure his ends. D'Artagnan, interested in adventure for the sake of adventure, was devoted to the king.

As the affair between Louise and the king continued, Madame, the sister-in-law of Louis, also in love with him, grew jealous and determined to send for Raoul and have him marry Louise at once. The queen mother and the young queen disapproved thoroughly of the flirtation of Madame with the king and told her so. Madame then decided that the quickest solution would be to send Mademoiselle de la Vallière away from the court. At the same time the king learned that Louise had at one time returned Raoul de Bragelonne's affection, and in a fit of envy and jealousy he decided to forget her. Madame ordered Louise to leave at once.

Broken-hearted, the girl resolved to enter a convent. In her flight, however, she encountered D'Artagnan, who took her under his protection and informed the king of her whereabouts. Louis went to her immediately. Convinced of her love, he returned with her to the court. Plotters in the king's pay had a secret trapdoor constructed from Louise's rooms to those of Saint-Aignan, a gentleman of the king, and Louis and Louise were able to meet there after Madame had made other meetings between them impossible. In London Raoul heard what was happening and rushed to France. He arrived at Louise's apartments just as the king was entering by the secret door. Realizing that the rumors he had heard were true, he went away in despair.

Aramis, who had now become General of the Jesuits, who visited by an elderly duchess who wished to sell him certain letters from Mazarin which would ruin his friend Fouquet. When he refused to buy them, she sold them to Colbert, Fouquet's rival and enemy. Aramis, learning of the transaction, hurried to warn Fouquet, who assured Aramis that the supposed theft of state funds attributed to him in the letters was credited by a receipt in his possession. The receipt, however, had been stolen. Furthermore, Colbert had arranged for Fouquet to sell his position of procureur-general. Aramis, with his immense financial backing, was able to rescue Fouquet.

Raoul de Bragelonne, grieved and angry at Louise's faithlessness, challenged Saint-Aignan to a duel and Porthos promised to act as his foster son's second. Saint-Aignan, however, revealed the matter to the king. Then Athos publicly denounced Louis over the proposed duel. When the king ordered D'Artagnan to arrest Athos, D'Artagnan, by his honest fearlessness, won a pardon for his old friend.

Fouquet, backed by Aramis, grandly and recklessly humiliated Colbert in the king's presence. He announced a great fête at his estate in honor of the king. Colbert, although temporarily eclipsed, vowed revenge. Fouquet, as minister of the king's finances, was tottering under the growing strength of his enemy Colbert, and he hoped the fête would secure his position.

Aramis, through his influence with M. de Baisemeaux, the governor of the Bastille, visited a prisoner there and revealed to him that he was actually the twin brother of Louis XIV. The conspirators planned to put him on the throne in place of Louis. Aramis then busied himself to learn the details of the king's costume for the fête, for he planned to substitute the twin brother Philippe for Louis during the grand ball. Although both D'Artagnan and Porthos were suspicious of Aramis, they could prove nothing.

Aramis freed the young prince from the Bastille and coached him thoroughly in the details of the role he was to play. By means of trapdoors in Fouquet's house,

Aramis overpowered Louis XIV and hustled him off to the Bastille to replace the released prince. Philippe, in gratitude, was to make Aramis as powerful in the kingdom as Richelieu had been.

But Aramis made a grave error in revealing his deeds to Fouquet. When Fouquet heard of the abduction of the king, the minister, hoping to win the king's gratitude, rushed to the Bastille and freed Louis. Aramis and Porthos fled hastily. D'Artagnan was instructed to capture Philippe, cover his face with an iron mask to hide his resemblance to the king, and imprison him for life in the Ile Sainte-Marguerite fortress. These orders he executed faithfully.

Raoul de Bragelonne, who had never forgiven the king for stealing Louise de la Vallière, decided to kill himself as soon as possible and joined the Duc de Beaufort on a campaign to Africa. When he went to say goodbye to his father, Athos realized sadly that he would never see his son again.

Louis XIV insisted that D'Artagnan arrest Fouquet, despite Fouquet's efforts in the king's behalf. After a mad chase in which both of their horses were raced to death, D'Artagnan captured Fouquet. Colbert then rose completely to power.

D'Artagnan was ordered by the king to go to Belle-Isle-en-Mer and take the fortress in which Aramis and Porthos were hiding and shoot the conspirators. D'Artagnan, too good a friend of each of the plotters to take their lives, planned to capture the fortress but to allow the two to escape. Louis had realized that this possibility might occur and had forewarned his officers so that D'Artagnan's scheme failed and he was ordered to return to France. A fierce battle ensued at Belle-Isle and Porthos was killed after many deeds of great heroism. Aramis escaped to Bayonne.

D'Artagnan, out of favor with the king over his disobedience to orders, resigned his position as captain of the musketeers and the king accepted, only to send for him later and ask him to take back his resignation. D'Artagnan agreed and won a pardon from the king for Aramis, who had settled in Spain.

Athos died of shock upon hearing that his son had been killed in Africa; they were buried in a double funeral. Louise de la Vallière, who had been replaced as the king's mistress by a younger favorite, attended the funeral. There D'Artagnan reproached her for causing the deaths of both Athos and Raoul de Bragelonne.

D'Artagnan remained in the service of Louis XIV and died four years later while fighting against the Dutch. His death came only a few moments after he had received the baton of a marshal of France.

VICTORY

Type of work: Novel
Author: Joseph Conrad (Teodor Józef Konrad Korzeniowski, 1857-1924)
Type of plot: Psychological romance
Time of plot: Early twentieth century
Locale: East Indies
First published: 1915

Principal characters:
AXEL HEYST, an idealist
LENA, whom he befriends
MR. SCHOMBERG, a hotel owner
MR. JONES, and
MARTIN RICARDO, gamblers
PEDRO, their servant
DAVIDSON, a sea captain
WANG, Heyst's servant

Critique:

Axel Heyst was not looking for material gain in his world. He had escaped life's demands by retreating to the East Indies, and there he found the one true value in his own life, love of a woman. But the victory was not Heyst's; it was Lena's. Every tense moment of the drama enacted on the island between the three bandits and the two innocent victims points tragically to Lena's final triumph. Although English was not Joseph Conrad's native tongue, he was able to use the English language with stylistic force and vigor. One startling feature of this novelist is his ability to encompass a mass of ideas into the force of one cryptic word or phrase. Victory is a romance between a man who is sensitive only to truth and honesty and a woman who had never known such things from other men.

The Story:

After the Tropical Belt Coal Company had gone into liquidation, Axel Heyst continued to live at the No. 1 coaling station on Samburan. Strange in his manners and desires, he was a legend among the islanders; they called him a Utopist. The coal company had come into existence after Heyst had met Morrison in a Portuguese seaport where the Englishman was about to lose his trading ship Capricorn because of an unpaid debt. Heyst, always sympathetic, had offered him a loan. Because Heyst was anxious to keep his generosity a secret and Morrison eager to conceal his shaky finances, the two men pledged secrecy, with the understanding that Heyst would thereafter have a share of the Capricorn's shipping business.

Schomberg, the owner of a hotel in Sourabaya, heard of the partnership and said that Heyst maintained some kind of hold over Morrison. Morrison instigated the coal company and then died in England. After that Schomberg, who for some reason hated Heyst, constructed a mysterious kind of villainy around Morrison's partner, and he was gleeful when the coal company liquidated.

After Heyst had retired from the human society of the islands, Davidson, a ship's captain, came upon him living alone on Samburan. Worrying over Heyst's welfare, Davidson adopted the habit of sailing ten miles out of his way around the north side of Samburan in case Heyst were to need aid. Once Davidson brought the hermit around to Sourabaya, where he put up at Schomberg's hotel. Later, Davidson heard bits of a story that Heyst had run off with a girl who was at the hotel with a troupe of entertainers. He was baffled that the shy, quiet Heyst would take a girl back to Samburan with him. Mrs. Schomberg, pitying the girl, had helped Heyst spirit the girl away. The affair had caused quite a hubbub on the island because it concerned Heyst.

When Heyst had come to the hotel, he ha.l been unaware of Schomberg's hatred. The entertainers were not very attractive to his fastidious mind, but one white-muslined girl seemed younger than the others. Noticing her distress at being ordered to join a guest at a table, Heyst was prompted by the same instinct which had led him to help Morrison. He invited the girl to sit with him. Lena told Heyst about herself. Her father in England had taught her to play the violin. After his death, she had joined the group of entertainers with whom she now worked. Schomberg had been stalking her ever since the troupe came to the hotel. The contrast between Heyst and the other men she had met was enough to cause the girl to be attracted to her new friend, and she welcomed his promise of help. After Heyst had taken her away, Schomberg's hatred was tremendous.

To Schomberg's hotel came three strangers, Mr. Jones, Martin Ricardo, his secretary, and a beast-like, hairy creature whom they called Pedro. Before long these men had transformed Schomberg's hotel into a professional gambling house. Schomberg's obsession for Lena was increased by the notion that with her at his side he could rid his hotel of the gamblers. One afternoon Ricardo told Schomberg that he had been employed on a yacht where he was first attracted by Jones' polished manners. The two had stolen the captain's cash box and jumped the ship. Later Pedro became attached to them. Schomberg decided that these thieves might leave his hotel if he could arouse their greed by the prospect of richer plunder. He offhandedly mentioned Heyst's alleged wealth and told how Heyst lived on a lonely island with a girl and a hoard of money. Together Ricardo and Schomberg began to plan their pillage of the island where Heyst lived.

On his island Heyst had lived with only his Chinese servant, Wang, until Lena joined him. She told him that he had saved her from more than misery and despair. Heyst told her the story of his own background. His father had been a cynical, domineering man whom he disliked. After his death Heyst had drifted, searching for some meaning in life, a meaning never glimpsed until he met Lena.

One evening Wang appeared to announce that he had seen a boat drifting offshore. Heyst went to investigate. He discovered Ricardo, Jones, and the beast-like Pedro perishing of thirst in a boat moored beside a small jetty. Heyst helped the men to shore and took them to an abandoned bungalow for temporary quarters. That night Heyst found that his gun was missing from his desk; Wang, frightened, had taken it. Meanwhile Ricardo and Jones speculated about locating Heyst's money.

Early in the morning Ricardo stole into Heyst's bungalow and saw Lena combing her hair. He jumped at her hungrily, but she was able to defend herself. When the struggle was over and the repulsed man saw that she raised no outcry, his admiration for her increased. She asked him what the men wanted on the island. Surprised that they had come for money which she knew Heyst did not possess, she determined to protect Heyst from Schomberg's evil design. Loving Heyst, she could repay his kindness by leading Ricardo and his partners on to their destruction.

Observing Ricardo's attack on Lena, Wang had decided to withdraw from this confusion of white men's affairs; he fled to the forest. When Heyst reported the loss of his servant to Jones and Ricardo, they offered him the service of Pedro. Because their manner made it impossible for him to refuse, Lena and Heyst knew then that they were lost. Davidson would not sail past the island for three more weeks. Their only weapon having been stolen, they were left defenseless.

That night Ricardo came to the bungalow for dinner with Heyst and Lena. When Heyst had regretted his helpless position without any weapon of defense, Lena had recalled that during their scuffle she had glimpsed the knife Ricardo wore under his trouser leg. During the evening Ricardo indicated that Jones wished Heyst to visit him. Before he left, Heyst insisted that Pedro be sent out of the way, and Ricardo ordered the brute to go down to the jetty.

After Heyst had gone, Lena allowed Ricardo to make love to her so that she could take possession of his knife. Heyst told Jones about her presence in the bungalow. Jones, who suffered a path-ological hatred for women, had not known of Lena's existence. Heyst convinced him that Schomberg had lied to get rid of the gamblers and to inflict upon Heyst a revenge Schomberg was too cowardly to inflict himself. Enraged by what he considered Ricardo's treachery, Jones suggested that they go to Heyst's bungalow.

Meanwhile Lena had taken Ricardo's knife. As the two men entered the bungalow, Jones fired over Heyst's shoulder, the bullet piercing Lena's breast. Ricardo sprang through the doorway. Jones followed his partner outside and shot him in the darkness. Heyst carried Lena to the bed, and as she lay there, deathly pale in the candlelight, she demanded the knife, her symbol of victory. She died as Heyst took her in his arms and for the first time spoke words that came from the depths of his heart.

VILE BODIES

Type of work: Novel
Author: Evelyn Waugh (1903-   )
Type of plot: Social satire
Time of plot: A twentieth-century interval between wars
Locale: England
First published: 1930

> *Principal characters:*
> ADAM FENWICK-SYMES, a young writer
> NINA BLOUNT, his fiancée
> COLONEL BLOUNT, her eccentric father
> AGATHA RUNCIBLE, one of the Bright Young People
> MILES MALPRACTICE, another of the Bright Young People
> LOTTIE CRUMP, proprietress of Shepheard's Hotel
> CAPTAIN EDDY (GINGER) LITTLEJOHN, in love with Nina
> MRS. MELROSE APE, a female evangelist
> FATHER ROTHSCHILD, a Jesuit
> A DRUNKEN MAJOR

Critique:

Vile Bodies is a witty satire on English life during the period between wars. It is also Mr. Waugh's valediction to the Bright Young People, a generation running to waste in a manner that is personal as well as social. As in his earlier *Decline and Fall*, the novel contains many elements which make for grotesque humor, but the sinister and often tragic ends that his characters meet provoke thoughtful reflection as well. No solution is offered. The writer merely presents his brief episodes in brilliant juxtaposition and leaves the reader to draw his own conclusions. The result is subtle but effective social criticism. Here is T. S. Eliot's modern Waste Land, with all of the poet's insight and bitterness but without his solemnity.

The Story:

During the rough channel crossing almost everyone was in some stage of seasickness. Some became tipsy and took to their berths. The Bright Young People, led by Agatha Runcible and effeminate Miles Malpractice, strapped themselves with sticking plaster and hoped for the best. A few hardy souls gathered in the smoking room where Mrs. Melrose Ape, a famous female evangelist traveling with her troupe of singing angels, bullied them into singing hymns. Father Rothschild, S.J., contemplated the sufferings of the saints.

Adam Fenwick-Symes, a young writer, was hurrying home to marry Nina Blount. To his dismay, the Dover customs authorities confiscated and burned the manuscript of the autobiography he had written while in Paris. Almost as bad was the case of Agatha Runcible, who was stripped and searched after being mistaken for a notorious jewel smuggler.

In London, Adam's publisher offered him a contract to write a novel, but no advance in royalties. With only ten shillings to his name Adam wondered how he was going to get married. Luckily, he was staying at Shepheard's Hotel. Lottie Crump, the proprietress, bullied kings and advised members of Parliament, and if she liked her guests she was careless about bills. Most of her guests were drunk. One young man made a foolish bet with Adam and lost a thousand pounds. Adam called Nina and told her they could get married immediately, but before he left the hotel a drunken major persuaded him to put the money on Indian Runner in the November Handicap. Then the major disappeared and Adam was forced to call Nina again and tell her that their marriage would have to be postponed.

Adam and Nina went to Archie Schwert's costume party. Finding the affair dull, some of the Bright Young People went off to Lottie Crump's for a drink. Judge Skimp, an American guest, was entertaining. One young woman had fallen while swinging on a chandelier; she died in spite of the champagne used to bathe her forehead.

The party was about to break up when a Miss Brown invited the group to her house, which happened to be No. 10 Downing Street, for her father was Sir James Brown, the Prime Minister. Agatha Runcible stayed all night because she had forgotten the key to her own house. The next morning, still in her Hawaiian grass skirt, she found reporters and photographers waiting when she went out the front door. Reports of midnight orgies at No. 10 Downing Street caused a change of government, and Mr. Outrage, whose dreams were filled with visions of nude Japanese ladies, became the new Prime Minister.

On Nina's advice Adam called on Colonel Blount to ask if that eccentric gentleman would not finance his daughter's wedding. The colonel generously gave him a check for a thousand pounds. Jubilant, Adam took Nina to a country hotel where they stayed overnight. He was so happy that she waited until the next morning to tell him that her father, an absent-minded movie fan, had signed Charlie Chaplin's name to the worthless check. The wedding was postponed once more.

At Lady Metroland's party for Mrs. Ape, Baron Balcairn, a gossip columnist known as Mr. Chatterbox, showed up in disguise after the hostess had refused to send him an invitation. Suspected of spying on a secret political conference between Lord Metroland, Father Rothschild, and Mr. Outrage, he was exposed. Deciding to give his paper the scoop of scoops, he reported a sensational but false account of indiscreet confessions made by aristocrats whom the evangelist had converted. Then he went home, put his head into the oven, turned on the gas, and quietly died.

Adam became Mr. Chatterbox. In the meantime Balcairn's hoax had swamped the courts with libel suits against the Daily Excess. Mrs. Ape confirmed the story in a special interview and then departed with her angels to pep up religion at Oberammergau. Forbidden to mention the names of those suing the paper, Adam was forced to invent fictitious people for his column. Among his creations was a man named Ginger, a model of fashion and a popular figure in society.

He was rather surprised when he finally encountered a man whom everyone called Ginger. He was Captain Eddy Littlejohn; Adam and Nina met him at the November Handicap, where Indian Runner came in first, paying thirty-five to one. A few minutes after the race Adam spied the drunken major, but he disappeared before Adam could push his way through the crowd to collect his winnings.

Adam promised Nina that he would speak to her father again. He found the colonel making a film based on the life of John Wesley and too busy to pay any attention to Adam. During his absence Nina wrote his column and mentioned green bowlers, a fashion item tabooed in the Daily Excess. So Adam lost his job and Miles Malpractice became Mr. Chatterbox. Miles took the post because he needed the money. His brother, Lord Throbbing, had returned unexpectedly from Canada and thrown Miles, along with his disreputable boxing and racing friends, out of Throbbing House.

Adam, Agatha, Miles, and Archie Schwert went to the auto races where, in order to get into the pits, they wore brassards indicating that they belonged to the crew of car 13. Between heats Adam again met the drunken major, who, after assuring him that his thirty-five thousand pounds were safe in the bank, borrowed five pounds to make a bet.

When the driver of car 13 was disabled by an Italian rival, Agatha, who wore a brassard designating her as spare driver, took the wheel. Careening madly, she established a course record for the lap before she left the track and drove across country until she crashed the car into a monument. Found wandering about in a dazed condition, she died in a nursing home, still thinking that she was driving in a spinning world of speed and sound.

Adam had no money to pay Lottie Crump's bill for seventy-eight pounds sixteen and twopence. Meeting Ginger Littlejohn, he borrowed that amount and promised in return that Ginger could marry Nina.

Shortly after Ginger and Nina returned from their honeymoon Ginger was called up for military service. Adam went with Nina to spend Christmas with Colonel Blount. The Wesley picture had been finished, and the colonel, planning to show it as a Christmas treat, was too preoccupied to notice that his supposed son-in-law was a writer he had met previously as Fenwick-Symes. On Christmas night they heard that war had been declared.

Adam met his drunken major again on a blasted battlefield during a lull in the fighting. The officer, who insisted that he was now a general, announced that he had lost his division. Adam was not quite so badly off; he had lost only one platoon. The general offered to pay the thirty-five thousand pounds on the spot, but Adam thought the money would be useless. They did find the general's car and in it a case of champagne and Chastity, who had been one of Mrs. Ape's singing angels. Adam drank some of the wine and fell asleep, leaving the general and Chastity to entertain each other.

THE VILLAGE

Type of work: Novel
Author: Ivan Alexeyevich Bunin (1870-1953)
Type of plot: Social criticism
Time of plot: Early twentieth century
Locale: Russia
First published: 1910

Principal characters:
TIKHON ILITCH KRASOFF, a self-made landowner
KUZMA ILITCH KRASOFF, his imaginative brother
THE BRIDE, a peasant woman employed by Tikhon
RODKA, a peasant, husband of the Bride

Critique:

Bunin himself, in an autobiographical introduction to the American edition of this novel, stated that it was one of a series of novels written to portray the character of the Russian people. In the series, said Bunin, he attempted to lay bare the Russian soul in all its complexity and depth, and in its invariably tragic state. Bunin also stated that no one who knew the Russian people as he did could have been surprised by the beastliness of the Russian revolution and its effect on Russia. Some critics have called Bunin cruel in his portrayal of the Russian people, for he showed them as vicious, egocentric, hatred-filled individuals who care little for anyone but themselves. Bunin himself has stated that he is content to have painted a more realistic picture of the Russian people than the idealized conception usually given in the literature of his land, a land from which he was, of course, an exile after the revolution. For his truthful account Bunin has received the Nobel Prize for Literature.

The Story:

The ancestors of Tikhon and Kuzma Ilitch Krasoff were nothing to be proud of: their great-grandfather had been hunted from Durnovka with wolfhounds; their grandfather had distinguished himself by becoming a thief; and their father, a petty huckster, had died early in life as a result of overdrinking. The sons, after serving for a time as clerks in town stores, took to the road as itinerant peddlers. After they had traveled together for many years, the partnership was mutually dissolved during an argument over the division of profits. The two parted very bitterly.

After the partnership was broken, Tikhon took over a posting-station a few miles from Durnovka, the little village where his ancestors had lived for many generations. Along with the station he operated a liquor dispensary and general mercantile establishment. Tikhon, determined to become a man of some consequence, began to build up his fortune when he was already in his forties. His plan was to follow the tax collectors and buy land at forced sales, and he paid the lowest possible prices for what he purchased.

Tikhon's private life was anything but rich. He lived with his cook, a dumb woman, who became the mother of his child. The child was accidentally smothered, however, and soon afterward Tikhon sent the woman away and married a waiting-woman to a noblewoman, by whom he tried to have children. His efforts were fruitless, however, for the children were always born ahead of their time and dead. As if to make up, temporarily at least, for his wife's failure to present him with children, fate gave Tikhon the opportunity of finishing off, economically speaking, the last member of the family that had held his own ancestors in serfdom through previous centuries.

Life was not easy for Tikhon. A government order closed all the dram shops, including his, and made liquor a state monopoly. Tikhon also continued to be disturbed over the fact that he had no children; he felt that it indicated a failure in life.

The summer following the government order closing his liquor business proved to be a bad one. There was no rain and a great deal of heat, and so the grain harvest on his lands was only a fraction of what it should have been. During that fall Tikhon went to a fair to do some horse trading; while he was there, he became disgusted with himself and with life in general, for life seemed to him suddenly to have no point to it. He began to take to drink, downing immense quantities of vodka, although not enough to interfere with the conduct of his business.

Tikhon's life was little affected by the war with Japan that broke out soon afterward; he was more affected by persistent rumors of an attempt at a socialist revolution in the Russian legislative body. When he learned that the great landowners, those who owned more than a thousand acres of ground, were likely to have their estates taken from them for redistribution, he even began to agitate a little for the new laws. But he soon changed his mind when he discovered that the peasants on his own land were plotting against him. One Sunday he heard that they were meeting at Durnovka to rise in rebellion against him. He immediately drove over to the village, but the peasants, refusing to listen to him, drove him away with force. But the uprising was short-lived, and within a few days the peasants were back to deal with him again. He no longer trusted them, however, and he thought of them as little better than treacherous animals.

One of the workers on Tikhon's land was a young peasant named Rodka, married to a young girl of some beauty who was always called the Bride. The girl was a source of annoyance to Tikhon because she aroused him sensually. On several occasions she resisted his unwelcome attentions, but finally he had his way with her. The Bride did not complain; she simply endured, much as she endured the terrible beatings that her husband administered to her with a knout. The beatings made Tikhon afraid of Rodka, and so he plotted to do away with the man. Such scheming proved unnecessary, however, for the Bride herself poisoned her husband. Tikhon, at least, was sure that she had poisoned her husband, even though no one else thought so.

Chance brought to Tikhon's perusal a volume of poems written by his brother Kuzma. Stirred by the knowledge that his brother was still alive and also an author, Tikhon wrote a letter telling Kuzma that it was high time they buried past differences and became friends again. Kuzma went to Durnovka, and the two became, at least on the surface, friendly. Tikhon offered his brother the overseership of the estate at Durnovka, and Kuzma accepted because he had no other prospects for making a living.

Kuzma Krasoff had done nothing with his life. Following the dissolution of the partnership with Tikhon years before, he had worked here and there, as a drover, a teamster, a general worker. Then he had fallen in love with a woman at Voronezh and had lived with her for ten years, until she died. In that decade he busied himself by trading in grain and horses and by writing occasionally for the local newspaper. All his life he had wanted to become a writer. He had never been educated, except for short periods of instruction at the hands of a shoemaker out of work and from books he had borrowed occasionally. He considered his life a complete waste, for he had never been able to settle down to writing seriously.

In his maturity Kuzma blamed all his troubles, and the troubles of Russians in general, on a lack of education. Education, he believed, was the answer to every problem confronting him and his fellowmen, and he claimed that the Russians, whom he regarded as little better than barbarians with a wide streak of hatred in their makeup, would have been better folk if they had been educated.

Kuzma's life as bailiff on his brother's estate was not a happy one. He felt that the position was a last resort, and he disliked the people with whom he had to deal, including Tikhon. He was also perturbed by the Bride, who had been sent by Tikhon to cook and keep house for him. She did not arouse him as she had Tikhon, but Kuzma was bothered by her presence, and he felt extremely sorry for her because, a few years before, a group of men had raped her. The incident, Kuzma felt, lingered like a cloud over her existence. When at last he spoke to Tikhon about the matter, Tikhon, supposing that Kuzma had been sampling the same favors that the owner had enjoyed in the past, laughed at his brother's scruples. He did arrange to marry off the woman, however, and the Bride became the wife of a peasant on the estate. On the wedding day only Kuzma realized that the prospect of a husband was but a makeshift in the Bride's mind, and that she, like himself, would never really be happy.

THE VILLAGE

Type of work: Poetry
Author: George Crabbe (1754-1832)
First published: 1783

Although George Crabbe's poem, *The Village*, contains two books, the anthologists have been largely justified in printing Book I as a separate poem. This book is in part a bitter answer to Oliver Goldsmith's sentimental picture of rural life in *The Deserted Village*: "I paint the cot/ As Truth will paint it, and as Bards will not." Book II continues the theme of the first book for over a hundred lines, then turns into a memorial eulogy of Lord Robert Manners, the brother of Crabbe's patron, the Duke of Rutland.

Crabbe's long life spanned the periods of eighteenth-century classicism and nineteenth-century romanticism, and his work contains elements of both schools. His friends included Samuel Johnson among the earlier poets and Sir Walter Scott among the later. Johnson "corrected" some of Crabbe's poetry and, according to Boswell, revised lines 15-20 of *The Village*:

On Mincio's banks, in Caesar's boun-
   teous reign,
If Tityrus found the Golden Age again,
Must sleepy bards the flattering dream
   prolong,
Mechanic echoes of the Mantuan song?
From Truth and Nature shall we widely
   stray,
Where Virgin, not where Fancy, leads
   the way?

These lines do have a Johnsonian flavor; and although they fit into the structure of the poem, they are not entirely typical of Crabbe. Francis Jeffrey, one of Crabbe's admiring later contemporaries, wrote: "The scope of the poem is to show that the villagers of real life have no resemblance to the villagers of poetry; that poverty, in sober truth, is very uncomfortable; and vice by no means confined to the opulent."

Jeffrey set the tone for much subsequent criticism of Crabbe: "His characteristic, certainly, is force and truth of description, joined for the most part to great selection and condensation of expression. . . . With a taste less disciplined and less fastidious than that of Goldsmith, he has, in our apprehension, a keener eye for observation, and a readier hand for the delineation of what he has observed." Crabbe has frequently been compared with the Dutch realistic painters, and *The Village* is rich with vigorous, natural word-painting. A dismal landscape with infertile soil and hardy weeds, listed and described by name, serves as background for group and individual portraits of a surly, selfish, unscrupulous, vicious, often miserable population. Particularly notable is his interior scene of the poorhouse:

Theirs is yon house that holds the parish poor,
Whose walls of mud scarce bear the
   broken door;
There, where the putrid vapors, flag-
   ging play,
And the dull wheel hums doleful
   through the day—
There children dwell, who know no
   parents' care;
Parents, who know no children's love,
   dwell there!
Heart-broken matrons on their joyless
   bed,
Forsaken wives, and mothers never
   wed;
Dejected widows with unheeded tears,
And crippled age with more than child-
   hood fears;
The lame, the blind, and, far the hap-
   piest they!
The moping idiot and the madman gay.

In this miserable house one of the aged inmates is dying. In connection with this death Crabbe introduces two of his most savage caricatures. First, he presents the doctor:

Anon, a figure enters, quaintly neat,
All pride and business, bustle and conceit;

4017

With looks unalter'd by these scenes of
woe,
With speed that, entering, speaks his
haste to go,
He bids the gazing throng around him
fly,
And carries fate and physic in his eye:
A potent quack, long versed in human
ills,
Who first insults the victim whom he
kills;
Whose murd'rous hand a drowsy Bench
protect,
And whose most tender mercy is neglect.

After the departure of the doctor, the
dying man asks for the parish priest. This
character is a direct antithesis to the
venerable vicar of Goldsmith's *The Deserted Village* or *The Vicar of Wakefield*.
He is concerned with hunting in the
daytime and whist at night. He not only
fails to answer the summons before the
death, but cannot be troubled with saying the funeral service until the following Sunday:

And waiting long, the crowd retire distress'd,

To think a poor man's bones should lie
unbless'd.

These lines end the first book.

The smugglers and drunkards of Book
I are forerunners of an equally vicious or
more vicious group in the first part of
Book II. In both books death is spoken
of as a deliverer and equalizer. The elegy
on Manners occupies the final hundred
lines of the poem and is really complete
in itself.

Crabbe has had warm admirers ever
since *The Village* was published. In our
time Edwin Arlington Robinson paid him
tribute in a strong-fibered sonnet; he felt
that changing fashions in literature could
not obscure Crabbe's "hard, human
pulse" or his "plain excellence and stubborn skill." In his opera *Peter Grimes*,
based on one of the tales in *The Bor-
ough*, Benjamin Britten has brought
Crabbe to the attention of many who
knew little about the old poet; but *The
Village*, which first made Crabbe's poetic
reputation, still best sustains it, and
remains his most familiar and frequently
read poem.

VILLETTE

Type of work: Novel
Author: Charlotte Brontë (1816-1855)
Type of plot: Psychological romance
Time of plot: Nineteenth century
Locale: France
First published: 1853

Principal characters:
LUCY SNOWE, a young teacher
JOHN GRAHAM BRETTON, a physician
MRS. BRETTON, his mother
POLLY HOME, in love with Bretton
GINEVRA FANSHAWE, a schoolgirl
MONSIEUR PAUL EMANUEL, a teacher of literature
MADAME BECK, mistress of a girls' school

Critique:

In spite of its apparent flaws, Villette remains a superior novel, for the sure hand of Charlotte Brontë overcame most of the weaknesses of her story. One of the most obvious faults is the flat characterization of Dr. John Bretton, and the novel itself is broken in construction when the doctor is replaced in the leading role by Monsieur Paul Emanuel. Typical of the period is the repetition of coincidental meetings between characters who have had previous relationship. Lucy meets Dr. John Bretton on the streets of Villette before she comes to know him as the physician of Madame Beck's establishment, and she meets the priest in a church before she finds him in the Walravens home. It is enough that John Bretton and Lucy are brought together again, but that Polly Home should also arrive strains at credibility. The narrative proper shows that Charlotte Brontë had in this novel finally mastered her autobiographical material; there is a quality of artistic strength here, and more profound character portrayal, than in the ingenuous but perennially popular Jane Eyre.

The Story:

When Lucy Snowe was a young girl, she went to visit her godmother, Mrs. Bretton, about twice each year. It was a warm, active household, and Lucy loved Mrs. Bretton.

During one of her visits, a small girl, whose widowed father was leaving England for a sojourn on the continent, came to stay with the Brettons. The girl, Polly Home, developed a strange and tender fondness for Mrs. Bretton's son Graham, who was a kind and compassionate boy. Mature and worldly for her years, Polly exhibited an almost maternal attachment toward Graham. Since Lucy shared a room with the young visitor, she became the recipient of the child's confidence. Although Polly's father had originally intended to deposit his daughter at Mrs. Bretton's home for an extended stay, he became lonely for her and returned to take his daughter back to Europe with him.

Lucy's visits with the Brettons came to an end when they lost their property and moved away. After that Lucy lost track of her godmother.

As a grown woman Lucy earned her living by acting as a companion to elderly women. Tiring of her humdrum existence, she went to France. There an unusual chain of circumstances led her to the city of Villette and to a boarding school run by Madame Beck and her kinsman, Monsieur Paul Emanuel. Lucy's calm disposition, ready wit, firm character, and advanced intellect soon led to her appointment as instructress of English.

Attending the school was Ginevra Fanshawe, a pretty but flighty and selfish girl whose relations with Lucy took the form of a scornful friendship. Madame Beck was a clever schoolmistress. She conducted her pension by a system of spying which included occasional furtive searches among the personal possessions of others and also a constant stealthy watching from her window. In spite of her behavior, Lucy felt a firm respect for Madame Beck. Her system was steady and unflagging. Monsieur Paul was a voluble and brilliant instructor. He seemed always to be at Lucy's elbow admonishing her, tantalizing her intellect, attempting to lead her. Often Lucy attributed the peculiar notions of the pair to their Catholicism, which Lucy abhorred.

Dr. John was a general favorite at the institute; he was a handsome, generous young practitioner who attended the children of Madame Beck's school. Lucy, although she did not betray her knowledge, recognized him as the John Graham Bretton whom she had known years before.

In her characteristically scornful and triumphant manner toward Lucy, Ginevra Fanshawe confided that she had a pair of ardent suitors. One, whom she called Isidore. was madly in love with her; the other was Colonel de Hamal, whom Ginevra herself preferred.

One night, in the garden, Lucy found a letter intended for someone in the school. Dr. John appeared in time to assist Lucy in disposing of the missive before Madame Beck, spying, could interfere. The young doctor knew, apparently, the person for whom the letter was intended. Some time later Lucy learned that Ginevra's Isidore was Dr. John himself. Thus the mystery of the nocturnal letter was solved. De Hamal had sent it and Dr. John was attempting to protect his beloved. In discussing his hopeless passion for Ginevra, Dr. John confessed that he hoped to marry the schoolgirl.

During a vacation Lucy, left alone at the pension, was overcome by depression. She had been haunted in the past by the apparition of a nun, and the reappearance of this specter so aggravated the already turbulent emotions of the young teacher

that she fled into the streets of the town. There she wandered, driven to despair by her inner conflicts, until she came to a Catholic church. A strange fascination drove her to confession, but she later regretted her action. While trying to find her way back to the school, she fainted. When she regained consciousness, she found herself in a room that contained familiar furnishings. She was in a Villette chateau occupied by her godmother, Mrs. Bretton, and Graham Bretton. Graham, who was giving Lucy medical attention, was the Dr. John whom Lucy had recognized at the pension. For the first time he recognized her as the young girl who had so often stayed in his home in England.

Lucy became a frequent visitor in the Bretton home, and before long she realized that she was in love with Dr. John. The warm friendship between the two young people was constantly put upon by the ubiquitous Monsieur Paul and his sarcastic raillery.

While at a concert one evening with Dr. John and Mrs. Bretton, Lucy noticed Ginevra Fanshawe in the audience. Ginevra, having located the doctor's party, began to mimic Mrs. Bretton, who was unaware of the young girl. Dr. John was not. At once he sensed the weakness and the selfishness of Ginevra, who could so irreverently make fun of a woman as good as his mother. His infatuation for Ginevra ended in disgust.

Again at a concert with Lucy, Dr. John rescued a young girl named Paulina from a rough crowd of people. Bringing Paulina Bassompierre to his own home, Dr. John discovered that she was in reality Polly Home, who had stayed at the old Bretton house in England. All the old acquaintances were together again.

Repeated meetings between Polly, now called Paulina, and Dr. John fostered the doctor's love for the girl who had loved him since childhood. Lucy, closing her eyes and ears to this grief, believed that Dr. John was lost to her.

Lucy began a new phase in her life at the school. Madame Beck gave her greater freedom in her work, and Monsieur Paul showed a hearty interest in her mind and in her heart. The only flaw remaining in Lucy's tranquillity was the reappearance of the apparition of the nun.

Once Madame Beck sent Lucy on an errand to the home of Madame Walravens. There Lucy was told a touching story about Monsieur Paul. He had loved a girl, Justine Marie, in his youth, but cruel relatives refused his suit and she subsequently died. Filled with remorse, Monsieur Paul undertook to care for Justine Marie's relatives. There survived old Madame Walravens and a priest, the same man to whom Lucy had confessed. The priest, Father Silas, had been Monsieur Paul's tutor; he was anxious to keep Monsieur Paul from coming under the influence of Lucy, a heretic.

Lucy's affection for the truculent professor grew, but suddenly all her hopes toppled about her. Monsieur Paul was leaving France for the West Indies. Madame Beck, always present when Monsieur Paul and Lucy met, kept the distraught teacher from talking to him.

Ginevra Fanshawe eloped with de Hamal. A letter from the runaway girl explained Lucy's ghostly nun. De Hamal had thus attired himself when making nocturnal visits to Ginevra.

But Monsieur Paul refused to abandon Lucy without an explanation of his sudden forced departure. On the eve of his sailing he arranged a meeting with her and explained his recent silence. Surrounded by his possessive relatives, he had occupied his time with secret arrangements to make Lucy mistress of the school. To avoid the temptation of telling Lucy about his plans before they were consummated, he had remained apart from her. Upon his return, in three years, he promised to rid himself of all his encumbrances, so that he would be free to marry Lucy Snowe.

A VINDICATION OF NATURAL SOCIETY

Type of work: Political satire
Author: Edmund Burke (1729-1797)
First published: 1756

Edmund Burke's first important publication, *A Vindication of Natural Society,* subtitled *A View of the Miseries and Evils arising to Mankind from every Species of Civil Society, in a Letter to Lord* ——, *by a late Noble Writer,* satirically attacked the views of Lord Bolingbroke (the late Noble Writer), whose philosophical works had been published posthumously in 1754. By adopting Bolingbroke's manner, Burke hoped to give a tone of irony and satire to his own opinions on society. So well did he succeed in imitating his model's polished style, however, that *A Vindication of Natural Society* was generally received as Bolingbroke's own, even by such critics as Chesterfield and Warburton.

Burke's central point was to show that Bolingbroke's arguments in favor of natural against revealed religion were equally applicable in favor of natural as against artificial society. Two years before *A Vindication of Natural Society* appeared, Rousseau had in fact developed the thesis that a simple society close to nature was morally superior to the refined society of Europe. Burke understood the revolutionary nature of this doctrine and its threat to the established order, and he consistently maintained that any society was preferable to the hypothetical "state of nature." To prove that he understood the implications of his opponents' arguments better than they themselves did, he assumed their position with massive irony: "In vain you tell me that artificial government is good, but that I fall out only with the abuse. The thing! the thing itself is the abuse!" His irony is so cleverly disguised that J.B. Bury commented, "*A Vindication* . . . worked out in detail a historical picture of the evils of civilization which is far more telling than Rousseau's generalities."

Burke begins by distinguishing between a *natural society* and the *political* society which came into being when man, observing the advantages of the family union, assumed that larger unions would be beneficial as well. Because the society so created was artificial, man was forced to invent laws. By stating the case so baldly, Burke hoped to ridicule Bolingbroke's straightforward rationalism. He puts a major part of the blame for social corruption on religious institutions in a covert attempt to identify Bolingbroke's deism with an attack on the social order: "Civil government borrows a strength from ecclesiastical; and artificial laws receive a sanction from artificial revelations. The ideas of religion and government are closely connected; and whilst we receive government as a thing necessary . . . we shall in spite of us draw in . . . an artificial religion of some kind or other." Although Burke's Noble Writer disavows any attack on English society, the sweeping nature of his generalizations obviously implicates him.

The state, the Noble Writer goes on, can be viewed in two different lights, in its external relationship to other states, and in its internal relationship to the governed. He finds that a description of the honorable conduct between nations would not fill ten pages, but their record of war and treachery is beyond human accounting. With deliberately exaggerated concern in proving his point, Burke devotes about one-sixth of his essay to the history of war. He caps his summary with the estimate that the number of men slaughtered in battle was seventy times the five hundred million then inhabiting the earth. The Noble Writer concludes that ". . . political society is justly chargeable with much the greatest part of this destruction of the species." In this passage Burke's irony attains a subtle level of complexity. Thoughtful men could hardly deny the general truth that Burke seemingly offered to his opposition. Burke's irony is perhaps intended to demonstrate that such righteousness is easy, and that his own views were based upon principle, and not upon a justification of the *status quo.*

The Noble Writer finds that governments are no less cruel and unjust to those they govern. "All writers on the science of policy are agreed . . . that all governments must frequently infringe the rules of justice to support themselves; that truth must give way to dissimulation; honesty to convenience; and humanity itself to the reigning interest." Why, he wonders, should Machiavelli be so detested for merely unveiling the mechanisms of government? The oppression of rulers can everywhere be seen in the dungeons, whips, chains, racks, and gibbets which they need to support themselves. "What sort of protection is this of the general right," the Noble Writer asks in mock triumph, "that is maintained bv infringing the rights of particulars? What sort of justice is this, which is enforced by breaches of its own laws?" Burke contrives to give the Noble Writer a strong emotional argument in words that were even quoted against him. Underlying the irony, however, is the quiet conviction that man is not essentially good and that some kind of government is necessary to regulate human affairs.

The Noble Writer then divides governments into three kinds, despotism, aristocracy, and democracy, and he gives a historical sketch of each. Despotism is the simplest and most general kind. In such a system power is usually given to the weakest and most foolish. The life and welfare of all are given over to the whim of one man, such as Nero, who had a learned scholar put to death because he did not like his face. Even the sincere and virtuous despot is corrupted by servile ministers who serve their own selfish ends. Under this system the greater part of the people are considered as cattle, and, having lost all pride and dignity, they soon become no better. Such a government is actually worse than anarchy (Burke actually thought that an-

archy was the worst possible civil order), yet the greater part of mankind throughout history has groaned under despotism.

Aristocracy has arisen whenever a society, finding the rule of one man intolerable, entrusts the public welfare to a group of leaders. Burke ironically presents the oversimplified assumptions about human nature implicit in this view: "They hoped it would be impossible that such a number [of aristocrats] could ever join in any design against the general good; and they promised themselves a great deal of security and happiness from the united counsels of so many able and experienced persons." The Noble Writer finds, however, that aristocracy differs little from despotism in practice. Once in power, the aristocrats use every means possible to maintain their position. In one important respect aristocracy is worse than despotism: one ruler can be overthrown and may be succeeded by a better one, but an aristocracy clings tenaciously to its body of traditions. In actuality, Burke valued the force of tradition as a bulwark against anarchy.

The third type of government, democracy, imposes the tyranny of the majority. The ignorance and fickleness of a popular assembly leads to the same kind of abuses as those of despotism and aristocracy. Although Athens has been much admired for its democracy, it was "a city of wise men, in which a minister could not exercise his functions; a warlike people, amongst whom a general did not dare either to gain or lose a battle: a learned nation, in which a philosopher could not venture on a free inquiry." The mixed society, the union of regal, aristocratic, and popular power, is equally insupportable. At this point Burke has his Noble Writer come dangerously close to attacking the foundations of eighteenth-century English society. The mixed society is represented as torn with strife over rights and powers, and as dominated by factions more interested in partisan advantage than in the general welfare.

The Noble Writer returns to a humanitarian appeal in his discussion of the rich and the poor. To him it is obvious that the whole function of the poor is to provide idleness and luxury for the rich. "In a state of nature," he says, with a simplicity that Burke intended to be ridiculous, "it is an invariable law, that a man's acquisitions are in proportion to his labors. In a state of artificial society, it is a law as constant and as invariable, that those who labor most enjoy the fewest things; and that those who labor not at all have the greatest number of enjoyments." The Noble Writer is eloquent, however, in describing the horrible life of the poor. The worker in the mine and factory is little more than a slave; the rich, on the other hand, corrupt themselves with lives of idleness.

Burke's mock indictment of society is thus complete: it slaughters and enslaves and corrupts. In answer to these genuine criticisms, however, Burke attributes to his Noble Writer only a naïve and dangerous sentimentality, hopelessly out of touch with man's true nature. The Noble Writer argues from lofty first principles; Burke consistently appealed for a practical, flexible, and conservative wisdom. *A Vindication of Natural Society* prophetically reveals the intellectual and moral debate in which Burke struggled all his life.

THE VIOLENT LAND

Type of work: Novel
Author: Jorge Amado (1913-   )
Type of plot: Historical romance
Time of plot: Late nineteenth century
Locale: State of Bahia, Brazil
First published: 1942

Principal characters:

COLONEL HORACIO DA SILVEIRA, a cacao planter
COLONEL SINHÔ BADARÓ, another planter
DOÑA ESTER DA SILVEIRA, Colonel da Silveira's wife
DOÑA ANA BADARÓ, Colonel Badaró's daughter
CAPTAIN JOÃO MAGALHÃES, in love with Doña Ana
DR. VIRGILIO CABRAL, Doña Ester's lover and da Silveira's lawyer
MARGOT, a prostitute
JUCA BADARÓ, Colonel Badaró's younger brother

Critique:

This novel, skillfully plotted and impressive in its evocation of the spirit of a region, reflects the violence of the struggle to produce and market the raw material for chocolate. The action covers the early years of cacao production in the State of Bahia, Brazil, a corner of the world that was a late frontier. Like most frontiers, it was a lawless area that attracted people anxious to get rich quickly, people who did not care whether others, or they themselves, lived or died. Bahia was, at the same time, a land where courageous men carved fortunes out of the wilderness and the labor of other men, a place where the strong lived and the weak succumbed. Its history is the Brazilian counterpart of an era in the development of the western United States. Wherever it is found, the frontier is always a violent land.

The Story:

In the minds of most Brazilians the São Jorge dos Ilhéos was a semi-barbarous country ruled by a handful of rich planters who styled themselves colonels. These men had risen, almost without exception, from humble origins by means of courage, bravado, and murder. The two most important planters were Colonel Horacio da Silveira and Colonel Sinhô Badaró. Between their lands lay a large forest, upon which both men had long cast covetous eyes. The forest, actually a jungle, could be cleared to uncover an almost fabulous cacao-growing soil.

Among the strangers who poured into the region in search of wealth at the time were several people who were to range themselves on one side or the other in the coming struggle. Dr. Virgilio Cabral, a cultured and talented lawyer, was to ally himself with da Silveira. With the lawyer came Margot, a beautiful prostitute who had fallen in love with him and become his mistress while he was a student. Another arrival was Captain João Magalhães, a professional gambler and a courageous opportunist who called himself a military engineer. Among his admirers were Juca Badaró, Colonel Badaró's younger brother, and Doña Ana Badaró, the colonel's daughter, who was also the heiress to the Badaró fortunes.

Soon after his arrival Cabral fell in love with Ester, da Silveira's beautiful wife. The woman, who hated her semi-barbarous husband, quickly returned the affection of the more cultured man. When she became his mistress, both knew that they would be killed if the husband found them out. As his ardor for Ester da Silveira increased, the lawyer's affection for his former mistress waned, and soon Margot found herself unwanted by her lover. In retaliation, and because she needed someone to support her, Margot became the mistress of Juca Badaró. Out of spite she also furnished him with scandal about the opposition, gossip which he turned to account in the newspaper which favored the Badarós.

Professionally, as well as amorously, Cabral was a success, for he found an old survey of the contested lands and registered the title in da Silveira's name after he had bribed the registry officials. The Badaró family quickly retaliated by burning the registry office and all the records on file. In addition, the Badarós hired Magalhães to run a survey for them. He made the survey, even though he lacked the proper knowledge to do so. His presence at the Badaró plantation earned him the respect of the Badaró brothers and the love of Doña Ana Badaró. The self-styled captain, always an opportunist, permitted himself to fall in love with the girl and pay court to her.

Because the Badaró family was the more powerful of the two factions, da Silveira went to several small planters and promised to let them divide half of the forest land if they, as a group, would help him hold it against the Badarós. There was bloody fighting on both sides of the forest and within it, for both factions hired many assassins and bodyguards to back up their interests with bullets. The Badarós controlled the local government, and the state government was in opposition to the federal government of Brazil.

Juca Badaró was assassinated by a hired gunman after he had insulted Cabral. Juca had found the lawyer dancing with Margot, at the girl's request, and had insulted the lawyer for daring to do so. On the other side, too, there were disappointments and deaths. Both Cabral and da Silveira were deterred in their plans when the colonel fell ill with a fever. The planter recovered, but his wife, the lawyer's mistress, became ill as a result of nursing her husband. Her death removed one incentive in the efforts of both her husband and her lover, but they stubbornly continued the fight.

As the struggle in the courts and in the fields continued, the Badarós spent more and more money. They not only sold their current crop of cacao pods, but also sold their next year's crop in order to raise funds immediately. Before his assassination Juca Badaró had seen to it that his niece, Doña Ana, was married to the gambler, for he saw in Magalhães an ambitious man willing to fight for money and power. So tempting was the proposal the Badarós made that the captain agreed to take his wife's name, her father insisting that he do so in order to carry on the Badaró line.

At first, by tacit consent, the contending parties did no damage to one another's cacao trees, but as the Badarós became desperate they instructed their desperadoes to burn the cacao groves. Their opponents saw that the matter had to be settled at once, lest both parties be irretrievably ruined and become victims of someone stronger than they. Colonel da Silveira and his henchman, along with their paid gunmen, attacked the Badaró plantation in force and drove off the family, after killing all the men except a handful led by Magalhães.

Da Silveira and his men thought that the women of the Badaró household had been sent away, but the attackers were greeted by gunfire from Doña Ana herself as they entered the house. When she ran out of ammunition, she gave up, expecting to be killed. The attackers let her go, however, because she was a woman.

The Badaró rout was completed by an announcement from the Brazilian capital that the political party favoring da Silveira had come into power and was sending troops and government agents to the district to quiet the violence. The jungle lands were ceded to the da Silveira faction by the government's action. Da Silveira was forced to stand trial for the murder of Juca Badaró, but the trial, having been staged more to clear the colonel than to find him guilty, was a mere formality.

The district quickly settled down after the great feud had ended and the new government had started its operations. But there was to be one more assassination. While going through his dead wife's effects, da Silveira discovered the letters Cabral had written to her. He was horrified and embarrassed to learn of her infidelity, which he had not suspected, and his lawyer's duplicity. After thinking about the matter for some time, he sent a gunman to clear his honor by killing the man who had made him a cuckold.

To symbolize the new peace that had come into the frontier district, the Church made the city of Ilhéos the seat of a newly created diocese and sent a bishop to officiate as its representative there. As if to show the value of the former jungle land, the cacao trees planted there produced a crop in the fourth year, a full twelve months earlier than usual.

VIRGIN SOIL

Type of work: Novel
Author: Ivan Turgenev (1818-1883)
Type of plot: Social criticism
Time of plot: 1868
Locale: Russia
First published: 1872

Principal characters:
NEZHDÁNOFF, a student
PÁHKLIN, his friend
SIPYÁGIN, a nobleman
VALENTÍNA, his wife
MARKÉLOFF, Valentína's brother
MARIANNA, Sipyágin's niece
SOLÓMIN, a factory superintendent

Critique:

Virgin Soil is in many respects typical of Turgenev. It is realistic, almost photographically so, reflecting the dominant pessimism of the author. Here we have a sensitive and sympathetic portrayal of the beginnings of Russian liberalism after the emancipation of the serfs. We see also the essential humanitarianism of the socialists and the frivolity of the aristocracy as both sides struggle in the developing industrialization. But in the conflict the chief liberal protagonists prove incapable and seal their own doom.

The Story:

Miss Mashúrin and Ostrodúmoff, both socialists, were waiting in Nezhdánoff's room in a poor quarter of St. Petersburg. A letter from a high leader had made a conference necessary, for another vague revolutionary project was under way. While they waited they were joined by Páhklin, a sly hanger-on of the intelligentsia, who wanted to discuss a critical matter with Nezhdánoff the student.

Nezhdánoff was late, but when he came they plunged into a discussion of their project. They needed money for a trip to Moscow, and they were all poor. Nezhdánoff, however, was the illegitimate son of a nobleman, and in a pinch he could secure small sums of money from his father. He promised to have the required sum the next day.

The conspirators were interrupted by the arrival of the elegant and noble Sipyágin, who had sat next to Nezhdánoff at the theater. A dilettante liberal, he had been attracted by the opinions and views of the poor student, and he came to offer Nezhdánoff a post as tutor to his young son at a salary of a hundred roubles a month. Sipyágin was generous, even offering to pay a month's salary in advance. So with the blessing of his socialist comrades, Nezhdánoff accepted the offer and went to live on the country estate of Sipyágin.

The household of Sipyágin was interesting, and after Nezhdánoff got over his shyness he made good progress with nine-year-old Kolya, his student. For a time, Nezhdánoff was content to live a leisurely life, for his duties were light. Although she scarcely spoke to him, Marianna, the penniless niece, attracted Nezhdánoff greatly. She was evidently unhappy, and she was abrupt and forthright in her attitude toward her rich relatives.

Valentína, Sipyágin's wife, was a beautiful woman without much heart. Although she herself was coldly virtuous, she enjoyed snaring men to see them dance at her bidding. She invited Nezhdánoff to her boudoir ostensibly to discuss her son's education, but in reality to captivate the young tutor. When he failed to respond to her attractions, she was nettled at his indifference. Then it became apparent that Nezhdánoff was attracted to Marianna, and Valentína became jealous.

Markéloff, Valentína's brother, came to visit the family. He was a savage, intense man who expressed his liberal opinions with great emphasis and alienated most of the company with his boorish ways. During a walk Nezhdánoff surprised Marianna and Markéloff in a lonely wood; he heard Marianna refuse something vigorously. Later, in an impulsive outburst, Marianna confided that Markéloff had proposed marriage.

This confidence strengthened the bond between Marianna and Nezhdánoff. That evening the tutor was surprised by an invitation to Markéloff's room. There he learned that Markéloff was a party member and a vigorous exponent of immediate action, who had been ordered to question Nezhdánoff about party activities on Sipyágin's estate and in his factory. Nezhdánoff had done nothing to stir up discontent among the peasants or workers, for he had been apathetic toward socialism for some time. Under Markéloff's urging he resolved to spread propaganda among the workmen.

Nezhdánoff confided his aims and problems to Marianna, who became a ready convert to revolutionary thought, her zeal surpassing that of Nezhdánoff. With Markéloff, Nezhdánoff visited some of the party members in the neighborhood, among them a man named Solómin.

Solómin was a factory manager and a good one, a calm, taciturn man of great strength of character. Sipyágin had tried to hire him to manage Sipyágin's own factory, but Solómin had refused. He was content where he was and he could scarcely conceal his contempt for the whole aristocracy. Sipyágin had taken the refusal with bad grace, and now began to show suspicion of Nezhdánoff.

From time to time Marianna and Nezhdánoff met in her room at night to discuss socialism. Although they were in love, they did not act as lovers. Valentína spied on the girl constantly. She made insinuations about her niece's character, and the atmosphere in the house-hold became quite unpleasant. At length Sipyágin discharged Nezhdánoff. Early the next morning Nezhdánoff returned with a cart for Marianna, and the two fled for shelter to the factory where Solómin was employed. The manager concealed them in his living quarters, and Nezhdánoff and Marianna lived together as brother and sister, waiting for the time when Nezhdánoff could be sure enough of his love to marry.

Marianna put on peasant clothes and tried to learn peasant ways so that she would be a good worker for the revolution. Nezhdánoff, roughly clothed, made many trips among the farmers and mill hands to talk to them of liberty and freedom. He was unsuccessful in his attempts, however, for he was far too impetuous and harangued peasant groups in words they could not understand. On one occasion Nezhdánoff tried to drink vodka to ingratiate himself with the workers, but strong drink only made him sick. More and more he became conscious of failure, and felt that he could not marry Marianna. She, in turn, became more aware of Nezhdánoff's weakness and Solómin's strength.

When the peasants in Markéloff's district rebelled against paying their taxes, Markéloff rashly urged complete and armed rebellion, but his manner was so abusive that the peasants turned against him, beat him severely, and delivered him to the general commanding the district police. This disquieting news reached Solómin's factory, and the conspirators there made plans to flee.

Páhklin, misguided in his sympathy, decided to appeal to Sipyágin to intercede for his brother-in-law, Markéloff. Foolishly he babbled the hiding place of Marianna and Nezhdánoff. Sipyágin kept Páhklin under close surveillance and went to see the general. So great was Sipyágin's influence that the general consented to release Markéloff if he would confess his crime and promise to stir up no more trouble. But Markéloff was stubborn. He repeated his belief in the revolution and refused to acknowledge any errors. The general had no choice but to imprison him. Then at the instigation of Sipyágin, the police prepared to raid Solómin's factory.

Solómin quietly made plans to disappear. Nezhdánoff, confronted by his own weakness and by his inability to love Marianna enough to marry her, wrote a last letter and killed himself with a revolver. In the letter he asked that Marianna marry Solómin. An obliging priest performed the ceremony quickly and Solómin and Marianna departed. When the police arrived, they discovered only the suicide of Nezhdánoff.

Markéloff was tried and sentenced to Siberia. Solómin reappeared, but was released because the police had no evidence against him. He rejoined Marianna, who had by that time agreed to live with him as his wife. They were busy with Solómin's new factory.

Back in St. Petersburg, Páhklin was unhappy, for the liberals now called him a spy. By chance he met Miss Mashúrin in the street. She was now supposedly an Italian countess. Somewhere she had secured an Italian passport and funds for traveling. Páhklin invited her to have tea with him. Although she despised him, she accepted, for he had been Nezhdánoff's friend. From Páhklin Miss Mashúrin got a photograph of Nezhdánoff, with whom she had always been in love.

THE VIRGINIA COMEDIANS

Type of work: Novel
Author: John Esten Cooke (1830-1886)
Type of plot: Sentimental romance
Time of plot: 1763-1765
Locale: Colonial Virginia
First published: 1854

Principal characters:
CHAMP EFFINGHAM, foppish scion of a wealthy planter
BEATRICE HALLAM, a young actress with whom Effingham falls in love
CLARE LEE, Effingham's cousin and fiancée
CHARLES WATERS, Effingham's rival for Beatrice Hallam
CAPTAIN RALPH WATERS, Charles Waters' brother
JACK HAMILTON, friend of Effingham, his sister's fiancé

Critique:

John Esten Cooke was one of the last of the historical romanticists who followed the footsteps of James Fenimore Cooper. He was also the first of a long line of authors who continue to idealize the pre-Civil War South. Unlike some of the imitators of Cooper, Cooke wrote books which are well grounded in the history of Virginia, especially that of the James River section, in which most of them are laid. While Cooke's novels display a keen sense of the dramatic, his books have too much elegance and too much sentimentality for most modern tastes. This novel survives, however, for its vivid pictures of places and events in the early history of the state.

The Story:

In the spring of 1763, Williamsburg, the Colonial capital of Virginia, was treated to its first professional dramatic presentation by an English company called The Virginia Comedians. The Colony, rich and poor, was highly excited over the event. The day the company was to arrive in Williamsburg, young Champ Effingham, son of a wealthy planter, rode to town for a holiday. Young Effingham, educated at Oxford, had taken up the ways of the London fops while in England. His dress was extraordinary; his manners were artificial.

On the way to Williamsburg he met a beautiful young woman on horseback who asked him the way. When questioned by him, she refused to give her name, stating only that she was unknown to him because she was not a lady. The mystery was solved the next day at the play, when Effingham discovered that the girl was an actress with the traveling company. Despite the fact that he was engaged to marry one of the most beautiful and wealthy of the Virginia girls, Effingham became infatuated with the actress, whose name was Beatrice Hallam. She was the daughter of the manager of the company.

There was scandal in the neighborhood when it became known that Champ Effingham was paying court to the actress. Everyone among the gentry was perturbed, for actresses were considered low in the social scale. When word came to Effingham's father, the old gentleman ordered his son to desist. The son's answer was to leave the house and take up residence at the inn in Williamsburg where the players were lodging. Effingham had little success with Beatrice Hallam, however. She despised him because of his artificial manners and his condescending attitude. She was really in love with a commoner, a young man named Charles Waters, who had rescued her from the James River on a stormy day when she had fallen overboard while boating.

Beatrice's father, on the other hand, wanted his daughter to encourage young

4031

Effingham. Mr. Hallam saw in Effingham a chance for his daughter to marry into a wealthy family, thus gaining an honest reputation for herself and a comfortable life for him.

At the opening of the session of the House of Burgesses, the governor gave a ball for the gentry of the colony. When an invitation was sent to Effingham, he resolved to take Beatrice to the ball, but his friends warned him not to do so because of the scandal. Although Beatrice did not want to go with him to the ball, her father finally browbeat her into agreeing. Effingham, daring his friends to prevent his appearance with an actress, vowed to fight duels with all who tried to hinder him or who insulted the girl.

At the ball everything went smoothly, for the Virginians, too well-mannered to make a disturbance over Effingham's actions, were all coolly polite to the actress. Their coolness only made the girl miserable, however, particularly when she knew how she was hurting Clare Lee, to whom Effingham had been engaged.

After the ball Effingham resolved to turn actor and join the company under the direction of Mr. Hallam. The manager was happy to have the young Virginian. In trying to find a costume for himself, Effingham inadvertently uncovered a little girl's dress and a letter, both of which he dropped in Beatrice's room. The dress and letter proved to her that she was not Hallam's daughter, and that her name was really Beatrice Waters. After some investigation, she learned that she was the cousin of the Charles Waters who had rescued her from the river and death by drowning.

Effingham was furious when he discovered the relationship between Beatrice and Charles Waters. Rather than fight a duel with the girl's cousin, he kidnaped her and took her away on his boat. But Charles and a friend followed and boarded Effingham's craft. In the fight to rescue Beatrice, Effingham wounded his rival. Thinking he had killed him, Effingham, in his extremity, went home to his father, who arranged for his son's escape to Europe.

After Effingham left for Europe, Beatrice nursed her cousin and restored him to health. Before long they were married and moved to a home in the uplands of the Piedmont region of Virginia. They left behind Captain Ralph Waters, Charles' brother, who had vowed to fight a duel with Champ Effingham on his brother's behalf. The planters were glad to see Charles Waters leave for another area; he had been heard to speak against the British government and to advocate a revolution.

Two years passed before Champ Effingham returned to Virginia, after learning that his sword thrust had not killed Charles Waters. Young Effingham, thoroughly cured of his infatuation for Beatrice, had also lost his foppishness of dress and manner. Although he returned a changed and acceptable young man, he was given to periods of moodiness, and nothing his family could do restored him to mental health. Then his boyhood friend, Jack Hamilton, secretly engaged to Effingham's sister, resolved to try to restore the young man. He encouraged, even forced Effingham to ride out to hounds and to visit other houses. He brought Captain Ralph Waters and Effingham together and made them friends. Still young Effingham remained moody and gloomy.

At last Hamilton resolved to try the power of jealousy, for he knew that Effingham was still very much in love with Clare Lee, whom he had thrown aside in his infatuation for Beatrice. In addition, Hamilton knew that Clare still loved Effingham and would accept him as her husband, in spite of all that had happened. Hamilton pretended to be in love with Clare; he even talked to Effingham about his suit for her hand. Such talk was too much for Effingham, who stirred himself to threaten Hamilton until he learned that Hamilton was really engaged to his sister. His sister and Hamilton finally persuaded him to go see

Clare, who readily accepted his suit and promised to become Mrs. Champ Effingham.

Happiness reigned in the Colony. Hamilton and Effingham's sister were married a few days after the wedding of Effingham and Clare. Captain Ralph Waters and Clare's sister were also married. The marriages seemed to mark the end of an era, however, for at the time of their celebration news came to the Colony of the passage of the Stamp Act, which everyone hated. Before long many began to speak of revolt against the British Crown. A leader of the agitators was Charles Waters, who returned to Williamsburg after the death of his wife Beatrice.

THE VIRGINIAN

Type of work: Novel
Author: Owen Wister (1860-1938)
Type of plot: Regional romance
Time of plot: Late nineteenth century
Locale: Wyoming
First published: 1902

> *Principal characters:*
> THE VIRGINIAN, a cowboy
> JUDGE HENRY, the Virginian's employer
> TRAMPAS, a cowboy, the Virginian's enemy
> STEVE, a cowboy friend of the Virginian
> SHORTY, a cowboy at Judge Henry's ranch
> MOLLY WOOD, a young schoolteacher at Bear Creek, Wyoming

Critique:

The Virginian is one of the classic novels of the American West. Owen Wister was familiar with Wyoming and the cowboys who worked there, for he himself had spent several years in the Western country. Wister saw that although the mountains and the plains would remain, the picturesque cowboy was rapidly disappearing, along with the antelope, the buffalo, and the unfenced grazing lands.

The Story:

The Virginian had been sent by his employer to meet an Eastern guest at Medicine Bow and escort him the two hundred and sixty miles from the town to Sunk Creek Ranch. While the Virginian and the guest were awaiting the arrival of the Easterner's trunk on the following westbound train, the cowboy entered into a poker game. One of the players, a cowboy named Trampas, accused the Virginian of cheating. The man backed down, however, before the gun of the cowboy from Sunk Creek. It was apparent to everyone that the Virginian had made an implacable enemy.

A few months later, in the fall, a schoolmistress came West from Vermont to teach in the new school at Bear Creek, Wyoming. All the single men, and there were many of them in the territory, anxiously awaited the arrival of the new teacher, Molly Wood. The Virginian was fortunate in his first meeting with her. A drunken stage driver tried to ford a creek in high water and marooned his coach and passenger. The Virginian, passing by, rode to the stage, lifted out the young woman, and deposited her safely on the bank of the stream. After he had ridden away, Molly missed her handkerchief and realized the young cowboy had somehow contrived to take it.

The next time the Virginian saw Molly, she was a guest at a barbecue. The cowboy had ridden his horse for two days for an opportunity to see her, but she coquettishly refused to notice him. The Virginian and another cowboy, piqued by her attitude, got drunk and played a prank on all the people who had brought their children to the barbecue. They switched the babies and their clothing, so that when the barbecue was over many of the mothers carried off the wrong babies. Before he left for Sunk Creek, the Virginian warned Molly that she was going to love him eventually, no matter what she thought of him then.

During the next year the Virginian began to read books for the first time since he had left school in the sixth grade. He borrowed the books from Molly in order to ride to Bear Creek to see her at intervals. In the meantime he had risen high in the estimation of his employer. Judge Henry put him in charge of a party of men who were to escort two trainloads of steers to the Chicago market.

On the trip back to the ranch the Virginian's men threatened to desert the train to go prospecting for gold which had been discovered in the Black Hills. The ringleader of the insurgents was Trampas.

The Virginian saw that the best way to win over the men was to make a fool of Trampas. His chance came when the train stopped near a bridge that was being repaired. Since there was no food on the train, the Virginian went out and gathered a sackful of frogs to cook. Then he began a story about frogs. a tall story by which Trampas was completely taken in. As soon as the rest of the cowboys saw how foolish Trampas appeared, they were willing to return to the ranch, much to the discomfiture of their ringleader.

Back at Sunk Creek, the Virginian found a pleasant surprise awaiting him. The foreman of the ranch had been forced to leave because of an invalid wife, and the judge had made the Virginian his foreman.

Trampas had expected to be discharged from his job as soon as the Virginian became foreman at the Sunk Creek Ranch. The Virginian, however, decided it was better to have his enemy in sight, and so Trampas stayed on, sullen and defiant in his behavior.

The following spring the Virginian made a trip to a neighboring ranch. On the way back he was attacked by Indians and severely wounded. He managed to escape from the Indians and make his way to a spring. There he was found, half dead, by Molly Wood. The girl stayed with him at the risk of her life, for the Indians were still in the vicinity. She then bound his wounds and took him back to her cabin and called a doctor.

Molly, meanwhile, had packed her possessions, for she was preparing to leave for her home in the East. By the time the Virginian had recovered sufficiently to go back to work, she had decided not to leave Wyoming. She was sure by then that she was in love with the cowboy foreman. When the Virginian left her cabin for Sunk Creek, Molly had promised to marry him.

Upon returning to work, the Virginian found that his enemy, Trampas, had disappeared, taking another of the cowboys, Shorty, with him. About the same time the ranches in that territory began to lose cattle to rustlers, and a posse was formed to track down the cattle thieves. After several weeks of searching, two of the thieves were caught. Since the rustlers had somehow managed to gain control of the local courts and had already been freed on one charge, the posse hanged both of them. It was a terrible experience for the Virginian. because one of the men, Steve, had been a close friend. The Virginian hated to think he had hanged his friend, and the hurt was made worse by the fact that the condemned man had refused to say a word to his former companion.

On his way back to Sunk Creek, the Virginian came across the trail of the other two rustlers. They were Trampas and Shorty. Because they had only one horse between them, Trampas murdered Shorty in order to escape.

When Molly Wood heard of the lynching and the Virginian's part in it, she refused to marry him. But after a conversation with Judge Henry, she realized that the Virginian had done no more than his duty. She and the Virginian were reconciled and a date was set for their wedding.

On the day before their wedding, Molly and the Virginian started to ride to Medicine Bow. On the way they met Trampas, who galloped ahead of them into the town. Molly questioned the Virginian about the man and discovered the enmity between the two. When they arrived in town, they were warned that Trampas had said he would shoot the Virginian if he were not out of town by sunset. Molly told him that she could never marry him if he fought with

Trampas and killed him. The Virginian, knowing that his honor was at stake, left her in the hotel and went out to face his enemy. Trampas fired first and missed. Then the Virginian fired and killed Trampas.

When the Virginian returned to the hotel, Molly was too glad to see him alive to remember her threat. Hearing the shots, she had been afraid that the Virginian had been killed. They were married the following day, as they had planned, and spent two months of their honeymoon high in the Rocky Mountains where no other humans ever went.

THE VIRGINIANS

Type of work: Novel
Author: William Makepeace Thackeray (1811-1863)
Type of plot: Historical romance
Time of plot: Late eighteenth century
Locale: England and the Colony of Virginia
First published: 1857-1859

Principal characters:
GEORGE, and
HARRY WARRINGTON, the Virginians
RACHEL ESMOND WARRINGTON, their mother
GEORGE WASHINGTON, a family friend
LORD CASTLEWOOD, an English kinsman
MARIA CASTLEWOOD, Lord Castlewood's sister
BARONESS BERNSTEIN, Rachel Warrington's half-sister, formerly Beatrix Esmond
COLONEL LAMBERT, a friend
THEO LAMBERT, Colonel Lambert's daughter and George's wife
HETTY LAMBERT, Colonel Lambert's other daughter
FANNY MOUNTAIN WARRINGTON, Harry's wife

Critique:

The *Virginians* might almost be studied as a group of portraits of the lesser nobility of England and the gentry of Virginia. The author shows us many pictures: a despotic mother who is the head of a great Colonial estate; her two sons, one to become a great soldier under Washington, the other an English gentleman. We see England in the time of Johnson and Richardson and David Garrick and America in the early days of her struggle for independence. For his material Thackeray studied the letters, either real or imagined, of two brothers who lived on opposite sides of the ocean and who had opposing views on the Revolutionary War. From these letters he created his story of romance and adventure.

The Story:

Although Harry and George Warrington were twins, George was declared the heir to their father's estate by virtue of having been born half an hour before his brother. Both were headstrong lads, greatly pampered by their widowed mother, Rachel Esmond Warrington, who managed her Virginia estate, Castlewood, much as she would have managed the mansion in the old country. She never let her sons forget their high birth, and she herself had dropped the name of Warrington in favor of her maiden name, Esmond, in order that everyone would remember she was of noble rank. Rachel was a dictator on her plantation, and although she was respected by many, she was loved by few.

Harry and George were trained according to the place and the time. They learned to ride and shoot and gamble like gentlemen, but had little formal education other than a small knowledge of Latin and French. Their mother hoped they might pattern themselves after Colonel George Washington, who was their neighbor and her close friend. Harry worshipped Washington from his youth to his death, but George and Colonel Washington were never to be friends.

When General Braddock arrived from England to command the English troops in the war against the French, Washington and George Warrington joined his forces. Although Harry was the better soldier, George represented the family because of his position as elder son. Braddock was defeated and George was reported captured and killed by the French. George's mother blamed Colonel Washington for not guarding her son, and Washington was no longer welcome at Castlewood.

Upon George's death, Harry became

the heir, and his mother sent him to visit his relatives in England. There he met his mother's kinsman, Lord Castlewood; her half-sister, Baroness Bernstein; and Will, Maria, and Fanny Esmond, his cousins. Of all his relatives, only Baroness Bernstein was fond of him. Harry and Will were enemies from their first meeting, and the rest of the family thought him a savage and tolerated him only because he would some day inherit the estate in Virginia. Harry thought himself in love with Maria, who was his mother's age, and sent her many gifts and passionate letters declaring himself hers and asking for her hand in marriage.

Harry was the toast of the country. He spent money lavishly on fine clothes and horses and at first won thousands of pounds at cards. But when his luck turned and he lost all his money, most of his former friends had only unkind words for him. Matters became so desperate that he was jailed for his debts, and Baroness Bernstein was the only one of his relatives who offered to help him. But there was a string attached to her offer. She was violently opposed to his intended marriage to Maria and would pay his debts only if he promised to break his word to that lady. Harry was tired of Maria, but he felt it was beneath a gentleman of his position to break his word, and he refused the baroness' help under her conditions. He would rather remain in prison.

There his brother George found him. For George had escaped from the French after eighteen months in prison and had returned to his home in Virginia, where he and his mother had decided that he, too, should visit England. He paid his brother's debts, and the two boys had a joyful reunion. Harry now had to return to his status as younger brother and George assumed his place as heir to Castlewood in Virginia.

Before Harry's imprisonment and George's arrival in England, Harry had made the acquaintance of Colonel Lambert and his family. There were two daughters, Theo and Hetty, whom the twin brothers found most charming. Theo and George fell in love, and after overcoming her father's objections, they were married. At first they lived in poverty, for George had spent all his money to rescue Harry from debtor's prison and to buy for him a commission in the army. George's only income for a time was from two tragedies he had written, one a success and the other a failure.

Shortly after Harry received his commission he joined General Wolfe and sailed for America to fight the French in the Colonies. Maria had released him from his promise to her, and he gladly took leave of his English relatives. About this time George inherited a title and an estate from an unexpected source. Sir Miles Warrington, his father's brother, died; and as young Miles Warrington, the only male heir, had been killed in an accident, the title and the estate fell to George. Now he and Theo lived in comparative luxury. They traveled extensively, and one day they decided to visit George's mother and brother in Virginia.

When they arrived in America they found the Colonies to be in a state of unrest. The colonists were determined not to pay all the taxes which the British crown levied against them, and there was much talk of war. At Castlewood there was also trouble. Harry had married Fanny Mountain, the daughter of his mother's housekeeper, and his mother refused to accept the girl. Harry had moved to his own smaller estate, but there was a great tension between the members of the family. George and Theo and their mother were loyal to the king. Harry became a true Virginian and followed General George Washington into battle. In spite of their different loyalties the brothers remained friends.

Shortly before the end of the war George and Theo returned to England. Although they were grieved at the outcome of the war, it made little difference in their lives. Harry visited them in England after the death of his wife, but their mother never again left her native

Virginia. George and Theo tried to persuade Hetty to marry Harry, whom she had once loved deeply, but she refused to leave her widowed father. The only departure from their quiet life came when Lord Castlewood tried to steal Castlewood in Virginia from their mother after her deed and title were burned during the war. But George was able to prevent the fraud and save the estate. Intending never to leave England again, he renounced his right to the Virginia land. Harry returned to Virginia, where he was made a general, to live out his life at Castlewood in the company of his mother. The brothers were destined never to meet again, but their love for each other went with them throughout their lives.

VISIÓN DE ANÁHUAC

Type of work: Essay
Author: Alfonso Reyes (1889-1959)
First published: 1917

For more than fifty years, in book after book, Alfonso Reyes has demonstrated the excellence and universality of Hispano-American letters. Poet, short story writer, essayist, critic, theoretician, metaphysicist, and a scholar in the best humanist tradition, he has ranged for his themes and materials from Athens in the classic age to the Indian pueblos and the history of his native Mexico. Under these circumstances it may seem somewhat arbitrary to let a single essay, even one commonly found in separate publication, represent a writer of such variety and scope. But *Visión de Anáhuac,* written in Madrid in 1915 and published in San José de Costa Rica two years later, is one of those seminal works in which significance or influence bears no relationship to bulk. It is a prose poem, a landscape painting, a patriotic invocation, a study in history, an archaeological reconstruction, a literary critique, an exercise in style. The late Gabriela Mistral, Chilean poet, called it the best single piece of Latin American prose.

Anáhuac was the Nahuatl name for the Valley of Mexico, site of the great city of Tenochtitlán and the center of the Aztec civilization which fell to the rapacity of the conquistadores under Hernán Cortés in 1521. In a style that is subtle, evocative, and varied, Alfonso Reyes re-creates the wonder of that place and time when two races, two societies, confronted each other and the feudal barbarism of the Old World performed its act of violence upon the Indian barbarism of the New. Years later Bernal Díaz del Castillo, chronicler of the conquest, voiced his lament for a despoiled culture that was passionate and cruel but also beautiful and splendid: "Now all is lost, razed, so that there is nothing."

In the epigraph to his essay Reyes welcomes the traveler to the most crystalline region of the air. In this luminous prose and vivid imagery every object stands out, distinct and immaculate in color and form, bathed in the blue and gold intensity of sky and sun. For the sake of analogy Reyes invokes the name of Giovanni Battista Ramusio, who began to publish his collection *Delle Navigazioni e Viaggi* in Venice in 1550. Among the illustrations in this old work are scenes of the New World as the explorers saw them and wrote about them. These pictures, ingenuous in conception, meticulous in design, present an exotic world of nature in the vegetation of New Spain: the ear of corn, the clustered banana, the strange tropical fruits distilling their own fragrance and honey, and in stiff array the varieties of cacti, emblematic plants of a semi-arid land where the cactus, the eagle, and the serpent are the appropriate heraldic devices for a coat of arms.

To the priests and warriors of the tribe that entered the valley early in the fourteenth century—the last of such migrations into Anáhuac—the legendary vision of the eagle and the serpent was the fulfillment of a prophecy. Behind that roving band lay a history of many wanderings and wars in which memory and fact faded into a primitive myth of warriors who came out of the Seven Caves to which the seven tribes traced their dim beginnings. There they built a city, a flower of stone on water, and the city became an empire, cyclopean like those of Egypt and Babylon, over which Moctezuma the magnificent but weak ruled in the ill-omened days that heralded the coming of the white man. The stage had been set for the last act in an ancient drama of conquest and settlement when Cortés and his followers crossed the snow-capped mountains and descended through fields of maize and maguey to the valley floor.

Ahead of them, connected with the

mainland by three stone causeways two lances in width, Tenochtitlán rose like a mirage from waters that caught and held the color of the sky. In that clear atmosphere every detail of the city and its environs could be viewed as if through crystal, an intricate pattern of temples, palaces, public squares, streets, canals, and gardens bright with flowers. Over the city loomed the bulk of the great temple, with wide streets radiating from its four corners. Smoke rose from the sanctuaries atop the holy pyramid, and through the still air came the echoing rumble of drums and the thin music of flutes.

To the Spaniards the sight was like some vision of enchantment, for the conquistadores carried in their blood the same strain of wonder that had produced the romantic story of Amadís of Gaul. "As soon as we saw so many cities and towns in the water," Díaz del Castillo wrote, "we were struck with amazement and said that it seemed like things from the book of Amadís because of the great towers and temples and houses which they had built in the water, and all of them of stone and mortar, and even some of our soldiers spoke of what they saw as if they were in a land of dreams. . . ."

As Alfonso Reyes points out, the life of the city revolved around three central points: the temple, the market place, and Moctezuma's palace. In all sections of the city, the pattern was repeated in the smaller shrines, the market squares, the palaces of the nobles. The proud, somber Indian of Anáhuac was a worshiper of fierce gods, a shrewd trader, a lover of ceremony and display.

Within the serpent-carved wall of the sacred enclosure stood the great temple, a terraced, monolithic pyramid built of basalt and porphyry slabs quarried from the surrounding hills. Inside this precinct the apartments of the priests, the study halls, and rooms for the storage of sacrificial utensils and books of ritual covered an area which could have enclosed a village of five hundred persons. One hundred and fourteen steps led to the highest platform on which were images of the gods, housed in sanctuaries decorated with carvings of men and monsters in wood and stone. The giant idols, made of cereals and blood, were decorated with precious metals and jewels. Sacred fires burned on the altars. Close at hand were trumpets, censers, flutes, conch shells, and the flint knives used for human sacrifice. There also was the ceremonial serpent-skin drum which could be heard two leagues away. Blood spattered the altars and floors. The priests wore black robes and their hair was matted with gore. They were the guardians of savage rituals, the ministers of a faith reaching downward toward that concept of earth and blood which is the dark mystery at the heart of mankind's remote origins.

From the horrors of the temple the Spaniards turned to the bustle of the market place. It was, said Cortés, twice as large as that of Salamanca and there every day some sixty thousand people engaged in buying and selling under the supervision of inspectors and twelve presiding magistrates. All the produce of the land was offered for sale, each in its separate quarter under deep porticoes: jewelry of precious stones and metals, collars, bracelets, earrings, lip plugs of jade, crystal, emerald, turquoise, gold, silver, and copper; beautiful featherwork, shimmering as a hummingbird poised in sunlight; flowers from Xochimilco; textiles that reminded Cortés of the silk market in Granada; game of all kinds, partridge, quail, wild ducks, rabbits, deer, and small dogs bred for eating; vegetables of every description, onions, leeks, cresses, sorrel, artichokes, beans, and golden thistles; corn, red, black, yellow, and blue, sold green on the ear or dried or ground or baked into loaves and tortillas; fish, fruits, cacao, syrups of corn and maguey; building materials, stone, bricks, timber; firewood and charcoal for cooking and heating; pottery for every use, painted and glazed; eggs, cakes, sweets, hides, tobacco. There was a quarter for apothecaries—Indian herbalists acquainted the Spaniards with more than twelve hundred medicinal plants and roots—and another for barbers. There were houses where food was cooked and served. In another quarter was the slave market where traders cried their human merchandise. The Indian market, according to Díaz del Castillo, surprised even those who had been to Constantinople and Rome.

Those familiar with the Spanish court were equally astonished by the pomp and splendor that surrounded Moctezuma. To their awed gaze he seemed another Midas whose touch turned everything to gold, so that it was necessary for him to uncover himself to show Cortés that he was, like other men, of human flesh. As the poet has said, if there is poetry in America it is Moctezuma on his throne of gold. In his palaces he had reproduced in precious stones, gold, silver, or feathers every natural object in his kingdom. Six hundred lords attended him daily. When he dined, three hundred noble youths were needed to serve him, for he had put before him every variety of meat, fish, vegetables, and fruits in the land. Four times a day he changed his dress, and his garments, like the dishes from which he was served, were never used again. Those who approached his person wore poor clothing and abased themselves in humility. When he took his ease, dancers, buffoons, and acrobats entertained him.

In his great palace the walls were of porphyry, jasper, and marble, roofed with carved beams and richly carpeted with cotton carpets, skins, and featherwork. Fountains played in the courtyards. He had other palaces for his recreation. One contained pools of water, salt and sweet, for every kind of aquatic bird. Another section contained birds prized for the beauty of their plumage. Still another housed birds of prey, for the king was skilled in falconry. There was a palace in which wild animals and reptiles were kept. Another was given over to the raising of flowers—no vegetables or fruit trees ever grew in the Indian garden—fragrant shrubs, and scented herbs.

In a land where nature was so insep-arably joined to the daily lives of the people, the flower, not the snakeskin drum or the sacrificial knife, was the symbol of their culture, a symbol of the love of art and beauty that redeemed in part the cruelty of their religion. The Aztec noble carried flowers in his hand when he walked abroad; garlands decked him on ceremonial occasions. Flowers filled the markets, the palaces, the adobe houses of the poor. Floral designs decorated the pottery of Cholula. Floating gardens covered the lakes. In the calendrical codices a shower of flowers is shown descending upon the earth at the end of the fourth sun-cycle. The flower also had its consecration in art. Stylized in picture writing and in sculpture, appears in place names and as the designation of the exquisite qualities of things. And as the surviving fragments or corrupted translations show, the flower provided the themes and imagery in both the secular and religious poetry of the period before the conquest.

Alfonso Reyes laments the loss of the indigenous poetry of the Indians. Although scholars may unearth portions of their hymns, rituals, or festive songs, and although others still exist in the versions of the Spanish friars, nothing can ever compensate for the loss of that body of literature which reflected the religious and social experience of the people of Anáhuac. Findings and reconstructions contain only suggestions of what that poetry must have been, for even altered and indirect in the surviving versions it exhibits a degree of sensibility not characteristic of the translating Spanish missionaries who possessed more pity than imagination. One poem, "Ninoyolonotza," is quoted as an example of man's search through the world of the senses for a concept of the ideal. Another, paraphrased in part from the Quetzalcoatl cycle, contains echoes of an ancient fertility myth similar to those of Tammuz and Adonis. The likeness becomes cause for reflection. The promise of rebirth in the Quetzalcoatl legend, if fulfilled, might have destroyed the blood-drinking gods of the Aztecs and so altered the somber history of Anáhuac.

Discussion can do no more than suggest the magnificence of the writing in *Visión de Anáhuac*. All of pre-conquest Mexico is seen here, evoked out of a vast and prodigal storehouse of history and legend, every detail viewed through the eyes of a poet conferring impressions of sense and details of fact like a radiant gift. The style is in keeping with the theme, language rising from the page to the slow swing of its rhythms and the sudden thrust of its images, a mingling of grace and violence, of the concrete and the hauntingly allusive. It has been said that *Visión de Anáhuac* set a standard for a new kind of poetry. Certainly its auditory and visual effects have been echoed by a number of modern poets. Among others, Valéry Larbaud and Juan José Domenchina have called attention to similarities of tone and style between this prose poem by Alfonso Reyes and the *Anabasis* of St.-John Perse. It should be pointed out also that *Visión de Anáhuac* is the antecedent work.

THE VISION OF WILLIAM, CONCERNING PIERS THE PLOWMAN

Type of work: Poem
Author: William Langland (c. 1332-c. 1400)
Time: The fourteenth century
Locale: England
First transcribed: c. 1362, c. 1377; complete version c. 1395

Principal characters:
THE POET
PIERS THE PLOWMAN, an English plowman who becomes an allegorical
    figure of Christ incarnate
LADY MEDE, an allegorical figure representing both just reward and
    bribery
CONSCIENCE,
REASON,
THOUGHT,
WIT,
STUDY,
CLERGY,
SCRIPTURE,
FAITH,
HOPE,
CHARITY, and other allegorical figures

Like Geoffrey Chaucer's *Canterbury Tales*, William Langland's *The Vision of William, Concerning Piers the Plowman* is one of the great vernacular works of the fourteenth century. Unlike Chaucer's poetry, however, Langland's work is apparently of and for the people, rather than the court. That the poem was popular is attested to by the meter in which it was written and by the fact that more than fifty manuscripts of the poem are still extant. Within the manuscripts are three different texts, the second and third being revisions containing additions to the first and earliest. The three versions have been dated respectively by scholars at about 1362, 1377, and 1395.

Langland's poem is in part a work of social protest, written from the viewpoint of the common man. The last half of the fourteenth century was a period of disaster and social unrest, the time of severe visitations of the plague (with accompanying moral, social, and economic upheavals), of the Peasant Revolt of 1381, and of John Wycliffe's Lollard movement. Langland often inserted, on behalf of the common folk, protests against unfair dealings by the crown, the courts, the clergy, and even the tradesmen. Being of the common folk himself, the poet recognized the trouble visited upon them, and he cried out bitterly against the cheating of the poor by the butcher, the baker, the miller, and others.

Most authorities now grant that the poem was probably written by one man, although some doubt had been expressed in the past on this point. Internal evidence indicates the author to be William Langland, a recipient of minor orders in the Church and a married man living in London. Despite allusions and references to himself and to happenings of the times, however, the author has retained the anonymity typical of the medieval author. The alliterative verse, much like the metrical structure used in *Beowulf* and other Anglo-Saxon poems, was the native style of versification lost when the conventions of our present metrical system were popularized by the court poetry. In the hands of medieval writers, including Langland, the Old English alliterative verse had not the subtlety and power it had once had in the ninth and tenth centuries. As used by Langland the measure consisted of lines of any number of syllables, divided into half-lines. Each half-line was given two heavy beats in important words, with the heavy beats accentuated by alliteration, as in such a line as "And wo in winter-tyme—with wakynge a nyghtes."

To emphasize the social or metrical aspects of *Piers Plowman* seems totally unfair to the poem, for it is essentially a religious work, filled with the religious doctrines, dogma, views, and sentiments of medieval Catholicism. In the poem the poet has a series of visions which he relates to the reader, each vision concerned with man's relationships to God, relationships which concerned every aspect of life, according to medieval thought. In the first vision, which is probably the best known, the poet dreamed of a vast field of people going about all the tasks and activities of the poet's world. The vision was explained to him by a lady named Holy Church, who informed him that the castle at one end of the field was the home of Truth, or God, and that in the dungeon in the valley dwelt the Father of Falsehood, or Satan. When asked by the poet how he might save his soul, the lady replied that he should learn to accept Truth, along with love and pity for his fellow man. The poet then envisioned a long, involved sequence in which appeared Lady Mede, representing at the same time just reward and bribery. A king proposed to marry Lady Mede to Conscience, after her rescue from False, but Conscience proclaimed against her and refused. Bribery, it is implied, cannot be reconciled with conscience. Reason, sent for by the king, promised to serve him, too, if Conscience would be another counselor. One interesting part of this sequence of the poem is Conscience's explanation of Latin grammar, with its declension and agreement of noun and adjective, as a symbolic representation of the relationship between man and God. The king in the vision demanded a full explanation because, as he pointed out, English, the only language he knew, had no such grammatical relationships.

In another vision the poet viewed the seven deadly sins. After a sermon by Conscience, Piers Plowman offered to show the company the way to Holy Truth, but only after he had plowed a half-acre field. Mentioned in this section are Piers' wife and children: Dame Work-while-I-am-Able, Daughter Do-this-or-thy-Dame-shall-beat-thee, and Son Suffer-thy-Sovereigns-to-have-their-Wishes-Dare-not-Judge-them-for-if-thou-Dost-thou-shalt-Dearly-Abide-it. At the end of this vision Piers Plowman was granted a pardon for himself and his heirs forever.

In the next sequence the poet took up Piers Plowman's quest for Truth. This quest is divided somewhat ambiguously into three parts, searches for Do-Well, Do-Better, and Do-Best. To achieve the state of Do-Well, the poet learned, one must fear God, be honest, be obedient, and love one's fellow man; this seems to be the task of the ordinary man. Do-Better, the seeming lot of the priest, represents the teaching of the gospel and helping everyone. Do-Best, the seeming lot of the bishop, involves everything in the first two categories, as well as the wise administration of the Church to save all souls.

Piers Plowman appears again and again in the poem, each time being more clearly an incarnation of the Christ. Seen at first as a hardworking, sincere, and honest plowman, Piers later shows up in the poem as the figure who can explain to the poet the Tree of Charity and the nature of the Trinity of God. He appears also as the Good Samaritan and, later, as the builder of the Church and the one who will joust in God's armor against Satan. These appearances serve to hold the poem together; without them the work would be a too loosely coupled series of episodes and digressions.

Much Biblical lore is presented, both from the Old and New Testaments. The events in Eden, Job's trials, the perfidy of Judas, Jesus' suffering and crucifixion, along with many other familiar and traditional Christian elements are recorded in the poem. There are digressions on sin and virtue, on the nature and value of learning, and on the activities of laity and clergy, some good and some bad. These individual portions of the poem are beautifully executed and deeply moving. They are probably of more worth when considered by themselves insofar as a present day reader is concerned. To read Piers Plowman in its entirety is tedious, largely because of its rambling qualities; and few general readers will have the patience to do so nowadays, even with the help of a translation into modern English.

THE VITA NUOVA

Type of work: Poetry with prose comments
Author: Dante Alighieri (1265-1321)
First transcribed: c. 1292

In that part of the book of my mind before which there would be little to read is found a chapter heading which says: "Here begins the new life." It is my intention to copy into this little book the words I find written there; if not all of them, at least their essential doctrine.

So begins Dante's *Vita Nuova,* a celebration in prose and poetry of the great poet's love for Beatrice Portinari. Perhaps it is revealing to realize that this love was a poet's love; that is, Dante's love was not ordinary and practical, leading to forthright pursuit, engagement, marriage, and children. When Dante first saw Beatrice he was nine and she was eight. He was so affected by the sight of her that his "vital spirit" trembled, his "animal spirit" was amazed, and his "natural spirit" wept. At least, this is how it was if we may trust the *Vita Nuova.*

Dante realized that, whatever a poet's passion, such early love could hardly be convincing to anyone save the victim. After a few more sentences of praise the *Vita Nuova* proceeds to a description of an encounter nine years after the first, when Beatrice stood between two ladies and greeted Dante. It was the ninth hour of the day, and nine had already become a symbol of their love. We do not know what Beatrice said, and it probably does not matter; the important thing is that her greeting inspired Dante's first poem of love for Beatrice. We are told that in a dream after being greeted by Beatrice, Dante had a vision of Love holding Beatrice in his arms "nude except for a scanty, crimson cloth." Holding forth a fiery object, Love said, "Behold your heart," and shortly thereafter persuaded Beatrice to eat the heart. Then Love wept and ascended toward the heavens with the lady in his arms. This dream is the subject of the poem.

We know from other sources that the poem, a sonnet, was sent to Guido Cavalcanti, who wrote a sonnet in return, initiating a strong friendship between the poets. In the *Vita Nuova* Dante merely refers to "my first friend" and quotes the beginning of Cavalcanti's sonnet: "I think that you beheld all worth."

Dante reports that love so weakened him that everyone noticed that he was not himself. When his glances at Beatrice were misinterpreted as being directed at another lady, Dante, seizing upon the opportunity to disguise the true object of his love, pretended that the other lady was his love, and he wrote several "trifles" for her. When the lady who served as his screen left Florence on a journey, Dante knew that he should pretend to be dismayed. In fact, he was, but not from love; he was upset because his lover's scheming had been frustrated. Despite the complications, the resultant sonnet satisfied Dante, and it is included in the collection. A comparison of the first part of the sonnet with the translation by Mark Musa will give even those ignorant of Italian a sense of Dante's poetic genius:

O voi che per la via d'Amor passate,
Attendete e guardate
S'elli è dolore alcun, quanto 'l mio,
   grave;
E prego sol ch'audir mi sofferiate,
E poi imaginate
S'io son d'ogni tormento ostale e chiave.

O you who travel on the road of Love,
Pause here and look about
For any man whose grief surpasses
   mine.
I ask this only; hear me out, then judge
If I am not indeed
Of every torment keeper and shade.

Despite the attraction of Dante's poetry, it would be a mistake to take the *Vita Nuova* as primarily a collection of poems, leaving the prose passages for those interested in biography and the poet's comments on style and intent. The prose passages are charming in themselves, and they reveal an intelligent, sensitive man who is always the poet. Perhaps it is truer to say that Beatrice was for the poems, rather than the poems were for Beatrice. But we cannot say the same of the prose; it is not merely an instrument to provide a setting for the poetry, but together with the poetry it forms an organic work of art. Dante's account of his love is so clear and ingenuous in style that it is only the cold analyst looking back on what he has read who can say that the entire affair was largely a matter of the poet's imagination extravagantly at work. Although it may have been the imagination or the animal spirit that stirred Dante, the effect created convinces that the passion was genuine (as it probably was, however engendered) and under poetic control.

Upon observing the body of a young lady who had died and was being mourned by weeping ladies, Dante suddenly realized that he had seen her in the company of the lady whom he pretended to love in order to hide his love for Beatrice. Although this knowledge means that the departed lady is two times removed from Beatrice, Dante is moved to write two sonnets about death. The first begins, "If Love himself weep, shall not lovers weep,/Hearing for what sad cause he pours his tears?" and the second begins, "Brute death, the enemy of tenderness,/Timeless mother of grief . . . My tongue consumes itself with cursing you."

Since the lady who had served as Dante's screen had left the city, Dante imagined that Love directed him to another lady in order that, pretending to love her, he might hide his love for Beatrice. This device, celebrated in a sonnet, was so effective that Beatrice herself must have believed the stories concerning him—rumors which he himself initiated —and one day she refused to greet him as he passed by. In the midst of Dante's grief, described in long prose passages, Love again appeared to him and told him to write a poem explaining that it was Love's idea, not Dante's, that he pretend to love someone other than Beatrice.

Several poems which follow work out the implications of Beatrice's refusal to greet him. He explains in a sonnet that Love is both good and evil—the poet's way of saying that the lover, especially a poetic one like Dante, has difficulty in staying out of trouble.

A long *canzone*, directed to ladies "refined and sensitive in Love," contains some of Dante's most effective passages. Even Love says of Beatrice, "How can flesh drawn from clay,/Achieve such purity?" and Dante adds, "She is the highest nature can achieve/And by her mold all beauty tests itself. . . ."

After a *canzone* on the nature of Love ("Love and the gracious heart are but one thing . . ."), Dante wrote a sonnet explaining that the power of Love is awakened by Beatrice. This comparatively pleasant and romantic interlude was interrupted by the death of Beatrice's father. Two sonnets recount, with fine poetic elaboration, how Dante wept for her sorrow; but it was only after these poetic tasks and after a serious illness during which Dante realized how frail his own existence was that he finally thought, "Some day the most gracious Beatrice will surely have to die." In his delirium he imagined that Beatrice had died and that he called upon Death to take him; then the ladies at his bedside woke him. The result is a long, dramatic *canzone* in which the events of the dream are told.

One of the most entertaining of the prose sections of the *Vita Nuova* is Section XXV, in which Dante defends his speaking of Love as if it were a thing in itself, a bodily substance. The defense is as charming as it is sophistical. He explains that as a poet writing in the vernacular, not in Latin, it is his duty to make what he writes understandable to ladies. Since the vernacular was invented in order to talk about love, poets using the vernacular to write about love enjoy the same privileges granted to the Latin poets. Also, because Latin poets often spoke of inanimate objects as if they were beings—and Dante gives examples from Vergil, Lucan, Horace, and Ovid—Dante, as a vernacular poet writing of love, has the same right to speak of Love as if it were a human being.

In subsequent poems and prose passages Dante celebrates Beatrice's capacity to delight all persons by her presence; he explains how a word from her revives his spirit when it is overcome by Love; and he argues that her power is such that even remembering her is enough to make one feel her influence.

In Section XXVIII Dante reveals that Beatrice has died. He explains that it would not be proper in this book to discuss the *canzone* he was writing at the time, and he then devotes Section XXIX to a rather involved discussion of the significance of the number nine in connection with Beatrice. We know that Beatrice—who in 1285 had married Simone de' Bardi—died on June 8, 1290. How, then, can Dante read the number nine into the time of her death? He argues that, counting in the Arabian fashion, she departed "during the first hour of the ninth day of the month," and using the Syrian calendar which has a first month corresponding to our October, she departed in the ninth month. Other ingenious calculations are used to argue that Beatrice was a miracle since nine was her number and three is its root and the Trinity is the sole factor of all miracles.

A lengthy *canzone* tells of Dante's grief, after which he presents a sonnet cleverly devised to express a brother's sorrow in the first half—for Dante later sent the poem to Beatrice's brother—and the poet's own sorrow in the second half. As he tells us in the remarks prefacing the sonnet, only a person examining the sonnet carefully can tell that the dramatic speaker changes.

Dante writes that he was observed while weeping and that the young woman who observed him did so with such compassion that he wrote a sonnet to her. The sonnet was followed by another, and the second by a third, the third a self-chastisement for taking such pleasure in writing poetry for the compassionate lady.

After a few more sonnets Dante decided that he had better cease writing about Beatrice until he could honor her in his writing as no other lady had ever been honored. We know that this hope was not mere sentiment or poetic falsehood, for Beatrice appears again as one of the most favored of Heaven, guiding Dante through the Paradise of *The Divine Comedy*.

The *Vita Nuova* leaves the reader with an impression of Dante the poetic artist, constructing in his walks about Florence the ideas and lines so charmingly used in his book. Although one may be convinced that much of Dante's love was created by the artist for the sake of his poetry, there is so much skill and poetic grace in his work that the distinction between man and artist no longer seems important.

VIVIAN GREY

Type of work: Novel
Author: Benjamin Disraeli (1804-1881)
Type of plot: Political romance
Time of plot: Early nineteenth century
Locale: England and Germany
First published: 1826-1827

Principal characters:
VIVIAN GREY, an ambitious young Englishman
SIDNEY LORRAINE, Marquess of Carabas
MRS. FELIX LORRAINE, sister-in-law of Lord Carabas
BARON VON KONIGSTEIN, a German nobleman
LADY MADELEINE TREVOR, Vivian's friend
SYBILLA, an Austrian baroness
ESSPER GEORGE, Vivian's servant

Critique:

That such a story could achieve popularity in its time is neither a discredit to the youth of the author nor to popular taste. In *Vivian Grey* are reflected characteristics of the romantic concept of the young man struggling with his soul, of the nature of the frightening elements when the utmost in horror and terror are presented. However, there are more than the qualities of an Ann Radcliffe or Monk Lewis in this book, for precepts and truisms of a particular nature are scattered throughout the length of the narrative. Many of these reflect the political life of the times, and all of them reflect the mind of the nineteenth century. As such they deserve the study of any scholar or enthusiast for the activities of men. To read this novel is to understand better Lord Byron, Shelley, or William Godwin, and the intellectual world in which they participated.

The Story:

In school Vivian Grey was more popular with his fellow students than he was with his masters. After his expulsion from a private school conducted by Mr. Dallas, he continued his studies at home. Because he had decided on a career in politics, he flattered a nobleman who occasionally visited his father. This man was the Marquess of Carabas, an office holder who had been turned out because of his blundering incompetence. Vivian,

who hoped to obtain the patronage of a noble name and the backing of a privileged aristocracy, flattered the vain, stupid peer who still hoped to play an active part in the world of politics. As a result, Lord Carabas invited Vivian to visit his country seat, Chateau Desir. There Vivian met the fashionable Mrs. Felix Lorraine, his lordship's sister-in-law. During his visit Vivian took advantage of his opportunities by making love to the wives while securing the confidence of the husbands.

At a brilliant dinner Vivian made his entrance late, secured the best seat in the house, and began a discussion of Goethe's *Sorrows of Werther* before he had been among the company three minutes. As usual, Vivian continued his art of flattering everyone in order to curry favor.

At the first opportunity Vivian planned to bring together a group of gentlemen out of office to form a new political party. As leader of the party Vivian had selected Frederick Cleveland, a former minister of state who, disappointed in public life, had retired to Wales. There Vivian sought him out and won the support of the older, more experienced statesman. His mission successful, Vivian returned to his fashionable friends. He spent a harrowing night with Mrs. Lorraine, who vowed she had seen a ghost and fainted in his arms.

Mrs. Lorraine was no less confusing to Cleveland when he met her, for to that gentleman's discomfiture she insisted on falling in love with him.

Before long, because of Vivian's unscrupulous conduct, his new-found friends deserted him and his political ambitions were terminated by Lord Carabas, who had learned that Vivian had used the old nobleman as a pawn in the political game he was playing with names of rank and fortune.

At the same time Vivian announced to Mrs. Lorraine that he had purposely kept Cleveland from liking her by interfering with her mail. In his arrogance Vivian insulted Cleveland in his London club, and Cleveland challenged him to a duel. Vivian killed Cleveland.

When Vivian had recovered from a fever brought on by excitement, he left England and made his home in Germany. There he took a course of studies at Heidelberg, where he met Baron von Konigstein. Vivian and the clever, worldly baron became close friends. At a fair in Frankfort they were entertained by a conjurer who called himself Essper George. George attached himself to Vivian as his valet.

Shortly thereafter, while vacationing in Ems, Vivian met Lady Madeleine Trevor, who knew Vivian's father. She was accompanied by her brother, Mr. St. George, and a friend, Violet Fane. Vivian soon became a member of her party on expeditions about the countryside. Lady Madeleine disliked the baron because the German had figured in a scandal over cards which had caused the death of Violet Fane's brother. For her friend's sake, Madeleine was anxious not to renew her own acquaintance with the baron.

One night a card game began at the baron's apartment. St. George was one of the players. Vivian remembered the card game which had ended fatally for Miss Fane's brother. When the game had gone long enough, Vivian revealed the fact that the cards were marked. The next day Baron von Konigstein left

Ems. Vivian had learned of the marked cards from Essper George, who had seen the pack in the possession of the baron's servant.

A week after the episode of the baron two young men, formerly Vivian's fellow students, made their appearance and joined Lady Madeleine's party. The pleasures of the company were shortlived, however. Miss Fane, who was in delicate health, overexerted herself and had an attack from which she never recovered. She died in Vivian's arms and he was overcome by grief.

Vivian and his servant, Essper George, set out across Germany toward Vienna. One night Vivian had a narrow escape from some Germans engaged in a great drinking spree. Essper George saved him from their drunken wrath.

Vivian was a guest for a time at the home of Mr. Beckendorff, an odd recluse. There he stayed until Mr. Beckendorff objected to the presence of Essper George. Another guest, the Prince of Little Lilliput, was permitted to remain. Vivian, who had been the friend of the prince and who on one occasion had even saved the prince's life, was ready to take his departure because he realized that he was becoming involved in secret political upheavals. He admired Mr. Beckendorff, who seemed to be successfully following the same policies which had ruined Vivian in London.

News came that Beckendorff had become prime minister of the Duchy of Reisenberg and that the prince was to be rewarded by a high position of state. Vivian spent some time at the court with the prince. At brilliant balls and on all public occasions Vivian observed closely but with great detachment the machinations of court intrigue. He fell in love with Sybilla, a young baroness, much to the dismay of Mr. Beckendorff, who planned to kill Vivian. His life was spared, however, on the condition that he leave the duchy at once. Vivian now learned that the baroness was in reality an Austrian archduchess whose marriage with the deformed, half-witted crown prince had been arranged as a matter of state. This final revelation into the nature of power politics sickened Vivian thoroughly. He continued on his way to Vienna.

When his carriage broke down, he was invited to stay with the lord of the village, who was soon to celebrate his daughter's marriage. Vivian was amazed to discover that the bridegroom was his former friend, Baron von Konigstein.

Leaving the carnival which followed the wedding celebration, Vivian and Essper George were not far from the village when a terrible storm began. Its fury smashed against the unprotected hamlet and a mountain river overflowed its banks, cutting away the hillside, destroying the village, drowning its inhabitants. Essper George was killed. Vivian, his horse dying under him, was flung to the earth. It was as if this upheaval of the elements matched the tumult of Vivian's own nature. He had yet to learn that the delusions and desires of youth give way to the disappointments of manhood on the road by which man travels toward old age.

VOLPONE

Type of work: Drama
Author: Ben Jonson (1572?-1637)
Type of plot: Social satire
Time of plot: Sixteenth century
Locale: Venice
First presented: 1605

> Principal characters:
> VOLPONE, a knave
> MOSCA, his servant
> CORBACCIO, an old gentleman
> CORVINO, a merchant
> VOLTORE, an advocate
> LORD POLITICK WOULD-BE, a knight
> LADY POLITICK WOULD-BE, his wife
> BONARIO, Corbaccio's son
> CELIA, Corvino's wife
> PEREGRINE, a gentleman traveler

Critique:

Although the extant copies of *Volpone, or, The Fox,* are revised versions of the original drama, the plan in its printed form is essentially Jonson's. The story is intricately plotted, so much so that it is likely to be confusing. The drama points toward the seventeenth-century theater with its sermonized ending. Jonson attempted to teach the social lesson that mischief leads to its own undoing.

The Story:

Volpone and his servant, Mosca, were playing a cunning game with all who professed to be Volpone's friends, and the two conspirators boasted to themselves that Volpone acquired his riches not by the common means of trade but by a method which cheated no one in a commercial sense. Volpone had no heirs. Since it was believed he possessed a large fortune, many people were courting his favor in hopes of rich rewards after his death.

For three years, while the foxy Volpone feigned gout, catarrh, palsy, and consumption, valuable gifts had been given him. Mosca's role in the grand deception was to assure each hopeful donor that he was the one whom Volpone had honored in an alleged will.

To Voltore, one of the dupes, Mosca boasted that particular attention was being paid to Voltore's interests. When Voltore the vulture left, Corbaccio the crow followed. He brought a potion to help Volpone, or so he claimed. But Mosca knew better than to give his master medicine from those who were awaiting the fox's death. Mosca suggested that to influence Volpone, Corbaccio should go home, disinherit his own son, and leave his fortune to Volpone. In return for this generous deed, Volpone, soon to die, would leave his fortune to Corbaccio, whose son would benefit eventually.

Next came Corvino, who was assured by Mosca that Volpone, now near death, had named him in a will. After the merchant had gone, Mosca told Volpone that Corvino had a beautiful wife whom he guarded at all times. Volpone resolved to go in disguise to see this woman.

Sir Politick Would-Be and his wife were traveling in Venice. Another English visitor, Peregrine, met Sir Politick on the street and gave him news from home. While the two Englishmen were trying to impress one another, Mosca and a servant came to the street and erected a stage for a medicine vendor to display his wares. Volpone, disguised as a mountebank, mounted the platform. While he haggled with Sir Politick and Peregrine over the price of his medicine, Celia appeared at her window and tossed down her handkerchief. Struck by Celia's beauty, Volpone resolved to possess her. Meanwhile Corvino brutally scolded Celia and told her that henceforth he would confine her to her room.

Mosca went to Corvino with news that physicians had recommended a healthy young girl to sleep by Volpone's side and that other men were striving to be the first to win Volpone's gratitude in this manner. Not to be outdone, Corvino promised that Celia would be sent to Volpone.

Mosca also told Bonario, Corbaccio's son, that his father was about to disinherit him. He promised to lead Bonario to a place where he could witness his father's betrayal.

When Lady Politick Would-Be came to visit Volpone, she was so talkative Volpone feared she would make him sick in actuality. To relieve Volpone's distress, the servant told the lady that Sir Politick was in a gondola with a young girl. Lady Would-Be hurried off in pursuit of her husband. Volpone retired to a private closet while Mosca led Bonario behind a curtain so the young man could spy on Corbaccio. At that moment, eager to win favor with Volpone, Corvino arrived with Celia, and Mosca had to send Bonario off to another room so he would not know of her presence. Meanwhile Corvino had told Celia what she must do to prove her chastity. To quiet her fears, and to guarantee the inheritance from Volpone, Corvino assured his distressed wife that Volpone was so decrepit he could not harm her.

When they were alone, Volpone leaped from his couch and displayed himself as an ardent lover. As he was about to force himself upon Celia, Bonario appeared from his hiding place and saved her. While Mosca and Volpone, in terror of exposure, bewailed their ruined plot, Corbaccio knocked. Volpone dashed back

to his couch. As Mosca was assuring Corbaccio of Volpone's forthcoming death, Voltore entered the room and overheard the discussion. Mosca drew Voltore aside and assured the lawyer that he was attempting to get possession of Corbaccio's money so that Voltore would inherit more from Volpone. Mosca further explained that Bonario had mistaken Celia's visit and had burst upon Volpone and threatened to kill him. Taken in by Mosca's lies, Voltore promised to keep Bonario from accusing Volpone of rape and Corvino of villainy; he ordered the young man arrested.

Mosca proceeded with his case against Celia and Bonario. He had assured Corvino, Corbaccio, and Voltore, independently, that each would be the sole heir of Volpone. Now he added Lady Would-Be as a witness against Celia. In court Voltore presented Celia and Bonario as schemers against Corvino, and he further showed that Bonario's father had disinherited his son and that Bonario had dragged Volpone out of bed and had attacked him. Both Corvino and Corbaccio testified against Celia and Bonario, while Mosca whispered to the avaricious old gentlemen that they were helping justice. To add to the testimony, Mosca presented Lady Would-Be, who told the court she had seen Celia beguiling Sir Politick in a gondola. Mosca promised Lady Would-Be that as a reward for her testimony her name would stand first on Volpone's list of heirs.

When the trial was over, Volpone sent his servants to announce that he was dead and that Mosca was his heir. While Volpone hid behind a curtain, Mosca sat at a desk taking an inventory of the inheritance as the hopefuls arrived. The next step in Volpone's plan was to escape from Venice with his loot. Mosca helped him disguise himself as a commodore. Mosca also put on a disguise.

Having lost his hopes for the inheritance, Voltore withdrew his false testimony at the trial, and Corbaccio and Corvino trembled lest their own cowardly acts be revealed. The court ordered Mosca to appear. Suspecting that Mosca planned to keep the fortune for himself, the disguised Volpone went to the court. When the dupes, learning that Volpone was still alive, began to bargain for the wealth Mosca held, Volpone threw off his disguise and exposed to the court the foolish behavior of Corbaccio, Corvino, and Voltore, and the innocence of Celia and Bonario. The court then sentenced each conspirator according to the severity of his crime. Bonario was restored to his father's inheritance, and Celia was allowed to return to her father because Corvino had attempted to barter her honor for wealth.

The court announced that evil could go only so far and then it killed itself.

VOLUPTÉ

Type of work: Novel
Author: Charles Augustin Sainte-Beuve (1804-1869)
Type of plot: Psychological romance
Time of plot: Early nineteenth century
Locale: France
First published: 1832

Principal characters:
AMAURY, the narrator, a man of sensibility
THE MARQUIS DE COUAËN, a royalist
MADAME DE COUAËN, his wife
AMÉLIE DE LINIERS, a girl in love with Amaury
MADAME R., wife of a royalist sympathizer

Critique:

Volupté is partly autobiographical, not in its material details but in its psychological content. Sainte-Beuve had met with little success in his attempts to write poetry, and he suffered from a lack of self-confidence in spite of his literary friendships with such men as Victor Hugo and Alphonse Lamartine. In addition, an affair with Madame Hugo had left him uneasy and confused. The result was that at thirty he experienced a feeling of complete failure. A harsh self-critic, he was analyzing himself to discover the causes of his failure. Volupté is actually the transposition, in fiction, of his process of introspection. The novel baffled Sainte-Beuve's contemporaries, thereby increasing his feeling of insecurity. From that time on he devoted himself exclusively to criticism, in which field he achieved fame.

The Story:

On the ship that was taking him to the United States, probably forever, Amaury undertook to tell the story of his life to a young friend. Having renounced his past life to live a new one abroad, he was afraid that he might find more pleasure than he should in those past memories; but he felt that his experience could prove useful to the young man, in whom he had recognized so many of his own tendencies.

Amaury, having lost his parents, had been reared by an uncle in Brittany. In his youth he had been sheltered from the outside world, which at that time was slowly recovering from the effects of the French Revolution. He spent most of his time studying and, prone to dreaming, he was actually more concerned with the adventures of Cyrus, Alexander, and Constantine than he was with the men and events of his own day. His Latin teacher was Monsieur Ploa, a man absolutely devoid of personal ambition; only a misinterpretation of Vergil or Cicero could momentarily get him excited. Monsieur Ploa had Amaury translate the voluptuous passages of the *Aeneid* or the odes of Horace with a complete candor which his disciple did not share.

When Amaury was about fifteen he spent six weeks at a neighboring castle. His life there, no longer checked by his regular schedule, helped to develop his tendency to melancholy; he would disappear into the woods reciting poetry with tears in his eyes, and he would forget to come back for meals.

At the age of eighteen he began visiting friends in the neighborhood. He would often visit Monsieur and Madame de Greneuc, in whose household lived two granddaughters orphaned during the revolution. The older, Amélie de Liniers, was a charming girl who soon considered herself engaged to him. Amaury, however, did not feel like settling down in life without first learning something of the world.

During a hunting party Amaury met

the Marquis de Couaën, an influential figure in royalist circles, who invited the young man to his castle. There Amaury met Madame de Couaën, the Irish wife of the marquis.

One day, as Amaury, lost in his thoughts, was emerging from the woods, Madame de Couaën called to him from the window and asked him to pick up an ivory needle she had lost. When he took it up to her, she asked him if he would, in the absence of her husband, accompany her to the little chapel of Saint-Pierre-de-Mer before the sun set. As they were walking along, she explained to Amaury that she was making a pilgrimage for her mother in Ireland, from whom she had received bad news.

That walk was more or less the beginning of a hopeless love relationship between Amaury and Madame de Couaën, an affair in which his respect for the marquis and the true love of Madame de Couaën for her husband left him with the sole possibility of platonic adoration. To escape such a situation, he attempted to retire as a hermit on a nearby deserted island which had been once inhabited by Druids, but after spending only one night there he abandoned that project. He then decided to go to Ireland on a boat that had brought the marquis some secret dispatches; he would see Madame de Couaën's mother and possibly establish some useful political connections for the marquis. As he was embarking, having left a letter of explanation in his room, Madame de Couaën came running to the beach with word that her mother had just died. While he was trying to comfort her she tearfully begged him never to get married but to stay with them, help her husband, and understand her as no one else could.

The Marquis de Couaën, having to go to Paris for some political meetings, took his wife, son, and daughter with him in order to avoid raising suspicions, and Amaury accompanied them. When they returned to Couaën they found the coast occupied by soldiers.

Amaury went to see Amélie, who was preparing to follow her grandmother to Normandy. When he insisted they ought to delay for two years before making a decision concerning their future, Amélie simply asked him to be prudent.

On his way home Amaury learned that the marquis had been arrested in Paris; he rushed immediately to Couaën to destroy some papers before the police officers would arrive there. Without objection or thanks, Madame de Couaën accepted his help, and the next day they left for Paris with the two children. There Amaury communicated with Monsieur D. and Monsieur R. in an effort to secure their help.

Meanwhile, the marquis was allowed to receive visitors, and his wife went to see him every day. Amaury spent every evening with her. At the same time he was beginning to feel attracted to Madame R., a lonely and disillusioned woman who often visited Madame de Couaën. Having decided also to experience physical love with a prostitute, Amaury accomplished his purpose but with no real pleasure.

In the midst of these circumstances Amaury could see no future for himself. He became involved in a royalist conspiracy, more to find self-fulfillment in a chivalric cause than to satisfy any political convictions. Faced with imminent action, he realized that his position might endanger the future of the marquis, bring grief to Madame de Couaën, and show ingratitude toward Monsieur R. and Monsieur D. Fortunately, his secret political involvement was never disclosed.

When the marquis was sent to Blois, Amaury did not accompany his friends, although they had wanted him to come with them. Left in Paris, he visited Madame R. and wrote to Blois, where the royalist political leaders were being tried. Madame R., while refusing to become his mistress, liked to be seen with him in public and demanded the most foolish proofs of his attachment. They never really trusted one another, and she was always jealous of his love for

Madame de Couaën.

A letter from the marquis having announced the death of his son and the alarming state of his wife's health, the nobleman asked for a two-week pass to bring her to Paris for medical attention. Madame de Couaën, who considered the death of her son a punishment for her own weakness, was unhappy to discover the relationship between Amaury and Madame R.

On a day when Amélie came to visit Madame de Couaën, Madame R. was also present, and Amaury realized that his instability had caused the unhappiness of three women. Caught in his youth in the web of illegitimate love, he had been unable to choose either true virtue or carefree disorder. He never saw Amélie again.

Back in Blois, Madame de Couaën sent him a medallion of her mother and a souvenir of her son. Shortly afterward he ended his affair with Madame R. Years later he was to hear that Monsieur R. had received a post of importance and that Madame R. had become the mother of a son.

Having thus reached the bottom of a moral abyss, Amaury enlisted in the army with the idea of finding death on the battlefield; he arrived at Austerlitz only after the battle had been won. Convinced that there was no place for him in society, he decided to become a priest.

Several years later, after he had taken holy orders, he decided to visit again his uncle's farm and the castle at Couaën. Having received no news from Blois for several weeks, he was afraid that Madame de Couaën's health had not improved. On his arrival at Couaën he was surprised to find a flurry of activity; his friends had returned the day before. Although Madame de Couaën was very weak, she welcomed him warmly, adding that someone might soon need his assistance. As her condition became worse, Amaury administered the rites of absolution and extreme unction. Madame de Couaën died soon afterward and was buried in the chapel of Saint-Pierre-de-Mer.

This experience and the emotions it called forth proved extremely trying on Amaury, who immediately left Brittany and, a short time later, France. He hoped to find abroad some peace in obscure but useful activities.

THE VOYAGE OF THE BEAGLE

Type of work: Journal
Author: Charles Darwin (1809-1882)
Type of plot: Travel and Natural History
Time of plot: 1831-1836
Locale: South America and the South Seas
First published: 1839

Principal character:
CHARLES DARWIN, English naturalist

Critique:

In this book the reader finds Darwin's brilliant mind already at work upon the problems which led to his world-shaking theory of evolution. The title of the work is misleading, for the author has little to say about the voyage. What interests him is the natural history of the lands at which the *Beagle* stops. Nothing escapes Darwin's eye; his observations are exact and beautifully written.

The Story:

In December, 1831, the brig *Beagle* of the Royal Navy set sail from Devonport, England, on a voyage which would include surveys of Patagonia, Tierra del Fuego, Chile, Peru, and some of the islands of the Pacific. Also, some chronometric measurements were to be made while the ship circumnavigated the earth.

Charles Darwin shipped aboard as a naturalist at the wish of the *Beagle's* commander, Captain Fitz Roy. Darwin kept a record of the journey in the form of a journal, besides making observations in natural history and geology.

The ship sailed to the coast of South America by way of the Canary Islands, the Cape Verde Islands, and the island of St. Paul's Rocks. The first American seaport that the *Beagle* touched was Rio de Janeiro. There Darwin went inland with an Englishman who was going to visit his estate. Upon his return Darwin resided near Botofogo Bay, where he made natural history observations.

From Rio de Janeiro the expedition went southward to the mouth of the River Plate. Darwin remained there for several weeks collecting animals, birds, and reptiles. On his journeys to the interior he met gauchos for the first time and witnessed their skill with the lasso and the bolas in capturing horses and cattle.

The next anchorage was at Rio Negro. Between this river and Buenos Aires the land was mostly inhabited by hostile Indians. At the time, General Rosas was making war on the various native tribes. Darwin decided to go by land from the Rio Negro to Buenos Aires under the protection of the Spanish Army. On this journey he was able to observe the habits of the South American ostrich.

Upon his arrival in Buenos Aires, Darwin was struck by the large size of the city; it had about sixty thousand inhabitants. From there he set out for Santa Fe by means of a slow bullock wagon. He returned by boat down the Parana River to the seacoast and sailed in a small vessel to join the *Beagle* at Montevideo. On an excursion inland from that seaport, Darwin observed herds of sheep that were watched only by dogs. The dogs were brought up with the flocks from infancy; thus they acquired an uncommon attachment for the sheep.

The *Beagle* sailed for the coast of Patagonia, a land where Spanish settlement had been unsuccessful. There Darwin observed the guanaco, or wild llama. These animals were extremely wary. Once caught, however, they were easily domesticated.

From Patagonia the *Beagle* went to the Falkland Islands, where Darwin found horses, cattle, and rabbits thriving on the seemingly desolate land. Captain Fitz Roy soon set sail for Tierra del Fuego. There the natives were curious about their white visitors. The natives existed in an utterly savage state with barely enough food and clothing to maintain their miserable existence.

The Beagle had aboard three Fuegians who had been taken to England to receive education and be taught the Christian religion. A missionary accompanied them. The plan was to return these natives to their own tribes, and for that purpose the Beagle anchored in Ponsonby Sound. Four boats set out to carry the natives to their homeland. All the natives on shore congregated about the English wherever they landed and asked for gifts. When their wants were not entirely satisfied, they became hostile. The missionary decided that it would be useless for him to stay among them.

From Tierra del Fuego the Beagle proceeded to Valparaiso, Chile. From there Darwin set out to observe the geological formations of the base of the Andes Mountains. On that journey he saw copper and gold mines.

The Beagle sailed from Valparaiso southward to the island of Chiloe and the southern part of Chile. While the ship was anchored in a harbor of Chiloe, all those aboard were able to observe the eruption of a volcano on the mainland.

About a month later, after the Beagle had sailed northward for a distance, a great earthquake shook parts of the coast and the nearby islands. Darwin saw the damage caused by the earthquake in the harbor city of Concepción, where almost every building had been demolished. Part of the town had been swept also by a tremendous wave that had rushed in from the sea.

After the Beagle returned to Valparaiso, Darwin procured guides and mules and set out to cross the Andes to Mendoza. He went eastward through the Portillo Pass and returned through the Uspallata Pass. He reported the scenery beautiful, and he collected much interesting geological and natural history data.

Next, the Beagle sailed up the coast of northern Chile and continued northward to Peru. At Iquique, in Peru, Darwin visited a saltpeter works. Lima was the next port of call for the Beagle. Darwin was not impressed by the city. It was dirty and ugly, having suffered from many revolutions, and the people, living in an almost continual state of anarchy, were unable to take time to improve the city.

Lima was the last point at which the Beagle touched on the western coast of South America. The ship proceeded next to the Galapagos archipelago, where the most interesting feature was the prevalence of great tortoises. The inhabitants often killed these reptiles for their meat. Most of the birds on the islands were completely tame; they had not yet learned to regard man as their enemy.

The ship then sailed on the long passage of three thousand miles to Tahiti. There Darwin was impressed by the swimming ability of the Polynesians. He explored the mountains of the island with the help of guides.

From Tahiti the Beagle went south to New Zealand, New South Wales, and Australia. There Darwin first saw the social greeting of rubbing noses performed by the aborigines. This custom took the place of shaking hands, as practiced by Europeans.

After leaving this group of islands the ship headed back to Brazil in order to complete chronometric measurements that were to be made. On the way Darwin visited the island of St. Helena.

Now that the Beagle was on the last part of her journey, Darwin recorded in his journal his theories as to the formation of coral reefs, many of which he had observed during his stay in the South Seas.

Darwin was glad to leave Brazil for the second time; the practice of slavery in that country sickened him. In October of 1836 the Beagle reached the shores of England. At Falmouth, Darwin left the ship. He had spent nearly five years on his journey.

4060

WAITING FOR GODOT

Type of work: Drama
Author: Samuel Beckett (1906-   )
Type of plot: Tragi-comedy
Time of plot: The present
Locale: A country road
First presented: 1952

Principal characters:
VLADIMIR, a tramp
ESTRAGON, another tramp
POZZO, a success-blinded materialist
LUCKY, Pozzo's servant
A BOY, a messenger from Godot

Critique:

In this play Beckett expresses his personal view of the human condition through symbolism which has its roots in Freudian psychology, the Christian myth, and Existentialist philosophy. Although the action is negligible and there is no development of character, this play, when sensitively produced, is excellent theater. The two tramps are continually aware of pain, hunger, and cold, yet they joke about these things. They vacillate between hope and despair; they are obsessed by uncertainty and dominated by the absurd. Their lives, and we infer all life, is somehow meaningful because of their persistence, despite seeming hopelessness, and because of their refusal to be destroyed.

The Story:

Estragon tried to take off his boot but failed. Vladimir agreed with him that it sometimes appeared that there was nothing one could do. They were glad to be reunited after a night apart. With Vladimir's help, Estragon succeeded in removing his painful boot. Vladimir, also in pain, could not laugh in comfort; he tried smiling instead but it was not satisfactory.

Vladimir mused on the one gospel account that said Christ saved one of the thieves. Estragon wanted to leave. They could not leave because they were wait-

ing for Godot. They became confused about the arrangements and wondered if they were waiting at the right time, in the right place, and on the right day. They quarreled briefly but were, as always, reconciled.

They considered hanging themselves but decided that it would be safer to do nothing until they heard what Godot said. They did not know what they had asked Godot for. They concluded they had foregone their rights.

Vladimir gave Estragon a carrot, which he ate hungrily. They decided that although they were not bound to Godot, they were in fact unable to act.

Pozzo entered, driving Lucky, who was laden with luggage, by a rope around his neck. Estragon and Vladimir mistook him for Godot but accepted him as Pozzo. Although he attempted to intimidate them, he was glad of their company. After ordering Lucky to bring him his stool and his coat, he gave Lucky the whip. Lucky obeyed automatically. Vladimir and Estragon protested violently against Pozzo's treatment of Lucky. Pozzo deflected their outburst and the subject was dropped.

After smoking a pipe Pozzo rose. He then decided he did not want to leave, but his pride almost prevented him from reseating himself. The tramps wanted to know why Lucky never put down the luggage. Pozzo said that Lucky was trying to make him keep the fellow. When Pozzo added that he would sell Lucky rather than throw him out, Lucky wept; but when Estragon tried to dry his tears, Lucky kicked him away. Then Estragon wept. Pozzo philosophized on this and said that Lucky had taught him all the beautiful things he knew, but that the fellow had now become unbearable and was driving Pozzo mad. Estragon and Vladimir then abused Lucky for mistreating his master.

Pozzo broke into a monologue on the twilight, alternating between the lyrical and the commonplace and ending with the bitter thought that everything happened in the world when one was least prepared. He decided to reward Estragon and Vladimir for praising him by making Lucky entertain them. Lucky executed a feeble dance which Estragon mocked but failed to imitate.

Estragon stated that there had been no arrivals, no departures, and no action, and that everything was terrible. Pozzo next decided that Lucky should think for them. For this Vladimir replaced Lucky's derby hat. Lucky's thought was an incoherent flood of words which resembled a dissertation on the possible goodness of God, the tortures of hell fire, the prevalence of sport, and the vacuity of suburbs. He desperately upset his listeners, who attacked him and silenced him by seizing his hat. Having restored Lucky to his position as carrier, Pozzo and the tramps said many farewells before he and Lucky finally left.

The Boy called to Vladimir and Estragon. He came with a message from Godot, who would come the next evening. The Boy, a goatherd, said that Godot was kind to him, but that he beat his brother, a shepherd. Vladimir asked the Boy to tell Godot only that he had seen them.

By the time the Boy left, night had fallen. Estragon decided to abandon his boots to someone else. Vladimir protested and Estragon said that Christ had gone barefoot. Once again they considered and rejected the idea of separating. They de-cided to leave for the night. They stayed where they were.

The following evening the boots were still there and the tree had grown some leaves. The tramps had spent the night separately. Vladimir returned first. When Estragon came back he said he had been beaten again and Vladimir felt that he could have prevented such cruelty. Vladimir began to talk of the previous day, but Estragon could remember nothing but being kicked. Then they were overwhelmed by the thought of the whispering voices of the dead around them. They tried to break their silence but succeeded only in part. By a great effort Estragon recalled that the previous day had been spent chattering inanities. He reflected that they had spent fifty years doing no more than that.

They discovered that the boots left behind by Estragon had been exchanged for another old pair. After finding Lucky's hat, which assured them that they had returned to the right place, they started a wild exchange of the three hats, shifting them from hand to hand. Finally Vladimir kept Lucky's hat and Estragon kept his own.

Once more Estragon decided to leave. To distract him, Vladimir suggested that they "play" Pozzo and Lucky. Puzzled, Estragon left, but he returned almost immediately because some people were coming. Vladimir was jubilant, convinced that Godot was arriving. They tried to hide, but there was nowhere for them to go. Finally Lucky entered with Pozzo, who was now blind. Lucky fell and dragged Pozzo with him. Pozzo cried for help. Vladimir passionately wished to act while there was the opportunity—to do one good thing as a member of the human race, a species that appalled him. Pozzo was terrified, and Vladimir also fell in his attempts to raise him. Estragon fell too while trying to lift Vladimir. As they fought and argued on the ground, they called Pozzo "Cain" and "Abel." When he responded to both names they concluded that he was all humanity. Suddenly they got up without difficulty.

Pozzo prepared to leave, but Vladimir wanted Lucky to sing first. Pozzo explained that Lucky was dumb. They wanted to know when he had been afflicted. Angry, Pozzo said that all their lives were merely momentary and time did not matter. He left with Lucky.

While Estragon slept, the Boy entered to say that Godot would come, not that night but the next. The message for Godot was that the Boy had seen Vladimir. The Boy left and Estragon awoke. He immediately wanted to leave. Vladimir insisted that they could not go far because they must return the next night in order to wait for Godot, who would punish them if they did not wait.

Estragon and Vladimir remarked that only the tree in the landscape was alive and considered hanging themselves again. Instead, they decided that if Godot did not come to save them the next night, they would hang themselves. At last the tramps decided to go. They remained immobile.

WALDEN

Type of work: Essays
Author: Henry David Thoreau (1817-1862)
Type of treatise: Autobiography and nature notes
Time of treatise: 1845-1847
Locale: Walden Pond, near Concord, Massachusetts
First published: 1854

Principal character:

HENRY DAVID THOREAU, author, and a student of nature and man

Critique:

Walden, Or, Life in the Woods is like its author, Henry David Thoreau, in that both are unique in the annals of American literature. Thoreau went to live at Walden Pond because he wanted to think and write a book. Walden is that book, and Thoreau's thoughts and life while writing it are part and parcel of the volume. If one must categorize the book, which contains a range of interests as wide as those found in many volumes by other writers, it can probably best be pigeonholed as what Ralph Waldo Emerson called "Man Thinking." The incidents of his daily life at the pond, his likes and dislikes, his intellectual and physical activities—all these have been utilized by Thoreau as starting points for solid discussions on the meanings of life and the universe in which we find ourselves. Only to the casual reader does the book seem a loosely knit work. To the careful reader the book is obviously bound together by that most complex of organizations, the human mind working consciously to discover the hidden meanings of man's existence. No more original book has been produced in the Western Hemisphere, and no summary can adequately convey Thoreau's reflective wisdom or the beauty of his style.

The Story:

Early in the summer of 1845, Henry David Thoreau left his family home in the village of Concord, Massachusetts, to live for two years by himself in a rude house that he had constructed beside Walden Pond, in a far corner of Concord township. While there he wrote in his journal about many of the things he did and thought. He was not the owner of the land on which he settled, but had received the owner's permission to build his house and to live there. His objective was really to live simply and think and write; in addition, he proved to himself that the necessities of food, clothing, shelter, and fuel could be rather simply obtained for a man who desired only what he needed.

As early as March, 1845, Thoreau went out to Walden Pond and cut the timber he needed for the framework of his house, doing all the labor himself. When that was done and the framing in place, Thoreau bought a shanty from an Irish railroad worker. He then tore down the shanty and used the boards for the sidings of the house, even making use of many of the nails already in the boards. By July, then, the house was ready for his occupancy. Before the advent of cold weather the following fall, Thoreau also built himself a fireplace and a chimney for cooking and heating purposes. He also lathed and plastered the interior of the one-room house, in order that it would be warm and comfortable during the cold New England winter.

Having done all the work himself, and having used native materials wherever possible, he had built the house for the absurdly low cost of twenty-eight dollars. In addition to providing himself with a place to live, Thoreau believed he had taught himself a great lesson in the art of living. He was also vastly pleased that he had provided himself with a place to live for less than a year's lodging had cost him as a student at Harvard College.

In order to get the money needed to build the house, Thoreau had planted about two and a half acres of beans, peas, potatoes, corn, and turnips, which he sold at harvest time. The land on which they were grown was lent by a neighbor who believed, along with everyone else, that the land was good for nothing. In addition to selling enough produce to pay his building expenses, Thoreau had enough yield left from his gardening to provide himself with food. But he did not spend all his time working on the house or in the garden. One of his purposes in living at Walden Pond was to live so simply that he might have plenty of time to think, to write, and to observe nature; and so he spent only as much time in other labors as he had to. He had little respect for possessions and material things. He believed, for instance, that most men were really possessed by their belongings, and that such a literary work as the *Bhagavad-Gita* was worth more than all the towers and temples of the Orient.

Thoreau was quite proud of how little money he needed to live comfortably while at Walden Pond. The first eight months he was there he spent only slightly more than a dollar a month for food. In addition to some twenty-odd dollars he received for vegetables he raised, his income, within which he lived, was slightly more than thirteen dollars. His food consisted almost entirely of rye and Indian meal bread, potatoes, rice, a little salt pork, molasses, and salt. His drink was water. Seldom did he eat large portions of meat, and he never hunted. His interest in the animals that lived in the woods and fields near Walden Pond was the interest of a naturalist. Although he spent some time fishing, he felt that the time he had was too valuable to spend in catching fish to feed himself.

For the small amounts of cash he needed, Thoreau worked with his hands at many occupations, working only so long as was necessary to provide himself with the money his meager wants required. He kept as much time as possible free for thinking and studying. His study consisted more of man and nature than of books, although he kept a few well-selected volumes about him at all times.

While at Walden Pond, summer and winter, Thoreau lived independent of time: he refused to acknowledge days of the week or month. When he wished to spend some time observing certain birds or animals, or even the progress of the weather, he felt free to do so. About the only thing to remind him that men were rushing pell-mell to keep a schedule was the whistle of the Fitchburg Railway trains, which passed within a mile or so of his dwelling. Not that he disliked the railroad; he thought it, in fact, a marvel of man's ingenuity, and he was fascinated by the cargoes which the trains carried from place to place. But he was glad that he was not chained to the commerce those cargoes represented. As much as he sometimes enjoyed the sound of the train, he enjoyed far more the sounds of the birds and animals, most of which he knew, not only as a country dweller knows them, but as the naturalist knows them as well. The loons, the owls, the squirrels, the various kinds of fish in Walden Pond, the migratory birds, all of these were part of his conscious existence and environment.

People often dropped in to visit with Thoreau, who frankly confessed that he did not consider people very important. He failed, in fact, to tell who his most frequent visitors were. He preferred only one visitor, and that a thinking one, at a time. Whenever he had more visitors than could be accommodated by his small house and its three chairs, he took them into his larger drawing-room, the pine wood which lay about his home. From what he wrote about his treatment of all but a very few of the people who came to visit him, it is very probable that he was a crusty kind of host, one who, if he had nothing better to do, was willing to talk, but who usually had more to occupy him than ordinary conversation.

During the winter months Thoreau continued to live comfortably at Walden

Pond, though his activities changed. He spent more time at the pond itself, making a survey of its bottom, studying the ice conditions, and observing the animal life which centered about the pond, which had some open water throughout the year.

After two years of life at Walden, Thoreau left the pond. He felt no regret for having stayed there or for leaving; his attitude was that he had many lives to live and that he had finished with living at the pond. He had learned many lessons there, had had time to think and study, and had proved what he had set out to prove twenty-six months before, that living could be extremely simple and yet fulfill the individual.

WALLENSTEIN

Type of work: Drama
Author: Johann Christoph Friedrich von Schiller (1759-1805)
Type of plot: Historical romance
Time of plot: The Thirty Years' War
Locale: Germany
First presented: 1799

Principal characters:
WALLENSTEIN, Duke of Friedland, Generalissimo of the Imperial forces
in the Thirty Years' War
OCTAVIO PICCOLOMINI, a lieutenant general
MAX PICCOLOMINI, the general's son, a colonel
COUNT TERZKY, Wallenstein's brother-in-law
BUTLER, an Irish soldier of fortune
DUCHESS OF FRIEDLAND, Wallenstein's wife
THEKLA, Wallenstein's daughter

Critique:

Wallenstein is actually a dramatic series, composed of a one-act prelude, Wallenstein's Camp, and two full-length plays, The Piccolomini and The Death of Wallenstein. The prelude, relatively unimportant, merely shows the scene of the army camp and indicates the temper of the period and the attitude of the army toward its commander. Schiller is far less known for his historical plays than he is for his lyrical dramas. Yet Samuel Taylor Coleridge, who translated Schiller's works in the early nineteenth century, pointed out that the history plays form a vital part of his work; Coleridge further suggested a parallel between the historical drama of Shakespeare— Henry VI and Richard II—and this dramatic trilogy by the German playwright.

The Story:

Wallenstein, Duke of Friedland, had once been dismissed by the Emperor Ferdinand from his service, but during the Thirty Years' War, in which the countries of central Europe battled to prevent their annihilation by the forces of the Swedish Gustavus Adolphus, the emperor had recalled Wallenstein and given him extraordinary powers, to build up an army that could drive the Swedes out of central Europe. The army had been raised, but its leaders and its rank and file felt that they owed allegiance to their commander, rather than the emperor whom Wallenstein and they served.

As time passed, Wallenstein's army won many victories and the situation in central Europe became less tense. The threat to his dominions having decreased, the emperor wished to curtail Wallenstein's powers, lest the conquering hero should attempt to dictate to the crown. In those days of suspicion, it was difficult to separate cause from effect. Wallenstein, fearing for his powers and becoming suspicious of the emperor and his government, wavered on the verge of declaring himself for the Swedes. At the same time the emperor, afraid of Wallenstein, made arrangements to have the commander removed from his post. The court reflected the attitude of its ruler, and Wallenstein thought more and more of turning against his monarch.

The emperor finally sent a war commissioner, Von Questenberg, to Wallenstein's camp. The commissioner found the army so sensitive to its leader's wishes that the soldiers were ready to follow him if he were to turn traitor. The commissioner told his fears to Lieutenant General Piccolomini and gave the general the emperor's secret commission to take over the armies and to arrest Wallenstein. Wallenstein, not suspecting what had happened, believed that General Piccolomini was his trusted friend and brother officer. He did not realize that General Piccolomini was more loyal to his monarch than to his military commander.

General Piccolomini wished to have the help of his son, Colonel Max Piccolomini, in his plans, but the son, who had grown up under Wallenstein's tutelage, refused to believe that Wallenstein could ever be anything but virtuous. In addition, Max Piccolomini was in love with Thekla, Wallenstein's daughter, and had high hopes that the great general-duke would permit them to marry. Young Piccolomini did not know that Wallenstein, fired with ambition and filled with suspicion of the Emperor Ferdinand, was actually plotting to go over to the Swedes with his army in return for the kingship of Hungary. Wallenstein saw in his daughter a future queen, not the wife of a colonel.

Worried by the arrival of Von Questenberg, Wallenstein gave one of his trusted henchmen the task of seeing that all his great leaders signed a document containing a vow to follow him wherever he might lead, even if he led them away from the emperor. The henchman planned a great banquet to accomplish the deed. Before the banquet he showed the officers a document which he would not let them sign. After the banquet, when the men were drunk, another document containing a pledge of loyalty to Wallenstein was substituted. The leaders all signed, except for Max Piccolomini, who was sober and realized that he could not take a vow against the emperor without forfeiting his honor.

Wallenstein believed that the leaders would be compelled to follow him after signing the document, a paper which would compromise them in the emperor's eyes, regardless of how the signatures were obtained.

General Piccolomini signed the document, although he knew what he was doing. He wished to let Wallenstein proceed far enough to expose his traitorous hand. General Piccolomini knew it would be easier to turn the army away from Wallenstein if he were to reveal himself as a traitor.

A crisis arose when Wallenstein received orders to send a large part of his army to a distant point under the command of another leader. The same messenger also brought news that an army from Spain, not under Wallenstein's command, was due to arrive in a matter of days. Seeing his ambitions threatened, Wallenstein refused to break up his army and immediately pushed his negotiations with the Swedes in the hope that he could complete his arrangements within a few hours.

While Wallenstein prepared to move his army, General Piccolomini set his own plan in motion. First he went to all the officers and convinced them, with the exception of the colonels of two regiments, one of them his own son, that Wallenstein was ambitious and a traitor. The commanders agreed to move their troops and, under General Piccolomini, remain loyal to the emperor.

Meanwhile the Swedes, through their envoy, were making inordinate demands upon Wallenstein. Among other things they wished to have control of Prague and the fortress at Egra, to insure that Wallenstein would not turn traitor to them. At first Wallenstein refused to turn over the fortifications, but at last he agreed. Shortly afterward his brother-in-law, Count Terzky, informed him that various regiments had marched away. Wallenstein realized what had happened when the count told him about General Piccolomini's negotiations with Von Questenberg and the emperor's commission authorizing General Piccolomini to relieve Wallenstein of his command.

Although his grand design was collapsing, Wallenstein resolved to go ahead with his plan to join the Swedes. He was still busy with his preparations when his daughter came to him with Colonel Max Piccolomini, who was still loyal to his commander. The couple asked to be allowed to marry, but Wallenstein re-

4068

fused. During the interview Max Piccolomini realized Wallenstein's ambitions for himself and his daughter, including the duke's intent to turn traitor. The young officer then decided to join his father in the plan to arrest Wallenstein. When Wallenstein tried to keep Colonel Piccolomini prisoner, his regiment rescued him from Wallenstein's soldiers.

Wallenstein fled with his few remaining troops and his family to Egra, where he had planned to meet the Swedish forces. With him was Colonel Butler, an Irish soldier of fortune. Because Wallenstein had kept the emperor from making Butler a count, the Irish adventurer took his revenge by contriving Wallenstein's murder at Egra. Word also came to Egra, shortly before Wallenstein's assassination, that Max Piccolomini had met his death in a wild attack on the Swedish forces. Thekla fled from Egra to mourn at her dead lover's bier.

General Piccolomini, arriving at Egra within a matter of minutes after Wallenstein's death, was horrified to learn that the duke was dead., Butler, confused by the turn of events, fled to the emperor to explain his actions. After his departure a messenger arrived to inform General Piccolomini that the emperor had elevated him to the rank of prince.

THE WANDERER

Type of work: Novel
Author: Alain-Fournier (Henri Alain Fournier, 1886-1914)
Type of plot: Psychological romance
Time of plot: Nineteenth century
Locale: France
First published: 1913

Principal characters:
AUGUSTIN MEAULNES, the wanderer
FRANÇOIS SEUREL, his friend
FRANTZ DE GALAIS, a young aristocrat
YVONNE DE GALAIS, his sister
VALENTINE BLONDEAU, Frantz's fiancée

Critique:

Half fantasy and half reality, this dream-like story skillfully mixes the vague dream world with the material world. A dream of delightful wonder obsesses a young man all his life. But when he finds the material existence of his dream, he is disillusioned, for he would prefer to return to the dream.

The Story:

M. Seurel was head of the Middle School and one of the Higher Elementary classes, and Madame Seurel taught the infants at Sainte-Agathe's School. Living in the school with his parents and his sister Millie, François Seurel attended the classes along with the other pupils. Young Seurel, however, never played much with the village boys because of an infection in his hip.

When François Seurel was fifteen, Augustin Meaulnes entered the school. His arrival marked a new life for Seurel, for Meaulnes soon banished his contentment with his family and his love for his home. His hip healing, Seurel began to spend more time with Meaulnes in the village. Even the school became livelier, for Meaulnes always drew a crowd of people around him in the evenings.

The adventure began one Christmas when Meaulnes set out for the railroad station to meet Seurel's grandparents, M. and Mme. Charpentier. When the grandparents arrived, Meaulnes had disappeared. Three days later, he casually took his seat in the classroom where M. Seurel was conducting a lesson. No one knew where Meaulnes had gone and he claimed when questioned that he himself did not know. Sometimes at night, in the attic room they shared, Seurel would be awakened to find Meaulnes pacing the floor, fully clothed, eager to enter again a mysterious world which once he had glimpsed briefly. Meaulnes promised to take Seurel along the next time he left on a journey.

At last Meaulnes told Seurel the story of his adventure after he had run off from the school. It had been a very cold December day, and Meaulnes, losing his way, had found his horse lame and darkness falling. He had wandered to a cottage, where he was fed. Then he had stumbled on until he found a barn in which, cold and lost, he fell asleep. The next day he wandered a long distance, until that night he had come to a manor where small children and old people were merrily planning a wedding feast. Tired and cold, Meaulnes had crawled through a window and climbed into a bed. There he slept all night. The next day, thinking him one of the guests, some strolling players invited him to eat with them. Then Meaulnes discovered the reason for the feast. Frantz de Galais, the son of the man who owned the

THE WANDERER by Alain-Fournier. Translated by François Delisle. By permission of the publishers Houghton Mifflin Co. Copyright, 1928, by Houghton Mifflin Co.

manor, had gone off to fetch his fiancée for the wedding.

All the first day Meaulnes danced and played with the other guests. The next day he met a beautiful girl with whom he immediately fell in love. Although she sadly declined to see him again, she promised to wait for his return to the manor. Inquiring about the strange girl, Meaulnes learned that she was Yvonne de Galais, the sister of Frantz. Frantz returned to the manor without his bride and dismissed all the guests.

Meaulnes joined the crowd of children and old people as they dejectedly walked or rode away from the manor. He fell asleep in a cart and did not awake until he found himself again near Sainte-Agathe's School.

Meaulnes' story would have seemed too unreal to young Seurel if the arrival of a strange boy at Sainte-Agathe's had not brought the story to reality. The boy, dressed as a gipsy, reminded Meaulnes of those Bohemians he had seen at the manor. After the gipsy had stolen the map which Meaulnes had been making in order to find his way back to the manor, Meaulnes and Seurel learned that the gipsy was young Frantz de Galais, who in a fit of despair after losing his sweetheart had run away with a band of gipsies. The boys swore to Frantz that they would help him if they could. One night Frantz disappeared.

Meaulnes went at last to Paris and wrote only three letters to Seurel after his arrival there.

Months passed. Seurel finished his school days and went to a village to visit some relatives. There he heard that a mysterious manor was not far off. Eagerly Seurel took up his friend's quest. His cousins, he learned, knew Yvonne. The manor had been razed after the disappearance of Frantz, but his sister often came to visit Seurel's cousins. One night while Seurel was there she arrived. He told her that Meaulnes hoped someday to find her again. Seurel then learned from his aunt that Frantz's fiancée had feared to marry him because she was certain that such great happiness could not come to her, the daughter of peasants. She was now in Paris working as a dressmaker. Seurel recalled his promise to Frantz to help him if ever he could. But first Seurel intended to find Meaulnes and bring him to Yvonne de Galais.

When Seurel found Meaulnes, the adventurer was packing his clothes to go on a journey. Abandoning his plans, he and Yvonne married. But there was some mysterious element in their lives which kept them from being as happy as Seurel had expected them to be. One night Frantz appeared near the village. Seurel met him and listened to his complaint of loneliness and sorrow. The next morning Meaulnes left Yvonne to go on another adventure.

For months Seurel, now a teacher at Sainte-Agathe's, and Yvonne awaited the return of Meaulnes. When her baby was born, Yvonne died, leaving Seurel with an untold sadness. Searching through his friend's old papers, Seurel found a diary which told him why Meaulnes had been so troubled before his disappearance.

While Meaulnes had lived in Paris, he had met Valentine Blondeau, a girl who became his mistress. Valentine often spoke of her former lover, whom she had deserted because she feared to marry him. When she showed Meaulnes her lover's letters, he realized that Valentine was the fiancée for whom Frantz de Galais had never stopped searching. In anger, Meaulnes told her he would leave her, and Valentine cried that she would then return to Paris to become a street-walker. After he had returned to his mother's home, where Seurel had found him, Meaulnes began to feel remorse for his treatment of Valentine.

Seurel, reading the diary, realized that Meaulnes must have been packing to go in search of Valentine when Seurel brought the news that Yvonne had been found. He decided that Meaulnes had deserted Yvonne to go on the same quest.

As Yvonne's daughter grew into a lovable, pretty child, Seurel often went

4071

to play with her, but she would not allow him completely to possess her affections. She seemed always to be waiting for someone. One afternoon, while playing with the little girl, Seurel noticed a burly stranger approaching. As the man neared him, Seurel recognized Meaulnes. He told Seurel that he had brought Valentine and Frantz together at last. With tears in his eyes at the news of his wife's death, Meaulnes took his daughter into his arms.

Seurel watched the father and daughter play together, and the schoolmaster smilingly imagined that he could envision Meaulnes arising in the middle of the night, wrapping his daughter in a cloak, and silently slipping off with her on some new adventure.

THE WANDERING JEW

Type of work: Novel
Author: Eugène Sue (1804-1857)
Type of plot: Mystery melodrama
Time of plot: 1831-1832
Locale: France
First published: 1844-1845

Principal characters:
RODIN, an ambitious Jesuit
M. L'ABBE D'AIGRIGNY, Provincial of the Jesuits
BLANCHE SIMON,
ROSE SIMON,
FRANÇOIS HARDY,
PRINCE DJALMA,
JACQUES DE RENNEPONT (COUCHE-TOUT-NUD),
GABRIEL DE RENNEPONT, and
ADRIENNE DE CARDOVILLE, descendants of Marius de Rennepont
    and heirs to his legacy
SAMUEL, the Wandering Jew
HERODIAS, who demanded the head of John the Baptist

Critique:

The Wandering Jew is a sprawling narrative written in a pedestrian style and dealing with one-dimensional characters whose conversations and behavior are unrealistic. In spite of its limitations, however, the novel has survived; and more than a hundred years after its publication it has become a minor classic of sorts. Probably the reasons for its survival are twofold. First, the legend of the Wandering Jew has always commanded interest. Second, Sue has technical skill in building up effects of mystery and terror. In addition, Sue's vivid knowledge of social and economic conditions of the time lend added value to a romantic work which was also a novel of social protest.

The Story:

Down a bleak hill in Poland a solitary figure stalked. He was an old man, his face gentle and sad. His footsteps left in the soil imprints of a cross made by the seven large nails in his shoes. He was hurrying, for he must be in Paris on the thirteenth of February, 1832, when the surviving descendants of his sister would gather in that city—the last members of that family over which he had watched for eighteen centuries. The

lonely traveler was the Wandering Jew, that artisan of Jerusalem who mocked Christ on the day of the Crucifixion, the sinner condemned to wander undying through the centuries over all the world.

Far in the wilds of America a woman also set her face toward Paris, driven by that same power which guided the Wandering Jew. She was Herodias, who had demanded the head of John the Baptist on a charger, also condemned to live through centuries of sorrow.

François Baudoin, called Dagobert, a faithful friend of Marshal Simon, an old Bonapartist hero, never faltered in his loyalty toward the Simon family. Years before he had followed the marshal's Polish wife into Siberia, where she was exiled, and after her death he set out with her twin daughters, Blanche and Rose, for Paris where, on a certain day in February, 1832, a legacy awaited the two girls. This was the legacy of Marius de Rennepont, an ancestor who, despoiled by the Jesuits, had salvaged out of his ruined estate a house and a small sum of money. The money he had placed in the hands of a faithful Jewish friend named Samuel, who had promised to invest it profitably. A hundred and fifty years later the descendants of this ancestor were to gather at a house where each was to receive a share of the legacy. Blanche and Rose Simon were only half-aware of the fortune awaiting them, for they were too young to understand what Dagobert told them about their inheritance.

But if these heirs of Marius de Rennepont did not know of the legacy, others did. For many years the Jesuits, masters of an intricate and diabolical conspiracy, had plotted to prevent the descendants from acquiring the money. They were responsible for Marshal Simon's exile, for his wife's banishment to Siberia.

The plotters had been so meticulous, so thorough in their scheming, that they had persuaded young Gabriel de Rennepont to become a priest and a member of the Society of Jesus. Through Gabriel they hoped to acquire the tremendous fortune; for by preventing the other heirs from reaching Paris — and the society had agents all over the world who would do its bidding under any conditions—Gabriel would inherit the legacy. Then, since he was forbidden by his vow of poverty to possess money, the funds would revert to the society. With that money the Jesuits would be able to re-establish their supremacy over the French people, would be able once more to govern countries and guide the destiny of Europe.

As soon as Dagobert and the two girls arrived in Paris, the Jesuits arranged to have them spirited away to a convent. Adrienne de Cardoville, another descendant of the de Rennepont family, was declared insane and committed to an asylum. Jacques de Rennepont, a good-hearted sensualist named Couche-tout-Nud, was jailed for debt. Prince Djalma, who had left India in spite of the efforts of the Jesuits, was drugged. François Hardy, a benevolent manufacturer, was sent out of town through the treachery of a friend who was a Jesuit spy.

As a result of that Jesuit conspiracy, on that fateful day in February, 1832, only the priest, Gabriel de Rennepont,

went to claim the legacy at the house of an old Jew known as Samuel. With Gabriel were M. l'Abbé d'Aigrigny, Provincial of the Jesuits, and Rodin, his secretary. Before the reading of the will, Gabriel was persuaded to sign a paper in which he renounced all claims to the legacy. When the bequest was announced, the Jesuits were astounded at the incredible sum of the inheritance, which had grown from 150,000 francs to a fortune of 212,175,000 francs. But just as the money was being handed over to the priests, a strange woman appeared and produced a codicil to the will, a document suspending its execution for three months. The woman was Herodias, but none then called her by that name. The priests were enraged, and they feared that their conspiracy would be exposed. Adrienne de Cardoville was certain to be released from the asylum. General Simon was reported to be on his way back to France to claim his daughters. Couche-tout-Nud would borrow money from his friends to pay his debts. Prince Djalma would soon awaken. François Hardy would return to Paris from his fruitless errand.

Rodin immediately produced a paper which placed him in complete charge of the Jesuit cabal. He proclaimed that they had not lost, that they could and would win by employing psychological methods instead of violence. He would let each heir destroy himself by his own desires, passions, or vices.

During the three months that followed Rodin pretended that he had left the service of the Abbé d'Aigrigny and passed himself off as a friend of the de Rennepont heirs. He secured the release of the Simon girls and Adrienne, and by those acts became known as a good, unselfish man. One of Adrienne's servants confessed, shortly before her death, that she had been blackmailed into spying for the Jesuits, and she revealed the whole sordid, brutal, unprincipled conspiracy. But Rodin was not yet willing to accept defeat. At his direction, François Hardy's factory was burned to the ground, his best friend's treachery was revealed, and his beautiful young mistress was spirited away. A broken man, Hardy was taken to a Jesuit retreat, where he accepted the doctrines of the order and died as the result of the penances and fasts imposed upon him. Couche-tout-Nud, separated from his mistress, died a miserable death after an orgy induced by another Jesuit agent. The Simon girls were taken to a hospital during a cholera epidemic and died there of the disease. Prince Djalma, led to believe that Adrienne had become the mistress of Agricola Baudoin, Dagobert's son, attacked Agricola and killed a girl whom he mistook for Adrienne. He discovered his error too late, for in his remorse he had already swallowed poison. Adrienne chose to die with him.

When the time came for the final disposition of the de Rennepont legacy, Gabriel was the only survivor. Just as Rodin was about to claim the inheritance in the name of his churchly office, the casket containing the money and securities burst into flames and the fortune was lost forever. A moment later Rodin fell to the floor and writhed in agony. As he had left a church, shortly before claiming the legacy, he had taken holy water from the fingers of an Indian who had accompanied Prince Djalma from India and who had become a lay member of the Jesuits. Too late, Rodin realized that he had been poisoned in some manner by the Indian. He died a few minutes later.

Gabriel de Rennepont, shocked when he realized the crimes of greed and lust for power that the lost fortune had caused, retired to live out the rest of his brief life with his friends, the Beaudoin family.

After Gabriel's body had been laid in the de Rennepont tomb, old Samuel went to a secret spot where a great cross was set upon a lonely hill. There Herodias found him. In the dawn's light each saw upon the face of the other the marks that age had put upon them, but they had found peace and happiness at last. Samuel—for he was the Wandering Jew —gave praise that their long punishment was ended, and Herodias echoed his words.

THE WANDERING SCHOLAR FROM PARADISE

Type of work: Drama
Author: Hans Sachs (1494-1576)
Type of plot: Farce
Time of plot: Sixteenth century
Locale: Nuremberg, Germany
First presented: 1550

Principal characters:
THE FARMER, a crude peasant
HIS WIFE, an ignorant, dreaming *hausfrau*
THE STUDENT, a quick-witted young man, more adventurer than scholar

Critique:

This bucolic farce is a *Fastnachtspiel*, a type of short play given about the countryside on the night-before-fasting, or the night before Ash Wednesday. Its form is rhyming couplets and it is presented in one act with scene changes indicated only by momentary closing and opening of the curtain. The typical subjects treated in this sort of play, written specifically for simple, rough production by wandering players, were burgher life, infidelity, and peasant stupidity. Some were uncomplicated comedy; others, artful satire. Plot was negligible. The humor in this play is both bold and fine. Almost every line, if read separately, has at least a double or hidden meaning. Throughout most of the play the humor is so broad that few, if any, readers or listeners can miss it. Hans Sachs was an artist in this form of writing. His characters were delineated by exaggerations easily recognizable by the audiences of his day. With economy of words, characters, properties, and scenery, he was able to establish and sustain a mood. His manner of expression, not the story, makes his writing palatable to the modern reader. A prolific writer, he wrote more than four thousand master songs for the Nuremberg school, about two thousand fables and tales in verse, and 208 plays. His stature as a writer is reflected in his being one of the principal characters in Wagner's *Die Meistersinger*.

The Story:

A wife of Nuremberg claimed to all and sundry that her deceased first husband was still her truelove and her second husband no lover at all. She described him as scrimpy, mean, and sour of disposition. One day, while she was voicing her complaints, a wandering Student came by, doffed his hat in a polite gesture, and begged for alms. Rightly guessing that boasts about his successes in Paris would impress the dame, he quickly used the advantage the Wife gave him when, hearing incorrectly, she thought that he had said he came from Paradise:

The Wife's mind still rambling among her dreams of her first husband, she asked the Student if he knew the departed one. The Student granted that he did not, but he thought that perhaps on his return to Paradise the acquaintance would be effected. The Wife accepted the Student's offer to take gifts back to her husband, after the Student had caught her sympathy with his description of how ill-clothed, ill-fed, and completely destitute her late husband was.

As the Student prepared to leave, the Wife inquired when he might come again, bringing word of her first love. He earnestly assured her that the road was long and difficult and that he would not be likely to pass her way again. Without delay and with a minimum of ceremony, the Student took her gifts and strode off —and none too soon, for the Farmer appeared just as the young man was taking his departure.

The Wife again sang the love song that she had been singing just before meeting the Student, but this time she sang happily, as her husband noticed. Naïvely she told him of the visitor who had brought her happiness and of her having sent gifts to her first love. Craftily concealing his anger at her simplicity, the Farmer sarcastically ordered her to prepare more gifts that he might take them to the Student as additional presents to the man who, though dead, retained her devotion. Laden, he went off in search of the Student.

In a rough slough the Student was quickly stuffing his booty into the bushes when he heard the Farmer approaching. With cunning and a veil of innocent helpfulness, he directed the Farmer deeper into the furze, where he claimed the culprit was hiding. He also offered to help the Farmer by holding his horse while he went on his search. When the Farmer was out of sight, the Student rode off on the horse, with the Farmer's and the Wife's contributions across the saddle. Meanwhile, the Farmer stumbled through the slough, muddier and more scratched with each step in his vain effort to find the offending traveler from Paradise.

At the cottage, the Wife was peering into the distance for some sign of the Farmer. Her chief concern was that her husband might be lost in the mist on the moor and unable to overtake the Student to add to her gifts. Her doubts vanished as the Farmer trudged in slowly and wearily, hoping against hope that his horse had run home ahead of him. Not seeing the animal, he accepted the rude truth that he had been duped. What could he do or say to the Wife—the stupid one, the gullible one—whom he had intended to beat for giving away a few farthings and some worn-out clothes? She was indeed a lesser fool than he who had lost his swiftest horse.

Stirred to activity in an effort to ease her husband's anger, the Wife carried in the milk pails and asked about the success of his search. The Farmer mumbled a halting explanation about his altruism; he had decided, he said, to make a gift of his horse to the Student, since the young man was tired and had far to go. The Wife was overwhelmed by her husband's unexpected kindness. For his thoughtfulness in behalf of her first husband, she promised that were he to die that night, she would send him all manner of presents in Paradise. Such a generous husband should have the good-will of his neighbors, she declared, and she proceeded to circulate the story of her husband's generosity throughout the parish.

But man is not to be pleased. The angry Farmer decided that it was bad enough to be burdened with such a wife; it was unbearable, however, to think that his neighbors considered him the same kind of fool. The moral was that if married people were to get along, they must cover for each other's weaknesses and not let others see a flaw in the bonds of wedlock.

WAR AND PEACE

Type of work: Novel
Author: Count Leo Tolstoy (1828-1910)
Type of plot: Historical romance
Time of plot: 1805-1813
Locale: Russia
First published: 1865-1869

Principal characters:
PIERRE BEZUHOV, illegitimate son of a wealthy count
NATASHA ROSTOV, beautiful daughter of a well-to-do Moscow family
NIKOLAY ROSTOV, Natasha's older brother
ANDREY BOLKONSKY, wealthy Russian prince
ELLEN KURAGIN BEZUHOV, Pierre's beautiful and immoral wife
ANATOLE KURAGIN, Ellen's brother
PRINCESS MARYA BOLKONSKY, Andrey's sister
OLD PRINCE BOLKONSKY, Andrey's tyrannical father
KUTUZOV, Commander-in-Chief of the Russian Army, appointed in August, 1812
NAPOLEON BONAPARTE

Critique:

Count Leo Tolstoy's *War and Peace* is a panorama of Russian life in that active period of history known as the Napoleonic Era. The whole structure of the novel indicates that Tolstoy was writing a new kind of book. He was not concerned with plot, setting, or even people, as such. His purpose was simply to show that the continuity of life in history is eternal. Each human life holds its influence on history, and the developments of youth and age, war and peace, are so interrelated that in the simplest patterns of social behavior vast implications are recognizable. Tolstoy seemed to feel a moral responsibility to present history as it was influenced by every conceivable human force. To do this, it was necessary for him to create not a series of simple, well-linked incidents but a whole evolution of events and personalities. Each character must change, must affect those around him; these people in turn must influence others, until imperceptibly, the whole historical framework of the nation changes. *War and Peace*, then, is a moving record of historical progress, and the dual themes of this vast novel—Age and Youth, War and Peace—are shown as simultaneous developments of history.

The Story:

In 1805, it was evident to most well-informed Russians that war with Napoleon was inevitable. Austria and Russia joined forces at the battle of Austerlitz, where they were soundly defeated by the French. But in the highest Russian society, life went on quite as though nothing of tremendous import were impending. After all, it was really only by a political formality that Russia had joined with Austria. The fact that one day Napoleon might threaten the gates of Russia seemed ridiculous. And so soirees and balls were held, old women gossiped, young women fell in love. War, though inevitable, was being waged on foreign soil, and was, therefore, of little importance.

The attraction held by the army for the young noblemen of Russia was understandable enough, for the Russian army had always offered excellent opportunities for ambitious, politically inclined young men. It was a wholesome release for their energies. Young Nikolay Rostov, for example, joined the hussars simply because he felt drawn to that way of life. His family idolized him because of his loyalty to the tsar, because of his courage, and because he was so handsome in his uniform. Natasha, his sister, wept over him, and Sonya, his cousin, promptly fell in love with him.

While young Nikolay was applauded in St. Petersburg society, Pierre Bezuhov, a friend of the Rostov family, was looked upon as somewhat of a boor. He had just returned from Paris, where he had studied at the university, and he had not yet made up his mind what to do with his life. He would not join the army for he saw no sense in a military career. His father gave him a liberal allowance, and he spent it frivolously at gambling. In truth, he seemed like a man lost. He would start long arguments, loudly shouting in the most conspicuous manner in the quiet drawing-rooms, and then suddenly lapse into sullen silence. He was barely tolerated at soirees before his father died and left him millions. Then, suddenly, Pierre became popular, although he attributed his rise to some new personality development of his own. He was no longer sullen, but loved everyone, and it was quite clear that everyone loved him. His most dogged follower was Prince Vassily Kuragin, the father of a beautiful, unmarried daughter, Ellen, who was recognized everywhere as a prospective leader of St. Petersburg society. Pierre was forced into marrying her by the crafty prince, who knew a good catch when he saw one. The marriage was never a success.

Pierre Bezuhov's closest friend was Prince Andrey Bolkonsky, an arrogant, somewhat cynical man who also despised his wife. Lise, the "Little Princess," as she was called, was pregnant, but Prince Andrey could endure the bondage of domesticity no longer. When he received a commission in the army, he left his wife at the family estate, Bleak Hills, in the care of his sister Marya and his tyrannical old father, and went off to war. During his absence, Princess Lise bore him a son, but died in childbirth. Prince Andrey returned after the battle of Austerlitz to find himself free once more, but he enjoyed no feeling of satisfaction in his freedom. Seeking Pierre, Prince Andrey turned to his friend for answer to some of the eternal questions of loneliness and despair that tortured him.

Pierre, meanwhile, had joined the brotherhood of Freemasons, and through this contact had arrived at a philosophy of life which he sincerely believed to be the only true philosophy. Had Pierre realized that the order had initiated him solely because of his wealth, he would never have adopted their ideals. However, in true faith, Pierre restored some of Prince Andrey's lost courage by means of a wild if unreasoning enthusiasm. In the belief that he was now an unselfish, free individual, Pierre freed his peasants and set about improving his estate; but having absolutely no sense of business administration he lost a great deal of money. Finally, with his affairs in almost hopeless disorder, he left an overseer in charge and retired to Bleak Hills and Prince Andrey's sane company.

Meanwhile, Nikolay Rostov was in the thick of the fighting. Napoleon, having overcome the Prussian forces at Jena, had reached Berlin in October. The Russians once more had gone to the assistance of their neighbors, and the two opposing armies met in a terrible battle at Eylau in February, 1807. In June, Nikolay had entered the campaign at Friedland, where the Russians were beaten. In June of that year Nikolay naïvely thought the war was over, for Napoleon and Tsar Alexander signed the Peace of Tilsit. What the young officer did not know was that Napoleon possessed a remarkable gift for flattery, and had promised, with no intention of keeping his word, that Russia would be given a free hand with Turkey and Finland. For two years Nikolay enjoyed all the privileges of his post in the army, without having to endure any of the risks. Napoleon had gone to Spain.

Prince Andrey, having served in minor skirmishes as an adjutant under General Kutuzov, leader of the Russian forces, returned to the country. He had some business affairs to straighten out with Count Rostov, marshal of his district, and so he went to the Rostov estate at

Otradnoe. There Andrey fell almost immediately under the spell of Count Rostov's lovely young daughter, Natasha. He fancied himself in love as he had never loved before. Once again he turned to Pierre for advice. But Pierre had had an unfortunate quarrel with his wife, Ellen. They were now separated, and Pierre had fought a senseless duel with an innocent man because he had suspected his wife of being unfaithful. But at the sight of Prince Andrey, so hopelessly in love, Pierre's great heart was touched. He had always been fond of Natasha, whom he had known since childhood, and the match seemed to him ideal. With love once more flowing through his heart, he took his wife back, feeling very virtuous at his own generosity. Meanwhile he encouraged Prince Andrey in his suit.

Natasha had ignored previous offers of marriage. When dashing and wealthy Prince Andrey came upon the scene, however, she lost her heart to him instantly. He asked her parents for her hand, and they immediately consented to the match, an excellent one from their point of view. But when Prince Andrey broke the news to his quarrelsome and dictatorial old father, the ancient prince said he would not give his blessing until a year had elapsed. He felt that Natasha had little money and was much too young to take charge of Prince Andrey's home and his son. Marya, Prince Andrey' sister, also disapproved of the match. She was jealous of her brother's fiancée.

Natasha, heartbroken, agreed to wait a year, and Prince Andrey kept their betrothal a secret, in order, as he said, to let her have complete freedom. Natasha went to visit a family friend in Moscow. There her freedom was too complete. One night at the opera with Pierre's wife Ellen, who was now recognized as an important social leader, she met Ellen's disreputable brother, Anatole. Unknown to Natasha, Anatole had already been forced to marry a peasant girl, whom he had ruined. The young rake now determined to conquer Natasha. Aided by his unscrupulous sister, he forced his suit. Natasha became confused. She loved Prince Andrey, but he had joined the army again and she never saw him; and she loved Anatole, who was becoming more insistent every day. At last she agreed to run away with Anatole and marry him. Anatole arranged with an unfrocked priest to have a mock ceremony performed.

On the night set for the elopement Natasha's hostess discovered the plan. Natasha was confined to her room. Unfortunately, she had already written to Prince Andrey's sister asking to be relieved of her betrothal vows.

When Pierre heard the scandal, he forced Anatole to leave town. Then he went to see Natasha. Strangely, he was the only person whom she trusted and to whom she could speak freely. She looked upon him as if he were an older uncle, and was charmed with his gruff, friendly disposition. Pierre realized that he felt an attraction toward Natasha he should not have had, since he was not free. He managed to let her know his affection for her, however, and she was pleased over his attentions. She soon began to get well, although she was never again to be the frivolous girl whom Prince Andrey had loved.

Prince Andrey had suffered a terrible blow to his pride, but in the army there were many engrossing matters to take his attention away from himself. By 1810, the Franco-Russian alliance had gradually dissolved. When France threatened to free Russia of responsibility for Poland, the tsar finally understood that Napoleon's promises meant little. The dapper little French emperor had forsaken Russia in favor of Austria as the center of his European domination, had married Marie Louise, and in 1812, with his eyes unmistakably fixed on Moscow, crossed the Nieman River. From June to August Napoleon enjoyed an almost uninterrupted march to Smolensk.

In Smolensk he found burned and

wrecked houses. The city was deserted. By that time Napoleon began to run into fierce opposition. Old General Kutuzov, former leader of the army of the East and now in complete charge of the Russian forces, was determined to halt the French advance. Oddly enough, he was doing the very thing that kept the Russians from a decisive victory because of the tactics used to stop Napoleon. If he had not attempted to halt the French, but instead had drawn them deeper and deeper into Russia, lengthening their lines of communication and cutting them off in the rear, the Russians might have won their war earlier. It was odd, too, that Napoleon, in attempting to complete his march, also lessened his chances for victory. Both sides, it seemed, did the very things which would automatically insure defeat.

Battle after battle was fought, with heavy losses on both sides before Napoleon finally led his forces to Borodino. There the most senseless battle in the whole campaign was fought. The Russians, determined to hold Moscow, which was only a short distance away, lost nearly their whole army. The French forces dwindled in proportion. But it was clear that the Russians got the worst of the battle. General Kutuzov, bitter and war-weary, decided, against his will, that the army could not hold Moscow. Napoleon, triumphant, marched once more into a deserted city.

Prince Andrey was gravely wounded at Borodino. The Rostovs were already abandoning their estate to move into the interior, when many wagons loaded with wounded soldiers were brought to the house for shelter. Among these was Prince Andrey himself. Natasha nursed him and sent for Marya, his sister, and his son, Nikolushka. Old Prince Bolkonsky, suffering from the shock of having French soldiers almost upon his doorstep, had died of a stroke. Nikolay managed to move Marya and the boy to safer quarters. Although Prince Andrey welcomed his sister, it was evident that he no longer expected to recover. Natasha

nursed him tenderly, and they once more declared their love for each other. When his wound festered, Prince Andrey knew at last that he was dying. He died one night in his sleep. United in tragedy, Marya and Natasha became close friends, and young Nikolay found Prince Andrey's sister attractive.

Pierre Bezuhov, meanwhile, had decided to remain in Moscow. Fired with thoughts of becoming a national hero, he hit upon the plan of assassinating Napoleon. But in his efforts to rescue a Russian woman, who was being molested by French soldiers, Pierre was captured as a prisoner of war.

Napoleon's army completely disintegrated in Moscow. After waiting in vain for peace terms from the tsar, Napoleon decided to abandon Moscow and head for France. A ragged, irresponsible, pillaging group of men, who had once been the most powerful army in the world, gathered up their booty, threw away their supplies, and took the road back to Smolensk. Winter came on. Pierre Bezuhov, luckily, was robust and healthy. Traveling with the other prisoners, he learned from experience that happiness could consist of merely being warm and having enough to eat. His privations aged and matured him. He learned responsibility and gained courage. He developed a sense of humor at the irony of his plight. His simplicity and even temperament made him a favorite with French and Russians alike.

On the road to Smolensk the French forces became completely demoralized. Cossacks charged out of the forests, cutting the lines, taking countless French prisoners, and rescuing the Russian captives. Many Frenchmen deserted. Others fell ill and died on the road. Pierre, free at last, returned to Orel, where he fell ill with fever. Later he learned of the deaths of Prince Andrey and his own wife. Ellen had died in St. Petersburg after a short illness. These shocks, coupled with the news of the defeat of the French, seemed to deprive him of all feeling. When he finally recovered, he was overwhelmed with a joyous sense of freedom of soul, a sense that he had at last found himself, that he knew himself for what he really was. He knew the sheer joy of being alive, and he was humble and grateful. He had discovered a faith in God that he had never known before.

Pierre returned to Moscow and renewed his friendships with Marya Bolkonsky and the Rostovs. Once more Natasha charmed him, and Pierre suddenly realized that she was no longer a child. He loved her now, as always, and so when the opportunity presented itself he dutifully asked her parents for Natasha's hand. At the same time Nikolay Rostov entertained the thought of marrying Marya. Natasha and Pierre were married. They were very happy. Natasha was an efficient wife who dominated her husband, much to the amusement of their friends, but Pierre loved her and respected her because she knew how to take charge of everything. She managed his estates as well as her household.

Nikolay, though not entirely sure that he loved Marya, knew that to marry her would be a wise thing. The Rostovs were now poor, the old count having left his affairs in a deplorable state. At the insistence of his mother, Nikolay finally proposed to Marya and the two families were joined. The union proved happier than Nikolay had expected. They adopted Prince Andrey's son, Nikolushka.

After eight years of marriage, Pierre and Natasha had four fine children, of whom they were very proud. It was thought, in society, that Natasha carried her devotion to her husband and children to an extreme. But Natasha and Pierre were happier than they had ever been before, and they found their lives together a fulfillment of all their dreams.

THE WAR OF THE WORLDS

Type of work: Novel
Author: H. G. Wells (1866-1946)
Type of plot: Pseudo-scientific romance
Time of plot: Late nineteenth century
Locale: London and environs
First published: 1898

Principal characters:
THE NARRATOR
HIS WIFE
THE ARTILLERYMAN
THE CURATE

Critique:

This novel is representative of Wells' pseudo-scientific romances. Founded as it is on popular conceptions of Mars, it exploits interplanetary travel and warfare. In its day it was popular, but it has very little more than historical interest for the modern reader. We have advanced so far in scientific sophistication that the wonders of the *War of the Worlds* seem rather tame. The narrative method and the use of an unnamed I lend probability to the work. The novel contains little character study, and the plot is a bare narrative of a few days of horror.

The Story:

I was interested in Mars, interested enough to observe the planet often through a telescope. Mars, I knew, was smaller than the earth and probably much older. One night in the observatory I noticed a small pinpoint of light leave our neighboring planet. Later I saw three more shooting off into space. My astronomer friends speculated on these strange meteors.

One evening a meteor fell near our suburban house, and I went over with other curious sightseers to look at it. Only one end of its roughly cylindrical shape was visible. In size it had a diameter of about thirty yards. I looked for a while but went home little impressed. The next day there were strange stories of the projectile. Noises could be heard inside, a kind of pounding. The end was slowly turning around, and it seemed to be unscrewing. I could hear the pounding all night long.

In the morning I went to look again at the object. While I was there the cap came completely off. Then there emerged a strange creature, brownish in color, about the size of a man's torso. It had a head with two enormous eyes and a mouth without teeth. Around the mouth were many pairs of tentacles. The creature hopped off the projectile and began circling the huge cylinder. It moved with much difficulty. Probably the greatly increased pull of gravity on our planet made the creature comparatively heavier. The man from Mars began to dig industriously.

Then I noted that many more of these creatures were crawling from the cylinder and beginning to dig. Soon it became apparent that they were trying to make a big pit around their projectile.

Within a day or so the Martians had their huge pit completed, and they turned it into a workshop where they hammered night and day. The London papers paid little attention to the Martians or gibed at the fantastic news. We in the neighborhood saw that the creatures could not get out of their pit, and the few scientific men who came to observe asked us not to harm them.

One evening my wife and I heard a loud clanking and trembling. Rushing to the window we saw a giant metal frame about a hundred feet high and shaped like a big milk stool. The metal monster strode disjointedly over a field where it met two others. The three stood together, apparently looking around. Then a great beam of heat shot from each, and a forest disappeared, seared as if from a giant's breath. The three monsters clanked away.

Shortly thereafter refugees in carts and wagons, on bicycles and on foot, began to stream past our door. They were all panic-stricken and we learned that they were the few survivors of a town destroyed by the Martian heat rays. The war of the worlds had begun.

Before long we heard the reassuring sounds of army artillery moving up. As soon as Martians had been spotted, the soldiers fired their field pieces. But there was little at which to aim and the Martians were little affected. Then, luckily, a heavy gun made a direct hit on the solid portion at the top of one of the machines and it went out of control. From the top fell one of the brown octopuses, the man from Mars who was the guiding genius of the machine. The metal tripod continued on in a straight line until it fell over. We were horrified to see another monster go after it and transfer a Martian warrior to the prostrate frame. In a moment the tripod was up and on its path of destruction.

I hired a cart from my landlord and took my wife to Leatherhead. When I returned late that night, the roads were jammed with panicky crowds. My own house was somewhat damaged, but I spent the rest of the night there.

In the morning the countryside was alive with metal monsters. Our soldiers had no defense against their heat rays. The Martians quickly learned about guns. Before them as they strode they loosed heavy clouds of dense green smoke which killed everyone it touched. A detachment of artillery had no chance against them.

A weary artilleryman stumbled into my house that evening. The rest of his outfit had been killed by the smoke. While he was telling me his story, a monster came toward our street, destroying each house as he came. In my fear I would have fled immediately, but the artilleryman made us stop for provisions. Supplied with bread and mutton, we left the house and escaped by hiding in bushes and streams. Behind us clanked the monster.

I left the artilleryman along the road because I was intent on getting back to my wife in Leatherhead. I hid in cellars to escape the green smoke. On my wanderings I picked up a hysterical curate. One night, while we were sleeping in a deserted cellar, a loud explosion rocked our retreat. In the morning we saw that we were trapped by a Martian projectile resting against our refuge.

Forced to stay there, forced to keep still to avoid detection, I learned much about the Martians. They were all head. In their evolution they had learned to do without stomach, legs, and glands. They had a sensitive area where they could hear, but they had no noses. I even learned how they fed; from captured men they drained the blood and let it flow directly into their veins from a pipette. The curate went raving mad during our close confinement and I had to kill him. When the Martians explored the cellar with tentacles, I escaped, but they took the curate's body.

After twelve days the Martians left and I was free. In London I saw a ruined city. The Martian machines, however, were standing idle. The men from Mars had fallen victim to our bacteria and the world was saved. My wife found me in our London studio.

THE WARDEN

Type of work: Novel
Author: Anthony Trollope (1815-1882)
Type of plot: Domestic realism
Time of plot: Mid-nineteenth century
Locale: London and "Barchester," England
First published: 1855

Principal characters:

MR. HARDING, warden of Hiram's Hospital
ELEANOR HARDING, his younger daughter
JOHN BOLD, her lover
DR. GRANTLY, husband of Mr. Harding's older daughter
TOM TOWERS, a newspaperman
SIR ABRAHAM HAPHAZARD, Mr. Harding's counsel

Critique:

The Warden is a pleasant story about British ecclesiastical life in the time of Queen Victoria, and the amiable style of the novel fits the leisurely existence it describes. The narrative is frequently interrupted by the author, who comments on character, situation, or life in general, as his fancy strikes him. Trollope does not pretend to any depth, but he has produced here a delightful picture of life in a particular time and place.

The Story:

At the age of fifty the Reverend Septimus Harding was appointed precentor of Barchester Cathedral, a position which carried with it the wardenship of Hiram's Hospital. This institution had for over four hundred years provided a home for twelve men in their old age, and as the income had grown to a considerable size, the warden and the steward received substantial yearly salaries. With his income of eight hundred pounds a year, Mr. Harding was able to provide comfortably for his younger daughter, Eleanor. His older daughter, Susan, was married to Dr. Grantly, archdeacon of the cathedral.

John Bold, a young physician with a small practice, turned his energies to reform. On investigation he discovered that the will of John Hiram, donor of the hospital, made no stipulation which would result in such a discrepancy as existed between the warden's and the steward's incomes and those of the twelve inmates, and he felt that his duty obliged him to bring this discrepancy to light. He engaged the interest of a newspaper friend, Tom Towers, and the services of a solicitor named Finney. Finney explained the situation to the inmates and encouraged them to think in terms of an annual income of one hundred pounds a year. Most of them signed a petition addressed to the bishop, asking that justice be done.

The *Jupiter,* for which Towers worked, published editorials about the greediness of the church and unscrupulous clergymen. Mr. Harding was distressed. It had never entered his head that he was living off an income not his by rights, and he began to talk of resigning. Eleanor agreed that if her father were unhappy at Hiram's Hospital, they would be better off at Crabtree Parva, a small parish which belonged to Mr. Harding and which paid an annual income of fifty pounds.

Dr. Grantly, a worldly man, would not hear of Mr. Harding's resignation. He insisted that the warden had an obligation to the church and to his fellow members of the clergy which required a firm stand against the laity and the press. Besides, as he pointed out, the living at Crabtree Parva could not provide a suitable match for Eleanor.

Dr. Grantly came to the hospital and addressed the inmates. He told them John Hiram had intended simply to provide comfortable quarters for old single men who had no other homes. But Dr. Grantly's speech had little effect, except on John Bunce and his two cronies. John Bunce, who was especially close to Mr. Harding, served as a sub-warden of the old men. Tho others felt they had a right to a hundred pounds a year.

When Eleanor saw how unhappy the whole affair made her father, she begged him to resign. Finally she went to John Bold and begged him to give up the suit. After promising to do anything he could for her, Bold declared his love. Eleanor, who had hoped not to let matters go so far, confessed her love in return.

Bold went to see Dr. Grantly and told him that for reasons best known to himself he was withdrawing the charges he had made. Dr. Grantly replied that he did not think the defendants wished to have the suit withdrawn. He had been advised that Mr. Harding and the steward were, in effect, servants, and so were not responsible and could not be defendants in a suit.

Mr. Harding decided to go to London for a conference with Sir Abraham Haphazard, counsel for the defense. Eleanor had come home expecting to tell her father all that Bold had told her, but she could not bring herself to discuss her own affairs before those of the wardenship had been settled. Mr. Harding had decided that he had no right to the income from Hiram's Hospital.

Bold also was going to London. When he arrived there, he went to Tom Towers and asked him not to print any more editorials about the Barchester situation. Towers said he could not be responsible for the attitude of the *Jupiter*. Bold then went to the offices of his lawyer and told him to drop the suit. The lawyer sent word to Sir Abraham.

Mr. Harding arrived in London and was given an appointment with Sir Abraham the next night at ten. Having explained his intention in a note to Dr. Grantly, he was afraid that Dr. Grantly would arrive in London before he would have a chance to carry out his plan. He left his hotel at ten in the morning and spent most of the day in Westminster Abbey in order to avoid Dr. Grantly. That night he told Sir Abraham that he must in all conscience resign his post as warden. When he returned to his hotel, he found Dr. and Mrs. Grantly waiting for him, but their arguments could not make the warden change his mind. Back in Barchester, he wrote a formal letter of resignation to the bishop and sent a copy to Dr. Grantly.

The bishop offered him a position as chaplain in his household. Mr. Harding declined the offer. Then it was suggested that a trade be effected between Mr. Harding and Mr. Quiverful of Puddingdale. Mr. Quiverful, who had ten children, would be glad to double his annual income and would be impervious to any attacks from the press. But this arrangement, too, met with opposition, for Puddingdale was too far from Barchester for Mr. Harding to attend to his duties as precentor at the cathedral.

As the time for Mr. Harding's departure from Hiram's Hospital drew near, he called in all the inmates and had a last talk with them. They were disturbed, even those who had petitioned the bishop, for they felt that they were being deprived of a friendly and sympathetic warden.

Mr. Harding took lodgings and was given a tiny parish at the entrance to the cathedral close. His daughter Eleanor married John Bold. So Mr. Harding's income continued to be ample for his needs. He dined frequently with the bishop and kept his cello at Eleanor's house, where he often went to make music. In short, Mr. Harding was not an unhappy man.

WASHINGTON SQUARE

Type of work: Novel
Author: Henry James (1843-1916)
Type of plot: Psychological realism
Time of plot: About 1850
Locale: New York City
First published: 1881

Principal characters:
  DR. SLOPER, a prominent New York doctor
  CATHERINE SLOPER, his daughter
  MRS. PENNIMAN, his sister
  MORRIS TOWNSEND, Catherine's suitor

Critique:

The publication of *Washington Square* marked the end of what has been called the first period of its author's work. At that time Henry James was still twenty or more years away from the three great novels which climaxed his artistic efforts: *The Wings of the Dove* (1902), *The Ambassadors* (1903), and *The Golden Bowl* (1904). In spite of its early date and its differences from these later and more ambitious books, however, *Washington Square* has been called a work of great genius. The plot of the book, simple as it is, still appeals to a considerable audience. Nor are its merits visible, as in some other novels of James, only to readers of intellectual pretensions. A short novel, with a style much less involved than that which James was later to develop, *Washington Square* can be read in two or three hours. It is one of the few of the author's earlier works with scenes laid in America. It is also one of the few which are not preoccupied with the contrast existing between the civilization of Europe and that of America. Laid in New York City around the middle of the nineteenth century, it explores a family situation ruffling the peace of a rich and respected New York physician.

The Story:

Peace, especially of the domestic variety, was becoming increasingly important to Dr. Sloper as he entered his fifties. Intelligent, poised, distinguished in his profession, he was accustomed to meeting life on his own terms. Not entirely un-scarred by fate, he had suffered the loss of his wife and a young son many years before; but the passage of time had helped to soften even this blow. Now he dwelt quietly and comfortably in his mansion on Washington Square with his only remaining child, his daughter Catherine, and his widowed sister, Mrs. Penniman.

Neither of these companions, oddly enough, inspired the doctor with any great fondness. His sister had just the sort of nature, incurably romantic and deviously feminine, to set his teeth on edge; he saw her presence in his establishment as merely an inconvenience to be overlooked in the interest of providing female supervision of his growing daughter. Nor, regarding the daughter herself, was Dr. Sloper any less candid in his private appraisal. Catherine was a good girl, he thought, but incurably dull. Entering her twenties, she had never had a romantic interest or a prospect of any. She was shyly fond of her father and very much afraid of him, especially when an ironical tone crept into his voice. However, he was generally kind and courteous to her, even if more self-contained than an adoring daughter might always wish.

Catherine's taste for ornate dress was one of the characteristics which her father found especially trying. She had long cherished this taste without venturing to express it, but when she reached the age of twenty she bought a red satin gown trimmed with gold fringe. It made her look like a woman of thirty, and her father inwardly grimaced at the thought that a child of his should be both ugly

4087

and overdressed.

Catherine was wearing her red gown on the evening when she first met Morris Townsend. The occasion was a party, given by her aunt, Mrs. Almond. Catherine became quickly convinced that she had never met a young man so handsome, clever, and attentive. When his absorption with Catherine began to attract notice, Townsend quickly shifted his attentions to Mrs. Penniman, whose romantic sensibilities were soon aflutter with delight and anticipation. Before the evening ended, she had managed to intimate to this agreeable young man that he would be welcome to call in Washington Square.

The visit soon occurred, to be quickly followed by another; and presently young Townsend was in regular attendance upon Catherine. This development was far from unobserved by the other two members of the household, though their reactions were entirely different. Mrs. Penniman, undertaking the role of a middle-aged Cupid, pressed Townsend's claims and assisted his cause as ardently as she dared. Dr. Sloper, on the other hand, became first skeptical and then concerned. An interview with the young man strengthened his conviction that Townsend's charming manner was only a mask for irresponsibility and selfishness. He suspected that Townsend was living off the meager resources of the latter's sister, a widow with five children, and the doctor determined to investigate the matter. Before he could do so, however, Catherine brought him word that Morris Townsend had proposed to her and that she was anxious to accept him.

His suspicions confirmed by a talk with Mrs. Montgomery, Townsend's sister, the doctor came away from his call more convinced than ever that Catherine's young man was a fortune hunter. For once, however, his objections failed to sway the infatuated girl. As a last resort Dr. Sloper declared that if Catherine married Townsend he would disinherit her. This measure would not leave her penniless by any means, since an inheritance from her mother would still supply her with a comfortable income. Nevertheless it would reduce, by two-thirds, the amount Catherine could eventually expect; and the doctor's announcement gave both Townsend and Mrs. Penniman, also the object of her brother's displeasure, something to think about.

Mrs. Penniman, alarmed, counseled delay, and Townsend agreed to part with Catherine while she accompanied her father to Europe. Both Townsend and Mrs. Penniman hoped that the passage of time would soften the doctor's obdurate opposition to the match. Catherine, while agreeing to make the trip, cherished no such illusions. After several months the travelers returned; but the situation remained unchanged. Catherine was determined to go ahead with the marriage; Townsend kept putting her off. Suddenly he vanished from New York altogether.

Years passed before she saw him again. In the meantime Dr. Sloper had died and, fearful to the end that Townsend might re-enter Catherine's life, had left his own fortune to charity. One night while Catherine was sitting quietly at home, there was a ring at the door. Morris Townsend had come back, secretly encouraged by the unwearying Mrs. Penniman. Bearded, heavier, and forty-five years of age, he was still fluent and personable; his whole manner made it clear that he expected to be made welcome in Washington Square. The lapse of twenty years might have taken much from him, including the European wife of whom Catherine had vaguely heard, but he had not lost the bright assurance with which he now waited for his words to work their old-time magic on Catherine's heart.

He stood, hat in hand, murmuring his warm phrases, but Catherine did not ask him to sit down. She looked at him as if he were a stranger, repelling all advances and brushing off all explanations with a cool imperturbability which would have been worthy of the old doctor himself. With Catherine there was no longer any question of yielding to his charm: she had suffered too much. This time it would be she who sent him away; and she gave him his dismissal with a finality which he had no choice but to accept and understand.

THE WASPS

Type of work: Drama
Author: Aristophanes (c. 448-c. 385 B.C.)
Type of plot: Social satire
Time of plot: Fifth century B.C.
Locale: Athens
First presented: 422 B.C.

Principal characters:
PHILOCLEON, an Athenian
BDELYCLEON, his son
SOSIAS, and
XANTHIAS, slaves of Philocleon
CHORUS OF WASPS

Critique:

Although not generally considered one of Aristophanes' best plays, *The Wasps* does afford a very good example of the wit and artistry of Greek comedy. Here the author satirizes the abuses of the jury courts of Athens which, through the charging of admissions, provided the chief means of support of a large number of citizens. The subject matter is foreign to the modern reader, however, and the play necessarily loses some of the comic charm and sharp humor that it must have held for the Athenians. It was imitated in more modern times by Racine, in his *Les Plaideurs.*

The Story:

Because he was afflicted with a constant desire to judge and to convict the people brought before the courts of Athens, Philocleon was locked up in his own house by his son, Bdelycleon, who had previously tried all rational means of persuading his father to give up his mania and become a gentleman. Bdelycleon now resorted to a net cast around the house in order to keep his father from leaving. Two slaves, Sosias and Xanthias, were set to guard the house, and Bdelycleon, as an added precaution, watched from the roof.

The three men were kept busy thwarting Philocleon's attempts to escape. He tried to crawl out through the chimney, threatened to chew his way through the net, and, at last, was almost successful when he crawled beneath the belly of his ass, in the manner of Odysseus, and then insisted that the beast be taken out and sold. The ass moaned and groaned so intently, however, that Xanthias noticed the concealed burden. Philocleon was caught and thrust back into the house just before the other jurymen, the Wasps, arrived to escort him to the courts.

When the Wasps arrived, Philocleon appeared at an upper window, told them of his plight, and begged them to help him find some means of escape. Between them they decided that his only hope was to gnaw through the net and then lower himself to the ground. In this manner Philocleon had all but regained his freedom when Bdelycleon, who, worn out with watching, had fallen asleep, awoke and again detained him. Although the Wasps quickly came to the aid of their friend, they were no match for the stones and clubs used against them by Bdelycleon and the two slaves; and they were soon driven back.

In the argument that followed Bdelycleon explained that he simply wanted his father to lead the joyous, easy life of an old man, rather than concern himself constantly with the tyranny and conspiracy of the courts. He argued convincingly enough to force Philocleon into a debate on the merits of his profession. Philocleon agreed that if Bdelycleon could convince the Wasps, who were to act as judges, that a public career was disreputable, then he would give it up. The old man, speaking first, defended the jury system on the basis of the pleasures and benefits that he personally derived from it. Bdelycleon, on the other hand, proved that the jurists were no more than the slaves of the rulers, who themselves received the bulk of the revenue that should have gone to feed the hungry people.

Philocleon, along with the Chorus, was converted by Bdelycleon's persuasive argument. Because Philocleon felt that he could not live without judging, however, Bdelycleon consented to allow him to hold court at their home: he was to be allowed to judge the slaves and all other things about the house. This solution had the added advantage, as Bdelycleon carefully pointed out, of allowing the judge to eat and drink and enjoy all the comforts of home at the same time that he was following his profession.

Philocleon agreed to this solution and all the paraphernalia of a court were quickly assembled and the first case was called. Labes, one of the household dogs, was accused of stealing and devouring a Sicilian cheese all by himself, having refused to share it with any other animal. Bdelycleon himself undertook the defense of Labes and pleaded for mercy, but Philocleon felt it his duty as a judge to convict everyone and everything that was brought into his court. His son, however, tricked his father into acquitting the dog, an act that was foreign to his very nature.

Philocleon then felt that he had betrayed the one thing sacred to him and that he was, therefore, no longer capable of judging. Bdelycleon's problems were apparently solved at this point, for his father agreed to live a happy and carefree life. But such a plan entailed changing Philocleon's whole mode of being. His manner of dress, his speech—everything about him had to change; in short, he needed to acquire at least some of the elementary social skills. He was to learn how to walk, how to recline at dinner, what to talk about in order to appear a gentleman of leisure.

After a short period of training Bdelycleon took his father to a dinner party, where Philocleon quickly proved that he was as much a hard-headed old man as ever. He drank and ate too much; he insulted both his host and the other guests; he beat the slaves who waited on him, and, finally, he ran off with a nude flute girl. On his way home with the girl he struck everyone that he encountered.

By the time Philocleon arrived home, he naturally had a large following, all anxious to accuse him and bring him before those very courts he had so recently abandoned. He tried to appease the people by telling them stories that he had just learned and by using his other social skills, but to no avail; everyone clamored for justice. Philocleon, paying no attention to their cries, continued to talk and act as if he were far above such plebian concerns. Bdelycleon, who had hurried after his father, finally caught up with him and again used force to get him into the house. This time Bdelycleon was unable to keep the old man there. Philocleon immediately returned to the streets, now determined to prove his dancing skill, and led off the Chorus in a licentious, drunken dance.

THE WASTE LAND

Type of work: Poem
Author: T. S. Eliot (1888-   )
First published: 1922

By the early 1920's the "New Poetry" or the "Poetic Renascence," usually dated from 1912, had spent much of its initial force. The Imagists had come and gone; the reputations of Frost, Masters, and Sandburg had been established. Whatever was original in the new poetry—and, viewed in retrospect, this originality was not nearly so great as it then seemed—had been accomplished. It was time for American poetry to take a new direction. T. S. Eliot had already published two small volumes in 1917 and 1920, but he had not attracted a great deal of attention—not so much as had Amy Lowell or Vachel Lindsay, for example. In the early editions of Louis Untermeyer's Modern American Poetry, a book which was then very influential and which well represented the critical evaluations of that period, he was briefly dismissed as a "brilliant expatriate" whose work lacked "the exaltation which is the very breath of poetry." He was allowed "a certain perverse brilliance"; but his work was finally summed up as merely "mordant light verse; complex and disillusioned vers de société."

The Waste Land first appeared in The Dial and, having won that magazine's poetry award for the year, was published in book form in 1922. It may truthfully be said that seldom has a poet created such a sensation in the American literary world. To many readers, it seemed a deliberate hoax; perhaps the appearance, in 1916, of Spectra, by "Morgan and Knish," had left some critics with an abiding fear of again being caught out on a limb. The most common charge hurled by those who took the poem seriously was that of willful obscurantism: that the poet was deliberately making his work difficult for his readers when he could have written in a simpler fashion. The eleven pages of notes appended to a poem of but 430 lines only made matters worse; surely Eliot was pulling the reader's leg or he was piling obscurity on obscurity.

The truth of the matter was that the "New Poetry" of 1912 had not prepared the average reader for Eliot's peculiar style. The poets of the preceding decade had expanded the subject matter and vocabulary of poetry and they had substituted free verse for traditional poetic forms; but they had not greatly altered the conventionalities of poetic statement. To put it simply, their verse was not hard to understand, even though its form might be unusual. But Eliot, influenced by the English metaphysicals and the French Symbolists, had broken more sharply with nineteenth-century poetry than had any of his contemporaries and had achieved a genuinely new, though very difficult, style. The recent remark of A. Alvarez applies particularly to him: ". . . a great deal of modern poetry seems often as specialized as modern science; both require a degree of single-minded preparedness to which the general public is neither willing nor able to attain."

Eliot's verse has been subjected to such exhaustive critical analysis that the interested reader will find ample exegesis of almost every line, including translations of the phrases in half a dozen foreign languages and identifications of the quotations and echoes of English verse, all of which the poet used for their evocative effect. Eliot himself explained in his notes that the "plan and a good deal of the incidental symbolism of the poem" came from the Grail Legend and Sir James Frazer's *The Golden Bough*. This anthropological material deals with certain vegetation-fertility rites in which the god—Adonis, Attis, Osiris—must be slain each year so that by his death the land can again become fruitful; hence, the prevalence throughout the poem of images of drought and of water: the "dry sterile thunder" contrasted with the rain that restores life to the parched earth. This theme of sterility is applied to modern civilization which is dying of spiritual drought.

The poem opens with a picture of this modern world, a picture made up of broken fragments of idle conversation. And

What are the roots that clutch, what
 branches grow
Out of this stony rubbish?

Nothing can grow from this sterile civilization, from these unreal great cities where the living seem already dead, where "I had not thought death had undone so many"—Dante's exclamation on first seeing the crowds of the Futile, rejected by both Hell and Heaven, for they had lived "without blame and without praise." This is the modern massman. We then are given one of the several sharp contrasts between the past and the present: the deliberately rich description (with its echoes of *Antony and Cleopatra*), perhaps of the Renaissance, set against the equally deliberately banal scene in a pub. In the third section the same device is employed: the vulgar seduction of the typist by the "small house-agent's clerk" (love in the modern world reduced to a meaningless mechanical act) contrasted with the glimpse of Elizabeth and Leicester sailing on Spenser's "sweet Thames." All of this is seen by Tiresias who, Eliot tells us, is "the most important personage in the poem" because, having experienced life as both a man and a woman, he can unite all the characters. In the last section, according to the author's notes, the themes are: "the journey to Emmaus, the approach to the Chapel Perilous, and the present decay of eastern Europe"—that is, the disintegration of secular society which can be saved only by the King who sacrifices himself that his land may revive ("Shall I at least set my lands in order?"), the Risen Christ who, having died for his people, will bring them to a new life. Thus the poem ends on a profoundly religious note.

Just as one critic will write of the irony of the poem and another claim that its method is the obverse of irony, so there are many interpretations of individual lines and, indeed, of whole passages. Yet clearly the "Waste Land" is the modern great city inhabited by those for whom contemporary life provides only "a heap of broken images" and "fear in a handful of dust." It is a civilization dying of spiritual drought. The poem is an enormously complex one, making great demands upon the reader, yet the importance of its theme and the brilliance of its technique give it rank as one of the most significant literary works of our time.

WAVERLEY

Type of work: Novel
Author: Sir Walter Scott (1771-1832)
Type of plot: Historical romance
Time of plot: 1745
Locale: England and Scotland
First published: 1814

Principal characters:

EDWARD WAVERLEY, a young English officer
BARON BRADWARDINE, a Scottish nobleman
ROSE BRADWARDINE, the baron's daughter
EVAN DHU MACCOMBICH, follower of Fergus Mac Ivor
DONALD BEAN LEAN, a Highland bandit
FERGUS MAC IVOR VICH IAN VOHR, leader of the clan of Mac Ivor
FLORA MAC IVOR, Fergus' sister
PRINCE CHARLES EDWARD STUART, the Young Pretender

Critique:

When this novel was published anonymously in 1814, it created great interest among readers who sought to learn the identity of its author. Scott himself claimed, in his preface to the 1829 edition, that he had published his work anonymously to avoid political discussion. Because the book was written only sixty years after the invasion of Prince Charlie and because the dark and bloody days of 1745 still rankled in the minds of many living men and women, it is conceivable that Scott spoke the truth; however, observing the nineteenth-century fondness for publishing anonymous works, one might add the opinion that Sir Walter was also following a custom of the times. *Waverley* is a romantic novel in which Scott paid tribute to a group of people who had been considered no more than fierce, ignorant barbarians. In the person of Fergus Mac Ivor we find not only intellect and sentiment, but also formal, courtly manners. Especially contributing to the reader's delight in *Waverley* is a picturesque Scottish Highland background.

The Story:

The English family of Waverley had long been known for its Jacobite sympathies. In the year 1745, Waverley-Honour, the ancestral home of the family, was a quiet retreat for Sir Everard Waverley, an elderly Jacobite. His brother, Richard Waverley, seeking political advantage in London, had sworn loyalty to the king.

Edward Waverley, the son of Whig Richard, divided his time between his father and his Uncle Everard at Waverley-Honour. On that great estate Edward was free to come and go as he pleased, for his tutor Pembroke, a devout dissenter, was often too busy writing religious pamphlets to spend much time in the education of his young charge. When Edward became old enough, his father obtained for him a commission in the army. Shortly afterward he was ordered to Scotland to join the dragoons of Colonel Gardiner. Equipped with the necessary articles of dress, accompanied by a retinue of men who had been selected by Sir Everard, and weighed down by the dissenting tomes of Pembroke, Edward left Waverley-Honour in quixotic fashion to conquer his world.

He had been instructed by Sir Everard to visit an old friend, Sir Cosmo Comyne Bradwardine, whose estate was near the village of Tully-Veolan in the Scottish Lowlands. Edward, soon after his arrival at the post of Colonel Gardiner, obtained a leave in order to go to Tully-Veolan. There he found Sir Everard's friend both cordial and happy to see him. The few days spent at Tully-Veolan convinced Edward that Scotland was a wilder and more romantic land than his native England. He paid little attention to Rose Bradwardine, the baron's daughter, his youthful imagination being fired by the songs and dances of Davie Gellatley, the baron's servant, and by tales about the Scottish Highlanders and their rude ways. At Tully-Veolan he was also confronted by a political issue that had been but an idealistic quarrel in his former existence; these Scottish people were Jacobites, and Edward ostensibly was a Whig royalist because of his father's politics and his own rank in the army of Hanoverian George II of England.

During his stay at Tully-Veolan an event occurred which was to change Edward's life. It began with the unexpected arrival of Evan Dhu Maccombich, a Highlander in the service of the renowned clan chieftain, Fergus Mac Ivor Vich Ian Vohr, a friend of the baron's. His taste for romantic adventure having been aroused, Edward begged another extension of his leave in order to accompany Evan Dhu into the Highlands. In those rugged hills Edward was led to the cave that sheltered the band of Donald Bean Lean, an outlaw who robbed and plundered the wealthy Lowlanders. Staying with the bandit only long enough to discover the romantic attachment between Donald's daughter Alice and Evan Dhu, Edward again set out into the hills with his cheerful young guide. His curiosity had been sufficiently whetted by Evans' descriptions of Fergus Mac Ivor and his ancient castle deep in the Highland hills at Glennaquoich.

The welcome that Mac Ivor extended to Edward was open-handed and hearty. No less warm was the quiet greeting which Flora, Fergus Mac Ivor's sister. had for the English soldier. Flora was a beautiful woman of romantic, poetic nature, and Edward found himself before long deeply in love with the chieftain's sister. Mac Ivor himself seemed to sanction the idea of a marriage. That union could not be, however, for Flora had vowed her life to another cause—

that of placing Charles, the young Stuart prince, upon the throne of England. At Edward's proposal of marriage, Flora advised him to seek a woman who could attach herself wholeheartedly to his happiness; Flora claimed that she could not divide her attentions between the Jacobite cause and marriage to one who was not an ardent supporter of Charles Edward Stuart.

Edward's stay at Glennaquoich was interrupted by letters carried to him by Davie Gellatley from Tully-Veolan. The first was from Rose Bradwardine, who advised him that the Lowlands were in a state of revolt. Her father being absent, she warned Edward not to return to Tully-Veolan. The other letters informed him that Richard Waverley had engaged in some unfortunate political maneuvers which had caused his political downfall. On the heels of this news came orders from Colonel Gardiner, who, having heard reports of Edward's association with traitors, was relieving the young officer of his command. Repulsed by Flora and disgraced in his army career, Edward resolved to return to Waverley-Honour. He equipped himself suitably for the dangerous journey and set out toward the Lowlands.

Because of armed revolt in Scotland and the linking of the Waverley name with the Jacobite cause, Edward found himself under arrest for treason against King George. The dissenting pamphlets of Pembroke which he carried, his stay in the Highlands, and the company he had kept there, were suspicious circumstances which made it impossible for him to prove his innocence. Captured by some of the king's troopers, he was turned over to an armed guard with orders to take him to Stirling Castle for trial on a charge of treason.

But the friend of Fergus Mac Ivor Vich Ian Vohr was not to be treated in such a scurvy manner. On the road a quick ambush rescued Edward from his captors, and he found himself once again in the hands of some Highlanders whom he was able to recognize as a party of Donald Bean Lean's followers. Indeed, Alice once appeared among the men to slip a packet of letters to him, but at the time he had no opportunity to read the papers she had given him so secretively.

A few days' journey brought Edward to the center of Jacobite activities at Holyrood, the temporary court of Charles Edward Stuart, who had secretly crossed the Channel from France. There Edward Waverley found Fergus Mac Ivor awaiting him. When the Highlander presented Edward to Prince Charles, the Pretender welcomed the English youth because of the name he bore. The prince, trained in French courts, was a model of refinement and courtesy. His heartfelt trust gave Edward a feeling of belonging, after he had lost his commission, his cause unheard, in the English army. When Charles asked him to join in the Scottish uprising, Edward assented. Mac Ivor seemed quite happy about Edward's new allegiance. When the young Englishman asked about Flora, Mac Ivor explained that he had brought her along to the prince's court so that he could make use of her graces in gaining a political foothold when the battle was won. Edward resented this manner of using Flora as bait, but soon he perceived that the court of the Pretender functioned very much like the French court where Charles and his followers had learned statecraft. Mac Ivor pressed Edward to continue his courtship of Flora. The sister of Mac Ivor, however, met his advances coldly. In the company of the Highland beauty was Rose Bradwardine, whose father had also joined the Stuart cause.

Accepted as a cavalier by the women who clustered around the prince and under the influence of the Pretender's courtly manners, Edward soon became a favorite, but Mac Ivor's sister persisted in ignoring him. He began to compare the two women, Rose and Flora, the former gaining favor in his eyes as he watched them together.

The expedition of the Pretender and his Highlanders was doomed to failure. As they marched southward to England, they began to lose hope. The prince ordered a retreat to Scotland. Many of the clansmen were killed at the disastrous battle of Culloden. The survivors escaped to the Highlands, to spend their days in hiding from troops sent to track them down. A few were fortunate enough to make their way in safety to France.

Edward managed to get away and to find a friend who helped him to steal back to Scotland, where he hoped to find Rose Bradwardine. So far Edward had cleared himself of the earlier charges of treachery and desertion, which had been the initial cause of his joining the Pretender. It had been Donald Bean Lean who had deceived Colonel Gardiner with a false report of Edward's activities. The letters Alice had slipped to him had conveyed that information to Edward. Now he hoped to escape to France with Rose and wait for a pardon from England. Richard Waverley had died and Edward had inherited his fortune.

Fergus Mac Ivor and Evan Dhu Maccombich were executed for their crimes against the crown, and the power of the Highland clan was broken. Flora entered a Catholic convent in France, the country in which she had been reared. Edward Waverley and Rose were married after Edward was certain of his pardon. They returned to Tully-Veolan, where the baron's estate was awaiting its heirs.

THE WAVES

Type of work: Novel
Author: Virginia Woolf (1882-1941)
Type of plot: Psychological realism
Time of plot: The present
Locale: England
First published: 1931

Principal characters:
BERNARD
NEVILLE
SUSAN
RHODA
JINNY
LOUIS
PERCIVAL

Critique:

The Waves owes nothing whatever to the traditional form of the novel. In this book Virginia Woolf was attempting to give to fiction the subtle insights and revealing moments of perception which at one time were the function of poetry only. Her method is arbitrary and stylized. In a series of interlocking dramatic monologues six characters reveal the hidden essence of being at successive stages of their lives. The action, if anything so fleeting and inward can be called action, is a record of time passing as the six characters trace the course of their memories and sensations from childhood to old age and death. There is nothing irrelevant here; everything is observation, sensation, and naked intuition. Mrs. Woolf looked at life with a poet's vision, and in this novel she went even beyond Joyce in her use of symbols to make objects in the external world correspond to inner reality. Each section of her story is prefaced by a descriptive passage in which the movements of sun and waves through a single day stand for time and eternity. Uniting her people is the character of Percival, viewed only through their eyes, symbol of the natural man and also of the emotional certainty which all seek in life. At the end Bernard sums up the experiences of the group and sees in their lives man's challenge to death, the archfoeman. A novel daring in imagination and technique, The Waves marks the extreme of Virginia Woolf's experimental method.

The Story:

The waves rolled shoreward and at daybreak the children awoke. Watching the sunrise, Bernard, maker of phrases, seeker of causes, saw a loop of light—he would always think of it as a ring, the circle of experience giving life pattern and meaning. Neville, shy, passionate, imagined a globe dangling against the flank of day. Susan, lover of fields and seasons, saw a slab of yellow, the crusted loaf, the buttered slice, of tea time in the country. Rhoda, awkward, timid, heard wild cries of startled birds. Jinny, sensuous, pleasure-loving, saw a tassel of gold and crimson. Louis, of a race that had seen women carry red pitchers to the Nile, heard a chained beast stamping on the sands.

While the others played, Louis hid among the currants. Jinny, finding him there and pitying his loneliness, kissed him. Susan, suddenly jealous, ran away, and Bernard followed to comfort her. They walked across fields to Elvedon, where they saw a woman writing at a window. Later, in the schoolroom, Louis refused to recite because he was ashamed of his Australian accent. Rhoda, unable to do her sums, had to stay in. Louis pitied her, for she was the one he did not fear.

The day brightened. Bernard, older now, yawned through the headmaster's speech in chapel. Neville leaned sideways to watch Percival, who sat flicking the back of his neck. A glance, a gesture, Neville realized, and one could fall in love forever. Louis, liking order, sat quietly. As long as the head talked, Louis forgot snickers at his accent, his memories of kisses underneath a hedge. Susan, Jinny, and Rhoda were in a school where they sat primly under a portrait of Queen Alexandra. Susan thought of hay waving in the meadows at home. Jinny pictured a gold and crimson party dress. Rhoda dreamed of picking flowers and offering them to someone whose face she never saw.

So time passed and the last day of the term arrived. Louis went to work in London after his father, a Brisbane banker, failed. Sometimes, in his attic room, he heard the great beast stamping in the dark, but now the noise was that of city crowds and traffic. At Cambridge, Neville read Catullus and waited with uneasy eagerness for Percival's smile or nod. Bernard was Byron's young man one day, Shelley's or Dostoevski's the next. One day Neville brought him a poem. Reading it, Bernard felt that Neville would succeed while he would fail. Neville was one person in love with one person, Percival. Bernard in his phrase-making was many people, a plumber, a horse-breeder, an old woman in the street, as well as Byron's or Dostoevski's man. Susan, in Switzerland, dreamed of new-born lambs in baskets, of marsh mist and autumn rains, of the lover who would walk with her beside dusty hollyhocks. At a ball in London, Jinny, dancing, felt as if her body glowed with inward fire. Rhoda, at the same ball, sat and stared across the rooftops.

They all loved Percival, and so before he left for India they met at a dinner party in London to bid him goodbye.

Bernard, not knowing that Susan had loved him, was already engaged. Louis was learning to cover his shyness with brisk assurance; the poet had become a businessman. Rhoda was frightened by life. Waiters and diners looked up when Jinny entered, lovely, poised. Susan came dowdily, hating London. Neville, loving Percival in secret, dreaded the moment of parting that would carry him away. Here, thought Bernard, was the circle he had seen long ago. Youth was friendship and a stirring in the blood, like the notes of Percival's wild hunting-song.

The sun passed the zenith and shadows lengthened. When word came that Percival had been killed in India, Neville felt as if that doom had been his own. But he would go on, a famous poet and scholar after a time, but always as well a lonely man waiting in his rooms for the footstep on the stair of this young man or that whom he loved in place of Percival. Bernard was married then; his son had been born. He thought of Susan, whom Percival had loved. Rhoda also thought of Susan, engaged to her farmer in the country. She remembered the dream in which she had offered flowers to a man whose face had been hidden from her, and she knew at last that the man had been Percival.

Shadows grew longer over country and town. Louis, a successful businessman and wealthy, planned a place in Surrey with greenhouses and rare gardens. But he still kept his attic room where Rhoda often came; they had become lovers. Susan walked in the fields with her children or sat sewing by the firelight in a quiet room. Jinny groomed a body shaped for gayety and pleasure. Neville measured time by the hours he spent waiting for the footstep on the stair, the young face at the door. Bernard tried to snare in phrases the old man on the train, the lovers in the park. The only realities, he thought, were in common things. He realized that he had lost friends by death—Percival was one—and others because he had not wished to cross the street. After Louis and Rhoda parted, his new mistress was a vulgar cockney actress. Rhoda, always in flight, went to Spain. Climbing a hill to look across the sea toward Africa, she thought of rest and longed for death. Slowly the sun sank. At Hampton Court the six friends met again for dinner. They were old now,.and each had gone a different way after Percival had died in India years before. Bernard felt that he had failed. He had wrapped himself in phrases; he had sons and daughters, but he had ventured no farther than Rome. He had not become rich, like Louis, or famous, like Neville. Jinny had lived only for pleasure, little enough, as she was learning. After dinner Bernard and Susan walked by the lake. There was little of their true thoughts they could say to each other. But Bernard was still a maker of phrases. Percival, he said, had become like the flower on the table where they ate—six-sided, made from their six lives.

So it seemed to him years later, after Rhoda had jumped to her death and the rest were old. He wondered what the real truth had been—the middle-class respectability of Louis, Rhoda's haunted imagination, Neville's passion for one love, Susan's primitivism, Jinny's sensuous pleasures, his own attempt to catch reality in a phrase. He had been Byron's young man and Dostoevski's, and also the hairy old savage in the blood. Once he had seen a loop of light, a ring. But he had found no pattern and no meaning, only the knowledge that death is the great adversary against whom man rides in the darkness where the waves break on the shore.

THE WAY OF ALL FLESH

Type of work: Novel
Author: Samuel Butler (1835-1902)
Type of plot: Social criticism
Time of plot: Nineteeenth century
Locale: England
First published: 1903

Principal characters:
GEORGE PONTIFEX, a printer
THEOBALD PONTIFEX, George's son
ALTHEA PONTIFEX, George's daughter
CHRISTINA PONTIFEX, Theobald's wife
ERNEST, Theobald's oldest son
MR. OVERTON, Ernest's friend
ELLEN, Ernest's wife

Critique:

Reared in the family of a strict clergyman, Samuel Butler patterned Theobald Pontifex after his own father. Aimed at a type of parent-children relationship that bred maladjusted, introverted children, this novel depicts one son who broke the parental ties, thereby freeing himself to make his own way in life. Pointing to the foibles of his fellow man, probing the motive of an indignant parent or burlesquing a controversy of ideas, Butler's wit and sarcastic humor lighten at all times the heavy tones of his social study.

The Story:

Mr. and Mrs. Pontifex were well up in years when their son George was born. When the time came for George to learn a trade, they accepted the offer of Mr. Pontifex's brother-in-law to take George with him to London as an apprentice in his printing shop. George learned his trade well, and when the uncle died he willed the shop to his nephew.

George had married, and five children were born to him and his wife; John, Theobald, Eliza, Maria, and Althea, at whose birth Mrs. Pontifex died. George considered himself a parent motivated only by the desire to do the right thing by his children. When Theobald proved himself not as quick as John but more

persistent, George picked the clergy as Theobald's profession. Shortly before his ordination, Theobald wrote to his father that he did not wish to become a minister. George, in reply, threatened to disinherit his son. Submitting, Theobald was ordained. His next step was to wait for some older member of the clergy to die so that he could be given a living.

The Allabys had three daughters, all of marriageable age. After having selected Theobald as a possible husband for one of the daughters, Mr. Allaby suggested to his offspring that they play a game of cards to decide who would become Theobald's wife. Christina won. Theobald unwittingly fell in with Mr. Allaby's plans and obligingly courted Christina until he won her promise to marry him. George wrote to Theobald that he objected to his son's marriage into the impoverished Allaby family, but Theobald was too deeply embroiled in his engagement to untangle himself. In five years he obtained a decent living in a community called Battersby, where he and Christina settled. Their first child was a son. Since this child was the first new male Pontifex, George was pleased, and Theobald felt that for the first time in his life he had done something to satisfy his father. After Ernest came Joseph and then Charlotte. Theobald and Christina reared their children with strict adherence to principles which they believed would mold fine character. The children were disciplined rigorously and beaten when their parents deemed it appropriate. When George Pontifex died, he left seventeen thousand, five hundred pounds to Theobald and twenty-five hundred pounds to Ernest.

From an oppressive existence under the almost obsessed rule of his parents, Ernest was sent to Roughborough to be educated under Dr. Skinner, who was as strict a disciplinarian as Theobald. Ernest was physically weak and mentally morose. He might have succumbed completely to his overpowering environment had not he been rescued by an understanding and loving relative. Althea Pontifex, Theobald's sister, had retired to London, where she lived comfortably on an inheritance wisely invested. Looking about for someone to whom she could leave her money when she died, Althea hit upon Ernest. Not wishing to bestow her fortune blindly, she determined to learn more about the boy. She moved to Roughborough so that she could spend a great deal of time with Ernest.

From the first, she endeared herself to the lonely youngster. She encouraged him to develop his own talents, and when she learned that he had a passion for music she suggested that he learn how to build an organ. Enthusiastically he set about to learn wood construction and harmony. Theobald disapproved, but he did not forbid Ernest's activities because he and Christina were eager to have Ernest inherit Althea's money. Ernest's shrinking personality changed under the benevolent influence of his aunt. When Althea died, she left her money in the hands of her best friend, Mr. Overton, whom she had appointed to administer the estate which would go to Ernest on his twenty-eighth birthday.

After Ernest had completed his course at Roughborough, Theobald sent him to Cambridge to study for the ministry. At Cambridge Ernest made a few friends and took part in athletics. He was ordained soon after he received his degree. Then he went to London. Still innocent and unworldly, he entrusted to a friend named Pryer the income he had inherited from his grandfather. Pryer cheated him out of his legacy. Because he could not differentiate between good and evil in human character, Ernest also became entangled in a charge of assault and battery and was sentenced to a term in the workhouse. Theobald sent word that henceforth Ernest was to consider himself an orphan.

Ernest was twenty-three years old at the time. Mr. Overton, who held, unknown to Ernest, the estate Althea had left for her nephew, began to take an interest in Ernest's affairs. When Ernest was released from prison, he went to Mr. Overton for advice concerning his future, since it was no longer possible for him to be a clergyman.

While Ernest was still at Roughborough, Christina had hired as a maid a young girl named Ellen. She and Ernest had become good friends simply because Ellen was kinder to him than anyone else at home. When Ellen became pregnant and Christina learned of her condition, she sent Ellen away. Ernest, fearing that the girl might starve, followed her and gave her all the money he had. Theobald learned what Ernest had done through John, the coachman, who had been present when Ernest had given Ellen the money. Theobald became angry and dismissed the coachman.

Soon after his release from prison, Ernest met Ellen in a London street. Because both were lonely, they married and set up a small second-hand clothing and book shop with the help of Mr. Overton, who deplored the idea of Ernest's marrying Ellen. Unknown to Ernest, Ellen was a habitual drunkard. Before long she had so impoverished him with her drinking and her foul ways that he disliked her intensely, but he could not leave her because of the two children she had borne him.

One day Ernest again met John, his

father's former coachman, who revealed that he was the father of Ellen's illegitimate child and that he had married Ellen shortly after she had left Theobald's home in disgrace. Acting on this information, Mr. Overton arranged matters for Ernest. Ellen was promised an income of a pound a week if she would leave Ernest, a proposal she readily accepted. The children were sent to live in a family of happy, healthy children, for Ernest feared that his own upbringing would make him as bad a parent as Theobald had been.

When Ernest reached his twenty-eighth birthday, he inherited Althea's trust fund of seventy thousand pounds. By that time Ernest had become a writer. With a part of his inheritance he traveled abroad for a few years and then returned to England with material for a book he planned to write.

Before he died he published many successful books, but he never told his own story. Mr. Overton, who had access to all the Pontifex papers and who knew Ernest so well, wrote the history of the Pontifex family.

THE WAY OF THE WORLD

Type of work: Drama
Author: William Congreve (1670-1729)
Type of plot: Comedy of manners
Time of plot: Seventeenth century
Locale: London
First presented: 1700

Principal characters:
    LADY WISHFORT, an aged coquette
    MRS. FAINALL, her daughter
    MRS. MILLAMANT, Lady Wishfort's niece
    FOIBLE, a servant
    SIR WILFULL WITWOUD, Lady Wishfort's nephew
    WITWOUD, his half-brother
    MIRABELL, a gentleman of fashion
    WAITWELL, his servant
    FAINALL, married to Lady Wishfort's daughter
    MRS. MARWOOD, in love with Fainall

Critique:

The Way of the World is the best of the Restoration dramas, a true comedy of manners. Criticism had paid particular attention to this play, for some hold that the famous scene between Mirabell and Millamant is one of the most profound analyses of the marriage relation ever written. The play as a whole is a realistic statement of a problem every individual must face in his adjustment to society.

The Story:

Mrs. Millamant, who was by far the most beautiful and wittiest of all the fine ladies in London, was sought after by all the beaux in town. The niece of the rich Lady Wishfort, she was also an heiress in her own right, and was looked upon with great favor by Witwoud, a kinsman of Lady Wishfort. But Millamant's acknowledged preference among her suitors was for young Mirabell, who was the only man in London who could match that lady's devastating wit.

Mirabell himself was as great a favorite among the ladies in the town as Millamant was among the beaux. She was the perfect coquette; he was the perfect gallant. Among Mirabell's jealous admirers was Mrs. Marwood, the mistress of Fainall, Lady Wishfort's son-in-law. In fact, Mirabell had but one real enemy among the ladies, and that was Lady Wishfort herself. On one occasion, in order to further his suit with Millamant, Mirabell had falsely made love to the old lady. Discovering his subterfuge later, she had never forgiven him. She determined that he would never marry her niece so long as she controlled Millamant's fortune. In consequence, Mirabell was hard put to devise a scheme whereby he might force Lady Wishfort to consent to the marriage.

The plan he devised was an ingenious one. Realizing that Lady Wishfort would respond to anything which even resembled a man, he promptly invented an imaginary uncle, Sir Rowland, who, he said, had fallen madly in love with Lady Wishfort and wanted to marry her. He forced his servant, Waitwell, to impersonate this fictitious uncle. To placate Waitwell and further insure the success of his plan, he contrived his servant's marriage to Lady Wishfort's maid, Foible.

His scheme might have worked had it not been for the counterplans of the designing Mrs. Marwood and her unscrupulous lover, Fainall. Although she pretended to despise all men, Mrs. Marwood was secretly in love with Mirabell, and had no intention of allowing him to marry Millamant. Fainall, although he detested his wife heartily, realized that

4103

he was dependent upon her and her mother's fortune for his well-being, and he resolved to stop at nothing to make sure that fortune was in his control.

While these plans were proceeding, Millamant gave little thought to plots or counterplots. She had not the slightest intention of compromising with life, but insisted that the world's way must somehow be made to conform to her own desires. She had little use for the life around her, seeing through its shallow pretenses and its falsity, and yet she knew that it was the world in which she had to live. She realized that any attempt to escape from it into some idyllic pastoral existence, as her aunt often suggested, would be folly.

Millamant laid down to Mirabell the conditions under which she would marry him, and they were stringent conditions, not at all in conformity with the average wife's idea of her lot. She would have in her marriage no place for the ridiculous codes and conventions which governed the behavior of the people around her. She would be entirely free of the cant and hypocrisy of married life, which were only a cloak for the corruption or misery hidden underneath social custom. In short, she refused to be merely a married woman in her husband's or society's eyes. Mirabell, likewise, had certain conditions which must be fulfilled before he was turned from bachelor into husband. When his demands proved reasonable, both lovers realized that they saw life through much the same eyes. They decided that they were probably made for one another.

But the world had not come to the same conclusion. Lady Wishfort, still embittered against Mirabell for his gross deception, resolved that Millamant was to marry a cousin, Sir Wilfull Witwoud, a country lout many years her senior, who had just arrived in London. Fortunately for Millamant, Sir Wilfull turned out to be a harmless booby, who, when he was in his cups, became the most understanding of men.

There was a greater obstacle, however, in the scheme which Mirabell himself had planned. Waitwell, disguised as Mirabell's imaginary uncle, Sir Rowland, paid ardent court to Lady Wishfort, and would have been successful in inveigling her into marriage had it not been for a letter from Mrs. Marwood exposing the whole scheme. Lady Wishfort's maid, Foible, succeeded in intercepting the letter, but Mrs. Marwood appeared at Lady Wishfort's in person and disclosed the deception.

Lady Wishfort was furious, and more determined than ever to prevent any marriage between her niece and Mirabell. She angrily discharged Foible from her employ. But Mrs. Fainall, Lady Wishfort's daughter, was on the side of the two lovers. When Foible informed her that she had tangible proof of the relationship between Fainall and Mrs. Marwood, Mrs. Fainall resolved to prosecute her husband to the limit. Meanwhile the wily Fainall had taken pains to have all his wife's property transferred to his name by means of trumped up evidence of an affair between his wife and Mirabell.

In this act Lady Wishfort began to see for the first time the scheming villainy of her daughter's husband. Mirabell, with the aid of Foible and Millamant's servant, Mincing, exposed the double-dealing Mrs. Marwood and her lover, and further proved that while she was yet a widow Mrs. Fainall had conveyed her whole estate in trust to Mirabell. Lady Wishfort was so delighted that she forgave Mirabell all his deceptions, and consented to his marriage to Millamant.

THE WEALTH OF NATIONS

Type of work: Economic treatise
Author: Adam Smith (1723-1790)
First published: 1776

The classic statement of economic liberalism, the policy of laissez faire, was written over a ten-year period by Adam Smith, a Scottish professor of moral philosophy, and published under the title *An Inquiry into the Nature and Causes of the Wealth of Nations*. Its power derived from its ideas which were useful in encouraging the rise of new business enterprise in Europe, but the ideas could not have taken hold so readily had it not been for the scope of Smith's work and the effectiveness of his style.

As a philosopher, Smith was interested in finding intellectual justification for certain economic principles which he came to believe, but as an economist and writer he was interested in making his ideas prevail in the world of business. He was reacting against oppressive systems of economic control which were restricting the growth of business; but although he concerned himself with general principles and their practical application, he was aware of the value of the individual, whether employer or laborer. There is no reason to believe Smith would have sanctioned monopolistic excesses of big business or any unprincipled use of the free enterprise philosophy.

Smith began his work with the assumption that whatever a nation consumes is either the product of the annual labor of that nation or what is purchased with the products of labor. The wealth of the nation depends upon the proportion of the produce to the consumers, and that proportion depends partly upon the proportion of those who are employed to those who are not, but even more on the skill of the workers and the efficiency of the means of distribution.

Book I of *The Wealth of Nations* considers the question of how the skill of the laborers can best be increased; II is a study of capital stock, since it is argued that the proportion of workers to non-laborers is a function of the amount of capital stock available; III explains how Europe came to emphasize the industry of the towns at the expense of agriculture; IV presents various economic theories, some stressing the importance of industry in the towns, others, the importance of agriculture; and V considers the revenue of the sovereign, or commonwealth, with particular attention paid to the sources of that revenue and the consequences of governmental debt.

In Smith's view, the productive power of labor is increased most readily by the division of labor, for by giving each worker a specific job to do he becomes more skillful, time is saved, and machinery is invented which further speeds the rate of production. Smith believed that as a result of the increase in production which followed the division of labor, a well-governed community was able to enjoy a "universal opulence which extends itself to the lowest ranks of people."

Smith regarded the division of labor as a necessary consequence of the human propensity to trade or exchange one thing for another. The propensity to trade is itself a consequence of a more fundamental human trait: self-love. Thus, for Smith, the basic motivating force of any economic system, including successful ones, is the self-interest of each person involved in the system.

Money originates as a means of facilitating exchange when the products of those who wish to barter are not desired by those with whom they choose to trade. To use Smith's example, if a butcher has all the bread and beer he needs, he will not accept more bread or beer in exchange for meat. But if the man with bread or beer can exchange it elsewhere for money—whether it be shells, tobacco, salt, or cattle, or the most favored medium of exchange, metal—he can then use the money to buy meat from the butcher.

Among the most important ideas in *The Wealth of Nations* is Smith's claim that labor is the real measure of the exchangeable value of commodities. Commodities have a value in use, but for the producer this value becomes unimportant, and he seeks to exchange what he has made for something that he needs. The amount of work he can purchase with his commodity is the real exchangeable value of that commodity. Thus, Smith defines wealth as the power of purchasing labor. The nominal, as distinguished from the real, price of commodities is their money value.

Smith defined *natural* price as the average price of a commodity in a community, and *market* price as the actual selling price. He presents the familiar principle of supply and demand by stating that market price increases when the quantity of a commodity brought to market falls short of the demand.

Wherever there is perfect liberty the advantages and disadvantages of different uses of labor and stock must be either equal or tending to equality, according to Smith. However, there are counterbalancing circumstances which affect equality: the agreeableness of the job, the cost of learning the business, the constancy of employment, the amount of trust that must be put in the employee, and the probability of success.

Smith makes a distinction between productive and unproductive labor. Labor is productive when it adds to the value of something, unproductive when it does not. The labor of a manufacturer adds to the value of the material which is used, but the labor of a menial servant adds nothing to the value of the employer whom he serves. This distinction is important because it is by reference to the proportion of productive to unproductive labor that capital is explained.

There are four ways of using capital: for purchasing raw materials, for manufacturing, for transportation, and for distribution.

Adam Smith was confident that he could discover the natural order of economic matters, but to later critics it has appeared that he was mistaking his own preferred kind of economic situation for that which would prevail if economic relations among men were in no way affected by social habit. His inclination was to regard what would prevail in a civilized community free from governmental restraint as the natural state of affairs. This view is acceptable when he says, for example, "According to the natural course of things, therefore, the greater part of the capital of every growing society is, first, directed to agriculture, afterwards to manufactures, and last of all to foreign commerce"; but the following account of rent is more provocative: "Rent, considered as the price paid for the use of land, is naturally the highest which the tenant can afford to pay in the actual circumstances of the land." However, Smith wrote without any obvious interest in supporting one economic class against another, and his definitions of "natural" price, rent, and other economic factors are couched in neutral terms.

Smith's experiences as a teacher and philosopher are reflected most clearly in his account "Of the Expence of the Institutions for the Education of Youth." He is rather bitter about the quality of education when the teacher is not driven by economic necessity to do his best. In situations where the professor is responsible only to his colleagues, they are likely to allow one another to neglect their duties as teachers. The result is that "In the university of Oxford, the greater part of the public professors have, for these many years, given up altogether even the pretense of teaching." Smith favored giving the student a considerable part to play in the selection and retention of teachers, and he warned that if this were not done, the professors would devise ways of giving "sham-lectures" and would force their students to attend regularly and keep silent.

Smith thought that the wealthy and wellborn could see to the education of their young, but that the state should support education for those who could not otherwise afford it. He argued that it was important, particularly in free countries, that the public be educated in order to exercise the art of judgment.

In considering the revenue of the state, Smith proceeded on the principle that whatever expense was beneficial to the whole society could justly be defrayed by the general contribution of the whole society. Thus, defending the society, supporting the chief magistrate, administering justice, maintaining good roads and communications, supporting state institutions or public works, and, under certain circumstances, defraying the expenses of educational institutions and institutions for religious instruction are all properly supported by general contribution of the whole society.

Support of the institutions and activities of the state must come either from some fund belonging to the state or from the revenue of the people. Smith considers three sources of the revenue of individuals: rent, profit, and wages. His discussion of taxes is based upon four maxims: 1. The taxpayer ought to be taxed according to his ability to pay as determined by his revenue; 2. The tax should be certain in the sense that there should be no question as to the time, manner, or quantity of payment; 3. Taxes should be levied in a convenient manner, e.g., taxes on consumer goods are paid for when the goods are bought; 4. The tax should be economical in the sense that it should not be expensive to collect.

Adam Smith's *The Wealth of Nations* is a temperate, thorough, and even engrossing analysis of the economic facts of life in a free industrial society. In so far as it is to some extent a proposal, it is not surprising that it has not won universal approval; but it is a masterpiece of its kind, and its influence on modern thought and practice has been historically significant.

THE WEAVERS

Type of work: Drama
Author: Gerhart Hauptmann (1862-1946)
Type of plot: Social criticism
Time of plot: The 1840's
Locale: Germany
First presented: 1892

Principal characters:
DREISSIGER, a manufacturer
PFEIFER, his manager
BECKER, a weaver
MORITZ JAEGER, a returned soldier
OLD BAUMERT, a weaver
OLD HILSE, a weaver
GOTTLIEB HILSE, his son
LUISE HILSE, Gottlieb's wife

Critique:

The Weavers is usually rated the best of Hauptmann's dramatic works. It is almost wholly a socio-economic study in that the characters are types caught in irresistible forces of the social and industrial system under which they live. The dramatic incidents are a microcosm of the much wider industrial revolution, with the unemployment caused in part by the introduction of power looms. In this play no answer to the problem is given; rather, Hauptmann shows us people who react in the only way they can when misery becomes too oppressive.

The Story:

In a large room on the ground floor of Dreissiger's house the weavers were bringing in their finished webs. Pfeifer, manager for Dreissiger, inspected each piece and assessed its value. He had a sharp eye for flaws and the amounts he named were low. From the complaints aired, the weavers were near starvation. In general, however, the weavers were a docile, tractable lot.

Old Baumert came in carrying a bundle wrapped in cloth. It was the body of his pet dog. Baumert had not had the heart to kill the animal himself, but he had had it butchered to provide meat for his family. The dog was only a skinny, half-grown pup, not large enough to feed his destitute family.

Most of the weavers were squat and sickly, but Becker was a young, impudent giant. When he heard the price Pfeifer would allow for his web, he refused on the ground that such an amount was alms, not wages. In fury Pfeifer called for Dreissiger, who upheld his manager. A diversion was created when a child fainted. Dreissiger was angry because the child's parents had sent him so far with the heavy web; he ignored the crowd's explanation that the child was starving.

Because of the tension in the room, Dreissiger harangued the weavers. In his view he provided work; if the weavers did not want to do his work, they could go elsewhere. Then he made a portentous announcement: he was engaging two hundred more weavers, and the new rates of pay would be lower.

The Baumerts occupied one room in the house of William Ansorge, a former weaver. Old Baumert was too feeble to do much and his wife was crippled. One daughter, Emma, was twenty-two. She had a boy of four fathered by a consumptive weaver who had died before they could be married. Bertha, the second daughter, was a pallid girl of fifteen. The two sisters spent long hours at the loom. Their landlord, Ansorge, was too old to

THE WEAVERS by Gerhart Hauptmann. Translated by Horst Frenz and Miles Waggoner. By permission of the publishers, Rinehart & Co., Inc. Copyright, 1951, by Horst Frenz.

weave any more; he led a miserable existence mending baskets.

When old Baumert came in, he brought with him Moritz Jaeger, a returned soldier. Jaeger was a fine strapping youth with good clothes and money in his pockets, the center of interest as he told of his successes in the army. He kindly provided a bottle of brandy which cheered the family immensely.

Bertha cooked their dog meat in the oven. With meat and brandy they would have a feast. Ansorge joined them as the smell of cooking meat spread through the house. To his intense disgust, Baumert's stomach could not hold the meal; two years had passed since he had tasted meat.

Jaeger was appalled at the misery of the weavers. Able to read, he was pessimistic about any relief for the workers. The papers had recently published the report of the Berlin inspector who had been sent to investigate their living conditions. The bureaucrat had asserted solemnly that there was no one in want among them. Jaeger had found a different answer.

He began to read to them a marching song that told the woes of the weavers. Inflammatory in tone, it named Dreissiger as an oppressive villain. As he read the stanzas, Ansorge and Baumert caught some of its revolutionary spirit, and they were stirred to fight for their rights.

In the common room of the public house, Welzel, the publican, served a commercial traveler. The salesman, a competent city man, was flirting with Anna, Welzel's red-haired daughter. Wiegand, a joiner, had that day made a coffin for a dead weaver. The man had died of starvation; he needed only a light coffin. The traveler expressed his surprise that the supposedly destitute weavers should hold such elaborate funerals. Wiegand, who was a cunning man, was of the opinion that the weavers were a wrongheaded lot; no one need be in want if he were enterprising.

When Ansorge and Baumert came in, the talk grew more animated as other weavers aired their wrongs. A peasant happening in told the assembly that the weavers were poor only because they did not know how to do useful work. A forester joined in that opinion. The weavers retorted bitterly that they were forbidden to take even a broken branch from the forests.

After Jaeger and Becker came in at the head of a small group of young men, the talk centered even more strongly on the weavers' woes. The traveler, attempting a pompous remark on the amount of real destitution, was roughly silenced, and Welzel for safety led him into another room. Then Kutsche, the policeman, came to warn the weavers that they must not sing their song any more. But the mob spirit grew; the defiant song rang out.

In Dreissiger's private room, the growing tulmult had forced the manufacturer to interrupt his whist game with Pastor Kittelhaus. As Dreissiger came back in, he announced that he had had Becker seized. Weinhold, a tutor in the household, was young enough to feel sympathy for the weavers. When he voiced his opinions, he was summarily discharged. The coachman entered and told them he had the carriage ready, for it looked as if the family might be compelled to flee. The children were already prepared to travel.

The obsequious police superintendent hurried to congratulate Dreissiger on having the ringleader, Becker, apprehended. When five dyers led in the captured Becker, the superintendent began to upbraid the weaver, but Becker, cool and self-possessed, cried shame on the dyers for not joining their fellow workers. When Becker was led off to jail, the mob freed him and manhandled the police.

Pastor Kittelhaus, who had no sympathy for the rioters, attempted to talk to the crowd outside. He was shouted down and roughly treated. The Dreissiger family drove away just as the weavers broke into the house. Thoroughly aroused, the mob sacked the building and broke windows and doors.

Old Hilse, a weaver living in another village, could not believe the news when Hornig the rag dealer told him that the weavers were rioting for more pay. The doctor came to see Hilse's blind wife and verified the news. Hilse, a pious old soldier, was upset that his fellow weavers could forget law and order. His son's wife, Luise, sided with the rioters, but Gottlieb, her husband, believed as his father did. Old Hilse predicted that as soon as the soldiers came the weavers would be a sorry lot.

The ominous marching song came closer as the rioters, led by Jaeger and Becker, shouted for Hilse and Gottlieb to join them. Luise courageously went out with the mob, but the Hilse men stayed at their looms. Soon shots were heard; the soldiers were putting down the riot. When Gottlieb saw his wife standing defiantly in front of the line of bayonets, he could resist no longer, and he dashed out to join the throng.

Old Hilse stubbornly stayed at his loom near a window, where a chance bullet wounded him fatally. Mielchen, Gottlieb's little daughter, called to her grandfather that the soldiers had been driven off and that the mob was entering the house of Dittrich, another manufacturer. Old Hilse made no answer.

THE WEB AND THE ROCK

Type of work: Novel
Author: Thomas Wolfe (1900-1938)
Type of plot: Impressionistic realism
Time of plot: 1900-1928
Locale: North Carolina, New York, Europe
First published: 1939

Principal characters:
GEORGE WEBBER, a young writer
ESTHER JACK, whom he loved

Critique:

Critics have said that The Web and the Rock is at once the best and the worst novel that Thomas Wolfe wrote. Certainly the first part of the book, that describing George Webber's childhood in a Southern town, is an excellent regional chronicle. Here Wolfe's genius with words reaches new heights. But the rest of the novel drags somewhat from overdone treatment of a love story in which similar scenes are repeated until they become monotonous. From his own experience, Wolfe here retells the story of a young man's search for the meaning of life. Like his other novels, it is a book of passion and fury and wild rhetoric.

The Story:

George Webber's childhood was one of bleakness and misery. He was really a charity ward, even though he lived with his aunt and uncle. For George's father had deserted him and his mother, and had gone off to live with another woman. After the death of George's mother, her Joyner relatives took George into their home, where the boy was never allowed to forget that he had some of the blood of the Webbers mixed with his Joyner blood. Strangely, all his good and beautiful dreams were dreams of his father, and often he hotly and passionately defended his father to the Joyners. His love for his father made his childhood a divided one. George hated the people his aunt and uncle called good; and those they called bad,

he loved. A lonely child, George kept his thoughts and dreams to himself rather than expose them to the ridicule of the Joyners. But the picture of that happy, joyful world of his father, and others like him, stayed with him during those bleak years of his childhood.

When George was sixteen, his father died, leaving the boy a small inheritance. With that money, George left the little southern town of Libya Hill and went to college. There he found knowledge, freedom, life. Like many other young men, George wasted some of that freedom in sprees of riotous and loose living. But he also used his freedom to read everything he could get his hands on, and he was deeply impressed with the power of great writers. George was beginning to feel the need of getting down some of his thoughts and memories on paper. He wanted to write of the two sides of the world—the bright, gay world of the people who had everything and the horrible, dreary world of the derelicts and the poor.

His college years ended, George fulfilled the dream of every country boy in the nation; he went to the city, to the beautiful, wonderful enfabled rock, as he called New York.

The city was as great and as marvelous as George had known it would be. He shared an apartment with four other boys; it was a dingy, cheap place, but it was their own apartment, where they could do as they pleased. But George found the city a lonely place in spite of its millions of people and its bright lights. There was no one to whom he was responsible nor to whom he belonged. He thought he would burst with what he knew about people and about life, and, since there was no one he could talk to about those things, he tried to write them down. He began his first novel.

The next year was the loneliest one George had ever known. He drove himself mercilessly. He was wretched, for the words torturing his mind would not go on the paper as he wanted them to. At the end of a year he took the last of his inheritance and went to Europe. He hoped to find there the peace of mind he needed to finish his book.

The cities of Europe did not hold his salvation. He was still lonely and bitter because he could not find the answer to the riddle of life. He went back to New York. But the city was no longer an unfriendly enemy, for George had found Esther.

They had met on the ship bound for New York. Esther was Mrs. Esther Jack, a well-known and successful stage set designer. She was fifteen or twenty years older than George, but she was also younger in many ways, for Esther loved people and believed in them. Where George was silent and distrustful, Esther was open and trusting. George sometimes felt that theirs was the greatest love of all times, at once brutal and tender, passionate and friendly, so deep that it could not last. But for the next three years he was the king of the world. To Esther, George told all his dreams, all his memories, all his formerly wordless thoughts about life and people.

George failed to realize at first that Esther meant more than a lover to him. Gradually he came to know that through her he was becoming a new person, a man who loved everyone. For the first time in his life George Webber belonged to someone. Since he was no longer lonely, the torture and the torment left him. At last his book began to take shape, to become a reality. George Webber was happy.

Slowly the magic of his affair with Esther began to disappear. He still loved her more than he believed possible, knew that he would always love her; but they began to quarrel, to have horrible, name-calling scenes that left them both exhausted and empty, even the quarrels that ended with passionate love-making. At first George did not know the reason for those scenes, although he always knew that it was he who started them. Slowly he began to realize that he quarreled with Esther because she possessed him so completely. He had given her his pride, his individuality, his dreams, his manhood. Esther had also unknowingly been a factor in his disillusionment, for through her he had met and known the great people of the world —the artists, the writers, the actors— and he had found those people disgusting and cheap. They had destroyed his childhood illusions of fame and greatness, and he hated them for it.

When his novel was finished, Esther sent the manuscript to several publishers she knew. After months had passed without his hearing that it had been accepted, George turned on Esther in one final burst of savage abuse and told her to leave him and never return. Then he went to Europe again.

Although he had gone to Europe to forget Esther, he did nothing without thinking of her and longing for her. Esther wrote to him regularly, and he paced the floor if the expected letter did not arrive. But he was still determined to be himself, and to accomplish his purpose he must not see Esther again.

One night, in a German beer hall, George got into a drunken brawl and was badly beaten up. While he was in the hospital, a feeling of peace came over him for the first time in ten years. He looked into a mirror and saw his body as a thing apart from the rest of him. And he knew that his body had been true to him, that it had taken the abuse he had heaped upon it for almost thirty years. Often he had been almost mad, and he had driven that body beyond endurance in his insane quest—for what he did not know. Now he was ready to go home again. If his first novel should not be published, he would write another. He still had a lot to say. The next time he would put it down right, and then he would be at peace with himself. George Webber was beginning to find himself at last.

WESTWARD HO!

Type of work: Novel
Author: Charles Kingsley (1819-1875)
Type of plot: Historical romance
Time of plot: Sixteenth century
Locale: England and South America
First published: 1855

Principal characters:
AMYAS LEIGH, an adventurer
FRANK LEIGH, his brother
SIR RICHARD GRENVILE, Amyas' godfather
EUSTACE LEIGH, Amyas' and Frank's cousin
ROSE SALTERNE, loved by Amyas and Frank
SALVATION YEO, Amyas' friend
DON GUZMAN DE SOTO, a treacherous Spaniard
AYACANORA, an Indian maiden
MRS. LEIGH, Amyas' and Frank's mother

Critique:

In *Westward Ho!* Charles Kingsley has taken us back to the days of Queen Elizabeth, when such men as Sir Francis Drake, Sir Walter Raleigh, and Sir Richard Grenvile sailed the seas in search of adventure and treasure for their queen. He has shown us that were it not for such men, the history of the world would have been different, for these men won for England the supremacy of the sea and determined who would settle North America. *Westward Ho!* is a story of great sea battles, duels of honor, romantic rescues, and deeds of horror in the Spanish Inquisition. Kingsley has woven all these into one of the most romantic adventure stories in our literature.

The Story:

Amyas Leigh had always had a secret longing to go to sea, but he had not spoken of it because he knew his parents thought him too young for such a rough, hard life. When he met John Oxenham and Salvation Yeo, who were recruiting a crew to sail to the New World after Spanish treasure, he begged to be allowed to join them, but his parents and Sir Richard Grenvile, his godfather, persuaded him to wait a while. The next year his father died of fever and his brother Frank went to the court of Queen Elizabeth. Then Sir Richard Grenvile persuaded Amyas' mother to let the boy accompany Drake on that first English voyage around the world. Now Drake and his adventurers had returned, and Amyas, no longer a boy but a blond young giant, came back to his home at Bideford, in Devon.

One face in the village he remembered better than any, Rose Salterne, the mayor's daughter. All the young men loved and honored her, including Amyas and his brother Frank, who had returned from court. She was also loved by Eustace Leigh, the cousin of Amyas and Frank. Eustace was a Catholic, distrusted by his cousins because they suspected he was in league with the Jesuit priests. When Rose spurned his love he vowed revenge. The other young men who loved Rose formed the Brotherhood of the Rose, and all swore to protect her always and to remain friends, no matter who should win her.

Shortly after Amyas had returned from his voyage with Drake, Salvation Yeo came to him and Sir Richard Grenvile with a strange and horrible tale. The voyage which he had made with John Oxenham had been ill-fated, and Oxenham and most of the crew had been captured by Spanish Inquisitors. Oxenham had had a child by a Spanish lady, and before they were separated Yeo had vowed that he would protect the child. Yeo had done his best, but the child had been lost, and now Yeo begged that he might attach himself to Amyas and go wherever Amyas went. He thought that he might in his travels someday find the little maid again. Amyas and Sir Richard Grenvile were touched by the story, and Amyas promised to keep Yeo with him. Before long the two sailed with Sir Walter Raleigh for Ireland, there to fight the Spaniards.

In Ireland, Raleigh defeated the Spaniards, and Amyas took as hostage Don Guzman de Soto, a Spanish nobleman. Don Guzman accompanied him back to Bideford, there to wait for his ransom from Spain. Don Guzman was a charming gentleman, and it was not long before he had caught the eye of Rose Salterne. After his ransom had been paid, he left England, and then it was learned that Rose had also disappeared in the company of Lucy the witch. Her father was wild with grief, as were Amyas and Frank and the other young men of the Brotherhood of the Rose. All vowed to sail to La Guayra in Caracas, where Don Guzman had gone to be governor and where they felt Rose had fled to join him.

Their voyage was an eventful one. When they neared La Guayra they were seen by the Spaniards, and they had to fight many times before they reached shore. Amyas and Frank went ashore with a few men to try to rescue Rose. There they learned that Eustace had known of their voyage and had beaten them to their destination to warn Don Guzman of their approach. Frank and Amyas heard Rose tell Eustace that she was happily married to Don Guzman, and so they knew she would never leave with them. But they also heard Eustace beg her to run away with him, threatening to turn her over to the Inquisition if she refused. At that threat, Frank and Amyas attacked Eustace, but he escaped, never to be heard of again. Rose fled into the fort. As they made their way back to their ship, Frank was captured by Don Guzman's men. Amyas was knocked unconscious, but his men carried him back to the ship.

When the ship was damaged in a later encounter with the Spaniards, the crew beached her and began a march toward the fabled city of Manoa. It was a long and hazardous journey over high mountains and through a land of hostile Indians. They found no El Dorado, but a young priestess of one of the tribes fell in love with Amyas and followed him the rest of the journey. She was called Ayacanora, and although she was of an Indian tribe she seemed to have the look of a white woman.

After more than three years the little band reached the shore of New Granada and there, after a furious fight, captured a Spanish galleon. After they had secured her and set sail, they went into the hold and released the prisoners the Spaniards had aboard. One of them was Lucy the witch, who told them of the horrible fate of Rose and Frank. Before Eustace disappeared from La Guayra, he had reported to the Inquisition that Rose had kept her Protestant faith. She and Lucy were taken before that terrible tribunal, where Frank also had been turned over to the torturers. Lucy confessed that she had accepted the Catholic faith, but Frank and Rose, refusing to yield to the Inquisitors, had been tortured for many days before they were burned at the stake. When Amyas heard this story, he was like a madman, vowing never to rest until he had killed every Spaniard he saw. On the ship were two Spanish dignitaries who had .witnessed the burning of Frank and Rose, and Amyas had them hanged immediately.

At last the ship reached Devon and Amyas took Ayacanora to his home, where his mother welcomed her and treated her as a daughter. During the voyage Yeo had discovered that she was the little maid he had promised Oxenham

4115

to protect, and he became as a father to her. Amyas treated her as he might a sister; Ayacanora was not happy at his treatment.

After a time Amyas fitted out a ship and prepared to go with Drake to Virginia, but before they sailed the Spanish Armada arrived off English shores. Amyas with his ship joined the rest of the fleet in that famous battle. After twelve terrible days, the Armada was defeated and almost every Spanish ship destroyed. But Amyas was not satisfied. Don Guzman was aboard one of the Spanish ships, and though Amyas pursued him relentlessly he had to sit by and watch a storm tear the Spaniard's ship apart. And Amyas cursed that he himself had not been able to kill Don Guzman and thus avenge his brother's death.

As Don Guzman's ship broke apart, a bolt of lightning struck Amyas' ship, blinding him and killing Yeo. At first Amyas was full of despair. One day he had a vision. He saw Rose and Don Guzman together, and knew that the Spaniard had really loved her and mourned her until his death. Then he saw himself with Don Guzman, acknowledging their sins to each other, and asking forgiveness. After that he felt at peace with himself.

Amyas returned to his mother's home, and there she and Ayacanora cared for him. Realizing how much the girl loved him, he was so grateful for the tenderness she showed him that he gave her his heart. In Bideford the blind hero spent his remaining days dreaming of his past deeds and of the great glory to come for his country and his queen.

WHAT EVERY WOMAN KNOWS

Type of work: Drama
Author: James M. Barrie (1860-1937)
Type of plot: Social satire
Time of plot: Early twentieth century
Locale: Scotland and England
First presented: 1908

> Principal characters:
> MAGGIE WYLIE, plain and spinsterish
> ALICK WYLIE, her father
> JAMES WYLIE, and
> DAVID WYLIE, her brothers
> JOHN SHAND, a young student
> LADY SYBIL TENTERDEN, a young and beautiful aristocrat
> THE COMTESSE DE LA BRIÈRE, her aunt
> MR. CHARLES VENABLES, a minister of the Cabinet

Critique:

What Every Woman Knows is one of the most realistic of Barrie's plays, developing as it does the familiar theme that behind every man there is a woman who makes him either a success or a failure. There are, however, flashes of Barrie's sly humor and dramatic irony throughout. The play has been a popular success on both sides of the Atlantic, and a favorite role with many distinguished actresses.

The Story:

The Wylies, like most Scotsmen, were a clannish lot. They had built up their business, a granite quarry, on the spot where their father once worked as a stonemason. They called it *Wylie and Sons.* Alick Wylie wanted it called *Wylie Brothers,* but David, his brother James, and their sister Maggie all insisted that first credit for the business should go to Alick, their father.

Maggie, who kept house for her father and two brothers, was their only problem, for she had reached twenty-seven years, an age when a woman must marry or be regarded as an old maid, and they were considerably downcast because their latest prospect, the minister at Galashiels, had married another woman. There was no question but that Maggie was plain, a fact of which she

herself was only too conscious, and the brothers realized that if their sister were to find a husband they would have to do everything in their power to help her.

The opportunity came while the Wylies were at the dambrod board, their favorite pastime on Saturday evenings. Maggie was seated in a chair in the corner knitting, and the brothers were trying to get her off to bed so that they could be on the lookout for a burglar they thought they had seen prowling about the house the night before. At last the burglar appeared, but to their astonishment they discovered the intruder was young John Shand, a neighbor, who confessed that his purpose in entering the house was to read. He was a student preparing for the ministry, but since he was too poor to buy books he had to choose that method of study. David was impressed at such earnestness. After a brief conference with his brother he made the boy an offer. He promised to pay up to three hundred pounds for John Shand's education if, at the end of five years, he would marry Maggie, providing she were at that time still unmarried and wanted him. After some quibbling to decide whether the full three hundred pounds would be deposited in his name at the bank immediately, John Shand agreed to the transaction. Maggie, wanting him to go into the deal with his eyes open, admitted that she had never had an offer of marriage, and that she was five years older than he. But those matters meant little to ambitious young John Shand, who left the house content that he was free to browse in the Wylie library without being mistaken for a burglar.

Six years later, having in the meantime abandoned his ambitions for the ministry, John Shand was standing for Parliament. His great hour had come, the hour for which he and Maggie had waited. She might have forced him to marry her one year before, but they both agreed to wait for his triumph. Maggie was almost frantic between hope and anxiety. At one time, certain that John had lost, she promised herself that she and John would begin another six years of waiting that very night.

Her fears were groundless, however, for John Shand won the election by an overwhelming majority. Her real problem lay in his victory. Immediately after his election John was taken up and lionized by women with whom plain little Maggie could not hope to compete. Among these was Lady Sybil Tenterden. Maggie, overwhelmed by a sense of her own inferiority, offered to release John from his contract and tore up the document which bound him to her. But John Shand was a man of his word, and in his speech to the Cowcaddens Club he announced his forthcoming marriage and introduced Maggie as the Mrs. John Shand soon to be.

Before long it was apparent that Lady Sybil's aunt, the Comtesse de la Briere, had been perfectly right when she warned Maggie against allowing John to see too much of her niece. For John, tiring of his plain wife, fell in love with Lady Sybil. They spent most of their time together, and as a consequence John's speeches in the House of Commons grew more dull. Essentially a humorless man, John had nevertheless built up a reputation for sudden flashes of humor which were called Shandisms,

and which won him great popularity. There was a simple reason for his success. Maggie, who typed his speeches, supplied the humor without letting her husband know it. The Comtesse saw through the subterfuge, and thereby named Maggie The Pin, meaning that she was like the pin every successful man is supposed to pick up at the beginning of a successful career.

By that time John was so absorbed in Lady Sybil that he considered her his sole inspiration, and he even went so far as to forget completely his wedding anniversary. Maggie's brothers were shocked at his neglect, but Maggie covered the situation perfectly by reaching out her hand to Lady Sybil for her ruby pendant, displaying it as her anniversary present. She then forced John to admit that he had given the pendant to Lady Sybil. John was defiant, declaring to Maggie and her brothers that Lady Sybil was the great love of his life, and that he would sacrifice everything for her sake. The brothers reminded him that if he deserted Maggie he could count on no career. A short time before, Mr. Charles Venables, a cabinet minister and John's political mentor, had offered him the opportunity to be third speaker at Leeds on the same platform with two ministers, an occasion which would mean John's appointment to a ministerial post. Maggie suggested that John go away for a few weeks with Lady Sybil and write the speech under her inspiration. When Maggie promised to keep silent concerning the marital difficulties between them, John agreed to the arrangement.

When John read to Mr. Venables the speech he had written, the minister was greatly disappointed and said it lacked the spark of life his earlier speeches had contained. Maggie, realizing what was at stake, informed Venables that her husband had written another speech which she had typed for him; it was a speech Maggie herself had written from notes John had left at home.

In the meantime, Lady Sybil admitted

that she had tired of John and had no intention of going on with the affair. Her decision was a jolt to John's vanity, but the final blow came when Venables congratulated him on the speech which, he realized, only Maggie could have written for him. When they were alone, Maggie told him that every man who is high up likes to think he has climbed there by himself, but every wife knows better. It was, she said, every woman's private joke. Whereupon Maggie laughed, and for perhaps the first time in his life John Shand laughed at himself. His marriage and career were both saved.

WHAT MAISIE KNEW

Type of work: Novel
Author: Henry James (1843-1916)
Type of plot: Social morality
Time of plot: 1890's
Locale: London, Folkestone, Boulogne
First published: 1897

Principal characters:
MAISIE FARANGE, the daughter of divorced parents
IDA FARANGE, her mother
BEALE FARANGE, her father
MISS OVERMORE, a governess, later the second Mrs. Beale Farange
MRS. WIX, a governess
SIR CLAUDE, Ida Farange's second husband

Critique:

This novel, one of the greatest of Henry James's middle period, is the story of the growing moral and intellectual perception of the neglected daughter of divorced and irresponsible parents. The story is told as Maisie herself lived it. Her view of the events caused by her parents' second marriages and the final affair between her step-parents, is both droll and deeply moving. There is much of Henry James's characteristic and profound irony in this story. The moral core of the novel is Maisie's incorruptible innocence. Although in self-defense she often was forced into deceit, she always willingly gave her love to her mentors. In the end she was able, with the perceptive awareness that James gave to all his major characters, to make freely a morally responsible decision about her future.

The Story:

Beale and Ida Farange were divorced with much publicity. At first each fought to possess their daughter Maisie, but at last it was arranged that the girl should spend six months with each in turn. The first period was to be spent with her father.

Maisie was confused by the divorce. At first she truthfully reported to her parents what they said about each other, but finding that her candor provoked furious outbursts and that she was being used as an innocent messenger, she soon became silent on the subject of the absent parent and appeared to absorb no knowledge during her visits.

Ida engaged Miss Overmore, a pretty governess, for Maisie, and Maisie was unhappy to leave her when she returned to her father. Soon, however, Miss Overmore went to Beale Farange's house where she was, to Ida's fury, also engaged as Maisie's governess. Upon her subsequent return to Ida, Maisie was placed in the care of Mrs. Wix. She learned no lessons from Mrs. Wix, but adored her conversation and felt comfortable and secure with her.

During Maisie's next stay with Beale he went for a few days to Brighton with Miss Overmore. When the governess returned, she found Mrs. Wix waiting for her. Mrs. Wix alone was preoccupied with Maisie's welfare, and was outraged by the child's environment. She announced to Miss Overmore that Ida was about to remarry and she gave Maisie a photograph of Sir Claude, her future stepfather. Miss Overmore outdid her, as it were, by announcing that she had just married Beale Farange.

Some time after his marriage Sir Claude called and was received by the new Mrs. Beale Farange. Maisie was delighted by their apparent understanding and declared that she had brought them together. Sir Claude won Maisie's love by his gentleness toward her and by his declared intent to make her his respon-

4120

sibility. In spite of the pain of leaving the new Mrs. Farange, the girl was pleased to go home with him. But Ida's love for her new husband soon waned and she had several lovers. When she accused Sir Claude of basely stealing Maisie's affections, and threatened to drive Mrs. Wix out of the house for supporting him, Maisie felt that she belonged nowhere. In this disturbed situation Mrs. Wix was determined to meet her responsibility for Maisie, and she desired to "save" Sir Claude from Mrs. Beale Farange, whom he frequently visited. Also, fearing the loss of her livelihood, she wished that Sir Claude would take a house for himself where she and Maisie would also live.

On one outing Sir Claude took Maisie to her father's new house, which she was afraid to enter for fear of losing him if she remained there. Once in the house, however, she was again enthralled by Mrs. Farange's beauty and was interested to learn that Beale mattered no more to his wife than Sir Claude did to Ida. Maisie remained happily with her stepmother after Sir Claude had assured her that he would provide for Mrs. Wix and visit her frequently.

After a long absence Sir Claude visited Maisie again. While they were walking in the park they met Ida with an unknown, military-appearing man. Ida and Sir Claude were immensely angry at their meeting, and Maisie was sent to talk with Ida's escort, whom her mother had called the Captain, while they finished their argument. Maisie, who was by that time thoroughly aware that neither parent loved her, wept when the Captain praised her mother highly and was eager to agree that she was "good." After this episode Sir Claude, unable to learn from Maisie what the Captain had said to her, sent her home alone in a cab.

Mrs. Farange told Maisie that she met Sir Claude away from her home, but that he was reluctant to visit them and thus compromise Maisie. The three hoped to meet at a London exhibition; instead, they unexpectedly encountered Beale Farange. After a subdued but violent quarrel, Maisie was whisked away by her father to the house of his mistress. There he offered, in such a way that Maisie could only refuse, to take her to America with him.

Sir Claude, encouraged by Mrs. Wix, took Maisie to Folkestone as the first step toward making a home for them in France. There Ida arrived suddenly and surrendered Maisie to Sir Claude's guardianship. The following day they crossed to France, where Mrs. Wix joined them. Sir Claude was to return to England and to Mrs. Beale Farange, when Maisie's father had finally left. Sir Claude confessed that he feared Mrs. Farange as he had formerly feared Ida. Mrs. Wix, still strongly opposed to Mrs. Farange, asked to be sent to England to sever their relationship. This request was refused by Sir Claude, who went off to England alone.

While he was away Mrs. Wix explained to a bewildered Maisie that she refused to condone the immorality of Mrs. Farange and Sir Claude in living together with them. Also, she declared that she would never again leave Maisie. After several walks and much thought the full implications of what this situation might mean became apparent to Maisie. She realized, too, that she had no moral "sense," and having rapidly absorbed the idea of such a sense from vague but emphatic conversations with Mrs. Wix, she decided to show in her future responses that she did indeed possess it.

When they returned to their hotel after a morning walk, Maisie was unexpectedly greeted by her stepmother. Mrs. Wix's own "moral sense" was nearly destroyed by Mrs. Farange's charm and her determination to have the governess-companion as an ally. According to Mrs. Farange, now that the girl's father had left, Maisie was her own daughter. In this way she intended to hold Sir Claude, through his devotion to the girl. Mrs. Wix wavered, but Maisie declared that she would stay with Sir Claude only if he were alone.

The next morning Mrs. Wix awakened

Maisie with the news that Sir Claude had arrived. When Maisie breakfasted alone with him, he asked her if she would leave Mrs. Wix and live with him and Mrs. Farange. She asked to see Mrs. Wix before deciding. Later, while walking with Sir Claude, she said she would give up Mrs. Wix only if he would give up Mrs. Farange. Maisie made her decision when the four people confronted one another in a final struggle at the hotel. After she had failed in her appeal to have Mrs. Farange give up Sir Claude, Maisie decided to stay with Mrs. Wix.

WHEN THE MOUNTAIN FELL

Type of work: Novel
Author: Charles-Ferdinand Ramuz (1878-   )
Type of plot: Regional romance
Time of plot: Eighteenth century
Locale: Switzerland
First published: 1935

Principal characters:
SERAPHIN CARRUPT, an old man
ANTOINE PONT, a young man newly married
THÈRESE, his wife
PHILOMÈNE MAYE, Thèrese's mother
OLD PLON, a shepherd
MAURICE NENDAZ, a lame villager

Critique:

Every once in a while there is fire, pestilence, or earthquake. Sometimes, too, the mountains let loose an avalanche that wrecks a place, a town, perhaps just a pasture on which are a few cabins, fifteen or twenty men, and a hundred or so cattle. What happened two hundred years ago in Switzerland is the basis of *When the Mountain Fell.* Since there have been more recent newspaper tales of the same sort of disaster, one can be sure that Ramuz takes as his subject a real force of nature and sets it against the smallness and inadequacy of men in a setting that is majestic and awe-inspiring enough to make us other little men feel intensely the dread those people of Aire felt when the mountain fell. The original French title of this novel is *Derborence.*

The Story:

It was the evening of the twenty-second of June, about nine o'clock, and Seraphin Carrupt and Antoine Pont were sitting in their little shepherd's cabin at some pasture fields called Derborence. They were pasturing their cattle there for the summer, as was the custom of those people in the towns lower down in the mountains. In the summer the towns were left with women, children, and old men in them, while the able men went up to tend the cattle and goats. In those days Derborence was a lovely valley pasture, but that was before the twenty-second of June.

Antoine had been married only two months before he left Aire to come up to Derborence with Seraphin. He was already becoming bored with the daily milking and cheese-making, already anxious to go back to his wife Thèrese. That night, as they sat together, Seraphin suggested that Antoine go home for a weekend to see that Thèrese was all right. It was a beautifully moonlit night and the air was crackling, so much so that Seraphin said the Devil, up there on the peak called The Devil's Tower, must have told his children to get out the ninepins. What they tried to hit was a spot that hung right over the cabin, and when they missed you could see, particularly on such a bright moonlit night, the balls skidding over into space and falling down. When the two men went to sleep, the crackling had stopped; but they dreamed of strange noises in the night.

The men of nearby Anzeindaz said it all started like a salvo of cannon; then came a blast of wind, and finally a great pale cloud of dust. The noise was terrific. The wind pinned men in their beds, and the cloud obscured everything for a long time. When men dared to go near Derborence, and could see through the cloud, the fine pasture land was gone; everywhere rocks, large at the bottom, smaller at the top, covered the land where cabins and cattle had been.

One man, old Barthelemy, crept out of the cloud. Friends carried him down the mountain on an improvised stretcher, but there was a second beard of pink froth over his own black one before he got down. His chest had been crushed and he died before he reached the town.

All the people in Aire, except Maurice Nendaz, a lame man who walked with a cane, thought a storm had struck, though there was no lightning. Nendaz went up the mountain to investigate and sent back a boy to tell the mayor that all the men and cattle from Aire had been buried under the rocks.

Thèrese had told her mother the night of the twenty-second that she thought she was going to have a baby. Philomène, therefore, tried to keep from her daughter the news of the disaster. How can one do that in a small town with the houses close to each other? And how can a girl believe that a mountain has fallen on her husband?

Men figured that 150,000,000 cubic feet of rock had fallen when The Devil's Tower slipped into Derborence. Scientists of all sorts came to measure, to investigate, to survey. Two months passed.

Only Old Plon, the shepherd, went near Derborence, where his sheep could find grass around the edges if they kept on the move. He knew the Devil had been at work, and he said that at night he had heard those poor fellows imprisoned there, lamenting because they had not been put to rest.

One day a head appeared, though only an eagle would have been able to see it in the midst of that huge pile of rocks. A body followed the head, squirming its way out through cracks in the rocks. The man who appeared, looking like death itself after two months underground, remembered only that he was Antoine. He fought with his memory to find the way down to the village, only to be shot at as an evil spirit when he arrived.

He saw Thèrese in the fields and called to her, but his voice was strange and she, afraid, ran home. When the priest came with a cross and the townspeople could persuade Antoine to come out of hiding, Thèrese, at least, believed he was really her husband and not a spirit.

The mayor and the priest asked him questions, and people came from all over the district to hear, over and over, the story of how he had lived up there with just enough space under a fallen slab, with his mattress, with the new cheeses on the shelf by his bed, and finally the dribble of water that seeped through the rocks; how he had found spaces between the rocks that he investigated day after day, week and week, until, more than seven weeks after he was imprisoned, he had found an opening that finally led to the light overhead.

When Antoine got away from the townspeople and came home, he wanted to go back up the mountain because he was sure Seraphin was waiting to be let out. He slipped out early in the morning before anyone else was up. Thèrese wanted to follow, but she could get only the lame Nendaz to go with her. Even he stayed back when Old Plon warned them not to go on among the spirits. But Thèrese went on, higher and higher on the mountain. Then Nendaz and others who had gathered with him to watch saw two tiny dots start down. Thèrese had defied the mountain to bring Antoine safely home.

WHEN WE DEAD AWAKEN

Type of work: Drama
Author: Henrik Ibsen (1828-1906)
Type of plot: Psychological symbolism
Time of plot: Nineteenth century
Locale: A coastal town of Norway
First presented: 1900; published 1899

>Principal characters:
>ARNOLD RUBEK, a sculptor
>MAIA RUBEK, his wife
>IRENE VON SATOW, his former model
>ULFHEIM, a landed proprietor and hunter

Critique:

When We Dead Awaken departs from the principles of art to which Ibsen's earlier social and later psychological dramas conform, and for this reason it is sometimes considered inferior to them. It delves into the realm of pathology, dealing with improbabilities rather than probabilities, with symbolic motive rather than actual motive. Solely as an artistic creation, however, the play has enduring merit. Because it is Ibsen's last production, we may read in it the intention of the dramatist to express some deeply felt final message which could be clothed only in poetically suggestive and symbolic language.

The Story:

Professor Arnold Rubek, a noted sculptor, and his young wife Maia, had returned to their home on the coast of Norway after four years abroad. At the baths and the hotel they admitted to being bored, and to break the summer tedium they planned to sail northward around the coast. Rubek had become world-renowned with the fashioning of his masterpiece, "The Resurrection Day," and success had brought him worldly riches.

Other visitors at the baths were a sportsman named Ulfheim, called the bear-killer, and a strange pale woman, Madame von Satow, who, with a companion dressed in black like a Sister of Mercy, had taken the nearby pavilion for the summer. As Rubek and Ulfheim conversed, the dark Sister passed from the pavilion to the hotel, and Ulfheim said her passing was a portent of death. Maia accepted his invitation to see his sledge dogs fed, but Rubek remained seated on the lawn. The lady in white emerged from the pavilion. Rubek felt strangely drawn to her. Years before, he had wanted to create a sculpture which would represent Woman awakening from the Dead on the Resurrection Day after the sleep of Death. After he had found Irene, he saw in her the perfect model for his composition, and she became his great inspiration. Irene had wanted his human love but he had felt that if he touched her his soul would be profaned.

Now Rubek recognized the strange woman in white as Irene. When he questioned her about her life since she had left him, she declared that she had died then and was not really alive now, though she had married a South American diplomat who later committed suicide, and then a Russian who owned gold mines in the Urals. Rubek admitted that after she left him he had made no marble creations of lasting beauty but had begun doing portraits which were really double-faced works of art, for behind the visible face he hid the face of an animal which he maliciously considered the real person. He told Irene that he and Maia were leaving the next day on a sea voyage. She suggested that he might prefer the mountains where she was going. At that moment Maia returned and announced that she would not make the sea voyage; instead, she wanted to go to the mountains with the bear-killer. To her surprise Rubek did not object. Maia ran out to inform Ulfheim. Meanwhile, unseen near the pavilion door, the Sister of Mercy watched intently.

The next day the bear-killer went off to hunt with his dog trainer Lars and his dogs, and Maia accompanied them. Before they left, Rubek told Maia that he could no longer live a life of indolent enjoyment with her.

Rubek found Irene near a brook. She said she had returned from the dead and had made the journey for the sake of the statue, which she called their "child." She loved it and wanted to see it. When Rubek implored her not to, saying he had altered it since she had left, Irene covertly unsheathed a knife, but stayed her hand as he explained the changes he had made and told how he also was in the altered sculpture, a man eaten by remorse, imprisoned in a hell from which he could never rise. At this she sheathed her knife, rejoicing that he suffered. But she bitterly reminded him that when he had finally finished the statue he had shrugged off their years together.

Together they stood and watched the sun go down. He then asked her to return and live with him in his villa, to help him find his real life again, but Irene said that for the life they had led there was no resurrection. Suddenly Irene challenged Rubek to dare the mountain heights and spend a summer night with her. Joyfully he agreed. As he did so a face stared down at Irene, the face of the Sister of Mercy.

On the wild mountainside, cut by sheer precipices and overhung with snow-clad peaks, Maia and Ulfheim quarreled, but made up as they told each other of the disappointments of their youth. When the dangerous mountain mist began to close in, they decided to journey down together, but as they made ready to descend they saw Rubek and Irene climbing up. Ulfheim warned them of the impending storm and the dangers ahead and urged them to take shelter in a nearby hut. He said that he would send them help; he himself could assist only one person at a time down the precipice.

After Ulfheim and Maia had gone, Irene, terrified not by the approaching storm but that she might be taken away, that the woman in black might seize her and put her in a straitjacket, showed Rubek her knife ready for such an emergency. She added that the knife had been intended for him the previous evening. Startled, he asked why she had not used it; she told him she had then realized that he was already dead. But Rubek passionately assured her that their love was not dead, for he realized with glaring certainty that she was the woman of his dreams. Irene said that such a love came too late, that desire for life was dead in her, and that she looked on him, too, as dead.

With his whole soul Rubek called on her, even if they both seemed dead, to awaken and live life to its fullest before they were forever put away in the grave. Exalted, they spurned the safety of the hut and joyously fought their way up to the peaks, through mist and storm, toward the sunrise. Far below the voice of Maia sang out free as a bird. The Sister of Mercy suddenly appeared. As Rubek and Irene were carried along and buried in the snow, she made the sign of the cross and wished that peace be with them.

WHERE ANGELS FEAR TO TREAD

Type of work: Novel
Author: E. M. Forster (1879-)
Type of plot: Social criticism
Time of plot: Early twentieth century
Locale: England and Italy
First published: 1905

Principal characters:
LILIA HERRITON, a young English widow
GINO CARELLA, an Italian
PHILIP HERRITON, Lilia's brother-in-law
HARRIET HERRITON, her sister-in-law
MRS. HERRITON, Lilia's mother-in-law
IRMA HERRITON, Lilia's daughter
CAROLINE ABBOTT, a friend

Critique:

In this novel Forster again shows himself to be a slightly satiric observer of the world and the affairs of mankind. As usual, the characters are perfectly ordinary and commonplace; in fact, it should be noted that no really admirable person appears in any of his novels. Here he is primarily concerned with the gulf that is normally found between the northern temperament of an overcivilized Englishwoman and the natural impulses of the South which are personified in the Italian whom she marries.

The Story:

Lilia Herriton, a widow of several years who had been living with her husband's family since his death, cheerfully left Sawston, England, with her friend Caroline Abbott for an extended visit in Italy. The Herriton family had encouraged such a visit because of their concern over Lilia's growing relationship with a man whom they considered unsuitable for her, and also because they welcomed a chance to train her daughter without the mother's interference. The trip, which had been Philip's idea, had been quickly agreed to by everyone concerned. Fortunately, Caroline Abbott, a woman ten years younger but much more level-headed than Lilia, was also planning such a trip and needed a companion.

The winter passed peacefully for every-

one and the tour seemed to be a success. Lilia was apparently gaining some degree of culture and taste under the guidance of Miss Abbott, and her daughter Irma was being tremendously improved by Mrs. Herriton. In the spring, however, the Herriton plans were upset. Mrs. Herriton heard from Lilia's mother that Lilia was engaged to an Italian, supposedly someone she had met in a hotel. She immediately wired Miss Abbott for details, but was answered only by the terse comment that Lilia was engaged to an Italian nobleman. This she instinctively knew was a lie; she insisted that Philip go at once to Italy and stop the marriage.

Miss Abbott met Philip's train when he arrived at Monteriano, the village in which Lilia and Miss Abbott had been staying for a month. Nervously she agreed to tell him everything. According to her story, Lilia and the man had both professed love for each other so she had rather offhandedly suggested marriage. Unfortunately, Signor Carella, some twelve years younger than Lilia, was the son of a dentist in that provincial village, and he had no money. His social position, therefore, was little better than that of a peasant. Philip was even more appalled when he saw the man, for his manners and everything about him except his physique were extremely vulgar. Philip's attempts to stop the marriage were

4127

thwarted, however, for the couple had been married as soon as they heard he was coming. There was nothing for him to do but return home, taking Miss Abbott with him.

The Herriton family naturally refused to have anything more to do with Lilia, but they kept Irma with them, to be brought up as one who bore the Herriton name. It was some time before Lilia realized that she did not love her husband and could never be happy with him, or that he had married her only for her money. And she never understood that as an Italian wife she could neither expect nor receive from her husband the things that English wives received from theirs as a matter of course. By the time she realized her unhappiness she had been cut off from everything in England and there was nothing she could do. Once, at a time when she was particularly upset, she did write to her little daughter, telling of her unhappiness and the reasons for it, but the letter was intercepted by Mrs. Herriton and nothing ever came of it.

Lilia often thought that if she could present her husband with a son they might eventually gain some happiness. His one ambition was to be the father of a man like himself. Finally Lilia did have a son, but she died in childbirth. The Herritons decided that they must tell Irma about her mother's death, but that it would be best if no one knew about the child who was, after all, no real relation of theirs.

Irma soon found out about the child when she began receiving post cards sent her by the father. Her childish pride prevented her from keeping such an event a secret and soon all Sawston knew of it. Much to the chagrin of the Herritons, Miss Abbott, who still considered herself partly responsible for all that had happened, began to insist that something be done for the child, either by them or by herself. Mrs. Herriton, whose pride would not allow anyone else to do something that would in any way reflect on her family, immediately began negotiations which she hoped would enable her to adopt the boy.

When letters resulted only in praise and polite refusals she decided that Philip must again go to Monteriano and gain the custody of the child at any cost; Harriet was to go along to see that he accomplished his mission. On their arrival, however, they found that Miss Abbott had preceded them and was also intent on seeing that the child was taken back to England. Unfortunately, Philip and Miss Abbott soon began to be affected by the romantic and charming atmosphere. They were still determined to carry out their mission, but they quickly lost all feeling of urgency in the matter.

On their second day in the village, when the interview with Signor Carella was to take place, Miss Abbott went to the house early and alone: she was afraid that Philip would fail. While there, she was completely won over by the father's devotion to the son and soon found herself on the Italian's side and against the Herritons, even though she knew she could do nothing to hinder their plans. Philip also saw Carella that day, in the morning and in the afternoon, and he, although he would not openly admit that the Italian was right, found himself completely indifferent to the outcome of his mission, and on friendly terms with his adversary. Success in the affair was left to Harriet, who, after apparently accepting Philip's failure, prepared to leave the village. Shortly before it was time for them to catch the train she sent a note to Philip telling him to pick her up just outside the gate to the village. When he got there he found that she had also visited the Carella household and, not finding Carella at home, had simply picked up the baby and walked away.

On the way down the mountain to the train their carriage was accidentally overturned and the baby was killed. When Philip told Carella what had happened, the Italian almost killed him. Miss Abbott, whom Carella had always revered as something of a goddess, was the only person who could calm him and prevent

4128

more pain. By the time the English group had recuperated enough to leave Italy the two men were again good friends.

On the way back to England, however, Philip received another disappointment. Because of the romantic atmosphere and of the close association, he and Miss Abbott had somewhat ignored the normal English coldness and he had fallen in love with her. He almost proposed to her when they were talking about love and their futures, but she, thinking he had suspected it long before, told him of her passion for Carella. Philip, who had for years thought that he understood the world and who had considered himself merely a spectator of life, discovered that he really understood nothing.

THE WHITE COMPANY

Type of work: Novel
Author: Arthur Conan Doyle (1859-1930)
Type of plot: Historical romance
Time of plot: Fifteenth century
Locale: England, France, Spain
First published: 1891

Principal characters:
ALLEYNE EDRICSON, an English youth
SAMKIN AYLWARD, a bowman
HORDLE JOHN, a bowman
SIR NIGEL LORING, a nobleman
LADY MAUDE, his daughter

Critique:

The White Company is a story of exciting adventures near the end of the age of chivalry. From its pages we can get accurate pictures of many types of people in feudal times as well as some insight into the interminable and fruitless wars with France. The charm of the story, however, lies in its romantic plot. The English nobles are all valiant men, but none so valiant as Sir Nigel. Hordle John is the strongest Englishman ever seen, as Aylward is the lustiest bowman. Everything turns out well for the heroes, and the villains came to grief. For many years The White Company has been a favorite, especially with young people.

The Story:

The Abbot of Beaulieu was a stern judge, and the charges against Hordle John, the novitiate, were severe. John had drunk all the ale from the firkin when he had the first turn; John had held a monk's head down over the beans in protest against poor fare; worst of all, John had carried a woman across a stream. When she smiled at him, he did not keep his eyes on the ground.

At the trial, huge John seemed out of place in a monastery. He cheerfully admitted the charges and did not even have the grace to be ashamed. But when the monks advanced to punish him, he picked up an altar and threw it at them. Then he dived out of the window and was never seen again in Beaulieu.

Much disturbed, the abbot retired to his study to meditate. There he received another visitor, Alleyne Edricson. It was Alleyne's twentieth birthday, and according to his father's will the boy was to leave the abbey for a year. When he was twenty-one, he would choose either a monastic or a secular life. Alleyne had never known any other life than that of the abbey and he was hesitant about entering a world of sin and lust. The abbot solemnly warned Alleyne of the perils of the secular life; but true to his promise he sent the youth forth with his blessing.

Alleyne started on foot for the estate of Minstead, where his older brother was the socman. Alleyne had never seen his brother, but from all reports he was a rude and sinful man. On this, his first trip into the world, Alleyne was continually alarmed at the sin his eyes beheld on every hand. Two robbers who molested an old woman were summarily executed on the spot by the king's bailiffs. Shaken by what he saw, Alleyne thankfully turned into the shelter of the Pied Merlin Inn to spend his first night away from the abbey.

There he found a rough company drinking and quarreling. Hordle John was there, making merry in his cups but kindly disposed toward the timid clerk. When a minstrel took up his harp and began to sing a bawdy song, Alleyne stood up and cried shame on the company for listening. The rough travelers shouted him down and they would have done hurt to Alleyne if John had not risen to defend the clerk.

At that instant Samkin Aylward burst in, bearing letters from France to Sir Nigel of nearby Christchurch. The White Company of English bowmen wanted Sir Nigel to lead them in the war against Spain. Samkin was trying to recruit other bowmen, and Hordle John agreed to go with him. Alleyne refused because he was intent on seeing his brother.

The next morning Alleyne came to the park of the Socman of Minstead. There he saw a strange sight. A great, yellow-bearded man held a struggling girl, and appeared determined to drag her into the house. Alleyne ran up to the rescue, armed with his iron-tipped staff. Only after Alleyne had threatened to run his staff through the yellow-beard was he informed that his adversary was his brother. The socman, furious at being balked by clerkly Alleyne, ran to the stables and whistled for his hunting dogs. Alleyne and the girl escaped into the woods.

The girl's page soon found them, and she rode away with a brilliant, mocking smile of thanks. Alleyne resolved to join John and Aylward and take service with Sir Nigel. He hurried to catch up with them before they arrived at Christchurch.

Alleyne's first view of Sir Nigel was disappointing. The lord was a slight, squinting, soft-spoken man, apparently the least warlike of nobles. But Alleyne changed his mind. A giant bear broke his chain and charged down the road, where he scattered all in front of him. Sir Nigel, however, merely looked in his near-sighted way to see the cause of the disturbance. Then, unarmed as he was, he walked up to the maddened bear and flicked the animal across the snout with his silk handkerchief. Discomfited, the bear retired in confusion and was soon rechained by the bearward. Then Alleyne knew he would serve a true knight.

At the castle Sir Nigel was making all in readiness for his expedition to France. Alleyne worked diligently in the courtyard as he learned the trade of man-at-arms. His efforts soon made him a favorite and his good education set him above his fellows. Sir Nigel asked him to take charge of his daughter's reading that winter, and Alleyne went into the lord's quarters for the first time. There he found that his pupil was the girl he had rescued from his brother. Lady Maude was a high-spirited girl, but charming and gracious. Alleyne felt her charm keenly, but he was only a poor clerk and so he kept silent as his fondness for her grew.

Just before the expedition departed, Sir Nigel made Alleyne his squire. After receiving the honor, Alleyne sought out Lady Maude and stammered some words of love. Lady Maude rebuked him for his presumption, but she did give him her green veil to wear to the wars. As Squire Alleyne rode away behind his lord, he thought more of Lady Maude than of the fighting to come.

At Bordeaux Sir Nigel and his party were received with all honors by Edward, their prince. Edward needed all his knights, for the English were embarking upon a long, difficult campaign to put Don Pedro upon the throne of Spain. Then, too, the White Company was becoming a great nuisance, as it was pillaging the country roundabout and earning few friends for England.

One night, on their way to join the White Company, Sir Nigel and his party stayed with the notorious Seneschal of Villefranche. This knight, a rapacious and cruel lord, had reduced all the peasants on his lands to the status of animals. That night, while the party slept, the peasants broke into the castle, murdered all the men-at-arms, and foully desecrated the bodies of the seneschal and his lady. Although Sir Nigel and his Englishmen were innocent of the wrongs committed by the French lord, the peasants made no distinction between aristocrats. They set fire to the castle when they were afraid to face the sword of Sir Nigel and the mace of Hordle John, and Sir Nigel's bowmen retired to the keep.

The frenzied serfs fired the keep as well. The English party was rescued only by the timely arrival of the White Company, which had been attracted by the great fires. The peasants slunk away in the darkness.

The White Company, under Sir Nigel, marched with Edward's army through the Pyrenees. Selected for scouting duty, the White Company harried the Spanish forces successfully. One day the whole company was trapped on a small mesa by the main Spanish body. Despite great slaughter by the English arrows and the might of Sir Nigel, the Englishmen were in great danger of being wiped out.

Alleyne was chosen as a messenger to summon reinforcements. He carried out his mission valiantly despite his wounds, but the rescuers found only Hordle John and a handful of survivors still uncon-

quered. Even Sir Nigel and Aylward had been captured.

Alleyne returned to England with a heavy heart. His brother in the meantime had been killed while trying to assault Sir Nigel's castle, and now Alleyne, knighted by Prince Edward, was the Socman of Minstead. With his new position he could aspire to the hand of Lady Maude.

The happiness of all returned when Sir Nigel and Aylward finally came back from their captivity among the Moors. Aylward married the mistress of the Pied Merlin and Hordle John became Alleyne's squire. Alleyne lived a long and happy life with Lady Maude. He went back to France to fight several times, and on each occasion reaped great honors there. Toward the end of his life he spent much time at Windsor as adviser to Edward.

THE WHITE DEVIL

Type of work: Drama
Author: John Webster (?-Before 1635)
Type of plot: Revenge tragedy
Time of plot: Sixteenth century
Locale: Rome and Padua, Italy
First presented: c. 1612

Principal characters:
>VITTORIA COROMBONA, a Venetian lady
>PAULO GIORDANO URSINI, Duke of Brachiano
>FRANCISCO DE MEDICIS, Duke of Florence
>CARDINAL MONTICELSO, his brother
>CAMILLO, Vittoria's husband
>FLAMINEO, Vittoria's brother, secretary to Brachiano
>MARCELLO, another brother, attendant on Francisco de Medicis
>COUNT LODOVICO, a banished nobleman
>ISABELLA, sister of Francisco de Medicis, Brachiano's wife
>GIOVANNI, son of Isabella and Brachiano

Critique:

The White Devil; or, Vittoria Corombona is as tumultuous a melodrama as any written during the Elizabethan Age. Filled with violent deeds performed by heroic personages, its plot, involving love, treachery, and revenge, seems incredible; but it is based on actual events which took place in sixteenth-century Italy.

The Story:

Antonelli and Gasparo, courtiers of Francisco de Medicis, Duke of Florence, brought to Count Lodovico in Rome the news that he had been banished because of his notorious intrigues and bloody murders. Lodovico could not understand why he had been singled out for punishment when other noblemen, especially the Duke of Brachiano, were guilty of crimes just as heinous.

Brachiano was trying to seduce Vittoria Corombona, wife of the aging Camillo. Helping Brachiano in his scheme was Vittoria's unscrupulous brother Flamineo, who convinced Camillo that the best way to keep Vittoria virtuous was to give her unlimited freedom. This privilege granted, Vittoria kept an assignation with Brachiano. Through the transparent symbolism of a dream which she had fabricated, Vittoria urged her lover to murder Isabella, his wife, and Camillo, her husband. Just as Brachiano was declaring his love for Vittoria and his understanding of her design, Vittoria's mother, Cornelia, disclosed herself to denounce the two and to announce the arrival of Brachiano's wife in Rome.

Isabella's brothers, Francisco and Cardinal Monticelso, summoned Brachiano to remonstrate against his philandering. When their appeal to Brachiano's sense of virtue resulted only in mutual recrimination, the brothers produced Giovanni, Brachiano's son, whose youthful innocence, they hoped, would inspire Brachiano with a sense of family duty. Confronted alone by Isabella, Brachiano proved the folly of such a hope by berating his wife and vowing never again to sleep with her. To forestall the war which would surely ensue if Francisco learned of this vow, Isabella pretended that she was unable to forgive her husband and declared that she was abandoning her husband's bed. Her ruse and Brachiano's acquiescence in it fooled Francisco so completely that he denounced Isabella for mad jealousy.

Disgusted by their sister's vow but convinced that she would soon retract it, Francisco and Monticelso turned their attention to Camillo and Marcello, another of Vittoria's brothers, whom they had decided to appoint joint commissioners in charge of combating the pirates reportedly led by the banished Lodovico. Camillo objected because he feared he

4133

would be cuckolded during his absence from home, but Monticelso's promise to keep an eye on Vittoria quieted him. Actually, Monticelso and Francisco were giving Camillo the commission to get him away from Rome so that Brachiano might have free access to Vittoria. By this scheme the two brothers hoped to plunge Brachiano into a shameful scandal.

Brachiano, however, had made his own plans, having arranged for Flamineo to murder Camillo, and for Julio, a physician, to kill Isabella. Through the magic of a conjurer, Brachiano was able to watch the murders, Isabella dying from kissing a poisoned portrait of her husband, and Camillo, from being pushed off a vaulting horse in a gymnasium.

Monticelso and Francisco immediately brought Vittoria to trial for the murder of her husband, though they knew they had no evidence other than her ill repute. At her trial before the ambassadors to Rome, a hearing presided over by Monticelso, Brachiano admitted that he had stayed at Vittoria's house the night of the murder. This testimony, along with other incriminating but circumstantial evidence of her prostitution, was sufficient to convict Vittoria, although she protested her innocence and denounced the conduct of the trial. Monticelso sentenced her to confinement in a house of reformed prostitutes.

Immediately after the pronouncement of this sentence, Giovanni arrived to tell his uncles of his mother's death. Accompanying him was Lodovico, who secretly had been in love with Isabella and who, in fact, had witnessed her death. Francisco and Monticelso realized that Brachiano was responsible for the murder of their sister but disagreed on how to avenge it. Fearing that a war might result from an open attack on Brachiano, yet unwilling to defer vengeance, Francisco, inspired by a vision of Isabella's ghost, devised a trick. He wrote a letter to Vittoria, professing his love for her, and instructed his servant to deliver it when some of Brachiano's men were close by.

As Francisco hoped, Flamineo intercepted the letter and gave it to Brachiano, who was, of course, enraged by Vittoria's apparent infidelity. A violent quarrel ensued between the two, refereed by the pandering Flamineo. It ended in a reconciliation so sweet that Brachiano resolved to have Vittoria stolen away from the home for convertites and then to marry her. To trick Brachiano into marrying a prostitute was exactly what Francisco had hoped for, but his lust for revenge was not yet satisfied. He engaged Lodovico, who had been pardoned, to murder Brachiano.

Monticelso, who had just been elected Pope, excommunicated Brachiano and his bride; then, learning of the plotted murder, he forbade Lodovico to commit it. Monticelso's command was ignored, however, when Francisco sent Lodovico a thousand crowns in Monticelso's name, a gift which convinced Lodovico that the Pope had been craftily insincere.

Francisco apparently decided to oversee the murder himself, for he disguised himself as Mulinasser, a Moor, and proceeded to Brachiano's palace in Padua, accompanied by Lodovico and Gasparo, who were disguised as Knights of Malta. Welcomed by Brachiano, the trio planned a horrible death for him.

Before they could carry out their scheme, another murder was committed. A quarrel between Marcello and Flamineo over the latter's amorous attentions paid to Zanche, Vittoria's Moorish maid, resulted in Flamineo's killing his brother. While Brachiano was passing judgment on the murderer, Lodovico sprinkled Brachiano's helmet with poison. The poison drove Brachiano mad. Soon thereafter, Lodovico and Gasparo, dressed as Capuchins, entered the room where the count lay raving; they revealed their true identity and strangled him.

After his lord's death, Flamineo sued to Vittoria for a reward in payment of his long, treacherous service. Rebuffed, he produced two pairs of pistols, claiming that he had promised Brachiano to kill himself and Vittoria after Brachiano's death. Vittoria persuaded Flamineo to die first, but when she and Zanche fired the pistols at him they learned that Flamineo, to test Vittoria, had not loaded the weapons. Before he could murder the women, however, Lodovico and Gasparo rushed in and killed all three. Giovanni and a group of ambassadors discovered the murderers standing over the corpses. Wounded, Lodovico confessed and then disclosed the part Francisco had played in these bloody deeds. Giovanni swore vengeance on the Duke of Florence.

WHITE-JACKET

Type of work: Novel
Author: Herman Melville (1819-1891)
Type of plot: Adventure romance
Time of plot: The 1840's
Locale: A vessel of the U.S. Navy
First published: 1850

Principal characters:
    WHITE-JACKET, a sailor on board the U.S.S. *Neversink*
    JACK CHASE, captain of the maintop in the ship
    CAPTAIN CLARET, commander of the vessel

Critique:

White-Jacket, Melville's fifth book, reflected the experience he had when he returned to America on board the U.S. frigate *United States* from Honolulu in 1843-44. The loosely-knit narrative was thus formed from experience as well as fiction. The novel gives an astonishing portrait of life in an American naval vessel at the time, astonishing because of the detail and because of the practices then in vogue. Actual purpose of the novel was to help correct some of the vicious practices which Melville had seen at first-hand. Flogging, tyranny of commanders, issuance of spirituous liquors to sailors, and the poor messing facilities of naval vessels of a century ago were all condemned by Melville in vivid terms. Authorities have conceded that Melville's novel did more than any other single source to abolish at least one of those practices, the flogging of enlisted men.

The Story:

White-Jacket, as he was later nick-named, was a common sailor, a member of the crew of the United States frigate *Neversink* on a cruise of the Pacific Ocean during the 1840's. After the ship left Callao, Peru, the sailor tried to purchase a heavy jacket, needed protection when the *Neversink* passed into the colder climate off Cape Horn. Because a heavy jacket was not available from the ship's purser, the vessel having been at sea for over three years, the sailor had to make a canvas jacket for himself.

The jacket was full of pockets and quilted with odds and ends of rags and clothing for warmth. When the maker requested some paint to make it waterproof and darken its color, he was told that no paint was available for the purpose.

As the ship moved southward toward the Antarctic, the sailor gradually came to be called White-Jacket by the crew because of the strange garment he wore. Some of the sailors, superstitious as old wives, disliked him because of the jacket; they said that White-Jacket was too much like a ghost as he went about his duties high in the rigging of the frigate.

The offensiveness of White-Jacket's strange apparel was revealed only a few days after the ship's anchor had been weighed at Callao. White-Jacket was forced to leave the mess group to which he had been assigned, for the sailors told him openly that anyone who wore such a weird garment was unwelcome. That White-Jacket had proved himself a very poor cook during his tour of duty for the group had not helped his cause.

Forced from his original messmates' company, White-Jacket was taken into the mess to which belonged the petty officer of the maintop under whom White-Jacket served. The petty officer was Jack Chase, a gentlemanly Britisher who shared White-Jacket's love of literature. Chase, who had returned to the *Neversink* after an absence of months, during which he had served as an officer on a Peruvian insurrectionist vessel, was looked up to by the rough sailors and respected by all the officers aboard the ship.

As the *Neversink* sailed southward along the western coast of South America

4136

the general ship's duties continued. White-Jacket and his fellows set sails and took them in, washed down the decks, stood their watches, and prepared for colder weather. To relieve the tedium of the long voyage, Captain Claret gave out word that the men would be permitted to stage a theatrical entertainment. The captain had permitted such entertainments in the earlier stages of the cruise, but he had discontinued them because one of the actors had behaved in an objectionable manner. White-Jacket noted that before the play the captain perused and censored the script. Neither the captain nor the commodore who was aboard the *Neversink* dignified the men's entertainment by being present.

During the coastal voyage a man fell overboard and was drowned. The incident demonstrated to White-Jacket how risky life aboard a ship was and how quickly a lost man was forgotten.

The *Neversink* was becalmed in the waters off Cape Horn. After three days of cold and calm the captain gave the unusual order for the crew to "skylark." The men gave themselves over to all kinds of activity and games of a rougher sort, all in an attempt to keep warm and to prevent frozen hands and feet. Shortly thereafter a wind came up. The ship rounded the Cape and began to cruise steadily northward.

One day the lookout sighted a number of casks floating on the ocean. Word was given that they should be picked up, and when they were hauled aboard it was discovered that they contained very fine port wine. The discovery caused great joy among the crew. In the 1840's the navy still clung to the custom of serving spirits to the men twice a day, but the *Neversink's* steward, for some unaccountable reason, had neglected to replenish the ship's supply of rum during the stop at Callao.

The most significant happenings during the run from Cape Horn northward to Rio de Janeiro, so far as White-Jacket was concerned, were a series of floggings. At that time the American navy still made flogging a punishment for offenses at sea. White-Jacket hated the cruel whippings, which all crew members and officers were forced to watch. White-Jacket reflected that even in Rome no citizen could be flogged as punishment and that the great naval officers of the nineteenth century were opposed to a practice so brutal and unnecessary.

The *Neversink* finally reached Rio de Janeiro. During many days in port the men were not to be permitted ashore. At last the petty officers appointed Jack Chase, the captain of the maintop, to request shore leave for the men. At first the captain was unwilling to grant leave, but the commodore interceded and gave his approval to sending the men ashore. Once again Chase was the hero of the men aboard the vessel.

One day the Emperor of Brazil was expected to visit the vessel. White-Jacket, amazed at preparations made by men and officers for the royal visit, wondered how men from a democratic nation could so easily fawn upon royalty. He decided the men would have made fewer preparations to receive the President of the United States.

On the voyage northward along the eastern coast of South America one of White-Jacket's shipmates fell ill and died. White-Jacket watched the preparations for burial, including the traditional final stitch of the shroud through the nose, then stood by during the service. That event was as moving to him as an amputation demonstrated by the ship's doctor while the *Neversink* lay in the harbor at Rio de Janeiro. The operation was performed, White-Jacket believed, because the surgeon wished to show off to colleagues from other vessels anchored there at the same time. Convinced that the operation was unnecessary, White-Jacket was very bitter when the injured man died of shock.

White-Jacket himself had a close escape from death when the ship was off the Virginia capes. Sent aloft to reeve a line through some blocks, he lost his balance and fell from the rigging a hundred feet into the sea. He had to cut away his white jacket in order to keep afloat. He was barely out of his garment when a sailor, mistaking the jacket for a white shark, threw a harpoon into it. White-Jacket, rescued from the sea, was sent aloft ten minutes later to complete his task. White-Jacket was content to close his story of the voyage with the loss of his unlucky garment.

WICKFORD POINT

Type of work: Novel
Author: John P. Marquand (1893-1960)
Type of plot: Social satire
Time of plot: Twentieth century
Locale: New York and Wickford Point
First published: 1939

> Principal characters:
> JIM CALDER, a writer
> MRS. CLOTHILDE WRIGHT, his cousin, formerly Clothilde Brill
> BELLA BRILL, her daughter
> MARY BRILL, another daughter
> PATRICIA LEIGHTON, Jim's friend
> JOE STOWE, Bella's former husband

Critique:

Next to *The Late George Apley,* this novel is perhaps Marquand's best. His technique here is marked by the use of flashbacks to make the present meaningful and to explain the motives of his characters. His touch is deft, his theme well-handled, his story interesting, his irony amusing. The impact of the outside world upon the little, complacent society of Wickford Point is admirably demonstrated.

The Story:

Jim Calder made his living by writing fiction for popular magazines. For this reason the contradiction between the actual life of his relatives at Wickford Point and the fiction he was required to write was extremely obvious. His relatives, the Brills, were a group of New Englanders who had little money, but who were disinclined to make a living. Being himself close to the Brills, he had attempted to escape from them and the enervating atmosphere of Wickford Point. He was only a second cousin to the Brill children, but his continual association with them in his early life produced bonds that were exceedingly hard to break. No matter how many times he left Wickford Point, he always returned. No matter how many times he returned, he always planned to get away as soon as possible.

Jim attended Harvard and there met Joe Stowe. Harry Brill also attended Harvard, where he made sure that he knew the right people. All through his life Harry was concerned with meeting the right people, but he never did make the right connections. Jim and Joe were fortunate in the fact that they became fast friends and were never elected to the right campus clubs. This polite ostracism served only to strengthen their friendship and to bring with it the assurance that they at least would be more successful than many of their snobbish classmates in their dealings with people.

When World War I arrived and America became involved, Joe and Jim were among the first to go into service, and they were shipped overseas as first lieutenants before they had completed their officers' training. After the war they went to China and served with the forces of General Feng. Some years later Jim returned to America to find a new way of life; Joe went to Italy. Both decided upon writing as a career.

When Jim returned to Wickford Point, he found the Brills just the same and as inconsequential as when he had left. Cousin Clothilde was still unable to manage finances satisfactorily. When she received her check on the first of the month, her children all raced to get their share of the cash, the first one arriving getting the greater share. Cousin Clo thilde was always broke within a few hours after receiving her money.

Bella had grown into quite a beautiful young woman during Jim's absence from America, and at the moment of his return she was involved in a rather serious affair with a nice young man named Avery Gifford. Jim, who had always been Bella's confidant, continued in this role when Bella sought advice from him. Since she was not sure that she loved Avery, it was decided that she should wait until her return from Europe to decide whether she would marry him. She went to Italy with her stepfather, Archie Wright, and while there she met Joe Stowe and eloped with him.

Their marriage was doomed to failure from the start, and after some years it ended in divorce. Bella never really knew what she wanted. She seemed to want everything but could never be satisfied with anything she had. She went from one affair to another because she was extremely attractive to men, but her affairs always remained platonic. Sometimes Jim felt that he was Bella's only friend, for none of her other friendships ever lasted and she made new friends as fast as she lost old ones. She was always confident that whenever she got into difficulties she could fly to Jim and he would straighten out the situation for her.

Jim met Patricia Leighton, a woman of great executive ability who had a penthouse in New York City and an income of several thousand dollars a year. Jim's affair with her was a lasting one, each party contributing equally to the relationship. At first Jim went to Pat to escape the inanities of his relatives at Wickford Point. Pat was a very understanding woman who realized clearly what Jim's problem really was, and she tried in an unobtrusive manner to help him make the final break with his family background.

In spite of their divorce, Bella and Joe thought often of each other, even though they both realized that to remarry would lead only to another divorce. Joe, since his divorce, had become a famous novelist, well off financially. Bella expressed her selfishness to Jim in her regretful admission that when she divorced Joe she had no idea that he would ever be so successful.

Bella went from one contemplated marriage to another, led her admirers on, and finally put herself into a rather delicate situation with Avery Gifford and Howard Berg. When she called upon Jim to rescue her once more, Jim decided that this time Bella would have to extricate herself, his refusal being motivated by his memory of recent conversations with Pat. Into the midst of these misunderstandings and resolves came Joe as a result of a telegram sent to him by Bella. At first Bella and Joe seemed likely to try marriage once more. But as a result of Jim's attitude toward her, Bella did the first generous deed in her life; she told Joe that she would not marry him again.

Jim took Bella back to changeless Wickford Point to find the place, as usual, thronged with visitors. Pat Leighton, as had previously been arranged, came down to Wickford Point to visit. Allen Southby, a friend of Jim's and a professor of English at Harvard, came to stay with the Brills while gathering material for his novel about Wickford Point. Mary Brill looked upon Allen as her own particular conquest until Bella's arrival. All her life Bella had been stealing Mary's eligible young men.

With the arrival of Pat, she and Jim faced once more the problem of getting Jim to break away from Wickford Point and the Brills. Jim finally made the decision to leave, after telling Pat that a part of him would always remain at Wickford Point and that he would always have to return occasionally for short visits. Under the circumstances Pat agreed. Seeing Southby's apparent willingness to marry Bella, Jim felt free of Wickford Point and the clinging past. He began to pack his bag to return with Pat to New York.

WIELAND

Type of work: Novel
Author: Charles Brockden Brown (1771-1810)
Type of plot: Mystery romance
Time of plot: Eighteenth century
Locale: Pennsylvania
First published: 1798

Principal characters:
WIELAND, a madman
CLARA, his sister
CATHARINE PLEYEL, his wife
HENRY PLEYEL, Catharine's brother
CARWIN, a ventriloquist

Critique:

Charles Brockden Brown has been called "The Father of American Literature," and rightly so, for his was the first truly native American literature in the field of the novel. Undoubtedly the best of Brown's works is *Wieland*, a romantic tragedy in a genre of horror and remorse which Poe was to cultivate later on. Brown was a careless writer, never revising, but submitting manuscripts with mechanical errors as well as cumbersome sentence structures. In spite of his faults, the macabre effects of his writing can still stir readers curious enough to read the now old-fashioned romances of this forerunner of Poe and Melville.

The Story:

In a long letter to a friend, Clara Wieland told the story of the tragedy of her family. Her father had been almost a religious fanatic, a strange man who feared some dreadful punishment because he had not answered a call to the mission field. He became more and more depressed and withdrawn until his life ended in a horrible fashion. One night he visited a temple he had built for solitary meditation. His wife, fearing the appearance and manner of her husband, followed him and saw his clothing suddenly go up in flames. She found him insensible, muttering incoherently about having been struck down by an unseen hand. Soon afterward he died. Within a few months the mother followed her husband to the grave, leaving

Clara and her brother orphaned but wealthy. They were happily reared by an aunt who gave them love and comfort and a good education.

One of their companions was Catharine Pleyel, a rich and beautiful girl with whom Wieland fell in love when he reached young manhood. Catherine returned his love, and when Wieland came of age they were married. Wieland took possession of the family house and half of the fortune, Clara the other half of their inheritance. Since she and Catharine and Wieland were beloved friends as well as relatives, Clara took a house only a short distance from her brother and sister-in-law. The three spent much time together. Clara and Catharine were frank and cheerful, but Wieland was more somber and thoughtful in disposition. But he was always considerate of their happiness, and nobly devoted his life to it. His melancholy was not morbid, only sober. The temple in which their father had met his strange fate was used by the three as a setting for long and delightful conversations, although Wieland's talk dwelt too often on death to suit Clara and Catharine.

Their circle was soon augmented by the addition of Catharine's beloved brother Henry, who had been for some time in Europe. His boisterous mirth enlivened the little group. Henry and Wieland found one great difference in their beliefs: Wieland built his life on religious necessity; Henry, on intellectual liberty. But their fondness for each other allowed them to differ without altering their mutual affection.

Wieland's family was enlarged during the next six years by four natural children and a foster child whose mother had died while under his aunt's protection. About that time another strange occurrence took place in the Wieland family. One day Wieland went to the temple to pick up a letter which would settle a minor dispute. Before he reached the temple he was stopped by his wife's voice, telling him that danger lay in his path. Returning quickly to the house, he found his wife there. Clara and Henry verified her statement that she had not left the room. Although the others soon dismissed the incident from their minds, it preyed on the already melancholy Wieland to the exclusion of everything else.

Not long after that incident Henry Pleyel learned that Wieland had inherited some large estates in Europe and he wanted Wieland to go abroad to claim them. Henry would accompany his friend because he had left his heart with a baroness, now widowed and willing to accept his suit. When Wieland seemed reluctant to make the journey, Henry, in an effort to persuade him, asked him one night to go for a walk. Their walk was interrupted by a voice telling them that the baroness was dead. Again the voice was Catharine's, but again Catharine had been nowhere near the men when the voice was heard. More frightening was the verification of the baroness' death given to Henry a few days later. Some dread supernatural power, Wieland believed, had spoken to them.

Shortly after these two mysterious occurrences, a stranger appeared in the neighborhood. He was dressed like a clown or a pathetically humorous beggar, but his voice had the musical ring of an actor. Clara, who saw him before the others knew of his existence, was strangely drawn to him.

She forgot him, however, because of another frightening incident. One night, alone in her room, she heard two voices in the closet planning her murder. One voice advised shooting; the other, choking. She fled to her brother's house and fell at his door in a faint. Wieland and Henry came to her rescue in answer to a summons from an unknown source, a voice calling that a loved one lay dying at the door.

Henry insisted upon occupying a vacant apartment in Clara's home in order to protect her from her unknown enemies. Clara was beset with nightmares, the mystifying voice having warned her of danger from her brother. Soon after the affair of the voices in the closet, she met the stranger she had seen and to whom she had been unaccountably drawn. His name was Carwin, and he had known Henry in Spain. His intelligent conversation and his wide travels making him welcome in the little group, he joined them frequently. When they discussed the supernatural voices they had all heard, Carwin dismissed the voices as fancy or pranks.

Clara, beginning to feel herself in love with Henry, believed that he returned her love but feared to tell her of it because he did not know her feelings. Then he confronted her with the accusation that she was a wanton. He said that he had heard her and a lover, Carwin, talking and that her words made her a sinner and a fallen woman. Henry had also learned that Carwin was wanted for murder, and he heaped abuses on the innocent Clara for consorting with such a man. All her pleas of innocence went unheeded, and she was thrown into despair. Thinking that Carwin had set out to ruin her, she was enraged when she received a note in which he asked for an interview. Reluctantly she agreed to meet him and hear his story. He was to come to her home, but when she arrived there she found only a note warning her of a horrible sight awaiting her. In her room, she found Catharine on the bed. She had been murdered.

Wieland entered her room, his manner strange and exulted, and begged that this sacrifice not be demanded of him. Before he reached Clara, however, others came into the house. From them she learned that her brother's children were also dead, killed by the same hand that had murdered their mother.

Clara was taken by friends to the city. There, after a time, she learned the tragic story. The murderer had been Wieland, his hand guided, he said, by a voice from heaven demanding that he sacrifice his loved ones to God. But he felt no guilt, only glory at having been the instrument through whom God worked. Twice Wieland had broken out of prison, his belief being that he must also kill Clara and Henry. Clara suspected that Carwin had somehow influenced Wieland to kill.

Carwin went to Clara and protested his innocence of the crime. He admitted that his had been the other voices heard. He was a ventriloquist who had used his tricks either to play some prank or to escape detection while prying into other people's affairs. Clara refused to believe him. While they talked, Wieland entered the apartment. Prepared to kill Clara, he had again broken out of prison to fulfill his bloody destiny. But this time Carwin, using his skill to save Clara, called out to Wieland that no voice had told him to kill, that only his own lunatic brain had guided him. At his words Wieland regained his sanity and seemed to understand for the first time what he had done. Picking up a knife, he plunged it into his throat.

Three years passed before Clara knew peace. Her uncle cared for her and arranged a meeting between Carwin and Henry so that Carwin might confess his part in the defamation of Clara's character. Carwin had been jealous and thus tried to destroy Henry's affection for her. Henry learned also that his baroness was not dead; the report had been another of Carwin's tricks. Henry married the baroness and settled down near Boston. Carwin, not a murderer but the victim of a plot, escaped to the country and became a farmer. Henry's wife died soon after their marriage, and he and Clara renewed their love. Their later happiness was marred only by sad and tragic memories.

THE WILD ASS'S SKIN

Type of work: Novel
Author: Honoré de Balzac (1799-1850)
Type of plot: Philosophical allegory
Time of plot: Early nineteenth century
Locale: Paris
First published: 1830

Principal characters:
RAPHAEL DE VALENTIN, the hero
PAULINE, his wife
FOEDORA, a countess loved by Raphael
RASTIGNAC, Raphael's friend

Critique:

This novel, *La Peau de Chagrin,* is a philosophical allegory, usually placed rather high among Balzac's work; in his own time it was frequently compared with *Hamlet* and *Faust.* Today the plot appears thin at times and the characters do not always seem real; but the story does abundantly exemplify a philosophical law. Everything we receive, we must pay for—such is the moral presented. The payment is a kind of nemesis: try as we will we cannot escape a final reckoning. Viewed as an allegory, the book has considerable merit, for the theme is crystal clear. The novel also appears under the title *The Magic Skin.*

The Story:

In a low quarter of Paris, Raphael de Valentin walked hesitantly into a gaming room. Inside were the usual raffish hangers-on. To them the young man was marked for mischance. Raphael played his last coin on the turn of the wheel, and lost.

Resolved to commit suicide, he wandered to the Seine. For a time he leaned over the parapet of the Pont Royal and looked at the cold water below. Only the thought of the paid rescuers kept him from jumping in. He finally sought shelter in an antique shop, where he posed as a customer. Upstairs the proprietor, an ancient scarecrow, showed him a piece of shagreen upon which were engraved words in Sanskrit telling the power of the skin. If the possessor wished for anything, he would get it; but in return the wisher's life would belong to the talisman, and he

would die when the skin, shrinking with each wish, dwindled to nothingness. In spite of the antique dealer's warning, Raphael recklessly took the piece of skin and wished for a great banquet, furnished with much wine, carousing companions, and ladies of light virtue.

As he left the shop, he met his friends, Rastignac and Emile, two penniless adventurers. They had a great scheme in mind for him: he was to be the editor of a new periodical backed by a rich banker. To celebrate the appointment, the banker was giving a banquet in Raphael's honor that very evening. Disquieted only a little by the prompt and complete granting of his wish, Raphael went willingly enough to the banquet.

In the banker's apartment a rich table was laid. After eating and drinking far too much, the company of men withdrew to another room. There a group of joyous ladies waited for them. In his somewhat drunken state, the women all looked pure and beautiful to Raphael. Settling himself with two complaisant entertainers and Emile, Raphael decided to tell his story.

After his mother's death, his rather stern father did his best to train his son for a scholarly career. The boy was destined to be a lawyer, and to that end he read law diligently. Shortly before he was to take a law degree, however, his father died; but, instead of leaving the son well off, the estate amounted to only a few francs. Thinking to achieve a fortune, Raphael decided to shut himself up in a garret and produce works of genius. He found that by living strictly on cold meat, bread, and milk, he would have enough money to see him through.

He found a cheap room under the eaves of a modest house and settled into his laborious routine of writing. Soon he had begun his projects. He spent half of his time writing a comedy, and the rest of his efforts went into the composition of a discourse on the human will. The family from whom he rented his room consisted of a mother, Madame Gaudin, and her young daughter, Pauline. The father, an army captain, had been lost in Siberia; only his wife believed him still alive. Pauline was an attractive child. Raphael gave her piano lessons, and in return Pauline performed small household chores for him.

For a long time Raphael stuck to his spartan schedule, but at last the poor diet and the effort of intense concentration proved too much for him to endure. Going out for a short walk one day, he ran into Rastignac, who teased him about the way he lived. Rastignac had no money and owed many bills, yet he lived a life of luxury. Resourceful at finding jobs, he secured a hack writing commission for Raphael. The advance payment was enough to settle Raphael's bills and leave a little over.

After faithfully paying his account with Pauline's mother, Raphael took his remaining capital to Rastignac, who was to gamble with it. Fortunately, Rastignac won a large sum. Raphael bought new clothes before Rastignac took him to see the Countess Foedora, who entertained lavishly. Since he really was a well-educated man, Raphael was soon a favorite at Foedora's salons, and by hook or crook he managed to keep up appearances so as to stay in her circle of close friends. He even took Foedora driving when he was in funds. Pauline, ever the faithful friend, occasionally gave him small sums to tide him over.

Foedora was a woman of mystery. She was a young widow, wealthy and surrounded by admirers. But some dark secret in her past kept her from marrying again or even taking a lover. Although she looked on many men as her friends, she had no inclination for a serious affair. She finally explained her attitude very clearly to Raphael, who was much cast down.

Determined to win his lady, he secreted himself behind her bed one evening and waited while Foedora made her toilet and went to sleep. From this close observation Raphael romantically expected to learn how to break down her reserve. The effort, however, was all in vain. Convinced at last that he could not win Foedora, Raphael gave up his social life; not even Pauline could console him. Without funds and with no prospects, he began to think of suicide.

As he finished his story, he noticed that his hearers were not seriously interested; even Emile joked about his trials and discomfiture. Soon the whole company lay in drunken sleep. When they all awoke, Raphael was disgusted at the tawdry appearance of his fellow rioters. Going back to the banquet, he told of his piece of skin, and in a spirit of bravado wished for six million francs. Before he left the table a messenger came to announce the death of his mother's brother; the dead man had bequeathed his nephew six million francs. Even though he was elated by his good fortune, he was disturbed to see that the magic skin was growing smaller.

Riches brought no peace to Raphael. Although he now lived in greatest luxury, he also lived in fear. He constantly had to guard against any desires; even an inadvertent wish shrank the magic skin.

One night at the opera he saw Foedora again. Leaning aside so that he would not be seen, he brushed against his neighbor. As he turned to apologize, he discovered that the woman beside him was Pauline Gaudin. She was now wealthy, for her father had returned with a fortune. The two were married, and for a few weeks Raphael knew a little happiness.

Because the skin continued to shrink steadily, Raphael determined on stern measures. He visited a zoölogist, who informed him that his talisman was a piece of skin from a rare, wild Persian ass. Then he visited a mechanic who tried to stretch the skin in a press, but the press was powerless. Even in a white hot forge the skin remained cool and pliable. A chemist tried immersing the wild ass's skin in hydrofluoric acid, but to no avail; the skin would not stretch.

Since his health was failing fast, Raphael left his bride to seek safety in the mountains. But the change of air did him no good; his condition grew steadily worse. One day a braggart challenged him to a duel. Raphael accepted, knowing bitterly that his unspoken wish would make him the victor. After shooting his opponent in the heart, he fled back to Paris with his magic skin. It was now no larger than an oak leaf.

Although he consulted the best doctors available, they gave him no comfort or help. They could scarcely believe his story of the skin, yet they could find no cause for his grave illness. At last he lay dying. Wishing to have Pauline near him, but knowing that his desire would consume the last shred of the magic skin, he asked her to leave him. As he called her name, she saw the skin growing smaller. In despair she rushed into the next room and tried to kill herself by knotting a scarf around her neck. The dying man tottered after her, and as he tore away the cloth he tried vainly to utter a final wish. No words would come. He died while holding her in that last, desperate embrace.

THE WILD DUCK

Type of work: Drama
Author: Henrik Ibsen (1828-1906)
Type of plot: Social criticism
Time of plot: Nineteenth century
Locale: Norway
First presented: 1884

> *Principal characters:*
> WERLE, a wealthy merchant
> GREGERS WERLE, his son
> OLD EKDAL, Werle's former partner
> HJALMAR EKDAL, his son
> GINA EKDAL, Hjalmar's wife
> HEDVIG, their daughter
> RELLING, a doctor

Critique:

In this play Ibsen has made us feel as well as think his message, for in the symbolism of the wild duck he has paralleled perfectly the meaning of his story. The wild duck wounded by old Werle and retrieved by his dog is an image of the Ekdal family, hurt by the world, diving to the depths of self-deception and finally rescued only to be hurt the more. In the character of Gregers Werle Ibsen seems to be turning the knife upon his own youthful idealism.

The Story:

Gregers Werle, son of a wealthy merchant and of a sensitive and high-minded mother, had early in life developed a loathing for the unscrupulous means his father had used to amass his fortune. After his mother's death, young Werle left his father's house for a time, but eventually returned.

His father, hoping to persuade his son to accept a partnership in his business, gave a large dinner party to which Gregers took the liberty of inviting a thirteenth guest, his old school friend, Hjalmar Ekdal. This act displeased his father very much; first, because Hjalmar did not belong in the social set of the Werles; second, because he was the son of a former business partner old Werle had wronged. The older Ekdal now held a menial position in Werle's employ, to which he had been reduced after a term in prison had broken his mind and spirit.

Gregers was aware that his father's machinations had sent Ekdal to prison after a scandal in which both had been involved, and he hated his father for this injury to the father of his friend. He discovered also that the older Werle had arranged a marriage between Hjalmar Ekdal and Gina Hansen, a former maid in the Werle household and, Gregers suspected, his father's mistress. Therefore Gregers was not hospitable to Werle's offer of a partnership nor to his forthcoming marriage to Mrs. Sorby, his housekeeper. Gregers announced that his future mission in life was to open Hjalmar Ekdal's eyes to the lie he had been living for the past fifteen years.

Outwardly, the Ekdal home was a shabby one. Hjalmar Ekdal was a photographer, a business in which Werle had set him up after his marriage to Gina. But Gina ran the business while her husband worked on an invention intended to enable his aged father to recoup some of his fortune. Old Ekdal himself, now practically out of his mind, spent most of his time in a garret in which he kept a curious assortment of animals ranging all the way from chickens to rabbits. Ekdal was under the illusion

THE WILD DUCK by Henrik Ibsen. Published by Charles Scribner's Sons.

that this garret was a forest like the one in which he had hunted as a young man. There he would shoot an occasional rabbit, and on holidays and special occasions he would appear before the family dressed in his old military uniform.

Although it was based almost entirely on self-deception and illusion, the Ekdal home was actually a happy one. Gina took good care of her husband and his aged father, and Hedvig, the fourteen-year-old daughter, loved Hjalmar dearly. To Hjalmar, Hedvig was his whole life, and he and Gina kept from her the fact that she was rapidly losing her eyesight. Gregers Werle, intent on his new mission, was shocked at the depths to which his old friend had sunk. His feelings found expression when old Ekdal showed him Hedvig's prize possession, a wild duck that the older Werle had once shot. The wounded duck had dived to the bottom of the water, but Werle's dog had retrieved it and brought it to the surface again. Gregers saw himself as the clever dog destined to bring the Ekdal family, like the wild duck, out of the muck of their straitened circumstances.

To accomplish his end, he rented a room from the Ekdals, a room Gina was unwilling to let him have. Gina was not the only one to resent his presence in the house. Dr. Relling, another roomer, knew Gregers Werle, and was aware of his reputation for meddling in the affairs of others. He agreed that Gregers was the victim of a morbid conscience, probably derived from his hysterical mother. Hjalmar, in his innocence, however, saw nothing amiss in his friend's behavior and allowed him to stay.

Gregers set about the task of rehabilitating his friend in a systematic way. His first discovery was that the little family was indirectly supported by the older Werle, and not by the photographic studio, as Hjalmar supposed. Also, and more important, Hedvig's approaching blindness and his own father's weak eyesight too nearly coincided to make it reasonable that Hjalmar was the child's natural father. Gregers resolved to open Hjalmar's eyes to his true position in his own house, and during a long walk he laid bare all the facts he had learned except his suspicion of Hedvig's illegitimacy, which was as yet unproved.

Having no real integrity or resources within himself, Hjalmar naturally fell back on all the clichés in the stories he had read as to how a wronged husband should behave. He demanded from Gina an accounting of all the money paid into the household by Werle, and asserted that every cent should be paid back out of the proceeds from his hypothetical invention. His outburst did nothing but disturb Gina and frighten Hedvig.

Hjalmar's pride might have been placated and the whole matter straightened out had not a letter arrived from old Werle, who was giving Hedvig a small annuity. Hjalmar announced that Hedvig was no child of his and that he wanted nothing more to do with her. Hedvig was heartbroken at her father's behavior, and Gregers Werle, beginning to realize the unfortunate condition his meddling had caused, persuaded the girl that her one hope of winning back her father's love was to sacrifice the thing she loved most for his sake. He urged her to have her grandfather kill the wild duck.

In the meantime Gina had succeeded in convincing Hjalmar that he was quite helpless without her. As they were discussing their plans for the future, they heard a shot. At first they thought old Ekdal was firing at his rabbits. Hedvig, in her despair, had put a bullet through her breast.

Gregers Werle had righted no wrongs with his meddling. He had merely made his friend's tragedy complete.

WILHELM MEISTER'S APPRENTICESHIP

Type of work: Novel
Author: Johann Wolfgang von Goethe (1749-1832)
Type of plot: Philosophical romance
Time of plot: Eighteenth century
Locale: Germany
First published: 1795-1796

Principal characters:
WILHELM MEISTER, a wealthy burgher's son
MARIANA, his first beloved, an actress
PHILINA, an actress
AURELIA, an unhappy woman
NATALIA, a beautiful Amazon
MIGNON, in love with Wilhelm

Critique:

Although Goethe never expressed real sympathy for the romanticists, *Wilhelm Meister's Apprenticeship* shows the prevailing romantic style and outlook on life. The action is slow, particularly noticeable in such a long novel, and the characters are never sharply delineated. The scene is a series of vignettes, each setting shading off into the next and none well defined. The people in the novel make long, diffuse speeches on various facets of philosophy and esthetics. Yet in spite of its very evident defects, the work shows real power in its emotional insights, and Goethe's appreciation of Shakespeare is well exhibited in his discussion of *Hamlet*.

The Story:

Old Barbara waited with eagerness for the return of her mistress, for tonight she had a surprise. Norberg, Mariana's protector, had sent money to his beloved, and to Barbara fancy clothes and ornaments. Norberg would be gone another two weeks, but in the meantime the two women would have plenty to live on. Mariana earned a fair amount as an actress, and Norberg's generosity enabled them to indulge a taste for luxury.

Mariana came whirling in, paying no attention to Barbara. Mariana was in love! Truly, this time it was real love. Wilhelm Meister was very young and poetic by nature, and his youth appealed to her. At other times she would listen to Barbara's calculating schemes, but now she would follow only her heart. As soon as deep night came, Wilhelm would be with her.

Wilhelm's family was of sturdy merchant stock. To his father Wilhelm's predilection for poetry seemed extreme. Since early youth he had written verse, declaimed it, and acted in neighborhood plays. For a long time his father was sympathetic, even providing him a puppet show with which to practice. But as Wilhelm grew to young manhood he spent more and more time at the local theater. The tawdry tinsel and the artificial makeup drew him as a magnet. After he met Mariana, he spent every evening admiring her and her acting. At last his father forbade his attendance at the theater. After the ban, Wilhelm would wait until his family was asleep; then he would steal out to see Mariana.

At last, after his father had decided to send Wilhelm on a commercial mission, the youth determined to take Mariana with him and marry her once they were well away from home. His decision drew protests from his friends, especially from Werner, his prospective brother-in-law. He was warned of Mariana's lack of virtue, but he refused to listen.

When he called at the usual time that night, Mariana pleaded a headache and asked him to leave. Wilhelm wandered about until very late and at last engaged some minstrels to serenade his intended. Toward morning his suspicions were aroused when he saw a man leaving

4149

Mariana's house. Going into the entry, he found the doors locked, but Mariana had left a scarf in the vestibule. In the scarf he found a note, written by Norberg, which revealed that Mariana was a kept woman.

After this bitter blow Wilhelm renounced poetry and drama and resolutely set himself to work in his father's business. After a time he passed for a rising young businessman. His father, pleased with the change in his son, decided to trust Wilhelm on an important journey; he was to travel widely among the clients of the firm to collect debts and to further trade. Wilhelm was glad to leave, for away from home he could forget Mariana the more easily.

From the first he was successful, especially in collecting debts. In fact, he could complete his commissions in such short order that he had ample opportunity to seek adventures. On one occasion he came upon an unhappy scene: a couple had been too indiscreet in their love and had been arrested. Wilhelm pleaded with the girl's parents not to press charges, although they were very angry that their daughter had become entangled with Melina, a wandering player. Finally the parents gave their consent to a marriage if the couple would leave town. So happily the two set out. Melina was sure he could get an engagement in a company of actors.

In another town Wilhelm was greatly attracted by the lovely, light-hearted Philina and her merry escort, Laertes. Wilhelm passed many a pleasant day in their company, dining and dancing and playing tricks. One evening they were diverted by a troupe of acrobats who performed dazzling feats on the tight rope. Wilhelm grew angry at the ill treatment the performers accorded a pretty child, a graceful, boyish girl called Mignon. He rescued her and found that he had henceforth a faithful and loving slave.

Gradually a company of actors out of work gathered about Philina, including the Melinas, who were almost destitute. After much urging, Wilhelm lent money to Melina, and the latter immediately purchased an abandoned stock of costumes and properties and set himself up as an actor-manager. Gathering together the ragtail company and persuading Wilhelm to join them as critic and gentleman actor, Melina began rehearsals and gave occasional performances.

At length the company was invited by a count to give a long series of performances at his nearby castle, where the count planned to entertain the Prince of ——. In spite of a poor reception, the company soon was acclimated to the surroundings, and the court even seemed to like their presentations.

Wilhelm attracted notice by writing short occasional pieces and reading poetry in intimate chambers. Although Philina still looked longingly at him, Wilhelm was drawn to the lovely countess. She condescended graciously to him and allowed him to kiss her hand.

One of the guests proposed a trick to play on the countess. Since the count was away overnight, Wilhelm was to put on the count's dressing gown. He would sit in the count's bedroom until the countess came in for a good-night kiss. Then Wilhelm would reveal the jest. But instead of the countess, the count himself came in. Quiet and grave, he looked silently at the dim figure in his clothes, and cautiously withdrew, believing he had seen his doppelgänger. Wilhelm's love for the countess led him, on another occasion, to seize her and embrace her violently. She protested lightly at first, then banished him from her presence.

After this engagement had ended, the actors took to the road. In spite of roving bands of ruffians and thieves, Wilhelm advised them to continue on to the next big town. The company was attacked by robbers and all their goods were stolen or smashed. Wilhelm was gravely wounded. When he came to, he was lying in Philina's lap. He learned that they had been rescued by a party led by a beautiful Amazon. The lady so captivated Wilhelm that he remembered always her haunting loveliness.

During his convalescence Wilhelm stayed in the house of a pastor in a nearby village. Mignon, wounded in the attack, and an old harper who had attached himself to the company, remained with him. Philina also stayed behind to act as nurse when the other actors went away to give performances throughout the countryside.

Recovered, Wilhelm decided to seek his own fortunes on the stage. With his friends he went to see Serlo, a famous actor-manager, who offered him a contract. While working on a production of *Hamlet,* Wilhelm spent much time in the company of Aurelia, Serlo's sister, whose husband was dead and who had been deserted by a noble lover. Wilhelm believed that a small child of the household, Felix, was the result of her unhappy love affair.

Word arrived that his father had died, leaving Wilhelm considerable property. In spite of his grief he decided to go ahead with his theatrical career. During the performance of *Hamlet,* Wilhelm, playing the Danish prince, was much puzzled by a strange actor who had played the role of the ghost. No one could explain who the mysterious actor could have been.

The mystery was forgotten in the excitement of a fire which broke out that night. In the excitement Felix was placed in the care of the aged harper. While Wilhelm was helping to fight the blaze, Mignon appeared with word that the harper had carried the boy to the basement of the castle and there was trying to kill him. After this crazed deed Wilhelm placed the old man in the care of a clergyman whose medical training had led him to care for such unfortunates.

From that time on Wilhelm became the special protector of little Felix, and Mignon the child's constant companion. Aurelia died, but before her death she told Wilhelm the story of her sad love affair and asked him to deliver a letter she had written to Lothario, the nobleman who had broken her heart. On his arrival at Lothario's castle Wilhelm recognized his host as the brother of the Countess ——. He and the nobleman became friends. Through Lothario he was initiated into a strange secret society of intellectuals and aristocrats; many of his experiences, he realized, had been an apprenticeship to prove his fitness to join the society. At the castle he learned also that the old harper was a former priest who had seduced a young woman, a near relation, to whom a child had been born. The man believed that a small child would cause his death.

While on a mission for Lothario, Wilhelm encountered old Barbara, who was now a sewing-woman. She assured him that Felix was his own son. Mariana, the mother, had died of a broken heart, and Aurelia had taken the child as her ward. Wilhelm, grieved to hear of Mariana's death, rejoiced also to hear of her fidelity.

Mignon, meanwhile, had been sent to stay with Lothario's sister. When word arrived that she was gravely ill, Wilhelm, with Felix, set out to see her. There he met Natalia, another sister of Lothario's, whom he recognized as the beautiful Amazon who had saved his life in the forest. Mignon died. Soon after her death the true story of her birth was revealed. She was the daughter of a priest, an Italian of noble birth, who on learning that his beloved was his own sister had gone mad. Later the child, the mother having died in a convent, was stolen by some traveling players. Mignon, then, had been the daughter of the old harper whom Wilhelm had befriended.

Shortly after Mignon's death Wilhelm made Natalia his wife. He believed that his apprenticeship had set him free from former confusion and doubts. He had become a judicious, unbiased personality, a critic appreciating art and life.

WILHELM MEISTER'S TRAVELS

Type of work: Novel
Author: Johann Wolfgang von Goethe (1749-1832)
Type of plot: Philosophical romance
Time of plot: Early nineteenth century
Locale: Germany
First published: 1821-1829

Principal characters:
    WILHELM MEISTER, a Renunciant
    FELIX, his son
    HERSILIA, a girl admired by Felix
    HILARIA, a young girl
    LENARDO, Wilhelm's friend

Critique:

Wilhelm Meister's Travels is a continuation of the *Apprenticeship*. Many of the same characters reappear briefly, and some attempt is made to bring to a close the adventures of a large number of people. This novel is very difficult to follow. There is no plot in the usual sense, the work being a convenient vehicle for Goethe's views on geology, art, and labor; for lyric interpolations, and for digressions which lengthen the work without illuminating it. The general atmosphere seems romantically vague to a modern reader.

The Story:

Wilhelm Meister was traveling on foot with his young son Felix. As a consequence of his liberation from ordinary desire through the noble Lothario and the abbot, he had become a Renunciant. Under the terms of his pledge he must wander for years, never stopping in one place more than three days. His travels were intended to give a final philosophical polish to the once troubled Wilhelm. Gone forever were the counting-house and the stage; now he undertook a last purifying sacrifice.

While Felix played merrily on the mountainside, Wilhelm mused beside a steep path. Hearing voices, he turned to see his son with a group of children running downhill before a donkey driven by a holy-looking man. The beast carried a sweet-faced woman with a small baby. The adults smiled at Wilhelm, but the path was too steep for them to stop. When Wilhelm caught up with the party, the man invited him to visit his household, and his wife amiably seconded the invitation. It was decided that Felix should go on ahead with the family and Wilhelm would follow the next day, after he had retrieved his wallet left high on the mountain.

When he arrived, Wilhelm was charmed to find the family living in a restored chapel. He was struck by the fact that the man was Joseph and the wife was Mary; indeed, they seemed a holy family. When he learned their story, Wilhelm was reverent.

Joseph's father had been a rent collector for an absentee landlord. Joseph had been promised that if he grew to be a steady man and a competent craftsman, he could succeed his father. But he decided to be a woodworker, and when he was sufficiently skilled he began to restore the paneling in the old chapel. His best work was the skillful reworking of an elaborate panel depicting in wood the flight of the Holy Family into Egypt.

One day, as Joseph was wandering on the trail, he found a beautiful woman weeping beside the path. Her husband had been killed by robbers. Joseph, alarmed by the woman's distress and condition, took her to his home and summoned his mother. Soon the widow was delivered of a child. After a patient courtship Joseph married the widow, Mary, and took her to live in the old chapel.

Now he was the rent collector in his father's place and possessed of a loving family.

While playing, Felix came upon a box of stones which had been given to Joseph by a scientist who was searching for minerals in that region. Learning that the geologist's name was Montan, a name frequently used by his old friend Jarno, Wilhelm hoped to overtake the scientist in the course of his own wanderings. He and Felix started out, led by Fitz, a beggar-boy who had been a playmate for Felix during the stay with the collector and his wife. On the way they came to a barrier of fallen trees. While their guide was looking for another path, Felix wandered into a nearby cave and there found a small box, no larger than an octavo volume, rich-looking and decorated with gold. Wilhelm and his son decided to conceal the box among their belongings and to tell no one of its discovery for the time being.

A short time later Fitz led them to the place where Montan was prospecting. As Wilhelm had expected, the scientist was Jarno, whom Wilhelm had known in his acting days, now a Renunciant geologist. They stayed with Jarno for three days, while the scientist tried to satisfy the great curiosity Felix had about minerals and their properties.

Taking leave of Jarno, the party started off to survey a natural phenomenon known as the Giant's Castle. Sending the pack animals around by road, the travelers followed a rugged path until they came in sight of a beautiful garden, separated from them by a yawning chasm. Fitz led them into an aqueduct which gave entrance to the garden. Suddenly they heard a shot. At the same time two iron-grated doors began to close behind them. Fitz sprang backward and escaped, but Wilhelm and his son were trapped. Some armed men with torches appeared, and to them Wilhelm surrendered his knife, his only weapon. He told his son to have no fear, for there were pious mottoes carved on the walls leading to the castle to which their captors conducted them.

After spending the night in a well-appointed room, father and son breakfasted with the gay Hersilia and her older, more sedate sister Julietta. Felix was charmed with Hersilia, as was his father. Hersilia gave Wilhelm a romant'c manuscript to read. The next day the eccentric uncle of the girls appeared and took them to lunch in a shooting lodge.

Finding himself in such agreeable and learned company, Wilhelm exerted himself to please. Hersilia accepted him as one of the family, and to show her trust gave him a pack of letters to read, letters telling of her cousin Lenardo. Some years ago Lenardo had determined to set out on his travels. In order to get the necessary funds, his uncle had to collect all outstanding debts. While arranging his affairs, he dispossessed a tenant farmer with a beautiful daughter called the Nut-Brown Maid. Although the girl pleaded with Lenardo for mercy, she and her father were evicted. Now Lenardo wrote his aunt that he would not come home until he learned what had happened to the girl.

After reading the letters, Wilhelm took his son to visit the aunt, a wise woman called Makaria. In her castle Wilhelm met an astronomer who revealed to him many of the secrets of the stars. Advised by the savant, Wilhelm deposited the box Felix had found with an antiquarian until the key could be found.

At a distant castle a major came to visit his sister. His intention was to consolidate the family fortunes by marrying his son Flavio to his sister's daughter Hilaria. To his surprise Hilaria loved only her uncle. So the major, after getting a valet to make him look younger, went to tell Flavio the news. He was heartened to learn that Flavio was in love with a widow.

One night Flavio burst hysterically into his aunt's castle. The widow had repulsed him when he became too eager in his love making. Flavio soon found solace in Hilaria's company. When the major returned the atmosphere grew tense. The gloom was lifted only after Hilaria's mother wrote to Makaria for advice. That wise lady had the widow visit the major and tell him the true state of affairs, that the young Flavio and Hilaria were really in love. Then Hilaria and the pretty widow set out to travel to Italy.

In the meantime Wilhelm had come upon Lenardo in his wanderings. Lenardo begged his aid in learning what had become of the Nut-Brown Maid. When Wilhelm agreed to the quest, Felix was put in a school run by wise men who taught the dignity of labor and the beauty of art. Shortly after Wilhelm left the school he was able to send Lenardo word that the girl was now well off and happy, and the wandering nephew was then able to return to Makaria.

With an artist friend, Wilhelm traveled among the beautiful Italian lakes. This neighborhood was especially dear to him, for it was the home of his beloved Mignon, his foster daughter. The two men were lucky enough to meet Hilaria and the widow, but before any serious interests could develop the ladies disappeared.

Hersilia wrote to Wilhelm that she was keeping Felix's box, as the antiquarian had gone away, and that she also had a key to the chest. Returning to Germany, Wilhelm went to the school to get Felix. He was pleased to find him a well-grown young man with considerable artistic ability. Father and son, once more together after their long separation, began to visit their old friends.

They found that Hilaria and Flavio had married and that Flavio had become a prosperous merchant. Felix was greatly attracted to Hersilia. When he learned that she had both key and box, he persuaded her to let him try to open it. But the key was a magnetic key, and the halves came apart when he tried to turn the lock.

Felix tried to embrace Hersilia, and the girl pushed him away much harder than she meant to. Fearing she did not love him, Felix impetuously dashed away and was injured when he fell on the shore beside a stream. There Wilhelm found him unconscious. His old training in medicine stood him in good stead, however, and Wilhelm was able to bleed his son and restore him to consciousness.

WILLIAM TELL

Type of work: Drama
Author: Johann Christoph Friedrich von Schiller (1759-1805)
Type of plot: Historical romance
Time of plot: Fifteenth century
Locale: Switzerland
First presented: 1804

Principal characters:
  WILLIAM TELL, a forester
  WALTER TELL, his son
  WALTER FÜRST, William Tell's father-in-law
  GESSLER, Governor of the Swiss Forest Cantons
  WERNER, a nobleman
  ULRICH, his nephew
  BERTHA OF BRUNECK, a rich heiress

Critique:

William Tell is based on a popular legend which in time became localized in Switzerland. In it Schiller demonstrated his admiration for natural man in a setting of primitive beauty. The love of liberty dramatized by the plot shows how Schiller agreed with and differed from the principles of the French Revolution. Schiller was a strong proponent of the dignity and worth of the common man, but he would have each man acknowledge and serve his rightful master.

The Story:

A storm was rising on Lake Lucerne and the ferryman was making his boat fast to the shore as Baumgarten rushed up, pursued by the soldiers of the tyrant, Gessler. He implored the ferryman to take him across the lake to safety. First, however, the crowd made him tell the reason for the pursuit.

The Wolfshot, a nobleman who had been appointed seneschal of the castle, had come into Baumgarten's house and had ordered the wife to prepare him a bath. When he had started to take liberties with the woman, she had escaped and had run to her husband in the forest. Baumgarten had hurried back and with his ax had split the Wolfshot's skull. Now he had to leave the country.

Because the sympathies of the common people were with Baumgarten,

they begged the ferryman to take him across. But the storm was almost upon them, and the ferryman was afraid. Then William Tell came up, Tell the hunter, the only man in the crowd with courage to steer the boat in a tempest. As soon as he heard Baumgarten's story, Tell unhesitatingly embarked to take the fugitive to the other shore. As they cast off, the soldiers thundered up. When they saw their prey escaping, they took their revenge on the peasants by killing their sheep and burning their cottages.

The free Switzers were greatly troubled because the Emperor of Austria had sent Gessler to rule as viceroy over the Forest Cantons. Gessler, a younger son of no fortune, was envious of the prosperity of the thrifty Switzers and enraged by their calm and independent bearing, for the inhabitants held their lands directly in fief to the emperor and the rights and duties of the viceroy were carefully limited. To break the proud spirit of the Switzers, Gessler mounted a cap on a pole in a public place and required that each man bow to the cap.

Henry of Halden was an upright man. To his farm came the emissaries of Gessler, attempting to take from him his best team of oxen. When Arnold, his son, sprang on the men and struck them with his staff, they released the oxen and left. Arnold thought it best to go into hiding. While he was away,

4155

the soldiers came and tortured old Henry and put out his eyes. Arnold joined the malcontents against Gessler.

Fürst became the leader of the Switzers. It was agreed that ten men from the three Cantons would meet and plan to overthrow the viceroy.

At the mansion of Werner, the common people and their lord were gathered for the morning cup of friendship. Old Werner gladly drank with his men, but his nephew Ulrich refused. He had been attracted to the Austrian court by the fine dress and high positions of the rulers, and he felt no bond with free Switzerland. Werner upbraided him for being a turncoat and finally accused Ulrich of turning to Austria because of love for the rich Bertha.

In great secrecy the representatives of the people met at night under the leadership of Fürst. Feeling their wrongs too great to bear, they revived their ancient Diet. Some of the more fiery members were in favor of an immediate uprising, but the cooler heads followed Fürst and voted to wait until Christmas, when by tradition all the peasants would be present in the castle.

Ulrich at last approached Bertha and declared his love for her. A true Switzer at heart, she spurned him for his loyalty to Austria.

Tell with his sons came near the hated cap. When Tell, more by accident than by design, paid no attention to the symbol of authority, he was arrested by two guards who tried to bind him and lead him to prison. Although Fürst came and offered bail for his son-in-law, law-abiding Tell submitted to his captors and was being led away when Gessler himself rode by.

Gessler ordered an apple placed on Walter Tell's head. Then he commanded William Tell to shoot the apple from his son's head. Tell protested in vain. Ulrich courageously defied Gessler and spoke hot words of blame to the tyrant, but Gessler was unmoved. In the confusion Tell took out two arrows, fitted one to his crossbow, and neatly pierced the apple.

While the crowd rejoiced, Gessler asked Tell why he had taken two arrows, but Tell refused to answer until Gessler promised not to execute him no matter what the reply might be. Then Tell boldly declared that if he had missed the apple and hurt his son, he would have killed Gessler with the second arrow. Infuriated, Gessler ordered Tell led away to life imprisonment.

Chained, Tell was put on the boat which was to take him to Gessler's castle, and Gessler himself went along to gloat over his victim. Once again a terrible storm arose. To save his own life, Gessler had Tell unbound and made him helmsman. Watching his chance, Tell steered the boat close to shore and sprang to safety on a rocky ledge.

He came with his crossbow to a pass through which Gessler must travel if he escaped the fury of the storm. Under Tell's hiding place a poor woman and her children waited for Gessler. Her husband was in prison for a minor offense, and she intended to appeal to Gessler for clemency.

At last Gessler approached with his train. The woman blocked his way and appealed for mercy on behalf of her husband. Waiting long enough to hear her plea denied, Tell pierced the breast of the tyrant with a bolt from his crossbow. Dropping down on the road, Tell announced to the gathered people that he had killed Gessler; then he disappeared into the forest.

Gessler lay in the road, with no friendly hand to pull the arrow from the bleeding heart. So died Switzerland's oppressor.

The people had hoped that Werner would lead them in their revolt, but he was old and on his deathbed. He hoped to remain alive until Ulrich would come to receive from him the leadership, but Ulrich did not arrive until after his uncle's death. The assembled peasants, however, acknowledged Ulrich as their leader, and they found in him a hardy knignt, all the more anxious for war because the Austrians had abducted Bertha. At last the three Cantons rose up against harsh Austrian rule.

At the height of the revolt, the news came that the emperor himself had been assassinated. Duke John of Austria, his nephew, had struck down the emperor after being robbed of his estates. The Switzers despised the duke for the crime because assassination for robbery seemed to them unjust. When Duke John sought refuge with Tell, the forester was indignant. Tell was a soldier for freedom, not a murderer. But his natural humanity kept him from exposing John, and the duke left unharmed to seek a safer sanctuary in Italy.

Tell put away his crossbow for good when the announcement came that the Count of Luxembourg had been elected emperor. The Cantons settled down to peaceful days once more. Bertha gave her hand freely to Ulrich, as one proud Switzer to another.

THE WIND IN THE WILLOWS

Type of work: Novel
Author: Kenneth Grahame (1859-1932)
Type of plot: Fantasy and allegory
Time of plot: Early twentieth century
Locale: England
First published: 1908

Principal characters:
MOLE, an introvert
WATER RAT, an extrovert
TOAD, a playboy
BADGER, a philosophical recluse

Critique:

Like mathematician Charles Lutwidge Dodgson, whom the world knows as Lewis Carroll, Kenneth Grahame found in imaginative tales escape from his duties as secretary of the Bank of England. The animals who are his characters in *The Wind in the Willows* belong to the same world in which human beings live; here are the same foibles and excesses, the same motives and loyalties. Whether the author intended his book chiefly for children is a matter still open for discussion, but one of little consequence, for the story of Mole and his friends has become a delight to readers of all ages. Fantasy and allegory touched by gentle satire make this story one which can be read on more than one level of meaning.

The Story:

Mole had spring fever, for he had been busy about his cleaning and repairing too long. Because the new spring smells and the sight of budding green were everywhere about him, he just could not resist them. Throwing aside his tools and mops, together with his ambition, he left his little home under the ground and traveled up a lovely meadow. There he wandered through the grass and along the river. He had never seen a river before, and he was bewitched by its chuckling and glimmering in the sunlight.

As he watched, Mole saw a dark hole in the bank. From it protruded the be- whiskered face of Water Rat, who promptly invited Mole to visit him. Mole, of course, could not swim, and so Rat took his little boat and rowed across to get him. Such enchantment was almost too much for quiet Mole. As they glided across the gurgling water, he thought this the best day of his entire life. After a little accident they reached Rat's house. There they packed a picnic basket and set out on a real excursion. They stayed carefully away from the Wild Wood, for fierce animals lived there. Badger kept his home there, but nobody would dare bother Badger.

As they floated down the river, Rat told Mole about other animals and the Wide World. Rat had never seen the Wide World and never wanted to, but he warned Mole against it. It was no place for respectable animals.

When they stopped for their picnic lunch, they were joined by Otter. Badger looked in on them but would not join them. Badger hated Society. He liked People all right, but he hated Society. Rat promised that they would meet Badger later, for from Badger Mole could learn much valuable knowledge.

After another accident, which was Mole's fault, the two new friends went to Rat's home and ate supper. Following the meal, Rat entertained Mole with many wonderful tales. It was a sleepy but happy Mole who was helped into bed by the kind Rat that night. From then on the two remained friends. Rat taught Mole to swim and to row, to listen to the music of the running water, and to catch a little of the meaning of the song the wind sang as it whispered in the willows.

One day the two went to call on Toad at Toad Hall. It was the most beautiful residence in animal land, for Toad was wealthy. He was also a playboy. Every new fad that came along attracted him. When Rat and Mole arrived, Toad was busy getting together a gipsy caravan. He persuaded the others to join him on the open road. Although the venture was much against Rat's better judgment, poor Mole was so desirous of joining Toad that Rat finally gave in.

Their adventure was short-lived. When the wagon was upset by a racing motorcar, Rat was so furious that he wanted to prosecute the owners of the car to the limit. Toad had other ideas; he must have the biggest, fastest, gaudiest car that money could buy.

Spring, summer, and fall passed—days filled with pleasure for Mole and Rat. Then, one cold winter day, Mole went out alone and got lost. Finding himself in the Wild Wood, he was terrified by the strange noises and evil faces he saw around him. Rat finally found him, but before they could reach Rat's home snow began to fall. By luck, they stumbled upon Badger's home, where the old philosopher welcomed them, even though he hated being distrubed from his winter's sleep. Badger asked for news of the other animals, particularly of Toad. He was not surprised to learn that Toad had been in trouble constantly because of his motorcars. There had been seven smash-ups, and seven new cars. He had been hospitalized three times and had paid innumerable fines. Badger promised that when the proper time came he would attend to Toad.

When their visit was over, Badger led Rat and Mole through a labyrinth of tunnels and underground passages until they reached the far edge of the Wild Wood. Then he bade them goodbye and they scampered for home. Not long afterward, in December, Mole felt a great desire to return to his own house that he had left on that spring day so long ago. Rat understood the feeling and gladly went with Mole to find his old home. It was a shabby place, not at all as fine as Toad Hall or Rat's house, but Rat was polite about it and praised it to Mole. On their first night there they gave a party for the field mice, then rolled into bed and slept the sleep of weary travelers.

Early the next summer Badger turned up and said that now he was ready to deal with Toad. Taking Mole and Rat with him, he went to Toad Hall and tried to persuade Toad to give up his cars and his reckless ways. Since force alone could accomplish that end, they locked Toad in his room until he should come to his senses. But Toad slipped out of the window and stole a car. Arrested, he was tried and sentenced to prison for twenty years. There Toad had ample time to think about his foolish ways. But not for long could he be restrained. Bribing the jailer's daughter, he escaped in the disguise of a washerwoman.

Finally, Mole learned the true meaning of the wind's song in the trees. One evening, when birds and insects were still, Mole suddenly felt the Awe that brought peace and contentment. He felt himself in the presence of Him who brought Life and Death. There was no terror, only peace. Then Mole and Rat really saw Him, his horns gleaming and his eyes smiling. The mood was over soon, and with its passing came complete forgetfulness. While the wind sang gently on through the willows, Mole and Rat felt only as if they had had an unremembered dream.

That fall Seafarer, a seafaring rat knocked on Rat's door and told wonderful tales of adventure throughout the Wide World. Rat had a dreamy look in his eye as Seafarer painted his pictures, and it was all Mole could do to remind

Rat of the fearsome things he had said about the Wide World. But the spell was broken at last, and Rat settled down again, contented with his narrow world.

Meanwhile Toad's escape was almost ruined by his conceit and his carelessness. As he was about to be caught again, Rat rescued him and took him home. There Rat told Toad that the weasels and stoats had taken over Toad Hall while Toad was in prison. Badger had a plan to recover Toad Hall. Through a tunnel known only to Badger, the four friends sneaked up on the intruders and captured Toad Hall again for its rightful owner. Toad, of course, took all the credit.

The four continued to live in joy and contentment. Unafraid, they walked in the Wild Wood, for the weasels had learned their lesson, and they heard the wind whispering its gentle song.

WINDSOR CASTLE

Type of work: Novel
Author: William Harrison Ainsworth (1805-1882)
Type of plot: Historical romance
Time of plot: Sixteenth century
Locale: England
First published: 1843

Principal characters:
HENRY THE EIGHTH, King of England
CATHERINE OF ARAGON, Queen of England
ANNE BOLEYN, Catherine's successor
CARDINAL WOLSEY, Lord High Chancellor
THE EARL OF SURREY, a member of the court
THE DUKE OF RICHMOND, Henry's natural son
LADY ELIZABETH FITZGERALD, the fair Geraldine
MABEL LYNDWOOD, granddaughter of a royal forester
MORGAN FENWOLF, a gamekeeper
HERNE THE HUNTER, a spectral demon

Critique:

This interesting novel of the reign of King Henry the Eighth combines two traditions of English fiction—the historical romance and the Gothic romance of mystery and terror. An element of the weird is imparted to the novel by the mysterious figure of Herne the Hunter, an apparition out of the imagination of medieval England and still a creature of legend in the history of Windsor Castle. In his novel Ainsworth gave Herne the function of a somewhat disorganized conscience. Linked to forces of evil as well as to those of good, he had a never clearly defined symbolic value, a representation of the inconsistency of man's nature, as illustrated in the person and acts of Henry Tudor.

The Story:

In April, 1529, the young Earl of Surrey was at Windsor Castle preparing for the arrival of King Henry the Eighth. One night, having dismissed his attendants with orders to meet him at the Garter Inn in the nearby village, he began a walk through the home park. On the way he passed near an ancient tree known as Herne's Oak, where a demon hunter was reported to lie in wait for wayfarers through the forest at night. Suddenly a blue light surrounded the old tree. Beneath its branches stood the figure of a man wearing upon his head the skull and antlers of a stag. From the left arm of the specter hung a heavy rusted chain; on its right wrist perched an owl with red, staring eyes.

When Surrey crossed himself in fear, the figure vanished. Hurrying from the haunted spot, he encountered another traveler through the park. The man was Morgan Fenwolf, a gamekeeper who led the earl to the inn where the young nobleman was to rejoin his companions.

Surrey arrived at the Garter in time to witness a quarrel between a butcher and an archer calling himself the Duke of Shoreditch. Speaking angry words that came close to treason, the butcher declared himself opposed to royal Henry's desire to put aside Catherine of Aragon. When words led to blows, Surrey and Fenwolf stepped in to halt the fight. The self-dubbed Duke of Shoreditch insisted that the butcher be imprisoned in the castle. As he was led away, the butcher charged that Fenwolf was a wizard. Surrey, much amused, rode off to Hampton Court to meet the royal procession.

Henry and his court arrived at Windsor Castle amid the shouts of the crowd and volleys of cannon from the walls. In his train Lady Anne Boleyn, dressed in ermine and cloth of gold, rode in a litter attended by Sir Thomas Wyat, the

4161

poet; the youthful Duke of Richmond, natural son of the king, and the Earl of Surrey. Also in the procession was Cardinal Wolsey, the Lord High Chancellor.

Informed on his arrival of the arrest of the treasonous butcher, Henry ordered his immediate execution. The body of the butcher was swinging from the battlements as Henry escorted Anne Boleyn into the castle.

After Surrey had told Richmond of his ghostly encounter in the park, the two young men agreed to go that night to Herne's Oak. There they watched a ghostly chase—the demon hunter pursuing a deer, a great owl flying before him and black hounds running silently beside his horse.

On their return to the castle, their haggard looks led to many questions from the ladies attending Anne Boleyn, among them Lady Elizabeth Fitzgerald, the fair Geraldine, as she was called, an Irish beauty with whom both Surrey and Richmond were in love. Later that night, suspecting that they may have been the victims of a hoax arranged by Morgan Fenwolf, Surrey and the duke returned to the forest in search of the gamekeeper. There they found the body of the hanged butcher. Pinned to his clothing was an inscription which indicated that a political party opposed to the king now considered the butcher a martyr to their cause.

Bad blood was brewing between Surrey and the duke over the fair Geraldine. Finding the girl and the young earl meeting in a secret tryst, the duke challenged Surrey to a duel. Royal guards stopped the fight and Surrey was imprisoned for drawing steel against the king's son.

Orders were given for a royal hunt. During the chase Anne Boleyn was endangered by the charge of a maddened stag, but her life was saved by a well-aimed arrow from Morgan Fenwolf's bow. To avoid the charging stag, Anne threw herself into the arms of Sir Thomas Wyat, who was riding by her side.

Henry, seeing her action, was furious.

Henry's jealousy immediately gave cheer to the supporters of Catherine of Aragon, who hoped that Henry would give up his plan to make Anne the next Queen of England. Shortly after the return of the party to Windsor, a spy informed Henry that Wyat was in Anne's apartment. Henry angrily went to see for himself, but before his arrival Surrey, just liberated from his cell to hear the king's judgment on his case, hurried to warn Wyat and Anne. Wyat escaped through a secret passage. Surrey explained that he had come to ask Anne's aid in obtaining a royal pardon for his rashness in quarreling with the Duke of Richmond. Through Anne's favor, his sentence was shortened to confinement for two months.

Herne the Hunter continued to haunt the home park. One night the Duke of Richmond went alone to the forest and there saw the demon accompanied by a band of spectral huntsmen, one of whom he recognized as the butcher. The horsemen rode rapidly through the forest and then plunged into a lake and disappeared. Sir Thomas Wyat, angry and wretched at having lost Anne to Henry, met the ghostly hunter and promised to give his soul to the powers of evil if he could only win back Anne. The demon assured him that he should have his wish. Soon afterward, however, Henry decided to send Wyat on a mission to France.

Cardinal Wolsey, thwarted in his attempt to make Wyat the agent of Anne's overthrow, planned to use Mabel Lyndwood, granddaughter of a royal forester, to attract Henry.

One night Herne the Hunter appeared to Surrey in his prison tower and showed the fair Geraldine to the young man in a vision. After the demon had disappeared Surrey was unable to find a holy relic that the girl had given him.

But Wyat had not gone to France. Kidnaped by the demon, he was imprisoned in a cave and forced to drink a strange brew which affected his reason and made him swear to become one of Herne's midnight huntsmen. Fenwolf, who was a member of the band, promised to betray the king into Wyat's hands. While riding through the home park, Henry and the Duke of Suffolk were attacked by Herne's followers. Henry, coming face to face with Wyat, was about to kill his rival, but Mabel Lyndwood suddenly appeared and asked the king to spare Wyat because he had saved Henry's life when the attack began. Henry sternly ordered Wyat, once more in possession of his senses, to continue on his way to France. Fenwolf, captured by royal guards who had ridden out in search of the king, was imprisoned in the castle. Later he escaped under mysterious circumstances. Henry, after failing to track down Herne, ordered the haunted oak felled and burned.

In disguise, Catherine of Aragon appeared at Windsor Castle and sought an audience with Henry in order to convince him of her love and to warn him against Anne's fickle and unfaithful nature. When Anne interrupted them, Catherine foretold Anne's bloody doom.

Shortly afterward Herne appeared before the king on the castle terrace and prophesied Henry's fearful end. A terrible storm broke at that moment and the demon disappeared.

Meanwhile Mabel Lyndwood had been brought to the castle, where her grandfather was being held for questioning following the attack on Henry. Finding her in the kitchen, Henry gave orders that she was to be cared for until he sent for her.

Questioned by the king, old Lyndwood refused to talk. Henry then ordered the guards to bring Mabel to her grandfather's cell. There Henry threatened them with death if the old forester refused to reveal his knowledge of the demon hunter. That night a strange messenger, after presenting the king's signet ring to the guards, led Mabel and her grandfather from the castle and told them to go to a secret cave. Meanwhile the castle was in an uproar. When the guards, led by Henry himself, cornered the demon in one of the upper chambers of the castle, the specter disappeared after pointing out to Henry a coffin containing the body of the hanged butcher.

Determined at last to put Catherine aside, and knowing that Wolsey would block his attempts so long as the cardinal remained in power, Henry removed Wolsey from office and disgraced him publicly. Anne Boleyn would be the next Queen of England.

Surrey, released from imprisonment, learned that the fair Geraldine had gone back to Ireland. Surrey and Richmond, riding near the castle, met Wyat, who had returned secretly from France to discover the whereabouts of Mabel Lyndwood and to rid the forest of the demon hunter.

His disclosure of his plans was overheard by the hunter and Fenwolf, who were hiding in the loft of a nearby cottage. A short time later Herne and Fenwolf quarreled over Mabel's favors. When Fenwolf tried to stab the demon, his dagger would not pierce the demon's body. Herne, who claimed that he was more than a hundred years old, asked Mabel to love him and to pray for his liberation from the spell which caused him to walk the earth and do evil. Wyat, who had been captured by the hunter, was offered his freedom if Mabel would accept the demon's love. Herne also promised her jewels and revealed that she was the unacknowledged daughter of the disgraced Cardinal Wolsey.

The hunter told her finally that whether she loved him or not he intended to marry her the next night near an ancient Druid ruin. Fenwolf, overhearing his declaration, promised to release Mabel if she would wed him. The girl refused; she said that Fenwolf was almost as evil as the demon himself.

The next day Mabel managed to free Wyat from the cave where he was confined and the two made their escape. Old Lyndwood and Fenwolf planned to destroy the hunter by setting off a blast of powder in the cave. In their flight

Wyat and Mabel were forced to swim their horse across a lake. Mabel fainted. On the opposite shore Wyat encountered Surrey, Richmond, and a party searching for the demon. Mabel was placed upon a litter of branches. At that moment Herne the Hunter rode up, seized the girl, and raced with her toward the cave, the others in pursuit until their way was blocked by a forest fire that followed the roar of an explosion from the direction of the cave. Fenwolf was burned in the blaze. The next morning Wyat, Surrey, and Richmond found old Lyndwood kneeling over his granddaughter, whose dead body he had dragged from the lake. The searchers found no trace of the demon hunter.

Seven years passed. Richmond had married Lady Mary Howard, the sister of Surrey. Surrey himself had been forced to wed Lady Frances Vere, for the king had refused permission to marry the fair Geraldine. Wolsey and Catherine were dead. Anne had become queen, but she was beginning to realize that Henry was growing cool toward her and their little daughter, Elizabeth. Although she was not faithful to the king, she would not allow another to share Henry's affection. Jealous of his attentions to Jane Seymour, she reproached and threatened her rival. Jane replied by accusing Anne of misconduct with Sir Henry Norris.

While the court was at Windsor Castle, Herne the Hunter appeared once more. Disguised as a monk, he led Anne and Norris to an apartment where they found the king and Jane Seymour together. Anne knew then what her end was to be; but when Norris asked her to flee with him she refused.

In May some jousts were held at the castle. Norris, who had formed a compact with the demon hunter, defeated the king in the tourney and as his reward Anne gave him a handkerchief which Henry had presented to her. Furious, Henry charged her with incontinence and sent Norris to the tower. Soon afterward Anne was also imprisoned. There Herne visited her and offered to carry her and her lover to a place of safety. Rather than sacrifice her soul, Anne refused. At her trial she was pronounced guilty and sentenced to die.

Henry was in retirement at Windsor Castle on the day of her execution. As her head rolled from the block, Herne the Hunter appeared before Henry, bowed mockingly, and told the king that he was free to wed once more.

WINESBURG, OHIO

Type of work: Short stories
Author: Sherwood Anderson (1876-1941)
Type of plot: Psychological realism
Time of plot: Late nineteenth century
Locale: Winesburg, Ohio
First published: 1919

Principal characters:
GEORGE WILLARD, a young reporter
ELIZABETH WILLARD, his mother
DR. REEFY, Elizabeth's confidant
HELEN WHITE, George's friend
KATE SWIFT, George's former teacher
REV. CURTIS HARTMAN, Kate's unknown admirer
WING BIDDLEBAUM, a berry picker

Critique:

Winesburg, Ohio has the stature of a modern classic. It is at once beautiful and tragic, realistic and poetic. Without being a novel in the usual sense of the word, the connected stories have the full range and emotional impact of a novel. In simple, though highly skillful and powerful language, Sherwood Anderson has told the story of a small town and the lonely, frustrated people who live there. Though regional in its setting and characters, the book is also intensely American. No one since Anderson has succeeded in interpreting the inner compulsions and loneliness of the national psyche with the same degree of accuracy and emotional impact.

The Story:

Young George Willard was the only child of Elizabeth and Tom Willard. His father, a dull, conventional, insensitive man, owned the local hotel. His mother had once been a popular young belle. She had never loved Tom Willard, but the young married women of the town seemed to her so happy, so satisfied, that she had married him in the hope that marriage would somehow change her own life for the better. Before long she realized that she was caught in the dull life of Winesburg,

her dreams turned to drab realities by her life with Tom Willard.

The only person who ever understood her was Dr. Reefy. Only in his small, untidy office did she feel free; only there did she achieve some measure of self-expression. Their relationship, doomed from the start, was nevertheless beautiful, a meeting of two lonely and sensitive people. For Dr. Reefy, too, had his sorrows. Once, years ago, a young girl, pregnant and unmarried, had come to his office, and shortly afterward he had married her. The following spring she had died, and from then on Dr. Reefy went around making little paper pills and stuffing his pockets with them. On the pieces of paper he had scribbled his thoughts about the beauty and strangeness of life.

Through her son George, Elizabeth Willard hoped to express herself, for she saw in him the fulfillment of her own hopes and desires. More than anything, she feared that George would settle down in Winesburg. When she learned that he wanted to be a writer, she was glad. Unknown to her husband, she had put away money enough to give her son a start. But before she could realize her ambition, Elizabeth Willard died. Lying on her bed, she did not seem dead to either George or Dr. Reefy. To both she was extremely beautiful. To George, she did not seem like his mother at all. To Dr. Reefy, she was the woman he had loved, now the symbol of another lost illusion.

Many people of the town sought out George Willard; they told him of their lives, of their compulsions, of their failures. Old Wing Biddlebaum, the berry picker, years before had been a schoolteacher. He had loved the boys in his charge, and he had been, in fact, one of those few teachers who understand young people. But one of his pupils, having conceived a strong affection for his teacher, had accused him of homosexuality. Wing Biddlebaum, though innocent, was driven out of town. In Winesburg, he became the best berry picker in the region. But always the same hands that earned his livelihood were a source of wonder and fear to him. When George Willard encountered him in the berry field Wing's hands went forward as if to caress the youth. But a wave of horror swept over him, and he hurriedly thrust them into his pockets. To George, also, Wing's hands seemed odd, mysterious.

Kate Swift, once George's teacher, saw in him a future writer. She tried to tell him what writing was, what it meant. George did not understand exactly, but he understood that Kate was speaking, not as his teacher, but as a woman. One night, in her house, she embraced him, for George was now a young man with whom she had fallen in love. On another night, when all of Winesburg seemed asleep, she went to his room. But just as she was on the point of yielding to him, she struck him and ran away, leaving George lonely and frustrated.

Kate lived across the street from the Presbyterian church. The pastor, Reverend Curtis Hartman, accidentally had learned that he could see into Kate's room from his study in the bell tower of the church. Night after night he looked through the window at Kate in her bed.

He wanted at first to prove his faith, but his flesh was weak. One night, the same night Kate had fled from George Willard, he saw her come into her room. He watched her. Naked, she threw herself on the bed and furiously pounded the pillows. Then she arose, knelt, and began to pray. With a cry, the minister got up from his chair, swept the Bible to the floor, smashed the glass in the window, and dashed out into the darkness. Running to the newspaper office, he burst in upon George. Wild-eyed, his fist dripping blood, he told the astonished young man that God had appeared to him in the person of a naked woman, that Kate Swift was the instrument of the Almighty, and that he was saved.

Besides Kate Swift, there were other women in George's life. There was Helen White, the banker's daughter. One night George and Helen went out together. At first they laughed and kissed, but then a strange new maturity overcame them and kept them apart. Louise Trunnion, a farm girl, wrote to George, saying that she was his if he wanted her. After dark he went out to the farm and they went for a walk. There, in a berry field, George Willard enjoyed the love that Helen White had refused him.

Like Louise Trunnion, Louise Bentley also wanted love. Before going to live in Winesburg, Louise had lived on a farm, forgotten and unloved by a greedy, fanatical father who had desired a boy instead of a daughter. In Winesburg she lived with the Hardy family while she went to school. She was a good student, praised by her teachers, but she was resented by the two Hardy girls, who believed that Louise was always showing off. More than ever, she wanted someone to love. One day she sent young John Hardy a note, and a few weeks later she gave herself to him. When it became clear that she was pregnant, Louise and John were married.

John reproached her for cruelty toward her son David. She would not nurse her child and for long periods of time she would ignore him. Since she had never really loved her husband, nor he her, the marriage was not a happy one. At last she and John separated, and shortly afterward her father took young David to live with him on the farm.

Old Jesse Bentley was convinced that God had manifested himself in his grandchild, that the young David, like the Biblical hero, would be a saviour, the conqueror of the Philistines who owned the land Jesse Bentley wanted for himself. One day the old man took the boy into the fields with him. Young David had brought along a little lamb, and the grandfather prepared to offer the animal as a sacrifice to the Almighty. The youngster, terrified, struck his grandfather and ran away, never to return to Winesburg.

The time came when George Willard had to choose between staying in Winesburg and starting out on his career as a writer. Shortly after his mother's death, George got up early one morning and walked to the railroad station. There, with the postmistress' expression of good luck in his ears, he boarded the train and left Winesburg behind him.

THE WINGS OF THE DOVE

Type of work: Novel
Author: Henry James (1843-1916)
Type of plot: Psychological realism
Time of plot: c. 1900
Locale: London and Venice
First published: 1902

Principal characters:
MILLY THEALE, a rich American girl
MRS. STRINGHAM, an American friend of Milly Theale
MRS. LOWDER, an English friend of Mrs. Stringham
KATE CROY, Mrs. Lowder's niece
MERTON DENSHER, Kate Croy's fiancé
LORD MARK, another suitor for Kate Croy's hand
SIR LUKE STRETT, an eminent British doctor

Critique:

The idea of a sick woman who strove to live a lifetime within a few months was on the mind of Henry James for many years before this book was written. He finally found the characters to fit the situation, and the result was *The Wings of the Dove,* one of his finest novels. The admirable character of "the dove," Milly Theale, was modeled avowedly on James' own cousin, Mary Temple. The charm of Milly Theale is that her sufferings are not overt. They are all the more poignant, however, because they are hidden.

The Story:

Kate Croy was dependent upon her aunt, Mrs. Lowder, because Kate's own father was a ne'er-do-well. Mrs. Lowder had great plans for her niece, and she encouraged Lord Mark as a suitor for Kate's hand. Kate's own mind was set on a young reporter, Merton Densher, who worked on one of the London papers. While Mrs. Lowder liked Densher, and even invited him to her home, she did not want him to marry her niece, for he had no apparent prospects of money or a place in society. Mrs. Lowder breathed easier when she learned that the young man was being sent by his newspaper to America, to write a series of articles on life in the United States.

While he was in New York, Densher made the acquaintance of a pretty young American, Milly Theale, who had recently inherited a large fortune through the death of her parents.

A few weeks later Milly Theale asked a Boston friend, Mrs. Stringham, an elderly widow and a writer, to go with her to Europe. Within a matter of days they had taken passage on a liner and soon arrived in Italy. They traveled up the Italian peninsula and into Switzerland. Restless, Milly soon decided that she would like to go to London.

When they had arrived in England, Mrs. Stringham sent word of her arrival to Mrs. Lowder, the one real acquaintance she had in that country from her schooldays many years before. Mrs. Stringham and Milly Theale immediately became familiar callers at Mrs. Lowder's home. Because of her beauty, money, and attractive personality, Milly was a great success. Lord Mark became infatuated with her. Milly and Kate Croy became fast friends.

Aware that she was ill, Milly went to see Sir Luke Strett, an eminent surgeon who informed her that there was nothing surgery or medicine could do to save her, and he advised her to make the best of the time she had left. Although Kate Croy, Mrs. Lowder, and Mrs. Stringham knew that she had only a few months to live, Milly requested them to keep silent in the matter. Her intention was to enjoy herself as much as possible.

Great friends as Kate Croy and Milly Theale were, they never mentioned their mutual acquaintance, Merton Densher. One day, while walking in the National Art Galleries, Milly saw him and her friend Kate together. Kate and Densher enlisted the aid of Mrs. Stringham and Milly to further their courtship. Milly, herself a little in love with Densher, was only too glad to help him be near Kate.

Soon Kate hit upon a way to bring her affair with Densher to a happy conclusion. She told the young man to marry Milly, thus making her happy for the few remaining months of her life. Kate had seen clearly that Milly was falling in love with Densher. Kate realized that Milly's fortune would be left after her death to Densher, who would then be free to marry Kate and would have sufficient money to allay any objections Mrs. Lowder might have to the match. Kate was sure that Mrs. Lowder or Mrs. Stringham would not try to prevent a marriage between Milly and Merton Densher, for she knew. that the two older women loved Milly enough to go to any lengths to make her final days happy.

The four women, accompanied by Densher, went to Venice for the winter months, Milly on the advice of Sir Luke Strett. Densher made little headway with his plan to marry Milly until Mrs. Lowder and Kate returned to England for a few weeks. Before they left, Kate made Densher promise that he would do as she had planned. Densher's conscience rebelled at the duplicity of the scheme, and he was not sure that when the plan was worked out to its finish Kate would still want him. As a sign that there was mutual trust between them, he asked Kate to go to his rooms with him. She did so the day before she left Venice, leaving her lover honor-bound to try to marry another woman.

One day, as Densher approached the house Milly had taken for the winter, he saw Lord Mark leaving. He soon found out from Mrs. Stringham that Lord Mark had proposed to Milly and had been rejected because the girl had detected unwanted sympathy in his proposal and had suspected that he was after her money rather than her love. Densher believed, rightly, that Lord Mark's rejection gave him some reason to be hopeful. He informed Milly that she was the only reason he was neglecting his work. She was highly pleased and hoped that he would propose.

Lord Mark disappeared from Venice for almost a month. Then Densher discovered him in a café, shortly after Densher had been refused admittance to Milly's house. Immediately Densher knew what had happened. Lord Mark had, in some way, discovered the engagement between Densher and Kate and had informed Milly. Densher attempted to hit upon some plan to right the situation. Three days later Mrs. Stringham came to him and told him what had happened. It was as he had guessed. What he had not guessed, however, was that Milly had ceased to take any interest in living and was refusing to eat or talk to anyone. Mrs. Stringham, desperate, had sent for Sir Luke Strett.

Densher returned to London but did not, at first, go to see Kate. He could not face her after the turn which their plans had taken, and he could not bear the idea of having hurt Milly as he had done. Finally, on Christmas Day, he had a premonition. He hurried to Sir Luke Strett's residence. There he found Mrs. Lowder, who told him that the previous day she had received a telegram telling of Milly's death. A few days later a letter arrived from Venice. Without opening it, Densher knew what the message was, for it was addressed in Milly's handwriting. He went immediately to see Kate, who also guessed that it was a letter informing Densher that she had left him part of her fortune so that he and Kate might marry. Neither of them dared to open the letter because they were ashamed of their conduct toward Milly. They burned the letter in the fireplace.

Within ten days another letter came from a New York law firm. Densher did not open it, but sent it with a short note to Kate. She came to his rooms with it. She wanted to know why he had sent it on to her. He replied that it was up to her to answer whether he should take the money that was offered by it, for he could never marry her with the money Milly had left him.

Kate refused to answer him or to open the letter, lest the large amount of the fortune tempt either of them into accepting it. Finally Densher said he wanted to marry her, but only as they had been before the arrival of Milly Theale. Kate left, after reminding him that they could never be the same, that such was impossible, for the events pertaining to Milly Theale had imbedded themselves into their souls.

THE WINTER'S TALE

Type of work: Drama
Author: William Shakespeare (1564-1616)
Type of plot: Tragi-comedy
Time of plot: The legendary past
Locale: Sicilia and Bohemia
First presented: 1611

Principal characters:
LEONTES, King of Sicilia
HERMIONE, his queen
POLIXENES, King of Bohemia
CAMILLO, Leontes' counselor
PERDITA, Leontes' daughter
FLORIZEL, Polixenes' son
PAULINA, Hermione's maid
AUTOLYCUS, a rogue

Critique:

Shakespeare defined a winter's tale as one of gentle melancholy, and this play, although it has the form of a romantic comedy, has many elements of real tragedy. This was one of the last of Shakespeare's plays, written in the decline of his life when he had become sad and embittered. The plot, motivated by unreasonable and cruel jealousy, is moderated by the charming romance of the young lovers, Perdita and Florizel. The source of the plot was Greene's *Pandosto, The Triumph of Time* (1588) which Shakespeare revised by adding some new characters and strengthening old ones.

The Story:

Polixenes, King of Bohemia, was the guest of Leontes, King of Sicilia. The two men had been friends since boyhood, and there was much celebrating and joyousness during the visit. At last Polixenes decided that he must return to his home country. Although Leontes urged him to extend his visit, Polixenes refused, saying that he had not seen his young son for a long time. Then Leontes asked Hermione, his wife, to do her part in persuading Polixenes to remain. Hermione did as her husband asked and finally Polixenes yielded to her pleas. The fact that Polixenes had listened to Hermione's request after refusing his own urgings aroused Leontes' suspicion. Quickly he decided that Hermione and Polixenes were lovers and that he had been cuckolded.

Leontes was of a jealous disposition, even seeking constant reassurance that his son Mamillius was his own offspring. Jealously misjudging his wife and his old friend, Leontes was so angered by this latest turn of events that he ordered Camillo, his chief counselor, to poison Polixenes. All Camillo's attempts to dissuade Leontes from his scheme only strengthened the jealous man's feelings of hate. Nothing could persuade the king that Hermione was true to him. Eventually Camillo agreed to poison Polixenes, but only on condition that Leontes return to Hermione with no more distrust.

Polixenes himself had noticed a change in Leontes' attitude toward him. When he questioned Camillo, the sympathetic lord revealed the whole plot to poison him. Together they hastily embarked for Bohemia.

Upon learning that Polixenes and Camillo had fled, Leontes was more than ever convinced that his guest and his wife had been guilty of carrying on an affair. He conjectured that Polixenes and Camillo had been plotting together all the while and planning his murder. Moreover, he decided that Hermione, who was pregnant, was in all likelihood bearing Polixenes' child and not his. Publicly he accused Hermione of adultery and commanded that her son be taken from her. She herself was put into prison. Although his servants protested the order, Leontes' mind could not be changed.

In prison Hermione gave birth to a baby girl. Paulina, her attendant, thought that the sight of the baby girl might cause Leontes to relent in his harshness, and so she carried the child to the palace. Instead of forgiving his wife, Leontes became more incensed and demanded that the child be put to death. He instructed Antigonus, Paulina's husband, to take the baby to a far-off desert shore and there abandon it. Although the lord pleaded release from this cruel command, he was at length forced to put out to sea with the intention of leaving the child to perish on some lonely coast.

Leontes had sent two messengers to consult the Oracle of Delphi to determine Hermione's guilt. When the men returned, Leontes summoned his wife and the whole court to hear the verdict. The messengers read a scroll which stated that Hermione was innocent, as well as Polixenes and Camillo, that Leontes was a tyrant, and that he would live without an heir until that which was lost was found.

The king, refusing to believe the oracle, declared its findings false, and again accused Hermione of infidelity. In the midst of his tirade a servant rushed in to say that young Mamillius had died because of sorrow and anxiety over his mother's plight. On hearing this news Hermione fell into a swoon and was carried to her chambers. Soon afterward Paulina returned to say that her mistress was dead. At this news Leontes, who had already begun to believe the oracle after news of his son's death, beat his breast with self-rage. He reproached himself bitterly for his insane jealousy which had led to these unhappy events. In repentance the king swore that he would have the legend of the deaths of his son and wife engraved on their tombstones and that he himself would do penance thereafter.

Meanwhile Antigonus took the baby girl to a desert country near the sea. Heartsick at having to abandon her, the old courtier laid a bag of gold and jewels by her with instructions that she should be called Perdita, a name revealed to him in a dream. After Antigonus completed these tasks, he was attacked and killed by a bear. Later his ship was wrecked in a storm and all hands were lost. Thus no news of the expedition reached Sicilia. A kind shepherd who had found Perdita watched, however, the deaths of Antigonus and his men.

Sixteen years passed, bringing with them many changes. Leontes was a broken man, grieving alone in his palace. Little Perdita had grown into a beautiful and charming young woman under the care of the shepherd. So lovely was she that Prince Florizel, heir to the throne of Bohemia and the son of Polixenes, had fallen madly in love with her.

Unaware of the girl's background, and knowing only that his son was in love with a young shepherdess, Polixenes and Camillo, now his most trusted servant, disguised themselves and visited a sheep-shearing festival, where they saw Florizel, dressed as a shepherd, dancing with a lovely young woman. Although he realized that the shepherdess was of noble bearing, Polixenes revealed himself when Florizel was about to become engaged to Perdita, and in great rage he forbade the marriage and threatened to punish his son.

Florizel then made secret plans to elope with Perdita to a foreign country in order to escape his father's wrath. Camillo, pitying the young couple, advised Florizel to embark for Sicilia and to pretend that he was a messenger of good-will from the King of Bohemia. Camillo supplied the young man with letters of introduction to Leontes. Camillo's plan was also to inform Polixenes of the lovers' escape, travel to Sicilia to find them, and thus enable himself to return home once more.

The poor shepherd, frightened by the king's wrath, decided to tell Polixenes how, years before, he had found the baby and a bag of gold and jewels by her side. Fate intervened, however, and the shepherd never reached the royal palace. Intercepted by the rogue Autolycus, he was put aboard the ship sailing to Sicilia.

Soon Florizel and Perdita arrived in Sicilia, followed by Polixenes and Camillo. When the old shepherd heard how Leontes had lost a daughter, he described the finding of Perdita. Leontes, convinced that Perdita and his own abandoned infant were the same, was joyfully reunited with his daughter. Polixenes immediately gave his consent to the marriage of Florizel and Perdita. The only sorrowful circumstance to mar the happiness of all concerned was the tragic death of Hermione.

One day Paulina asked Leontes to visit a newly erected statue of the dead woman in Hermione's chapel. Leontes, ever faithful to the memory of his dead wife—even to the point of promising Paulina never to marry again—gathered his guests and took them to view the statue. Standing in the chapel, amazed at the wonderful lifelike quality of the work, they heard strains of soft music. Suddenly the statue descended from its pedestal and was revealed as the living Hermione. She had spent the sixteen years in seclusion while awaiting some word of her daughter. The happy family once more united, Hermione completely forgave her repentant husband. He and Polixenes were again the best of friends, rejoicing in the happiness of Perdita and Florizel.

WINTERSET

Type of work: Drama
Author: Maxwell Anderson (1888-1959)
Type of plot: Romantic tragedy
Time of plot: Twentieth century
Locale: New York
First presented: 1935

Principal characters:
ESDRAS, an old man
GARTH, his son
MIRIAMNE, his daughter
TROCK, a murderer
SHADOW, his henchman
JUDGE GAUNT
MIO, Romagna's son

Critique:

The plot of Winterset is based upon the famous murder trial of Sacco and Vanzetti. Mio is a classical tragic character in the sense that his weakness lay in his desire to revenge his father's death, yet his love for Miriamne would not allow him to consummate his desire. He had lived all his seventeen years for the revenge which he could no longer fulfill without injuring the girl he loved. Because he still felt compelled to exonerate his father, there was no solution to his conflict, and he had to die.

The Story:

Trock and Shadow walked warily under the bridge by the tenement where Garth lived with his old father, Esdras, and his fifteen-year-old sister, Miriamne. Trock had just been released from jail, where he had served a sentence for his part in a murder for which Romagna had been electrocuted. Judge Gaunt, who had presided over the trial when Romagna had been convicted, was said to be mad and to be roaming the country telling people that the trial had been unfair. A college professor had also begun an investigation of the old murder trial. Trock had come to the tenement district to see Garth, who had witnessed the murder which Trock had really committed. Garth had not testified at the trial, and Trock wanted to warn him

never to tell what he had seen.

Trock threatened to kill Garth if he talked. Miriamne knew nothing about her brother's part in this crime, but after she heard Trock threaten her brother, she questioned him and learned a little about the killing. Miriamne loved Garth, but she knew that his silence about the murder was wrong. Old Esdras watched and comforted his two children.

To the same tenement district came Mio and his friend, Carr. Mio was seventeen, and he had learned that somewhere in the tenements lived a man who knew that Romagna was innocent. Mio and Miramne saw one another on the street and fell in love. Knowing that he had to speak to Miriamne, Mio sent Carr away. When Miriamne heard Mio's full name, Bartolemeo Romagna, she told him that he must go away and never see her again, for Miriamne knew then that Mio was the son of the man who had died for the murder Trock had committed. Mio told Miriamne that he had been four years old when his father had been electrocuted and that he lived only co prove his father's innocence.

While the lovers were talking, Shadow and Trock appeared on the street, and Miriamne hid Mio in the shadow so that the two men could not see him. The gangsters were looking for Judge Gaunt in order to silence him. The judge had also come to the tenement, and Garth, meeting him, had made the crazed man go to Esdras' apartment for safety. But Shadow wanted no part in killing the judge. As he left, Trock sent two henchmen after Shadow to kill him. Mio saw the shooting. Feeling that he had come to the right place to learn the truth of the old killing, he waited.

In Esdras' room the judge awoke, refreshed and normal once more. Realizing where he was and what he had done, the judge asked Garth and Esdras to say nothing of his mad claims that Romagna's trial had been unfair. The judge did not want the case to be reopened any more than did Trock. Esdras offered to guide Judge Gaunt part way back to his home.

After the two old men had left, Mio knocked on the door. He had been directed to Garth's home by neighbors. At the sight of Miriamne he was bewildered until she explained that Garth was her brother. She asked Mio to leave, but first she wanted him to tell her that he loved her. Garth angrily interrupted the lovers and ordered Mio to leave. As Mio was preparing to go, Judge Gaunt and Esdras returned, forced to turn back by driving sleet. Mio recognized the judge and began questioning him and Garth about the trial. Garth's story was that he had not witnessed the murder for which Mio's father had died. Judge Gaunt insisted that Romagna was guilty. Mio pointed out that evidence at the trial was biased because his father had been an anarchist. The judge said that if he had thought the trial unjust, he would have allowed a retrial.

The steady denials of Garth and Judge Gaunt nearly broke Mio's spirit. Suddenly Trock entered the apartment. Mio grew more suspicious. Then Shadow came to the door. The sight of the henchman he had thought dead terrified Trock. Shadow had been shot, but he lived long enough to accuse Trock of his murder. After Shadow died, Judge Gaunt again became deranged. He thought he was in court, and Mio tricked him into admitting that Romagna had been an anarchist and as such should have been put to death. When Trock threatened to kill them all, Mio knew that he was near the end of his search.

In the midst of Mio's glory the police came looking for Judge Gaunt, who had been missing from his home for many days. Mio accused Trock of murdering Shadow, but when he sent the police into an inner room where Garth had dragged the body, the corpse was not there. When Miriamne also denied his charges, Mio admitted that he must have been dreaming, for he had seen a pleading message in Miriamne's eyes that directed his decision.

As the police took Judge Gaunt away, Trock went also, leaving Garth to face Mio's accusations. But Mio was helpless because he loved Miriamne. Free at last to vindicate his father's name, he was tied by Miriamne's love for her brother. In spite of Miriamne's fears that his life was in danger, Mio left Esdras' home.

Mio felt that there was nothing left for him but to die, for he could not live and remain silent about his father's death. While he hesitated outside the tenement, Miriamne came to join him, and they saw Garth carrying the body of Shadow from the alley where it had fallen. Esdras joined Mio outside. The boy's search for justice and his courage had made the old man see that Garth's silence had been wrong. Esdras told Mio that he was going to the police to report Shadow's murder. Mio cautioned Esdras that he would not try to save Garth by remaining silent about the Romagna case, but Esdras said that Mio owed them nothing. He went to inform the police.

Alone with Mio, Miriamne tried to find hope of happiness for him. At last she reminded him that his father would have forgiven his killers, and Mio realized that she was right. Still, he was determined to reveal the truth. Then Esdras returned and told him that Trock's henchmen were guarding the streets and that there was no way of escape.

4175

As Mio dashed down a passage toward the river, Miriamne heard the sound of shooting. She ran to her lover and found him dying. Then she ran toward the same passage, into the fire of Trock's machine gun. Dying, she crawled back to Mio. Esdras and Garth, still alive, carried the dead lovers out of the cold, wet winter night.

4176

WITH FIRE AND SWORD

Type of work: Novel
Author: Henryk Sienkiewicz (1846-1916)
Type of plot: Historical romance
Time of plot: Seventeenth century
Locale: Poland and the Ukraine
First published: 1883

Principal characters:

PAN YAN SKSHETUSKI, a young Polish officer
PRINCESS HELENA KURTSEVICH, his beloved
HMELNITSKI, hetman of the Zaporojian Cossacks
BOGUN, a Cossack officer
PRINCE YEREMI VISHNYEVETSKI, general of the Polish forces

Critique:

With Fire and Sword is the first, and best, of three novels written by Sienkiewicz to dramatize Polish military history in the seventeenth century, at a time when the Poles were struggling to establish and preserve national unity. The background of this novel is the revolt of the Cossacks and the heroic defense of Zbaraź by the Poles in the days of the Commonwealth. Characterization is negligible. The writer's emphasis is always upon military valor and the wider panorama of history, and the exploits of Prince Yeremi Vishnyevetski, Polish national hero, and his captains overshadow a rather conventional love story.

The Story:

It was December, 1647, in the wilderness of steppeland and marsh, when Lieutenant Yan Skshetuski found a Cossack traveler who had been attacked by unknown enemies. Grateful to Skshetuski for assisting him, the Cossack rode off after pledging friendship with the young officer.

Prince Yeremi Vishnyevetski had sent Pan Yan Skshetuski to the Khan to obtain that ruler's aid in punishing certain Tartars who had raided the prince's estates beyond the Dnieper. Pan Yan broke his return journey at Chigirin. There, at the inn of Dopula, he learned that the man whose life he had saved was a rebel Cossack who had escaped to the Saitch, the Cossack territory, where he too could threaten Prince Yeremi's domain.

When Pan Yan left Chigirin, he was anxious to get to Lubni, where a pleased prince awaited him. Along the way Pan Yan had occasion to aid the widow of Prince Constantine Kurtsevich and her orphaned niece, Princess Helena, with whom the lieutenant fell in love. The five sons of Princess Kurtsevich and a young man named Bogun joined them. Bogun's animosity toward Pan Yan convinced the lieutenant that the man was jealous because of Helena. Bogun was an adopted sixth son of the Princess Kurtsevich.

The party stopped at the family estate, Rozlogi, which rightfully belonged to Helena, but which was in the hands of the aunt and her sons. Pan Yan offered not to interfere with the present ownership of Rozlogi if the princess would give him Helena as a wife. The princess promised to send Bogun away and to bring Helena to Lubni.

Confiding in Prince Yeremi, Pan Yan confessed his love for Helena. Much to Pan Yan's joy, the indulgent commander offered to care for Helena as a daughter. Later, wishing to learn about Hmelnitski's activities in the Saitch, Prince Yeremi sent Pan Yan there. This mission gave the lieutenant a chance to stop at Rozlogi on the way.

After Pan Yan had passed through Kudak, the key city commanding the Saitch, his party was attacked by a group of Tartars, Cossacks, and Zaporojians, and Pan Yan was taken prisoner.

Hmelnitski had become the hetman of

the Saitch. Tugai Bey, hetman of the Tartars, was his ally. Pan Yan had carried three letters in which Prince Yeremi requested safe conduct for his envoy. The men to whom these letters were addressed were massacred by the savage Cossack Brotherhood of the Saitch. Hmelnitski, recognizing Pan Yan as his rescuer on the steppes, persuaded Tugai Bey not to order the lieutenant's death.

From the Saitch rode Hmelnitski and the Zaporojians and Tartars. From Chigirin, under young Pototski, marched the armies of the king. In the enemy camp Pan Yan mourned his inability to help his ruler. After days of battle the Commonwealth army fell under the onslaught of the attackers. Next Prince Yeremi himself came to quell the rebellion. Deciding to retreat to the Dnieper, Hmelnitski released Pan Yan, who hurried at once to Rozlogi. He found the house in ruins.

During the battle Bogun had found out about Princess Kurtzevich's plan to marry Helena to Pan Yan. He went to Rozlogi, killed the princess and two of her sons, and was himself wounded. One of his allies, Zagloba, turned against him and rescued Helena. In disguise, the pair of fugitives escaped in the darkness to seek refuge and safety. After Bogun had burned Rozlogi, Prince Yeremi, learning of the raid, sent soldiers to find Helena. When the search proved unsuccessful, the prince tried vainly to console Pan Yan, whose grief nearly drove him mad.

The prince and his followers, forced to retreat from Lubni toward the Dnieper, left behind them their rich estates and towns. Harried by Tartars and Cossacks, they marched through forests set afire by the rebels. When they arrived at the Dnieper, the prince sent the women to Vilna. He, with his troops, headed toward the Ukraine. There he strengthened his forces and rested.

Hmelnitski followed a waiting course in hopes of averting a military campaign; his plan was to effect negotiations which might reward him with a high position. The king offered independence to the Zaporojian Cossacks in return for loyalty to the Commonwealth. If Prince Yeremi attacked and Hmelnitski resisted, it would appear that the hetman did not want peace. Therefore he urged part of his followers to oppose Prince Yeremi, while Hmelnitski himself seemed to hold the truce. Pan Kisel was the leader of a government faction that wished to negotiate with Hmelnitski. Prince Yeremi decided to act independently and attack.

While on an errand for Prince Yeremi, Pan Yan met Zagloba, who told the young lieutenant that Helena had found safety in a convent.

A battle between the Commonwealth troops and Hmelnitski's Cossacks began. Prince Yeremi gained in popularity and soon his army had greatly increased. Before long he was the greatest power in the Commonwealth.

At last Pan Yan petitioned his commander for two months' leave so that he could marry Helena. Prince Yeremi himself was undergoing severe inner conflict, for he realized that the future of the Commonwealth lay in his hands. After long deliberation he announced that he would place himself under the other commanders of the Polish forces. The night before Pan Yan was to take his leave, a messenger brought word that the convent where Helena was staying had been sacked by the Cossacks.

Bogun, her jealous lover, had led the attack. When he went to get Helena, however, she had stabbed herself and lay unconscious. When she revived, Bogun pleaded for her affections, but she refused him. He angrily threatened to murder Pan Yan.

Meanwhile Prince Yeremi had made Pan Yan colonel of a regiment. Prince Dominik Zaslavski Ostrogski was appointed commander-in-chief of the Commonwealth armies.

During a battle Bogun captured Zagloba, who then learned that Helena was still alive but in Bogun's keeping. Zagloba was rescued during a raid in which Bogun escaped alive. Pan Yan, Zagloba, and two other officers set out to hunt for Helena. When news that the

Commonwealth armies had been defeated and completely routed reached the searchers, they hurried to Lvoff to join Prince Yeremi's shattered forces. At Lvoff many loyal citizens gathered, clamoring for Prince Yeremi's leadership in the fight against the Cossacks and Tartars.

After accepting the command, the prince hurried to Warsaw to attend the election for king, disputed between Prince Karl and Prince Kazimir. The first advocated fighting Hmelnitski; the other favored negotiating with the Cossacks. At last Prince Karl withdrew in favor of Prince Kazimir. Bogun was reported killed in a duel. Because Hmelnitski was expected to withdraw his troops after the election of Kazimir, Prince Yeremi gave Pan Yan permission to seek Helena once more.

A delegation was sent to Hmelnitski to petition for peace. Although King Kazimir had officially appointed him hetman of the Cossacks, the greedy leader smirked at the delegation and treated them poorly. Among the Cossacks was Pan Yan, disguised, hunting for Bogun should he still be alive. Hmelnitski, still favoring Pan Yan, offered to help him find Helena.

An armistice was signed, but along the borders small bands of marauders kept the war afire. Hmelnitski had little control over his Cossack warriors.

From Pan Yan's faithful servant Jendzian, who had been captured by the Cossacks, Zagloba learned that Helena was held captive by Horpyna, a witch, and a party of Pan Yan's friends went to rescue the girl. Meanwhile Pan Yan, having heard that Helena was dead, was ill and grief-stricken. The rescue party, with Helena, began its perilous return journey through enemy country. On the way they learned that Bogun was still alive. As they rode toward safety they fell into the thick of a battle. Helena was entrusted to Jendzian, who led her through the lines unharmed.

Prince Yeremi and Hmelnitski again engaged in battle. The Cossacks and Tartars laid siege to the city of Zbaraż, to which Prince Yeremi had withdrawn, but could not break through the city walls. When supplies had run low, Pan Yan volunteered to slip past the Cossacks and summon help for the besieged city. After a perilous journey Pan Yan reached the king with news of Prince Yeremi's heroic stand against Hmelnitski and the Tartars. King Kazimir at once ordered an attack on the enemy. Exhausted and hungry, Pan Yan lay in the care of servants when Jendzian brought him news that Helena was alive and safe.

The Cossacks were routed in a decisive battle. When Bogun was found among the captured Cossacks, Prince Yeremi turned him over to Pan Yan for punishment. Pan Yan generously gave his old enemy his life. Prince Yeremi and his followers were called the lions of Zbaraż, even by the Cossacks. And Pan Yan, who had traveled through the enemy lines to bring help to the beleaguered city, was called the bravest of them all.

WITHIN THE GATES

Type of work: Drama
Author: Sean O'Casey (1884-
Type of plot: Morality play
Time of plot: Twentieth century
Locale: In a London park
First presented: 1933

Principal characters:
THE DREAMER, a young poet
THE YOUNG WOMAN, Jannice, a prostitute
THE OLD WOMAN, her mother, a drunkard
THE ATHEIST, foster father of Jannice
THE BISHOP, Jannice's father

Critique:

This expressionistic morality play, the least-produced play of a seldom-produced playwright, has had a very mixed reception by audiences and critics alike. It belongs to the Devon period of plays by an expatriate, though still very Irish, writer who followed Shaw into English exile and who became in part his successor in the theater. The play, in four parts or seasons, is a kind of war cry against the modern, impoverished spirit of man, weighed down by mass conformity, though protested against by the poet-dreamer. In its simplest outline, the play is a modern Everywoman—O'Casey's great concern for the life force is brought to focus here—who turns, in her final days on earth, to family, church, social agency, lover, and finally, poet. Though she dies making the sign of the cross, he alone sustains her with love and compassion.

The Story:

It was spring within the gates of a London park where a war memorial stood in strong contrast to the surrounding spring flowers. A group of young people, costumed like the spring vegetation, sang and danced to a poem newly written by The Dreamer. His song expressed hope for the world through the earth mother's renewal of old promises. Contrasted with this lively group were The Down-and-Outs, those bowed by the master classes and the prejudices they spawn.

The Dreamer, who sensed the independent spirit disguised by her conventional street-walker's appearance, followed The Young Woman, only to be rejected by her. His friend The Atheist urged the poet to leave her adrift. As the girl's foster father, he explained to the interested young man that she had a fine mind which forever darted first to the left, then to the right. A young divinity student named Gilbert had fathered and forgotten her. Her housemaid mother, turned away from the college gate, had placed her child in a church orphanage, where the nuns treated her as a child of sin and impressed fancifully on her mind the hell for which she was probably destined. The Atheist, smitten with the good looks and fierce spirit of the mother, took them both in, only to be deserted when the daughter became a prostitute and the mother a drunkard. Both were beset by their own vision of sin and full of hate for each other.

Since the godless man gave the girl no poetry but only intellectual exercises, The Dreamer suggested that The Atheist had taken her from one darkness into another. He begged the foster father to take her home again while there still was loveliness in her, but The Atheist was too fond of his independent life of rabble-rousing through speechifying and pamphleteering.

Within the park appeared vested interests represented by nursemaids and their aristocratic charges, a policewoman, The Bishop and his sister, chair attendants, a gardener, a Salvation Army officer, evangelists, and politicians in various types of hats which corresponded to their points of view. The Dreamer moved among them all and urged them to throw off their worldly bonds; for them he wrote the Song of the Down-and-Outs, a lament for those who whine through life with dread and who are sick with apprehension, the victims of dead traditions.

The Young Woman, in spite of a heart condition, ran after her foster father. Rebuffed, she still persisted in disclosing her dreams of hell and heaven. She turned next to a young Salvation Army officer who offered her the minimum security of the body, though he was interested in her for other reasons of the flesh. The Gardener, in love with physical love and unresponsive to her claim for affectionate understanding, rejected her and refused to marry her when he learned she was ill. The gates then closed on this satiric spring idyl.

Summer found the gates opening on the people's sensuous enjoyment of the lovely day, bellowing summer's deceptive pleasures. Conventional morality was the topic of discussion among the Down-and-Outs; The Bishop, guiltily avoiding his sister, who disliked the commoners, was their leader while on a kind of pilgrimage among the "lower classes." His morality was tested by chair attendants wanting charity and by The Young Woman, who wanted redemption. She vigorously parried dogma against dogma—to his chagrin, for he urged her to return to her mother and the church, only to discover himself as the guilty lover and irresponsible father. After this disjointed, highly emotional reunion, The Dreamer rescued The Young Woman from the mother's violence and the passivity of the priest-father (as yet not identified by anyone but himself), who could only give her money clandestinely. She again rejected the poet, who offered her a song, and departed with the somewhat guilty-acting Salvation Army officer. She mocked the priest who saved only himself but complimented the poet on his song as the gates closed on the departing couple.

On a lovely autumn day, the park gates opened on The Dreamer and The Young Woman, he ecstatic and she drunk with wine and joy. She begged him not to leave her because in his absence she might return to her Salvation Army lover. The young poet insisted that the officer could give her neither peace nor joy, for his peace brought a measured joy, whereas she needed joy to find peace.

The political forces came together armed with newspapers and debated the origin of God and the universe. The Young Woman ended the argument by stating that their combined knowledge could not fill a spoon. She, uneasy in her soul, sang the poet's song of love to the background chanting of despair. Her panic mounted as she felt death's clutch and she shouted for help, but the only solace she found was the conventional responses of The Bishop, responses she rejected with telling arguments against his stringent denial of life. Nor could The Atheist or Salvation Army arguments win her; only the kiss and embrace of man for woman took her through the gates.

Winter came through the gates into the desolate park as the bugle call, The Last Post, set the mood. The Bishop had returned with his sister, he now strongly moved to compassion, the desire to do the right thing, and she determined to prevent it.

The Old Woman, also touched by conscience, went looking for her daughter but presented her wreath to the war memorial because her one week of happiness had been spent with an Irish soldier killed later in a senseless battle. She accosted The Bishop, a thin thought of recollection assailing her, but he denied her and the girl and, prompted by his sister, reverted to his worship of self.

The men of argument proposed the riddles of modern psychology, again not filling a spoon with knowledge.

The Young Woman now wished to reject the poet-lover for The Bishop, knowing as she did so that life was fast going out of her. She revived long enough to revile her sob-saying mother, who in turn reviled The Bishop's sister in garbled ritual for oaths.

A great struggle for supremacy over the dying woman's thoughts ensued: The Bishop with Latin comfort, the Down-and-Outs with conventional sympathy, but the poet with song and dance of an Old Testament elegiac sort, a defiance of the world and a praise of God. The priest intoned as she haltingly made the sign of the cross, the hymn of Down-and-Outs praised oblivion, and the poet sang his song of praise to The Young Woman who was dying within the gates.

WOLF SOLENT

Type of work: Novel
Author: John Cowper Powys (1872-1963)
Type of plot: Psychological realism
Time of plot: Twentieth century
Locale: Devon, England
First published: 1929

Principal characters:

WOLF SOLENT
ANN SOLENT, his mother
GERDA TORP, his wife
MR. TORP, Gerda's father, a stonecutter
LOB TORP, his son
SELENA GAULT, Wolf's father's mistress
DARNLEY OTTER, Wolf's friend
JASON OTTER, Darnley's brother, a poet
SQUIRE URQUHART, a wealthy historian, Wolf's employer
CHRISTIE MALAKITE, Wolf's spiritual mate
MR. MALAKITE, her father, a bookseller
BOB WEEVIL, Gerda's friend
MATTIE SMITH, Wolf's half-sister
ALBERT SMITH, a hatter
OLWEN, a child living with the Smiths

Critique:

In this novel Powys presents against a contemporary setting some of his ideas on the mystical power that shapes all men's actions. The hero, Wolf Solent, attempts to find himself and his place in the universe, but he is constantly caught between the dictates of his own nature and the conventions of the world in which he lives. This world is not merely conventional, for Powys' Dorset is a mystic place of powerful spirits affecting human beings and conducive to strange nocturnal wanderings, as well as a community haunted by incest, disturbing graves, and sinister suggestions of murder. The powerful spirits are reflections of the animal nature of human beings, forces springing from man that defy his best efforts to impose a rational order on himself and his world. Many of the names of the characters, such as Wolf Solent and Jason Otter, suggest this idea of the animal nature of man. At times Powys has his characters dwell at great length on their own personalities and on the symbolic nature of all they have discovered

in experience. Despite the turgidity of some of these reflections and the loose structure of the novel, Wolf Solent is not without forceful appeal. For many modern readers it is too prolix to carry deep tragic meaning. For others it is a powerful demonstration of man's essential loneliness and lack of control.

The Story:

Wolf Solent, a thirty-five-year-old history master from London, decided to accept a post in the Dorset village that he and his mother had left when he was ten years old. His father, a teacher in the village school, had carried on several affairs with local women and had died in disgrace years before. When Wolf arrived in the village, Ramsgard, he had the promise of a job as secretary to Mr. Urquhart, the local squire, who was engaged in writing a history of the area. Wolf, haunted by the misery and poverty of the city and anticipating a peaceful existence in the area of his origin, looked forward to establishing himself in Ramsgard,

4183

where he planned to have his mother join him.

On his first day in Ramsgard, Wolf called on Selena Gault, his father's old mistress. She took him to his father's grave, which she tended with reverence, and praised his father's force and vitality in contrast to the rigid control Wolf's mother had always maintained. Wolf went to live with the Otters. There he found himself attracted to Darnley's sane kindness but repelled by Jason's erratic conversation and worship of mystic symbols.

When Wolf began to work for Squire Urquhart, he soon discovered that the Squire's proposed history was simply a chronicle of all the scandals and salacious stories of the county. About the same time Wolf met Gerda Torp, the beautiful daughter of the local stonecutter. Attracted by her beauty and worked on by all the natural symbols emerging in the long walks that he and Gerda took, he soon yielded to his own animal nature and seduced the girl in a bed of yellow bracken. Soon, following the conventions of village society, they made plans to marry. In the meantime Wolf had also met Christie Malakite, the daughter of the local bookseller. He often went to tea in Christie's small, book-filled sitting room. The spiritual attraction Christie held for him was as powerful as his physical attraction to Gerda.

Wolf had been in Ramsgard only a short time when his mother arrived. Because he could find no place for his mother to stay on her first night in Ramsgard, he accepted Selena Gault's suggestion that he take his mother to the home of Albert Smith, a local hatter. At the Smith cottage Wolf felt a sudden strong kinship with Mattie, apparently the daughter of Albert Smith. He later discovered that Mattie was, in fact, his half-sister, the illegitimate daughter of his father and Albert Smith's late wife. A young girl, Olwen, was also living at the Smiths. Olwen was the offspring of Mr. Malakite and his own oldest daughter. This knowledge of the animal spirit in-

fusing so much of Ramsgard's past made a deep impression on Wolf about the same time that he became aware of the conflict between his physical feelings for Gerda and his spiritual ties with Christie. In spite of his conflict he married Gerda.

As time passed he became more conscious of strange hints and references to the sudden death of Squire Urquhart's former secretary. He even bought Jason Otter's Mukalog, a God-figure that Jason associated with mystical and devilish powers. Wolf knew that he could not really afford the purchase, but he hoped that through ownership of the image he could rationally control the strange force of experience around him. Control, however, seemed to be breaking down for Wolf. His marriage with Gerda, a silent and impassive beauty, was not working out well, and he still felt impelled to call on Christie frequently. He suspected that Gerda was having an affair with a former suitor, Bob Weevil, a flashy young man who helped run his father's sausage shop. Only Wolf's mother seemed in full control of her destiny as she made careful plans to open a tea shop in the neighborhood.

Albert Smith died suddenly. After a great deal of discussion among the Otters, the Solents, and Selena Gault, Mattie and Olwen went to live with the Otters. There, Mattie and Darnley fell in love and eventually married, while Olwen, having come close to her sister, Christie, eventually went to live with her.

Wolf, revolting against Squire Urquhart's pornographic project, had quit his job on the history and, with Darnley Otter's help, secured a job as a teacher. In need of money, however, for he and Gerda lived in a fairly shabby house, Wolf returned to Squire Urquhart and agreed to finish the history by working evenings. Throughout the winter Wolf worked hard on the project. One evening, having been told that Christie would be alone for the night, he went to visit her. Although she was fully prepared for his visit, Wolf discovered that, bound as he was to keep Christie in the spiritual category he had created for her, he could not transform his spiritual passion into the physical. He realized then that their relationship would always remain spiritual.

When Wolf finished the history and delivered it to Squire Urquhart, he felt that he ought not to cash the check because the work had been so cheaply pornographic. Gerda, wanting the money for household improvements, could not see his point and became furious with him. In her anger she confirmed Wolf's jealous feelings and had an affair with Bob Weevil. Wolf later decided to cash the check and keep the money, but his decision came too late to heal the rupture with Gerda. However, after a few months they did achieve a kind of peace without love.

One evening, while drinking tea with Gerda, Wolf suddenly received a telepathic message from Christie. He hurried to her house to discover that old Mr. Malakite had fallen down the narrow stairs. Wolf stayed with Christie until after her father's death, comforting her and making the necessary arrangements. A short time later Christie, having no further reason to remain in Ramsgard since Wolf's love for her was simply spiritual, took Olwen and moved to Weymouth. Wolf stayed with Gerda, even though he realized more and more that she was a woman still attractive to men and that, having lost her loyalty to Wolf, she was probably having affairs with other men. Wolf realized his failure to master his feelings. Unable to control the forces within him in a sane and meaningful way, he would always struggle in his loneliness to know himself and the world of confusion around him.

THE WOMAN HATER

Type of work: Drama
Authors: Francis Beaumont (1585?-1616) and John Fletcher (1579-1625); sometimes attributed to Beaumont alone
Type of plot: Romantic comedy
Time of plot: Early seventeenth century
Locale: Milan
First presented: c. 1606

Principal characters:
ORIANA, a beautiful, witty, young girl
THE DUKE OF MILAN, in love with Oriana
COUNT VALORE, Oriana's brother
GONDARINO, general of Milan, the woman-hater
ARRIGO, a courtier
LUCIO, a lord
LAZARILLO, a glutton
A MERCER
A PANDERER
JULIA, a prostitute

Critique:

In this play Beaumont, possibly with some assistance from Fletcher, attempted to do more than could be successfully accomplished in one work. The result is a comedy which has some good moments, but which contains much undigested material. Gondarino, who gives the play its title, is a character of Jonsonian humours who is motivated solely by a pathological hatred of women. Little is done with him, however; at the end of the play he remains unregenerate, a speaker of satirical truth in his anti-feminine attitude. Lazarillo, whose only aim in life is the consumption of rare delicacies of the table, is a Gondarino on a different level. In spite of his foolishness, he carries about him such an air of genial absurdity that his punishment, marriage to a prostitute, seems unduly harsh. Oriana is an emancipated woman—beautiful, witty, bold, yet honest as well. However, with an almost incredible stupidity she allows Gondarino to maneuver her into a highly compromising position. In addition, the play also presents satirical glances at the stupidity of middle-class citizens, the affectations of courtiers, and the dishonesty of the lower class. The plot, unfortunately, is not constructed with sufficient care to carry all the burdens placed upon it.

The Story:

Wandering the streets late at night with Arrigo and Lucio, the Duke of Milan discussed various affairs of state and talked about his personal life. That day he had been presented with the head of an umbrana, a rare and delicious fish, and he had ordered it sent to Gondarino. More important, he confessed his love for Oriana, a maiden whom he had seen but never spoken with.

Although the Duke's passion was still a closely guarded secret, the news of the umbrana's head had spread abroad. It was of particular concern to Lazarillo, a courtier whose consuming passion was food. Every day Lazarillo's boy scoured the court for information concerning novel dishes to be served at the various tables, and Lazarillo exercised his wits to secure an invitation to share the most appetizing. When Lazarillo learned that umbrana was available, he was beside himself; unfortunately, however, he did not know that the Duke had already given away the fish's head.

Valore, meanwhile, was doing everything in his power to persuade his sister Oriana not to present herself at court. Because she was only fifteen and had no experience in the world, Valore feared that the temptations of the court would override her good judgment. But Oriana was determined, and, after hearing her brother's warnings, she set out. Valore, left at loose ends, was glad to see Lazarillo approaching because he could count on being amused by the glutton's foibles. Lazarillo quickly declined Valore's invitation to dine—he was after bigger game. His real business was to ask Valore to present him that morning to the Duke, from whom he hoped to extract in some manner an invitation to dinner. Valore was quite willing to make the presentation, but in order to increase the sport he ordered a professional intelligencer who happened to be at hand to shadow Lazarillo and to report any of his treasonable utterances to Lucio. While Valore was giving the spy these secret instructions, Lazarillo's boy learned that the fish's head was now to be found at Gondarino's house. Agreeing to meet Valore there later, Lazarillo hurried off in pursuit of a dinner invitation.

But Gondarino, having no use for the delicacy, had sent it off to his mercer, to whom he owed money, as a mollification. Gondarino, like Lazarillo, was ruled by one consuming passion, in his case a complete aversion to women. He was horrified, therefore, when a sudden hailstorm caused Oriana to take refuge in his house. He cursed her, reviled her, insulted her, not realizing that Oriana, who knew his reputation as a woman hater, had sought out his house deliberately in order to plague him. She answered his violence only with pleasantries. Oriana was not the only one who had been caught outdoors in the hailstorm, however; before long the Duke, Arrigo, and Lucio also made their way to Gondarino's house. Gondarino immediately petitioned to have Oriana removed, but the Duke, startled to find Oriana present, began to suspect that she had visited Gondarino for no virtuous purpose and that his host's bluster was feigned in an attempt to conceal a clandestine love affair. After a prolonged consultation with Arrigo and Lucio, the Duke decided to reserve judgment.

Meanwhile, Valore and Lazarillo also appeared, Lazarillo having sent his boy into the kitchens to inquire after the umbrana's head. Valore presented Lazarillo to the Duke, who received him cordially and even did him the honor of inviting him to dinner. Lazarillo declined, not wishing to be separated from the delicacy he had his heart set upon. Soon after the Duke's departure, however, Lazarillo was informed that the head was again missing. Once more he set out to track it down, Valore going with him. Oriana remained behind, vowing that she would dine with Gondarino; the more he protested, the more she resolved to pretend love for him in order to torment him.

Oriana was using all of her wiles on the woman hater when her campaign was interrupted by the return of the Duke, who was much distressed by his suspicions. After Oriana had left the room, he began to question Gondarino closely about his relationship with the girl. Gondarino, taking this opportunity to be revenged upon the troublesome baggage, swore to the Duke that all of his suspicions were true—that Oriana was a prostitute who had forced him to yield to her after she had pursued him for a long time. Believing, yet wishing to disbelieve, the Duke rushed out; but Gondarino's plans for Oriana were not yet terminated. When she reappeared, he pretended to have fallen in love with her. Having revealed that he had slandered her to the Duke, he swore to set matters straight again, and offered her a private house to which she could retire until the Duke should once more regard her with favor. Completely taken in, Oriana agreed.

During this time Valore and Lazarillo had reached the court, where they discussed the matter of the missing umbrana in detail and at last received a report from the boy that it was to be found at Gondarino's mercer's house. Lazarillo hurried off again. Unknown to him, Valore's intelligencers had copied down bits and snatches of his words in such a way that they constituted evidence for high treason. They, in turn, hastened to Lucio

4187

to report.

In the meantime Gondarino's mercer, a man with a foolish respect for learning but not the slightest idea of what true learning was, discussed with a panderer the possibility of obtaining a bride for himself. The panderer, who had disguised himself as a scholar, had convinced the mercer that he could, by means of his art, arrange a match with an heiress. That very afternoon, he promised, the mercer's bride would be compelled by magic to· appear at the panderer's house, and in order that she should be the less noticed as she was drawn irresistibly through the streets she would be dressed in a white waistcoat and torn stockings. Actually this woman was to be one of the panderer's stable of prostitutes. Just as the man was about to depart, the umbrana's head arrived from Gondarino; and the mercer, as a mark of favor, gave it to the panderer. Lazarillo, arriving a few moments later, learned the fish's new destination and set off after it again.

At the court Valore, closeted with the Duke, defended his sister's reputation while Gondarino waited outside the Duke's chambers with more lies to blacken it still further. When the two confronted each other, Gondarino offered to take Valore and the Duke to a place where Oriana's unchastity would be proved. Thus all parties began to converge upon a bagnio to which Gondarino had sent Oriana without her knowledge —the mercer to claim his bride, Lazarillo to seek the umbrana's head, and Gondarino, Valore, and the Duke to find out the truth about Oriana.

The mercer was the first to arrive. Having been assured by the panderer that the heiress waited within, he entered. Lazarillo next appeared upon the scene; he recognized the house for what it was, but, his appetite being stronger than his

virtue, he also entered. He had just secured from Julia, a prostitute, an invitation to a supper at which the coveted fish's head was to be served when he was arrested for treason by the intelligencers. As he was dragged away, he promised Julia marriage if she would only save the umbrana until his return. Finally, the Duke, Valore, and Gondarino arrived and caught sight of Oriana at an upper window of the house. The sight of her was almost enough to convince the Duke. When Gondarino hailed her, however, she replied by asking leave to write Va lore for her release.

The three noblemen returned to the palace, where a hot argument ensued. It was ultimately decided that Oriana's virtue would be put to a final test; if she failed it, she would die. As the Duke, Valore, and Gondarino watched from a concealed gallery, Arrigo confronted Oriana with the information that she was held guilty of unchastity and had been condemned to death. Oriana protested her innocence, but Arrigo was firm—she had been judged and she must die. Yet there was one way in which she could preserve her life; she could lie with Arrigo, who had the power to save her. When Oriana indignantly refused, declaring that she preferred death to dishonor, the Duke emerged from his hiding place to claim her for his bride. Gondarino was punished by being bound in a chair, helpless while, under Oriana's supervision, he was kissed and fondled by the ladies of the court.

Lazarillo, meanwhile, had been condemned by Lucio but pardoned through Valore's intervention. He returned to the bagnio, took Julia to the priest, and finally feasted on the umbrana's head. The mercer married the woman the panderer had produced. Thus he was taught the lesson that no man can be learned without labor.

THE WOMAN IN WHITE

Type of work: Novel
Author: Wilkie Collins (1824-1889)
Type of plot: Mystery romance
Time of plot: 1850's
Locale: England
First published: 1860

Principal characters:
WALTER HARTRIGHT, a young artist
FREDERICK FAIRLIE, owner of Limmeridge House
LAURA FAIRLIE, his niece and ward
MARIAN HALCOMBE, her half-sister
SIR PERCIVAL GLYDE, Laura Fairlie's suitor
COUNT FOSCO, a scheming nobleman
ANNE CATHERICK, the woman in white

Critique:

The story of *The Woman in White* is told by a collection of papers by different hands. This method gives Collins a chance to show the versatility of his style and to lend interest to the narrative. The plot, brought together with deftness, involves considerable suspense. The unusual characteristics of the villains and their victims are easily adaptable to motion picture versions of the story, and they have been successful in that form. There is not a great deal of background atmosphere or thought in the novel; its appeal is almost entirely on the basis of plot and characterization.

The Story:

Through the help of his Italian friend, Professor Pesca, Walter Hartright was engaged as drawing master to the nieces of Frederick Fairlie, of Limmeridge House, in Cumberland, England. On the day before he left to take up his new position, he met a girl dressed in white wandering about the outskirts of London. Walter discovered that she knew Limmeridge and had once gone to school there with Laura Fairlie. Suddenly the strange girl left him. Shortly afterward a coach came by. Its passenger leaned from the window to ask a policeman if he had seen a girl in white. The policeman had not, and Walter hesitated to intrude. As the coach went off, he heard the man say the girl had escaped from an asylum.

On arriving at Limmeridge, Walter met the first of his two pupils, Marian Halcombe. Marian was homely, but intelligent and charming in manner. Her half-sister, Laura, was the beauty of the family and heiress of Limmeridge House. The two girls were living under the protection of Laura's uncle, Frederick Fairlie, a selfish and fastidious hypochondriac. Walter fell in love with Laura almost at once. Hearing his story about the strange woman in white, Marian searched her mother's letters and discovered that the woman must have been a girl named Anne Catherick, in whom Mrs. Fairlie had taken great interest because she looked so much like Laura.

After several months, Marian realized that Walter was deeply in love with Laura. She advised him to leave, as Laura's father had asked her on his deathbed to marry Sir Percival Glyde. Then Walter met the girl in white again. She was in the graveyard cleaning the stone which bore Mrs. Fairlie's name. She admitted that she hoped to thwart Laura's coming marriage to Sir Percival. Told of this incident, Marian promised she would request a full explanation from Sir Percival.

Walter left Limmeridge. When Sir Percival arrived he explained to Marian that Anne Catherick was the daughter of a woman in his family's service in the past, and that she was in need of hospital treatment. He said he had kept her in an asylum at her mother's request, and he proved the statement with a letter from Mrs. Catherick. His explanation was accepted, and his marriage to Laura took place. Walter, heartbroken, went to Central America as a painter for an archaeological expedition. When Sir Percival and Laura came home from their wedding trip, some months later, Marian found them much changed. Laura was extremely unhappy, and Sir Percival was not at all pleased to have Marian live with them in his house at Blackwater Park. Count Fosco, a huge and very self-assured Italian, arrived with his wife, Laura's aunt, for a visit. Marian soon learned that the count was involved in money matters with Sir Percival. When Laura was asked to sign a document without looking at it, both she and Marian knew Sir Percival and Count Fosco were trying to get money from her by fraudulent means. Over Sir Percival's loud protests, Laura refused to sign the paper unless he would let her read it. The count interfered and made Sir Percival give up the matter for a time. Marian overheard a conversation between the count and Sir Percival in which they decided to get loans and wait three months before trying again to persuade Laura to sign away her money. The household became one of suspicion and fear.

By chance, one day, Laura met the woman in white and learned that there was some secret in Sir Percival's life, a secret involving both Anne Catherick and her mother. Before Anne could tell her the secret, Count Fosco appeared and frightened the girl away. As soon as Sir Percival learned Anne was in the neighborhood, he became alarmed. He tried to lock both Marian and Laura in their rooms. Marian spied on the two men by climbing to the roof during a pouring rain, where she overheard a plot to get Laura's money by killing her. Before she could act, however, Marian caught a fever from the chill of her rain-soaked clothing, and she was put to bed. Laura, too, became mysteriously ill.

When Laura was better, she was told that Marian had gone to London. She could not believe her sister had left her without saying goodbye and insisted on going to London herself. Actually, Marian had been moved to another room in the house. When Laura arrived in London, Count Fosco met her. She was given drugs, falsely declared insane, dressed in Anne Catherick's old clothes, and taken to the asylum from which Anne had escaped. In the meanwhile, Sir Percival had found Anne. Because of her resemblance to Laura, he planned to have her die and be buried under Laura's name. Anne was very ill anyway. When she died suddenly in London of natural causes, she was buried under the name of Laura, Lady Glyde.

After Marian recovered she was told that her sister was dead. She did not believe either the count or Sir Percival. She went to find Anne and discovered that the woman in the asylum was really Laura. Arranging Laura's escape, she took her back to Limmeridge. At Limmeridge, however, Frederick Fairlie refused to recognize the sickly Laura as anyone but Anne Catherick. Laura's memory had been so impaired by the experience that she could not prove who she was. Furious, Marian and Laura left, and went to look at the false tomb bearing the name of Lady Glyde. There they met Walter Hartright, recently returned from Central America. He had come to pay his respects at Laura's grave.

There was no possibility of returning Laura to her rightful estate as long as her mind was impaired by her terrible experience. Meanwhile Walter Hartright attempted to learn Sir Percival's secret. Finally he discovered that Sir Percival's father and mother had never been legally married. Hoping to destroy the evidence of his birth, Sir Percival attempted to burn an old church record that Walter needed. In the fire he set, Sir Percival burned up the church and himself as well. Mrs. Catherick, after his death, hinted that Laura's father had been the father of illegitimate Anne as well. After more searching, Walter found that this must be true.

Walter returned to London, and together the three planned to clear Laura by forcing the count to confess. Walter's old friend, Professor Pesca, revealed that Count Fosco was a traitor to the secret society to which both Pesca and the count had belonged. Through Pesca's help Walter was able to frighten the count into giving him a confession and written proof in Sir Percival's handwriting that Laura was still alive when Anne had been buried under the name of Lady Glyde. The count fled England, to be killed soon afterward by the secret society he had betrayed.

Walter, Marian, and Laura, who was now much improved, were happy to have proof of the substitution that had been made. Walter and Laura married and went to Limmeridge to confront Frederick Fairlie with the evidence. He was forced to admit Laura was really Laura and his heir. The friends then left, not to return until after Fairlie's death. After his death Laura's and Walter's son took over the estate. Marian lived with the happy family until she died.

A WOMAN KILLED WITH KINDNESS

Type of work: Drama
Author: Thomas Heywood (1570?-1641)
Type of plot: Domestic tragedy
Time of plot: Early seventeenth century
Locale: Yorkshire, England
First presented: 1603

Principal characters:
JOHN FRANKFORD, a provincial gentleman
ANNE, his wife
WENDOLL, her paramour
SIR FRANCIS ACTON, her brother
SIR CHARLES MOUNTFORD, a provincial nobleman
SUSAN, his sister
NICHOLAS, servant of the Frankfords
SHAFTON, a schemer

Critique:

This play marks a high point in the development of the domestic drama of the Elizabethan and Jacobean periods. Heywood was clearly well acquainted with the bourgeoisie of his time, and in his play he presented both an interesting story and a vivid documentation of the domestic life of the period. The source of *A Woman Killed With Kindness* was William Painter's collection of classical tales, *The Palace of Pleasure.* The play is marked by genuine dramatic force and considerable depth of feeling.

The Story:

John and Anne Frankford celebrated their marriage feast in the company of a group of relatives and friends. Everyone joined in complimenting the bride on her beauty and on her charming submission to her husband. As the group joined the crowd dancing in the great hall of the house, Sir Francis Acton and Sir Charles Mountford arranged a wager on hawking for the next day. Out in the courtyard, tenants of the Frankford estate celebrated their master's wedding.

Early the next morning Acton and Mountford and their companions went into the field to match their falcons. Acton lost the wager, but declared that Mountford's falcon had broken the rules of the hunt. Following an exchange of

hot words, the hunting party divided, and in the fighting Mountford killed two of Acton's men. Susan, Mountford's sister, went to him in the field and advised him to flee, but he declared that he could never leave her. The sheriff arrived and apprehended Mountford.

Frankford, at his home, felt himself supremely happy; he was affluent, well-educated, and blessed with a lovely and virtuous wife. As he reflected upon his felicity, Wendoll, who had been in the hunting party, excitedly arrived to report the details of the fatal fight. Frankford, already impressed by Wendoll's manner, invited the young gentleman to live in his house and to be his companion. Nicholas, Frankford's faithful servant, observed to himself that there was something about Wendoll that he did not like; he and the other servants expressed distaste that Wendoll should become a guest in the house.

Mountford, meanwhile, had been forced to spend almost his entire patrimony in order to gain his liberty. As he left the jail, he encountered Shafton, an unprincipled man who forced a large sum of money upon him. It was Shafton's purpose eventually to cheat Mountford out of a small ancestral house he still possessed and somehow to win the hand of Mountford's sister Susan.

Wendoll fell passionately in love with Anne Frankford. Conscience-stricken, he was distracted by the dreadful thoughts that went through his mind. But when Frankford rode away on business, Anne innocently told Wendoll that Frankford wished him to take his place in the household during his absence. Torn between reason and passion, Wendoll succumbed to passion and disclosed to Anne his great love for her. Anne at first resisted his blandishments, but she was soon overcome by his insistence that his love for her in no way reduced his great affection for and obligation to Frankford. Nicholas, undetected, overheard the conversation and vowed to bring the affair to light.

The term of Mountford's debt to Shafton having come due, the lender offered to buy Mountford's house, his last worldly possession. When Mountford refused to sell at any price, Shafton ordered a sergeant to handcuff Mountford and clap him in jail for debt. Hearing what had happened, Acton, who was filled with hatred for Mountford because of the violent dispute over the hawks, declared that he would seduce Susan Mountford. But when Acton actually saw Susan, he immediately fell in love with her.

On his return Frankford learned from Nicholas that Anne and Wendoll were unfaithful, she to her marriage vows, Wendoll to the bonds of friendship. When Frankford, Anne, Wendoll, and a guest, Cranwell, played cards after dinner, it seemed all too clear from the irony revealed in the conversation that Nicholas had indeed told the truth. Frankford planned to make certain that Anne was untrue to him.

Susan, meanwhile, asked her uncle, Old Mountford, to help her brother. The old man refused, as did other men to whom Mountford had been generous in former days. When Acton offered Susan a bag of gold, she spurned help from her brother's enemy. Acton cleared Mountford's debts anonymously. Mountford, released again from jail and from all of his debts, encountered Susan and, to her bewilderment, thanked her for her good work. When the jailer informed the pair that it was Acton who had aided them, Mountford, unable to accept the generosity of an enemy, proposed to return to jail. The jailer, having been paid, refused to admit him. At last Susan confessed that Acton had paid the debts because of his love for her. Knowing that fact, and shamed by his debt to Acton, Mountford felt that there was only one thing to do.

During supper at the Frankfords, Nicholas, by prearrangement, brought a letter to his master at the table. Frankford announced that he was called away immediately on legal business. After he had gone, Wendoll thanked fortune that matters worked out so well for him and Anne. Anne, however, was not happy in her affair with Wendoll; her conscience told her that she was lost in sin. Although she had succumbed to Wendoll because of his clever rhetoric, she suffered remorse. After dining with Wendoll in her chamber, she directed the servants to lock up the house and to bring her the keys.

Frankford, meanwhile, tied his horse to a tree near the house and with keys that he had made for the purpose he and Nicholas crept into the darkened house at midnight. Discovering Wendoll and his wife asleep in each other's arms, Frankford expressed a desire to turn back the clock so that the shame to his honor might have been prevented. Awaking the couple, he chased Wendoll with drawn sword, but a housemaid caught his arm and kept him from taking Wendoll's life. Anne, conscience-stricken, asked Frankford to end her life. He decided, however, that death was too good for her; he condemned her to live the rest of her life comfortably but in seclusion in a house on the estate. She was never to set eyes on him again.

In the meantime Mountford suggested to Susan that she give herself to Acton in return for his deed. When Susan

4193

objected on grounds of honor, Mountford declared that his soul would not rest until Acton had been repaid, and Susan finally agreed to this proposal. When Acton went to their house, Mountford bitterly offered his sister as payment. Acton was overcome by the magnanimous gesture. At one time he had not dreamed of marrying poverty-stricken Susan; now he declared that he would proudly take her as his wife.

As Anne, accompanied by her servants, prepared to start on her exile, Nicholas rode up and handed her a lute, the only one of her possessions she had left behind her. Tearfully, she declared that the lute, untuned as it was, was a symbol of her marriage. Wendoll, now repentant, met Anne on the road. When he began to express his remorse, she, fearful lest he tempt her again before she died, commanded the coachman to drive on to the house where she would end her days.

Later, learning that Anne was near death from a broken heart, Frankford went to her and forgave her sins. After her death Frankford declared that her epitaph would recall her as a woman killed by her husband's kindness.

THE WOMAN OF ROME

Type of work: Novel
Author: Alberto Moravia (Alberto Pincherle, 1907-   )
Type of plot: Naturalism
Time of plot: Twentieth century
Locale: Rome
First published: 1947

Principal characters:
ADRIANA, a prostitute
HER MOTHER
GINO, a chauffeur
MINO, a student
SONZOGNO, a thug
ASTARITA, a police official
GISELLA, Adriana's friend

Critique:

A keen study of several years in a prostitute's life, *The Woman of Rome* is an extreme example of one school of contemporary Italian writing. Details are piled up with scrupulous exactitude, and the first person method of getting the story told lends credence. The style is lucid and almost artless in its simplicity. Probably the subject matter would be repelling to many readers, as it is close to pornography at times, but the story is so compelling that as one reads one believes. Moravia has probed the social depths of a generation and its period in history.

The Story:

At sixteen Adriana was beautiful both in face and body. Her lips were red and full, her breasts high and firm. Her mother, a poor sewing woman, thought of 'her as her only capital; the family had been poverty-stricken since the illness and death of the father. Adriana's mother did not conceal her opinion that their poverty could be traced to her marriage and Adriana's unwanted birth.

Thinking her daughter mature enough, the mother took her to an artist to arrange for her career as a model. Adriana was not embarrassed by undressing before a strange man, nor was she much embarrassed when her mother punched and patted her naked body as she stressed her good points. But her mother's shrill arguing about the pay was quite ill-mannered. She was especially violent with polite people because they usually gave in before her temper displays.

The artist agreed to pay a higher fee with good grace. As he talked with Adriana afterward, he tried to tell her that her mother loved money above all else. Adriana was unconvinced. The artist was a man of about forty, always correct in his behavior. When his pictures did not sell, he had no more work for Adriana. She had little difficulty in obtaining other jobs, because her figure was so fine, even heroic in proportions.

When modeling did not pay well enough, her mother tried to get Adriana a job as a dancer, and she secured an interview with a vaudeville manager. Adriana did her best, but she was miserably conscious of her swelling thighs and her clumsy feet. Even the mother's shrewish scolding could not win her a job on the stage.

Adriana dutifully took as many modeling jobs as she could, built up a reputation for virtue among the artists, and sewed shirts afternoons and evenings. A turning point came when she met Gino.

THE WOMAN OF ROME by Alberto Moravia. Translated by Lydia Holland. By permission of the publishers, Farrar, Straus & Young, Inc. Copyright, 1949, by Valentino Bompiani & Co., S. A.

Gino was soft-spoken and gentle in spite of his rough workman's hands. He was a chauffeur for a wealthy family, and when he could possibly do so he took Adriana for long rides. Her mother objected to the friendship, for she thought Adriana's beauty could win her a gentleman.

Adriana did not object when Gino invited her to his employer's villa while the family was away. She willingly went to his room and afterward they slept until past midnight. Adriana had never been out so late before, and her suspecting mother was furious. She set on her daughter with her fists and beat her as long as she had strength. Then she took Adriana to an all night clinic and had her examined by a doctor. When the doctor confirmed her fears, she was glum but calm.

It was understood that Gino and Adriana would be married, but Gino found excuses for delaying the wedding. The mother was pessimistic about the marriage. Gisella, Adriana's friend, was also doubtful of Gino's intentions and urged her to accept a rich lover while she could. She finally induced Adriana to go out to dinner with Astarita, a rich police official who was anxious to meet her. At the dinner in a hotel Gisella almost forced Adriana to go into a bedroom with Astarita. On the way home Astarita gave Adriana money.

So Adriana was launched on a new career. She did not break with Gino, for she still thought that perhaps they would be married. That hope vanished, however, when Astarita produced evidence that Gino was married and had a daughter. For revenge, Adriana let Gino take her to the villa again, but she insisted on making love in the mistress' bed. After she told Gino that she knew the truth about his wife, she stole a compact from the dresser.

Adriana became a prostitute. She brought her clients home, usually, and her mother accepted the state of affairs with good grace because there was more money in the house. Adriana usually slept late and led an indolent, satisfied existence. She really liked men. Her mother became fat and much less attractive.

One night she met Gino again. He wondered about the compact. The wealthy family, on their return home, had missed it, and Gino suspected Adriana. Gino arranged to have suspicion fall on a maid, who was arrested and sent to jail. After getting the compact from Adriana, Gino planned to sell it to a fence. When he said he would divide the money with her, Adriana, filled with pity for the falsely arrested maid, refused.

She found Gino one night in company with Sonzogno, a strong man and a thug. When Gino and Adriana left a café together, she felt repelled by her former fiancé and on an impulse called to Sonzogno for help. He promptly knocked Gino down and went home with Adriana. Adriana was both attracted to Sonzogno and in terror of him. He had the stolen compact in his possession. Gino had given it to Sonzogno to sell and Sonzogno had murdered an old jeweler to whom he had taken it for that purpose. After listening to callous boasts of his crime, Adriana succeeded in getting the compact away from him. She passed rather a bad night, for Sonzogno beat her. Later she had her confessor give the compact to the police and the maid was released.

Out at night with Gisella, the girls were picked up by two men and the four went to Adriana's house. Gisella, soon afterward, became the mistress of her pickup and was installed in her own apartment. Adriana's pickup was Mino, a student of nineteen. Thin and withdrawn, he was not much interested in love making. His attitude attracted Adriana and thereafter she pursued him, even to his respectable rooming-house.

Adriana's affairs became more complicated. The friendly clinic doctor confirmed her fears; she was pregnant. As she thought back, she knew that Sonzogno was the father. She was rather pleased to have a child, but her baby would be born of a murderer and a prostitute. When Mino came to live at her house, she told him that he was the father of her expected baby.

Mino was an anti-Fascist engaged in subversive work. When he was arrested, he promptly betrayed his fellow conspirators under the sympathetic questioning of Astarita. As soon as he learned that Astarita was an admirer of Adriana, he proposed that she should invite him to her house, and there Mino would shoot him.

Sonzogno, sure that Adriana had betrayed him to the police, arrived just before Astarita was expected. When Astarita appeared, he slapped the submissive Sonzogno's face and sent him away. Then he told Adriana that Mino's confession had not been written down and the police had taken no action against his friends.

But Adriana was apprehensive. It was not like Sonzogno to be meek. When she went to the ministry, her fears were justified. Astarita was dead in the courtyard; Sonzogno had followed him to his office and had thrown him off a balcony. Adriana went home to find Mino gone. He had left a note saying that his parents would look after her and his son; he was going to kill himself. His body was found in a hotel near the station.

A WOMAN'S LIFE

Type of work: Novel
Author: Guy de Maupassant (1850-1893)
Type of plot: Naturalism
Time of plot: Early nineteenth century
Locale: Normandy and the island of Corsica
First published: 1883

Principal characters:
JEANNE DE LAMARE
JULIEN DE LAMARE, her husband
PAUL DE LAMARE, her son
BARON SIMON-JACQUES LE PERTHUIS DES VAUDS, her father
ROSALIE, her foster sister

Critique:

A *Woman's Life* is one of the masterful long fictions of that master of the short story, de Maupassant. The chronicle of a sheltered woman's life, her thoughts and misfortunes, it describes more than a quarter century of Jeanne de Lamare's existence. Such is the skill of the author that, though the book is short, neither the characterizations nor the narrative suffer from being briefly sketched.

The Story:

In the spring of 1819 Jeanne Le Perthuis des Vauds and her parents went to live in an old chateau, The Poplars, on the Normandy coast. Baron Simon-Jacques Le Perthuis des Vauds had been left a large inheritance, but he had so reduced it by his free-handedness that he was finally forced to reconcile himself to a simple country life for the remainder of his days.

Jeanne, who had spent the past five years in a convent, looked forward happily to her new life and dreamed of the day when she would find the man who loved her.

All of her expectations were fulfilled. She found a beautiful countryside to wander over, the sea to bathe in and to sail on. She met a neighbor, the handsome young Viscount Julien de Lamare, who came to call. M. de Lamare and Jeanne quickly became good friends. When the baron presented his daughter with a boat, he invited the village priest and his acolytes to christen it. To Jeanne the ceremony seemed like a wedding, and under the spell of her illusion she accepted his proposal when Julien asked her to marry him. The wedding took place that summer, six weeks after they became engaged.

At Jeanne's wish the couple journeyed to Corsica on their honeymoon. She had been romantically in love with her husband before her marriage, but during the two months she was away from home with him her emotion grew into a passion. Thus she was amazed, when they stopped in Paris on their way home, to find Julien not perfect. She had given him her filled purse, her mother's present, to look after, and when she requested it back to buy some gifts for her family he gruffly refused to dole out more than a hundred francs to her. Jeanne was afraid to ask for more.

When Jeanne and Julien returned to The Poplars, Julien took over the management of the estate. During the long, monotonous days of winter he began to wear old clothes and no longer bothered to shave. He paid little attention to his wife. Having sold the carriage horses to save the cost of their feed, he used the tenants' nags and became furious when Jeanne and her parents laughed at the ugly team.

In January Jeanne's parents went to Rouen and left the young couple alone.

A WOMAN'S LIFE by Guy de Maupassant. Published by The Viking Press, Inc.

It was then that Jeanne was completely disillusioned about her husband. One day the maid, her foster sister Rosalie, bore a child. Julien insisted that the mother and her illegitimate infant should be sent off immediately, but Jeanne, who was fond of Rosalie, opposed him. A few weeks later she found the pair in bed together.

The shock was so great that Jeanne could only think that she must get away from her husband. She ran out of the house in her night clothes, to the edge of the cliffs which hung over the sea. There Julien found her and brought her back to the house before she could jump.

For several weeks the young wife was ill as the result of her exposure. When she began to recover and could convince her parents of her discovery, Rosalie confessed that Julien had seduced her on the first day he had come to call at the house.

The maid and her baby were sent away. Jeanne would have preferred separation from her husband, but the knowledge that she herself was pregnant and the priest's intercession on Julien's behalf made her agree to a reconciliation.

Jeanne's baby was born in July, nearly a year after her marriage. On the infant, Paul, she lavished all the love which Julien had not accepted.

After the baby's birth the de Lamares became friendly with their neighbors, the Count and Countess de Fourville. The count was passionately in love with his wife, but Gilberte de Fourville rode alone with Julien almost every-day. One morning, as Jeanne was walking her horse through the woods in which Julien had proposed, she found her husband's and Gilberte's horses tied together.

Shortly afterward the baroness died after an illness which had kept her partly crippled for many years. To Jeanne, who had been deeply attached to her mother, it came as a great shock to find that she, too, had not been above an affair, documented in the letters she had saved.

Jeanne had kept the secret of Julien's latest intrigue to herself, fearful of the steps the count might take if he ever discovered his wife's unfaithfulness. The old village priest, Abbé Picot, also held his peace. Unfortunately, Abbé Picot was called elsewhere. His successor was not so liberal in his views.

Abbé Tolbiac, who was conscious of his parishioners' morals and determined to guard them, discovered by chance the philandering of Julien and Gilberte de Fourville. He had no hesitation about discussing the subject with Jeanne, and when she refused to desert her husband or to inform the count he took the story to Gilberte's husband.

One day, while the couple were in a shepherd's hut, the count, a powerful giant, pushed the building down an incline and into a ravine. He then managed to dash home without being seen. Under the wreckage of the hut lay the two mangled bodies.

That night, after Julien's body had been carried home, Jeanne bore her second child, a stillborn girl.

Although she suspected that Julien's death had not been an accident, she remained silent. The memories of her husband's infidelities faded quickly, leaving her at peace with her recollections of their early life together, as it had been on Corsica. Soon even these began to dim, and she turned all her attention to Paul.

Paul de Lamare did not go to school until he was fifteen. At home he was petted and indulged by his mother, grandfather, and a maiden aunt who had come to live at The Poplars after the death of the baroness. When he was finally sent off to Le Havre to school, Jeanne visited him so frequently that the principal had to beg her not to come so often.

The third year Paul was away from home he stopped spending his Sundays with his mother. When a usurer called on her to collect money for the youth's debts, Jeanne visited his school and learned that he had not been there for a month. While living with a mistress, he had signed his mother's name to letters stating that he was ill.

After his escapade Paul was taken home and watched. He managed to escape from The Poplars, however, and two days later Jeanne received a letter from him from London. It was the first of many begging notes he was to send her. In addition to asking for money, he announced that the woman he had known in Le Havre was living with him.

For over a year Paul sent a series of requests for financial help which were never ignored, even though they meant the mortgaging of The Poplars and the two farms that went with the estate. Anxiety over his grandson and his property caused the baron's death from apoplexy.

Soon after the baron's death, Jeanne's aunt followed him to the grave. Jeanne would have been alone then if Rosalie, who had since been married and widowed, had not returned to look after her. Her foster sister insisted on working without pay and on putting a much-needed check on Jeanne's expenditures. It was necessary to sell The Poplars, however, and the two women settled down in a small farmhouse.

Although Jeanne was forced to limit the sums she sent Paul, she did not curb her affection for him. When he had been away from home for seven years, she wrote begging him to come home. Paul's reply was that before he would return he wanted her consent to marry his mistress, who was living with him in Paris. Jeanne, who was not without a strain of jealousy, decided that she would persuade him to come without the woman.

As quickly as possible she set out for Paris. Although she had written to announce her visit, Paul did not meet her. In order to avoid his creditors, he had moved without leaving a forwarding address. His disconsolate mother returned to Normandy.

Some months later Jeanne heard from her son once more. His wife, whom he had at last married without his mother's blessing, was dying, and he entreated Jeanne to come for their little daughter. This time it was Rosalie who went to Paris. When she came back she had the infant with her, and she brought the news that Paul would follow her the next day.

THE WOMAN'S PRIZE

Type of work: Drama
Author: John Fletcher (1579-1625)
Type of plot: Farce
Time of plot: Sixteenth century
Locale: Italy
First presented: c. 1604

Principal characters:
PETRUCHIO, the wife-tamer
MARIA, Petruchio's bride
LIVIA, her sister
BIANCA, their cousin
MOROSO, an old man, in love with Livia
SOPHOCLES, a friend of Petruchio
TRANIO, another friend
PETRONIUS, father of Maria and Livia
ROWLAND, a young gentleman, in love with Livia
JACQUES, Petruchio's servant

Critique:

Attempting no doubt to capitalize on the earlier success of Shakespeare's *The Taming of the Shrew,* Fletcher in this play turns the tables on Petruchio by having a new wife bring him to heel. Although it is by no means a failure, *The Woman's Prize or, The Tamer Tamed* is considerably inferior to the comedy on which it is based. To cite only one point of difference, Shakespeare manages very skillfully to have Petruchio show Katharina her shortcomings by subtly mirroring her meanness and perversity; she is tamed, as it were, with love and emerges reformed but with her spirit unbroken. Fletcher is incapable of this kind of finesse. Maria, Katharina's successor, completely humiliates Petruchio by means of a series of extravagant tricks, all of which are ultimately made possible by taking advantage of her husband's unsatisfied desire for her. The resulting comedy of situation is, however, very tightly constructed; the subplot, which deals with the love affair between Livia and the rather ineffectual Rowland, is skillfully interwoven with the main plot. Much broadly comic business is introduced more or less for its own sake—notably the invasion of the townswomen—but the pace of the action is so fast and the matter so high-spirited that the whole play comes off successfully.

The Story:

As they gathered in Petruchio's house after the wedding, Moroso, Sophocles, and Tranio discussed the match that had been made between Petruchio, the shrew-tamer, and the soft and yielding Maria, daughter of Petronius. Although Moroso, an ancient dotard who was infatuated with Livia, Petronius' second daughter, held that Petruchio was not so terrible as some believed, the others agreed that his first wife, now dead, had so inflamed his ill humor that Maria was in for a very bad time indeed. As a man's man Petruchio left nothing to be desired, but as a woman's man he was fiery and unpredictable.

A different conversation occupied two other wedding guests. Young Rowland was half afraid that Livia, enticed by Moroso's gold, would renounce the love she had secretly sworn to him, and he was attempting to induce her to elope with him. But Livia, who was as practical as she was beautiful, was unwilling to sacrifice her marriage portion by marrying without her father's permission. Vowing that she had a plan which would make her legitimately his, she sent Rowland from her. She was immediately joined by the new bride Maria and her cousin Bianca.

Influenced by Bianca, Maria had undergone such a change that Livia was shocked. Gone were her soft and gentle manners; in their place Maria, urged on by Bianca, exhibited a firm resolution. She would fight a holy war for the salvation of all womanhood. Never would she yield herself to her husband until his spirit was broken, until the wifetamer was himself tamed. This she proclaimed in so imperious and immodest a tone that Livia left offended, but Maria's plans remained unchanged. When Jacques entered to inform her that Petruchio was ready to come to her, she replied that Petruchio could sleep elsewhere—he would share no bed with her. Dumbfounded, Jacques sought the impatient bridegroom.

Jacques interrupted Petruchio's boasts of his sexual prowess with the news that Maria and Bianca were firmly entrenched in the bedchamber with a month's rations and the determination that no man should enter until he had come to terms with them. Just then the window opened above the courtyard where Petruchio was standing, and Maria appeared to announce that she would remain barricaded until Petruchio signed the articles she proposed. Petruchio began to reason with her, gently at first but with increasing fire, but for every one of his arguments she had a counterargument of greater weight. Finally, in a blind rage, Petruchio swore that he would starve her into submission. Thus the engagement ended, with the bride inside and the bridegroom firmly locked out.

Livia, meanwhile, began to put her plan into action. With Moroso looking on, she purposely offended Rowland and bade him what seemed to be a final farewell as the young man stalked away, cursing women and all their works. Moroso took this as a sign that his suit had prospered; yet when he attempted to kiss Livia, she gave him a box on the ear. Somewhat discomfited, Moroso complained to Petronius, who assured him that within two hours the girl would be married to him. But Livia had other ideas. Approaching the sealed chamber, she begged to become a member of the women's party. Her admission was assured when Maria learned that she was laden with provisions.

Outside, the siege continued. Sophocles argued for a peaceful settlement, but Petruchio was adamant; he would assert his rights as a husband—no woman could daunt him. But Petruchio had reckoned without the townswomen, who had learned of Maria's stand. Armed with pot lids, ladles, and other household utensils, they formed a relief column and forced their way into the women's stronghold. The victory was celebrated with dancing and wine, and several of the victors drank rather more than they should have. The siege was lifted and the vanquished men agreed to a treaty. Petruchio yielded to Maria's terms, liberty and clothes; and Moroso agreed to Livia's, that she should be forced to marry no one for a month. Then victors and vanquished celebrated at a supper attended by all the townswomen.

Although the women had temporarily called a truce, the war was not yet over. As Rowland sulked and swore that he was forever through with love, Petruchio, attempting to bed his bride, met another cold rebuff. Once more in a rage, he offered half his land to the one who could make him stop loving her. Continuing to press her advantage, Maria first ordered an elaborate gown, then new horses and hawks for hunting, and new hangings for the house. Finally she considered having the house torn down altogether and rebuilt in a more pleasant location. Hard pressed, Petruchio again attempted to reason with her as sweetly as he could; however, he once more flew into a rage when Maria began to flirt openly with Sophocles. In despair, Petruchio resolved simply to die; he declared that only his death could shame his shrewish wife.

In the meantime Rowland was still having difficulties. Tranio had induced him to show how little he cared for Livia by attending her forthcoming wedding to Moroso. He returned to her the various favors she had given him during their courtship and gave her a parting kiss. Suddenly, his resolution beginning to weaken, he had to hurry from the scene to prevent love's stealing upon him again.

At the same time all was in confusion at Petruchio's. Declaring that her husband was sick of the plague, Maria was having the house stripped of all its furnishings. In spite of his protests that he was as healthy as anyone else, Petruchio was put under guard, and all of his friends deserted him for fear of infection. Left alone except for some members of the watch, the supposedly dying man burst open the door and put his guardians to flight by threatening them with a fowling piece. Only then did he realize that Maria had executed another maneuver in her campaign to humiliate him, but this blow was not the final one. Soon Maria returned and belabored him soundly for casting her off during his sickness. Stung beyond endurance, Petruchio nearly struck her, but caught himself because she vowed to repay any mistreatment by cuckolding him with the first man she met.

Moroso also was feeling the pangs of despised love, and Petronius again promised him that he should enjoy Livia soon. However, Bianca and Tranio were hatching a plot to aid Livia in her efforts to thwart her suitor. Tranio's task was to persuade Rowland to return to Petronius' house while Livia, under Bianca's tutelage, feigned illness. After she was safely abed and Tranio had lured Rowland to the scene, Bianca informed Moroso that although Livia was suffering an emotional upset she had renounced Rowland forever and would accept him instead. When the entire party had gathered around her bed, Livia, speaking in the weak voice of one desperately sick, contritely begged Moroso's pardon for the many tricks she had played upon him. She then sadly took her final leave of Rowland and had him sign a paper which she produced, a document in which he formally renounced any claim he had upon her. After Moroso and Petronius had affixed their signatures, the party left the ailing maid to recuperate. But as Rowland sadly walked toward his home, he looked more closely at his copy of the paper. To his delight, he found that it was not a renunciation at all, but a marriage contract. Livia's strange actions then became clear to him; she had tricked Moroso and her father into giving her and her dowry to the man she loved.

Petruchio, during this time, was attempting to meet Maria's strategy with some ruses of his own. Pretending that her treatment of him had killed any love he had felt for her, he threatened to set out on a journey. She took the announcement calmly and encouraged him to do so. This scheme failing, he had himself carried home in a coffin surrounded by mourners who lamented that his wife's evil ways had killed him. On seeing his body, Maria wept, but not for his death. Rather, she grieved that he had led such a misguided and foolish life.

This was the last straw; Petruchio sat up in the coffin. But at last he had to admit himself outwitted and defeated. Maria now had her wish; her campaign had been an unqualified success. Embracing her husband, she announced that from that moment she was entirely his to do with as he chose. With the tamer tamed, she vowed to be a humble and dutiful wife. And Petruchio, his lesson learned, forgave her.

WOMEN BEWARE WOMEN

Type of work: Drama
Author: Thomas Middleton (1580-1627)
Type of plot: Tragedy of revenge
Time of plot: Early seventeenth century
Locale: Florence, Italy
First presented: c. 1621

Principal characters:

LEANTIO, a Florentine clerk
BIANCA, his wife
FABRICIO, a Florentine gentleman
ISABELLA, his daughter
LIVIA, Fabricio's sister
HIPPOLITO, brother of Livia and Fabricio
THE DUKE OF FLORENCE
A CARDINAL, the Duke's brother
THE WARD
GUARDIANO, his uncle and guardian

Critique:

This Jacobean drama is set in Italy, the conventional background which in tragedies of the period implied luxury, vice, and violence. Within this framework Middleton dispassionately and ironically recorded human—especially feminine—motivation and passion. The moral ending is also conventional. The lasting impression left by the play is one of the movement of characters from deliberate scheming to uncontrollable involvement and destruction. The dramatic structure of the play is unbalanced, and the slow entanglement of destructive passions is abruptly changed to the final, almost farcical, holocaust. The tragedy is memorable not for its moral ending but for the nightmare quality of human passions revealed by the force of richly dramatic verse.

The Story:

Leantio, a Florentine merchant's clerk, married Bianca, a beautiful and well-born Venetian, and brought her to his mother's house. On her arrival there, she responded graciously to his mother's words of welcome and spoke of her love for Leantio. He in turn informed his mother of Bianca's luxurious background and of his inability to equal it. He explained also that Bianca was a great prize who must be kept hidden from other men's eyes. His mother feared that Bianca would be discontented with her new and poorer home.

In a richer house, Livia was entertaining her brother Fabricio, the father of Isabella, and Guardiano, the uncle of a rich and foolish boy called the Ward. They discussed the proposed marriage between the Ward and Isabella. Livia, protesting against loveless marriages, lectured Fabricio on man's unfaithfulness and woman's obedience, and declared that she would never remarry. When Isabella was sent for, Fabricio declared that her uncle Hippolito would surely follow her in her married state because they were as inseparable as links in a chain. Isabella's ideals, especially her ideas on marriage, were in marked contrast to the Ward's foolishness and vulgarity. She dreaded marriage to him and regarded it as slavery. This was her explanation to Livia, who sent Hippolito to comfort her. At that time Isabella's conscious feelings toward her uncle were those of deep friendship. Unaware at the time of any sexual attraction toward him, she was horrified and sadly left him when he told her he loved her as a man loves his wife.

When Leantio finally left Bianca at his mother's house and returned to his work, Bianca wept bitterly. She was distracted from her grief by the noise and excitement of the annual religious procession to the cathedral. Deeply impressed by the noble bearing of the Duke of Florence, Bianca was sure that he noticed her as she watched him passing by.

Meanwhile, Hippolito had told Livia of his love for Isabella and of her reaction, and Livia promised to procure the girl as his mistress. When Isabella confided her unhappiness to Livia, her aunt took the opportunity to tell her that Hippolito was not her uncle, that she was in fact the child of Fabricio's wife by a Spanish nobleman. She insisted, however, that Isabella keep this matter a secret because Fabricio and Hippolito were ignorant of it. Thus Isabella welcomed Hippolito with a kiss when he returned and he marveled at Livia's skill. Isabella decided that she would still marry the Ward in order to conceal her love affair with Hippolito.

While with Livia, Guardiano told her that the Duke of Florence was enamored of a girl he had seen on the balcony of Leantio's mother's house. Accordingly, Livia undertook to win her for the Duke and summoned Leantio's mother for a game of chess. Under pressure, the mother admitted that she had a daughter-in-law in her home, and Bianca was sent for. She was taken on a tour of the house by Guardiano, who thus led her to the Duke.

While the Duke spoke of his passion for her, Bianca pleaded for her honor, virtue, and safety. The Duke, continuing his token pleading, intimated to Bianca, however, that she did not have the power to refuse him. When she returned to the two chess players, Bianca was half pleased by the Duke but also eager to have revenge on Livia.

At home, Bianca's ensuing frustration and discontent infuriated her mother-in-law and she was glad that Leantio would soon return. On his arrival Leantio, delighted to be home, anticipated an ecstatic reunion with his wife, but he was greeted coldly by Bianca and angrily repulsed.

Before long, sent for by the Duke, she went to the palace with Leantio's mother. Left alone, Leantio abandoned himself to jealousy, but he failed to realize the extent of his betrayal until he too was summoned to dine with the Duke.

When offered the command of a distant city, Leantio was as powerless to refuse as he was to disrupt the affair between his wife and her noble lover, and he was forced to stand by when Bianca, bored by the banquet, left with the Duke.

In the meantime Livia, who had fallen in love at first sight with Leantio, was determined to woo him from his grief. When she indirectly offered herself as his mistress, he accepted because of the wealth and luxury she promised. Some weeks later Leantio visited Bianca in her apartment at the court and they jeered at each other's finery and new place in the world. Later Bianca told the Duke of her husband's visit and disclosed that he had become Livia's lover. Jealous of Leantio, the Duke informed Hippolito, who, as the ruler expected, threatened to kill his sister's lover in order to preserve publicly Livia's honor.

The Duke's pleasure at the idea of Leantio's death was increased when his brother, the Cardinal, threatened him with the fires of hell if he continued to live adulterously. Having vowed that he would reform, he decided that with Leantio dead he could lawfully marry Bianca. And so Leantio was murdered. Livia, finding Hippolito with her lover's body and driven almost to madness by grief, fury, and malice, betrayed him and Isabella and admitted that she had lied to Isabella about her parentage in order to make her Hippolito's mistress. Isabella, who had transgressed, unlike the others, through ignorance, resolved to leave Hippolito and in turn to avenge herself by destroying Livia.

The separate revenges plotted by these people resulted in their own deaths. At a masque held ostensibly in honor of the Duke's marriage to Bianca, poisoned incense killed Isabella and Livia. Hippolito stabbed himself, and Bianca had the Duke poisoned and then drank also from the poisoned cup.

THE WOMEN OF TRACHIS

Type of work: Drama
Author: Sophocles (c. 496-406 or 405 B.C.)
Type of plot: Classical tragedy
Time of plot: Remote antiquity
Locale: Trachis
First presented: Before 408 B.C.

Principal characters:
HERAKLES
DEIANIRA, his wife
HYLLUS, their son
LICHAS, herald of Herakles
IOLE, captive wife to Herakles
CHORUS OF TRACHINIAN MAIDENS

Critique:

The *Women of Trachis (Trachiniae)*, recounting the last crisis in the life of Herakles, is of interest for several reasons. It is the only surviving tragedy of Sophocles which ends in death for both of the chief characters. Also, though they are constantly in the mind of spectator or reader, neither appears on the stage at the same time. The gods, as in the Sophoclean drama, take an active part; but in this painful play they are unseen, though from beginning to end it is their will that is done, their oracles that are fulfilled. The tragedy is of universal interest because it emphasizes the devotion and love inherent in womanhood, while in the awful agonies of Herakles are embodied the heroic endurance and strength representative of ideal masculinity. Appropriately, the title is not derived from either hero or heroine but from the Chorus of Trachinian Maidens who are on the stage from beginning to end.

The Story:

Fifteen long months had passed since Deianira had received word from Herakles, her husband, who, when he left on his last journey, had given her a tablet setting forth the disposition of his estate and stating that it had been decreed that after a year and three moons had passed he would either die or live happily thereafter in untroubled peace. The fated day had arrived, and Deianira was filled with foreboding.

However, before she could send her son Hyllus to get accurate news of her husband, a messenger, outstripping the herald Lichas, arrived to announce that Herakles was living and would soon appear. Lichas himself followed shortly with a group of captive maidens and, answering Deianira's question, assured her that her husband, alive and sound of limb, was at that time sacrificing the fruits of his victories to great Zeus in fulfillment of a vow made when he took from towered Oechalia the captive women. Deianira was touched by the plight of the captives. Lichas told her they were from the city ruled by Eurytus, selected by Herakles as chosen possessions for himself and the gods; but, he added, it was not the taking of the city that had delayed the hero this long time. He had been detained in Lydia. Sold into bondage, he had passed a year as servant to Omphale, the barbaric queen. Before this bondage, Eurytus, an old friend, had taunted and so incensed him that Herakles, encountering Iphitus, one of Eurytus' four sons, without warning hurled him from a cliff. This act roused the ire of Olympian Zeus who, because Herakles had slain a foe by treachery and not in fair fight, drove him out to be sold as a slave to Omphale. But those who had reviled Herakles had been conquered, and now Lichas brought these virgins by Herakles' order to Deianira.

A strange pity came over Deianira as she gazed at the captives. One in particular, Iole, held her attention; but Lichas pretended not to know who she was; and

4207

Iole herself spoke no word, bearing in silence her grief and suffering. The messenger, however, informed Deianira that Lichas had not told the truth, which was that Herakles for love of Iole had destroyed Eurytus, the maiden's father; that it was not his adventures in Lydia, his serfdom with Omphale, nor the death of Iphitus which had held him these many moons, but love for this maid. Failing to persuade her father to give up his daughter, Herakles had attacked Oechalia, sacked the city, slain Eurytus, and taken Iole for his concubine. Deianira, cruelly hurt, called upon Lichas to tell her everything. He confirmed the news. Sorrowfully she asked the herald to wait while she had suitable gifts prepared for Herakles in return for those he had sent.

But Deianira could not bear the thought of having another share her husband's affections. Judging it unwise to give way to anger, she thought of another course. In an old urn she had long hid a keepsake of Nessus, the centaur whose work it was to ferry wayfarers across the river Evenus, carrying them in his arms. When Deianira, as a bride, was on her way to Herakles, she too was carried across by the centaur, but in midstream he lewdly sought to take her. Her screams brought from the waiting son of Zeus an arrow that pierced the centaur's lungs. Dying, he told Deianira that as the last to be ferried across the river she should profit by receiving from him a love philter made by taking the curdled gore from his wound. This would act as a charm so that Herakles would never find any other woman fairer than she. Now, recalling these words, Deianira selected a festal robe and smeared it with the magic ointment. Then she presented the robe to Lichas, telling him he was to instruct Herakles to put it on immediately, before sun or light struck it, and stand before the people with it on as he made his sacrifices to the gods.

No sooner had Lichas departed, however, than Deianira felt uneasy because she had resorted to magic to win back her husband's love. Quickly her fears were realized. She had faithfully followed the instructions of the centaur by preserving the drug unexposed to light or fire or sun until the moment of application. Secretly, indoors, she had spread the unguent on the robe with some wool and, folding the gift, had placed it securely in a chest. Now, by chance, she threw the tuft of wool on the flagstones in the blazing sun, whereupon there boiled up from it clots of foam as it consumed itself and disappeared into nothingness. In consternation Deianira realized that the black-venomed gore, instead of winning anew her husband's love, had been dying Nessus' trick to cause his death, and she would be his murderer. Overwhelmed, she determined to end her own life.

Hyllus returned. He had seen Herakles receive from Lichas the robe and put it on. Then, when the fierce rays of the sun had melted the venom with which the deadly garment was coated, it clung to his body, the sweat burst out, and, before the assembled company, he writhed in dreadful pain. Herakles in his agony called out to Lichas, who told him the robe was Deianira's gift, whereupon the unhappy man seized the messenger by the foot and dashed out his brains against a rock. When, shouting and shrieking, Herakles called on Hyllus to carry him away to die where no one might see him, they had placed him on a ship and brought him to his home.

Hyllus now accused his mother of her vile deed and called down on her the vengeance of the Erinyes. Silently Deianira went indoors and in the bedchamber of Herakles bade farewell to her bridal bed. Then with a sword she pierced her heart and died. Hyllus, told by others that his mother's gift of the robe to Herakles had been instigated by the centaur, realized too late her innocence, and he grieved to lose in one day both mother and sire.

Hyllus, still lamenting, left, but returned with attendants bearing his father on a litter. Herakles, fighting off the deadly spasms that shook him, entreated his son to end his miserable life. He recalled his great labors and the fact that he had never met defeat. But now death had come by a woman's wile. Hyllus told him that Deianira had been innocent of murderous intent in her act, that she had wished only to win back his love, that it was the centaur's venom that had brought about his undoing, and that Deianira, not wishing to live without him, now lay cold and dead.

Herakles admitted that it had been foreshown him that he would perish not by any living being but by a dweller in the realms of the Dead. Because the prophecy had also promised him release from his toils, he had misinterpreted it as meaning a happy life; instead, it had portended death, for with death comes the end of toil.

Knowing thus that it was the will of the gods, Herakles faced death nobly. He bade Hyllus bear him to the peak of Oeta, place him on a great funeral pyre of oak and olive, and ignite it. Hyllus consented to carry his sire to his destination and prepare the pyre, but he refused to light it. Herakles, not pressing him, asked as one other boon that Hyllus take Iole to wife and care for her. Unwillingly, but moved by filial obedience, Hyllus assented. In these dread matters he saw the will of immortal Zeus.

THE WOODLANDERS

Type of work: Novel
Author: Thomas Hardy (1840-1928)
Type of plot: Tragic romance
Time of plot: Nineteenth century
Locale: Rural England
First published: 1887

Principal characters:
GEORGE MELBURY, a timber merchant
GRACE MELBURY, his daughter
GILES WINTERBORNE, an itinerant farmer
FELICE CHARMOND, a lady of the manor
EDGAR FITZPIERS, a doctor

Critique:

One of the lesser known of the works of Thomas Hardy, *The Woodlanders* lacks some of his philosophical depth and insight. Perhaps neglect of the novel may lie in the fact that in it Hardy wrote neither his usual stark tragedy nor his occasional gentle, rustic romance; instead, he attempted to combine the two. But even though the book does not always measure up to Hardy's fiction at its best, it is still good reading. The writer's ability to portray and develop character is here and, as always, it is above reproach.

The Story:

Mr. George Melbury, timber merchant, had spared no expense in educating Grace, his only daughter. She had been gone from home a year, and he was eagerly awaiting her return. Another man also waited for Grace's homecoming. He was Giles Winterborne, an itinerant farmer and apple grower. Mr. Melbury had wronged Giles' father many years before, and in order to atone for this wrong he had half promised Giles that he should have Grace for his wife.

When Grace returned, it was soon evident that she was now much too cultured and refined for the ways of a simple farmer. But Grace knew that her father had promised her to Giles, and she meant to go through with the plans even though she shrank a little from his plainness. It was Mr. Melbury who was the most concerned. He was an honorable man and liked Giles, but he also loved his only child above everything else. He could not bear to see her throw herself away when she could no doubt marry better.

Giles agreed that he was not worthy of Grace, and so the three vacillated, no one wanting to make a decision. Then through a series of unfortunate and unforeseen circumstances Giles lost the houses that meant his living. His loss decided the issue. Although Mr. Melbury could easily have supported them both, it was unthinkable that such a lady as Grace should be tied to a man without a steady income. But when her father told her that she must forget Giles, Grace found herself for the first time thinking of her would-be lover with real affection.

Another person was destined to change the lives of all three. In the area was a doctor, Edgar Fitzpiers, descendant of a former fine family and in his own right a brilliant and charming man. The local folk thought he consorted with the devil, for he performed many weird experiments. From the first time Edgar saw Grace, he was enchanted with her beauty and her bearing. At first he thought she must be the lady of the manor, Mrs. Charmond, for he could not believe that the daughter of a merchant could be so well educated and charming. Before long the two young people met and Edgar asked Grace's father for her hand. Mr. Melbury gladly gave his permission, for Edgar was far above Grace in position. In spite of his sorrow at disappointing Giles and at failing to keep his pledge to the faithful fellow, Mr. Melbury encouraged Grace to accept Edgar. Since she had always obeyed her father in all things, she accepted Edgar even as she realized that she grew fonder of Giles each day.

When the young couple returned from a long honeymoon, they settled in a newly decorated wing of her father's house. Edgar continued his practice. It grew alarmingly smaller, however, for the country folk who had once looked up to him now felt him one of their own. He decided that perhaps he should accept a practice in a neighboring town.

Before he could make a final decision on this question, Mrs. Felice Charmond entered the picture. The lady of the manor was well known for her many love affairs and her questionable reputation. When she had a slight accident and sent for Edgar, he was attracted to her immediately. The few scratches she had suffered were enough to take him to her house day after day, until even the servants and farmers were talking about them. At last Mr. Melbury could no longer stand by idly and see his daughter suffer, and so he appealed in person to Mrs. Charmond to leave Edgar alone. Grace herself was rather immune to the whole affair, not caring enough for her husband to suffer any great jealousy.

The climax to the affair occurred when Mr. Melbury found Edgar near Mrs. Charmond's home after Edgar had been thrown from a horse. Mr. Melbury picked him up and placed him on his own mount. Edgar was drunk and not aware that he was riding with his father-in-law. He berated Mr. Melbury and Grace as ignorant peasants and cursed his ill luck in having married beneath himself. His drunken ravings were too much for the kind-hearted merchant, who threw Edgar off the horse and rode away. Edgar, who was injured in the first fall, made his way to Mrs. Charmond and begged her to hide him until he could travel. He must now leave the district; there could be no forgiveness for his many sins.

Mrs. Charmond left her home to travel on the continent and before long rumors came back that Edgar was with her. Grace was stoic through it all. Unknown to her husband, she was also aware that he had had an affair with a peasant girl of the neighborhood before his marriage. She would have let things stand as they were, but an unscrupulous lawyer persuaded her father that a new law would permit her to divorce Edgar. While he was making arrangements for the divorce, Mr. Melbury encouraged both Giles and Grace to renew their old plans to marry. By that time they both felt sure they loved each other, but they were more cautious than Grace's father. Thus when the word came that she could not be free of her husband, they were resigned to their unhappiness.

Grace and Giles did resume the friendship they had known since childhood, but decorously in all respects, for neither wished a hint of scandal to touch the other. Then, after many months, Grace heard from her husband that he wanted her to live with him again. Mrs. Charmond was dead, killed by a thwarted lover who afterward committed suicide. Edgar did not mention this fact, but a newspaper told the whole story. Grace and her father decided she should not meet Edgar as he had asked. When she failed to do so, he threatened to come to their home.

Hearing Edgar approaching, Grace slipped out of the house and ran into the woods. Stumbling and afraid, she came at last to the hut occupied by Giles. On learning that she did not wish to see her husband, Giles installed her in his hut and went out into the rain to sleep. What Grace did not know was that Giles had been very ill of a fever, and a few days and nights in the cold rain made him desperately ill. When she found her faithful friend so ill, she ran for Edgar, forgetting her desire not to see him in her anxiety for Giles. Edgar returned with her but there was nothing to be done. Grace held her one real love in her arms as he died, seeming not aware that her husband was present.

For a long time Grace would not listen to her husband's pleas to return to him. Wanting to hurt him as she had been hurt, she told him that she and Giles had lived together those last few days. Before he learned that her self-accusation was not true, Edgar realized that he truly loved her. When a man trap, set for Edgar by the husband of the peasant girl he had once wronged, almost caught Grace in its steel jaws, Edgar found his wife and helped her to safety. After he told her that he had bought a practice at a great distance from her old home and that he would be a faithful husband, devoting himself to her happiness, she went away with him. She intended to be a good wife, but part of her remained with Giles in the country churchyard grave.

WOODSTOCK

Type of work: Novel
Author: Sir Walter Scott (1771-1832)
Type of plot: Historical romance
Time of plot: 1651
Locale: England
First published: 1826

Principal characters:
SIR HENRY LEE, a Royalist
ALICE LEE, his daughter
ALBERT LEE, his son
COLONEL MARKHAM EVERARD, his nephew, a Puritan
ROGER WILDRAKE, Everard's friend, a Royalist
JOCELINE JOLIFFE, a lodgekeeper, a Royalist
JOSEPH TOMKINS, steward for the Puritans
DR. ROCHECLIFFE, chaplain of Woodstock, a Royalist
LOUIS KERNEGUY, a page, in reality Charles Stuart
OLIVER CROMWELL, Lord Protector of the Commonwealth

Critique:

Again mixing historical facts with fiction, Sir Walter Scott wrote a delightful novel originally called *The Cavalier* and later changed to *Woodstock.* This novel is primarily the story of a gallant old cavalier, Sir Henry Lee, and of his efforts in behalf of his fugitive king, Charles II of England. There is enough historical fact to make the story plausible, but it is fact highly colored by Scott's romantic imagination in a plot dealing with a monarch in disguise, thwarted lovers, a hateful villain. These characters are in turn overshadowed by the gallant old gentleman who could die happily at the instant he saw his king return to glory.

The Story:

Following the death of King Charles I, commissioners of the usurping Oliver Cromwell were sent to destroy the royal residences of England, including the royal lodge of Woodstock, occupied by Sir Henry Lee and his daughter Alice. Forced from their home by Cromwell's soldiers, the old Royalist and his daughter moved to a nearby hut occupied by the royal lodgekeeper, Joceline Joliffe. Arriving at the hut, they found Markham Everard, Sir Henry's nephew, whose opposite political views so enraged his uncle that the young man left the hut and moved into the lodge. There he composed a letter to Cromwell, in which he asked for the pres-

ervation of Woodstock as a personal favor. He sent the letter by his friend, Roger Wildrake, who, even though he was a Royalist, was a trustworthy friend.

Cromwell hated to grant the request, but he hoped to turn it to his own advantage. Young Charles Stuart, heir to the throne, had escaped the Puritans in the company of Albert Lee, Sir Henry's son. Hoping to capture the prince, Cromwell ordered his soldiers to leave the lodge because he believed that Albert might try to contact his father and in that way lead the royal fugitive into a trap. Cromwell ordered Wildrake to tell Everard to detain Albert and Charles, if they appeared at Woodstock, and turn them over to the Puritan troops. But Everard, even though he was a member of Cromwell's party, assured Wildrake that he would not only refuse to betray Charles, but would also, if he had an opportunity, help Charles to escape.

Sir Henry and Alice, accompanied by several servants, returned to Woodstock after the departure of the soldiers. Soon young Albert Lee did arrive at the lodge, and with him were the Woodstock chaplain, Dr. Rochecliffe, and a young Scottish page, Louis Kerneguy. The page was actually Charles Stuart in disguise. He had much fun acting the part of a churlish and mischievous page, and Albert and Dr.

Rochecliffe worried for his safety, although they realized that Woodstock was probably the safest refuge possible for him at the time. Albert and Rochecliffe were the only two certain of the page's real identity, but Joliffe, the lodgekeeper, suspected that the page was his monarch. He kept his eyes open for trouble, particularly from the Puritan steward, Tomkins, who had been left at the lodge by Cromwell to act as a spy. Albert feared too that Wildrake would discover the plot, but Rochecliffe assured Albert that Wildrake would not betray the prince.

The plan was to find a ship to take Charles Stuart to safety. While they waited for arrangements to be completed, Charles became interested in Alice Lee, who was in love with Everard. Hers was a hopeless love, however, for her father would not hear of an alliance between his daughter and a Puritan.

One afternoon, when Alice and Kerneguy—for she knew him only as such—were alone, he became angry because she would not pay proper attention to him. He stalked into the woods and was there confronted by a stranger who was in reality Everard. Everard accused the page of taking advantage of the hospitality offered him by making advances to Alice. The two drew their swords. At that moment Sir Henry appeared. He reprimanded them and escorted them back to the lodge. Everard and his uncle soon quarreled again, egged on by the mischievous page, and Everard left Woodstock. Charles, continuing his suit with Alice, told her that he was her sovereign. Still she would not accept him because of her love for Everard. Charles was greatly annoyed that she would prefer a Roundhead to a king, and when, a short time later, Wildrake delivered to him Everard's challenge to a duel, he accepted with alacrity.

Dr. Rochecliffe and Alice, attempting to prevent the duel, met the hot-blooded young men as they prepared to fight. Alice protested so violently against the duel that Everard thought she must be in love with Kerneguy. He withdrew from the duel and bade Alice goodbye. Then Kerneguy,

seeing her obvious distress, revealed himself to Everard as Charles Stuart. He told the miserable lover that only Alice's loyalty to the Stuarts made her act as she did. Everard assured Charles that his secret was safe with him, as did Wildrake, who was also present.

In the meantime Joliffe killed the Roundhead steward, Tomkins, for making unwelcome advances to Phoebe Mayflower, a maid with whom Joliffe was in love. His rash act increased the danger to the fugitive, for Cromwell depended on Tomkins for information from the lodge. Cromwell, visiting Everard, hinted that he knew Everard had betrayed him. Not knowing of Tomkins' death, Cromwell waited for a message from him before making definite accusations. Wildrake, also present during the interview with Cromwell, sent a message to Woodstock, warning the inhabitants that Cromwell would be there soon. Cromwell waited until midnight; then, hearing nothing from Tomkins, he arrested Everard and forced him to join the Commonwealth soldiers as they surrounded the lodge in an attempt to capture the prince.

Albert Lee, who had been away searching for a ship to take Charles to safety, also sent a letter to Woodstock. In it he stated that he would return that night and that Kerneguy must be ready to leave at once. Albert arrived about the same time that a messenger came with the warning from Wildrake. Then Sir Henry, informed of the true identity of his guest, hastily made arrangements for Charles to escape with a trusted forester as his guide. Alice led Charles to Joliffe's hut, where he was to meet his guide; Albert, remaining behind to delay Cromwell's troops, disguised himself as Charles and hid in a secret room to await the soldiers.

Cromwell and his men seized Rochecliffe and Joliffe as they were burying Tomkins' body. They also captured Sir Henry. Albert, leading the soldiers a merry chase, caused them to blow up a part of the lodge and kill some of their own men. At last they captured him, only to discover that he was not Charles Stuart.

When he refused to reveal the whereabouts of the fugitive, Cromwell sentenced him to death. Relenting, however, he changed the sentence to one of banishment from England. He also released the other prisoners, including Sir Henry, Joliffe, and Everard.

Alice returned from her mission with the news that Charles was safe and that he had asked Sir Henry to withdraw his objections to the marriage between her and Everard. Obedient to his monarch, the old cavalier gave his consent.

Years passed. Sir Henry living near Alice and Everard, was cared for by Joliffe, now married to Phoebe. Albert, after his release, had been killed in battle. At length Cromwell died and his son resigned the government. When Charles returned to England, the only incident marring his triumph was the death of his old and good friend, Sir Henry of Woodstock, who had lived only to see his rightful king restored to the throne of the Stuarts.

WORKS AND DAYS

Type of work: Poetry
Author: Hesiod (fl. c. 735 B.C.)
First transcribed: Eighth century B.C.

Proof of the existence of a writer who flourished about 2,500 years ago is hard to find. Herodotus, liking to exaggerate the antiquity of people, wrote that Hesiod lived "not more than 400 years before my time," putting him about 850 B.C. Most scholars, however, are inclined to place him a century later. Some, believing that the author of *Theogony,* a genealogy of the gods (from which Aeschylus took his *Prometheus Bound*), could not have written *Works and Days* because of different concepts and styles, solve the problem by guessing at two writers with the same name.

At any rate, Homer and Hesiod have left the only Greek writing of the Epic age. Hesiod, in his *Theogony,* shows his indebtedness to the Homeric concept of Zeus, his power and his family life, as set forth in the *Iliad.* Working with some of Homer's earlier material, Hesiod the traditionalist tried also to combine the concepts of his own times. In *Works and Days,* he is no longer concerned with the past. To him the gods are contemporary, directly influencing life in Boeotia. He was talking about his own environment, and not writing a story of the past.

From internal evidence (lines 636-640), it is assumed that the author's father migrated across the Aegean from Cyme in Aeolia on account of poverty. He settled at Ascra, a village of Boeotia, at the foot of Mt. Helicon. Ovid, in referring to Hesiod, used the adjective "ascraeus." The poet himself, heir to the traditions of minstrelsy in this colony of Hellas, says that he once sailed to Chalcis in Euboea, where he competed in a poetry contest held by Amphidamas, and won the prize, a tripod with handles, which he gave to the Muses of Helicon.

The poem also contains details of a lawsuit brought against Hesiod by his brother Perses. Apparently by bribery of the judges, Perses was awarded Hesiod's sheep. But the diligent Hesiod accumulated another fortune while Perses lost all he had and was forced to beg further help from the poet. Without hard feelings, Hesiod gave him assistance, with the warning not to ask again, and put his admonitions in a poem of 828 lines, of which the title well sums up its content: Rules for work and days on which luck is favorable.

Works and Days is neither a scientific treatise on farming nor a lesson on economic recovery through diligence, but rather a combination of moral precepts and an agricultural almanac. Under the symbols of Prometheus and Epimetheus (Forethought and Afterthought), Hesiod epitomized himself and his brother.

In epic style, Hesiod begins *Works and Days* with an appeal to the Muses of Pieria, to sing of their father Zeus, who determines man's fame or dishonor, provides the good and the bad, destroys the mighty, and rewards the humble. The poet adds that there are two kinds of Strife on earth, one good and one bad. The good Strife, the elder daughter of Dark Night and of Zeus the Son of Chronos, makes men industrious so that they strive to imitate and surpass their neighbors.

Then, addressing himself to his brother Perses, Hesiod begs him not to follow the other Strife, in market place or court house. First lay up food for a year, he advises, and then, if necessary, enter disputes of law. This section contains references to Perses' unbrotherly lawsuit to get more than his rightful share of their father's possessions.

Prometheus by craft recovered the fire that Zeus had taken from men, and in revenge Zeus created a woman of water and earth. Pandora ("The All-Endowed") received all the lures provided by the gods to deceive men. She was eagerly accepted by Epimetheus, who had forgotten his brother's warning against gifts from the gods.

Before her advent, men lived on earth free from wearying toil and death-bringing diseases. But Pandora removed the great lid from the jar and all the evils flew out and scattered over the earth.

Hesiod then tells another tale about the way gods and men came from the same seed. In the time of Chronos there existed a golden race of mortals, living like gods and ignorant of sorrow or old age. Everything good belonged to them: abundant flocks, fruits, the blessings of the gods. After the earth covered them, the gods created an inferior race of silver. After a hundred years of idiotic childhood, they came of age, only to kill one another off in warfare. A third race followed whose delight was war; they died and went to chill Hades. Then came the demi-gods, the heroes of Thebes and Troy, preceding the present race of iron, whose daily lot is weariness and woe. To them, might is right. They have no reverence for justice and oaths.

At this point in the poem Hesiod tells the first animal fable in Greek literature, the tale of a hawk who flew high into the sky with a nightingale, lecturing her against the folly of trying to compete with stronger people. To Perses, he adds a warning that violence is a bad quality in a poor man. For him, justice is better.

A city that provides honest judgments, says Hesiod, is blessed by Zeus who protects it from war and famine. Its citizens never have to make sea voyages (which Hesiod hated); their earth provides their living. But an insolent city, even one with a single insolent citizen, is plagued by the gods because Justice, the daughter of Zeus, is quick with rewards or punishment.

Then follows a series of homilies as encouragement to the lazy and improvident Perses: "Work is no disgrace; it is idleness that is disgraceful." "The idle envy the wealth of the hard worker and try to seize it violently. God-given wealth is better."

After these homilies the poet rhymes a sort of farmers' almanac: Plow when the Pleiades set (in November). After forty days they come back. Then sharpen your sickle. When the autumn rains come, cut your wood. Choose oak for ploughbeams, and bring home two, in case one breaks. Get two nine-year-old oxen to plow. A forty-year-old slave is most reliable in the fields. Have everything ready to start plowing when the cry of the crane is heard. If the cuckoo sings, plant quickly, for it will rain in three days. When winter comes, your slaves will need twice as much food, your oxen half their regular ration. Prune your grapes before the return of the swallow, sixty days after the sun turns. When Orion is overhead, it is time to harvest your grapes. Sun them for ten days, cover them for five, and then press out the wine.

His theories on husbandry extend into domestic life. The ideal time for a man to marry, he says, is at the age of thirty; for a woman, the fifth year after puberty. Marry a neighbor, but be sure the others will not laugh at your choice.

Finally, the poet records holy days and the lucky days for different tasks. He concludes that the wise man is the one who works blamelessly before the deathless gods, for he knows the propitious omens and avoids sin.

Works and Days served Vergil as the model for his *Georgics*.

4217

WORKS OF JONATHAN EDWARDS

Type of work: Essays and sermons
Author: Jonathan Edwards (1703-1758)
First published: 1731-1758 (Collected Works: 1808-1809)

Jonathan Edwards, Calvinist preacher and philosopher, was America's first eminent philosopher. Metaphysically, he was an idealist like Berkeley, but his primary concern was not with the traditional problems of philosophy but with theological issues that had a direct bearing on the religious practices of his time. He used his philosophy to assert the absolute sovereignty of God and to reaffirm the doctrine of original sin. He argued that reason and natural goodness are not enough to make a man virtuous: man needs revelation and disinterested benevolence if he is to be worth-while as a religious person. Showing the influence of Locke and Newton, Edwards argued that every event has a cause; he then went on to maintain that man is free, nevertheless, in that he can do as he wills and is therefore responsible for his actions.

The effect of Edwards' work was a strong revival of idealism and Calvinistic pietism. His own congregation responded with a surprising number of conversions, as he reports in his essay, "Narrative of Surprising Conversions" (1736). Edwards attributed what he called the "awakening" to God's influence, but it is clear that his efforts were at least instrumental. The Puritan revival grew to such proportions that the phrase "The Great Awakening" was devised to describe the period between 1740 and 1742.

Edwards' earliest philosophical efforts are preserved in his "Notes on the Mind," an early product of his reading of Locke's Essay Concerning Human Understanding. Edwards went beyond Locke in much the same critical manner as Berkeley, pointing out that the primary qualities of extension, motion, and figure, are as much dependent on the senses as are the secondary qualities of color, taste, sound, and odor. Like Berkeley, Edwards decided that objects are combinations of

ideas and that the "Substance of all Bodies, is the infinitely exact, and precise, and perfectly stable Idea, in God's mind. . . ." Edwards identified perceptions with ideas and attributed all ideas to the influence of God. Like later idealists, he defined truth as the consistency of ideas with themselves; to know that a proposition is true one perceives the relations between ideas, but to have a false idea is to suppose that certain relations obtain among the ideas which, as a matter of fact, do not so obtain. The essay also presented an analysis of value in terms of "the inclination and disposition of the mind." In Notes on the Mind we also find the claim that "all Virtue, which is the Excellency of minds, is resolved into Love to Being," an idea which was later developed in more detail in the essay titled "A Dissertation on the Nature of True Virtue."

In the essay on true virtue, written in 1755, Edwards wrote that "true virtue," by which he meant actual, as distinguished from merely apparent, moral excellence, "consists in benevolence to Being general. Or perhaps to speak more accurately, it is that consent, propensity and union of heart to Being in general, that is immediately exercised in a general good will." Edwards argued that all sin is the result of self-love which resists the directives of the "natural conscience." True virtue is the actual consent to Being, the acceptance of God, and must be distinguished from the natural conscience which approves of true virtue, although it is not itself the virtuous response to Being.

For many outside of Edwards' faith, the problem has always been that of reconciling the idea of God's sovereignty with the idea that God, as Being, should be the object of disinterested benevolence, or love. In his sermon, "Sinners in the Hands of an Angry God," for example,

Edwards spoke from the pulpit of the imminence of hell for the wicked: "There is nothing that keeps wicked men at any one moment out of hell, but the mere pleasure of God. By the mere pleasure of God, I mean his sovereign pleasure, his arbitrary will, restrained by no obligation. . . ." He went on to warn that "natural men are held in the hand of God over the pit of hell; they have deserved the fiery pit, and are already sentenced to it." He declared that the wrath of God is "everlasting" and that the torments of hell will continue for "millions and millions of ages. . . ." Finally, he concluded that "it would be a wonder if some that are now present should not be in hell in a very short time, before this year is out. And it would be no wonder if some persons, that now sit here in some seats of this meeting-house in health, and quiet and secure, should be there before tomorrow morning."

In his *Personal Narrative* (1765) Edwards wrote that the doctrine of God's sovereignty "used to appear like a horrible doctrine to me," but he had come to regard the doctrine as "exceeding pleasant, bright, and sweet." For a man who had learned to consent to Being, the change of attitude was inevitable. But how was Edwards to reconcile for his congregation the idea of a sovereign God whose nature and grace are beyond discovery with the idea of a God worthy of love? To understand the answer, one must consider, in turn, two such famous sermons as "God Glorified in Man's Dependence," delivered in 1731, and "A Divine and Supernatural Light, Immediately Imparted to the Soul by the Spirit of God, Shown to be Both a Scriptural and Rational Doctrine," delivered in 1734.

The former sermon was enthusiastically received by Calvinist ministers who sought, through its publication, to defend their faith from attack. In his sermon Edwards argued that the redeemed are absolutely dependent on God, that His grace is entirely free, that all good is in God, and that the fact of man's dependence glorifies God. To have any hope of an eternal life, a man should "abase himself, and reflect on his own exceeding unworthiness of such a favor, and to exalt God alone." Although Edwards insisted that the redeemed have spiritual joy because of their dependence, the emphasis was more on the fact of dependence and on God's glory than on the satisfaction of being redeemed.

In the sermon "A Divine and Supernatural Light," Edwards used the psychology he had learned from reading Locke to emphasize his claim that there is no natural way of coming to know and love God. The blessedness of some men, their spiritual happiness, resulted from God's having given them a spiritual light whereby they could come to be convinced of God's reality and excellence. Such a spiritual light cannot be explained in any of the ways by which we understand natural faculties of the understanding and will; it must be imparted by the Spirit of God. Edwards offered the doctrine as both scriptural and "rational." The sermon concluded with a reassuring statement of the value of the spiritual light: "It draws forth the heart in a sincere love to God, which is the only principle of a true, gracious, and universal obedience; and it convinces of the reality of those glorious rewards that God has promised to them that obey him."

By alternatively emphasizing the sovereignty of God and the joy of loving Him, Edwards achieved a balance between the harsh and the comforting aspects of his Calvinistic views.

Of his essays, the most famous is the essay on the freedom of the will, a book-length study entitled "A Careful and Strict Inquiry into the Modern Prevailing Notions of that Freedom of the Will, Which is Supposed to be Essential to Moral Agency, Virtue, and Vice, Reward and Punishment, Praise and Blame." The will is quickly and simply defined as the power to choose. Edwards then agreed that Locke was correct in distinguishing between will and desire, the latter being restricted to what is absent; but he argued that the distinction was not important in the problem of free will. The will is determined, he wrote, because in consequence of some influence a choice is made. The will is always determined by the strongest motive; i.e., by the prevailing inclination. Whether one considers natural or moral necessity, in either case one is considering the connection of cause and effect. By freedom is meant the power to do as one pleases or wills. Thus, even if the will is determined by the strongest motive, there is no contradiction involved in saying that a man is free if he can do what he wills. If a person is forced to do something, then he is not free; but even if the will is determined by cause, a man is free if he can do as he chooses.

Edwards would have rejected the question of the freedom or determination of the will. For him the answer was that the will is *both* determined and free: it is determined in that it acts from causes; it is free provided the person who wills is able to act as he wills.

Edwards concluded that whenever an act results from the exercise of a man's will, the agent is morally responsible for his act. By his philosophical resolution of the problem of free will Edwards was able to relate moral necessity to God's necessarily choosing the best. He rejected Arminian criticisms which attempted to support a conception of liberty as "indifferent"; i.e., a conception of the will as capable of acting entirely without determination.

Other important essays by Edwards are "The Great Christian Doctrine of Original Sin Defended" (1758), "True Grace" (1753), "Dissertation Concerning the End for which God Created the World" (1755), and "Treatise Concerning Religious Affections" (1746).

Edwards brought all of his philosophical powers to bear on the issues which kept Calvinism in the midst of religious controversy, and although few modern philosophical critics would grant that he in any way proved his case, it is generally conceded that he played a major role in the "Great Awakening" and gave American philosophy an initial impetus and influence that continued until realistic and pragmatic ideas effectively displaced religious idealism.

THE WORLD AS WILL AND IDEA

Type of work: Philosophy
Author: Arthur Schopenhauer (1788-1860)
First published: 1818

In his massive masterpiece, *The World as Will and Idea (Die Welt als Wille und Vorstellung),* Schopenhauer goes to great lengths, following Kant, to argue that everything that exists is a manifestation of will. Man's life should be an attempt to see this fact clearly and to recognize that the will brings nothing but suffering. The most satisfactory life, then, is one that finally succeeds in extinguishing itself, not by suicide but by an elimination of will.

It might be supposed that his philosophy made Schopenhauer a pessimist, but it is probably nearer to the truth to say that the pessimist Schopenhauer made his philosophy. If his mother, whom he hated, had not had a strong will, perhaps Schopenhauer would not have come to the conclusion that everything is will; but if he had not developed his philosophy, not only would there have been no great work for the melancholy Romantics, but there would have been no adequate stimulus for Nietzsche's idiosyncratic extension of Schopenhauer's ideas.

To persons who are not philosophers it is very difficult and sometimes impossible to imagine how anyone could suppose that the world is nothing but will. But there is a simple way of succeeding at this task: one has only to suppose that the philosopher's will is so strong and his preoccupation with his own ideas so great that he soon comes to believe that all talk about a physical world that is in no way will or idea must be nonsensical. Of course, he finds reasons for what he claims, but his reasons usually turn out to be ingenious academic constructions designed to disguise the limited concern which the philosophical view expresses.

Schopenhauer prefaces his work with an expression of indebtedness to Kant, Plato, and the Upanishads. He was in debt to Kant for the idea that the world as we know it is conditioned by our way of seeing and understanding it, and from Sanskrit literature and Indian philosophy he derived the basic belief that suffering is the inevitable consequence of the exercise of will and that Nirvana, the eternal calm that follows the elimination of will, is all that man can hope for. He modified Kant radically in claiming that the ultimate reality is will, and he did not share any positive conception of Nirvana but chose to emphasize the value of total extinction, coming to be nothing.

"'The world is my idea:'—this is a truth which holds good for everything that lives and knows, though man alone can bring it into reflective and abstract consciousness." So the book begins. The initial line of justification is acceptable to almost anyone; Schopenhauer argues that we do not know the sun and earth, for example, in any direct way but only in relation to our own experience. Put it another way: all that we ever know is known by means of the ideas we have about objects. But then Schopenhauer makes the typical idealist leap. From the proposition that we know only *by* our ideas he passes to the claim that we know *only* our ideas. He writes, "All that in any way belongs or can belong to the world is inevitably . . . conditioned through the subject, and exists only for the subject. The world is idea."

The subject is "That which knows all things and is known by none." Consequently, no one knows himself as subject. Everyone knows his body, for his body is an idea and can exist only for a subject; but no one knows that subject. The subject is not in space and time, for space and time (following Kant) are forms in which the subject knows objects. The subject's mode of understanding is such that only by perceiving objects spatially and temporally can he perceive them at all; but it would be a mistake to suppose that objects themselves, considered as something other than ideas, are in space and time. It would be a mistake on two counts. First, it would be a confusion of the object of our knowledge, an idea, with what could never be an object of knowledge, viz., something "outside," a thing-in-itself. Secondly, it would be an instance of the fallacy of attributing to the objects of our perception the conditions of our perception; that is, it would be like holding seriously that everything is green when the fact of the matter is that we are looking at everything through green glasses. (This is not Schopenhauer's analogy.)

Schopenhauer's way of making the point that space, time, and causality are features given to objects by the subject because of its way of understanding objects is by saying that "the essential and hence universal forms of all objects, space, time, and causality, may, without knowledge of the object, be discovered and fully known from a consideration of the subject; i.e., in Kantian language, they lie a priori in our consciousness."

Schopenhauer explicitly rejects realism and calls it a "grave error" to suppose that physical objects are the cause of our sensations. His basic argument in support of his rejection of realism consists in the claim that since causality is a condition of perception (we must understand objects as causally related to each other) it can hardly be a principle by reference to which one explains objects.

It is only because we, as knowing subjects, have bodies that we can come to have knowledge of the content of our ideas. Schopenhauer decides that what objectifies itself as body is will. The body is like other objects in being known as an idea, but it is different because we understand it "from the inside," so to speak, as a manifestation of will. Schopenhauer insists that he is not using the word "will" to mean force; he desires "that every force in nature should be thought of as will." He refers to insect and animal life in order to defend his

point: "The bird of a year old has no idea of the eggs for which it builds a nest; the young spider has no idea of the prey for which it spins a web. . . ."

For Schopenhauer, then, everything that is known to us is known as idea, and all ideas are conditioned by the knowing subject. Yet if the knowing subject were eliminated, there would still remain the "thing-in-itself," which Schopenhauer identifies as will.

Schopenhauer then goes on to argue that in recognizing will as the inner reality of the world he is agreeing with Plato, who maintained that the Ideas, or unchangeable forms, constitute that reality. He contends that the Platonic idea is the object of art, that art affords pleasure because it presents the "purely knowable side of the world" and allows the artist and the spectator to escape, for moments at a time, from the intimate knowledge of will as suffering.

The philosopher's interest in art as a way to the knowledge of Idea, the highest objectification of will, leads Schopenhauer into a number of chapters concerning the theory of art, drama, architecture, music, poetry, and beauty. The constant effort to explain art in terms of the will results, on occasion, in some interesting, if not acceptable, observations. For example, Schopenhauer claims that the beauty of a landscape derives from the "truth and consistency" of nature. He argues that wherever nature is left alone, natural beauty results. "Every neglected plant at once becomes beautiful," he assures us. The English garden allows the will of nature to express itself, but the French garden imposes man's will on hedges, plants, and trees, so that it is difficult, if not impossible, for a French garden to have any natural beauty.

If we consider the world as the objectification of will, then we must consider it as having no end of suffering. If the will were entirely content, it could not exist; will is a striving, and a striving or effort is a sign of defect. As long as there is striving, there is suffering; and satisfaction is always short-lived and only partial.

Having made these points, Schopenhauer then draws the conclusion that recognition of will as the only reality leads to a recognition of the value of denying the will. If man denies the will, he denies painful striving; although in eliminating will he eliminates the world, everything that exists; he escapes from suffering and attains a kind of peace. At that stage "only knowledge remains, the will has vanished." Even though the denial of the will results in nothingness—for if everything is will, the elimination of will is the elimination of everything—Schopenhauer prefers nothingness to the ceaseless striving and suffering of the will. In any case, he argues that nothingness is always relative to something, and that to achieve nothingness is nothing more than to be rid of something, namely, suffering.

One can understand how a pessimist who was at the same time a philosopher might come to prefer the peace of willing nothing to the pain of willing what always escapes, or changes, or dies. But why did Schopenhauer take the trouble to write several volumes on the subject, objectifying will at great length, rather than commit suicide and achieve nothingness in one fell swoop? His answer is that "suicide is a phenomenon of strong asser-tion of will. . . . The suicide wills life, and is only dissatisfied with the conditions under which it has presented itself to him." Schopenhauer's objection seems to be that since suicide is not a denial of the will but an affirmation of it, the death of an individual in no way eliminates will but only the place and time of its objectification. If a man bent on suicide were to argue that forcing the will to objectify itself elsewhere is the point of suicide, since in that way suffering is eliminated *for him*, Schopenhauer would reply that the suicide overemphasizes the value of the individual, forgetting that only will is real.

The World as Will and Idea is important as a philosophical expression of Western man's discontent as a result of falling away from the comforting dogmas of religion. Its weakness as a solution to the fundamental problem of life—finding a reason for being—is that it borrows an Eastern faith and tries to convert it into a Western metaphysics. The result is not only an endorsement of nothing through sanctioning the denial of the will to live, but also a philosophy in which other philosophers, for the most part, find nothing to endorse.

WORLD ENOUGH AND TIME

Type of work: Novel
Author: Robert Penn Warren (1905-   )
Type of plot: Philosophical romance
Time of plot: 1801-1826
Locale: Kentucky
First published: 1950

Principal characters:
JEREMIAH BEAUMONT, an idealist
COLONEL CASSIUS FORT, a frontier politician, Jeremiah's benefactor
RACHAEL JORDAN, betrayed by Fort, later Jeremiah's wife
WILKIE BARRON, an opportunist
DR. LEICESTER BURNHAM, Jeremiah's teacher
LA GRAND' BOSSE, a river pirate

Critique:

Colonel Solomon P. Sharp, Solicitor General of Kentucky, was killed by a masked assassin in 1825. Shortly afterward Jeroboam Beauchamp, a young lawyer and a member of the political party opposing Sharp, was arrested and charged with the crime. During the trial it was revealed that Beauchamp had married a planter's daughter whom Sharp had seduced. A dose of laudanum failing to kill them, husband and wife stabbed themselves. The wife died in her husband's cell. Beauchamp was hanged. The Kentucky Tragedy, as this story of intrigue and revenge was called, became a popular subject during the nineteenth century, among writers as dissimilar as Edgar Allan Poe, Charlotte Barnes, Thomas H. Chivers, Charles F. Hoffman, and William Gilmore Simms. Robert Penn Warren, reworking the old tale, has filled it with philosophical speculation and symbolic moral overtones. His Jeremiah Beaumont is an idealist confronted by the realities and compromises of the world, a man betrayed not only by an acquisitive and self-seeking society but also by the very idealism which sustains him in loneliness and doubt. The plot, centering about a theme of community guilt and expiation, illustrates the complex moral issues of the present age.

The Story:

Jeremiah Beaumont was born in Kentucky in 1801. His father was Jasper Beaumont, one of the first settlers in Glasgow County, his mother the disinherited daughter of a wealthy planter. Jasper Beaumont never prospered as he had hoped, and his unfulfilled ambitions bred in him a strain of awkward moodiness which was reflected in his son.

Jasper died, debt-ridden, when Jeremiah was thirteen. Before that time the boy had been put to school with Leicester Burnham. Hoping for a better life than his father's, Jeremiah was diligent in his studies. He was also stubbornly independent, for he refused to become his grandfather's heir because the old man insisted that he take his mother's maiden name, Marcher. When he was seventeen, Dr. Burnham introduced him to Colonel Cassius Fort, a famous frontier lawyer and politician who was looking for a young man to train in his law office at Bowling Green. Jeremiah was eager to accept Fort's offer but could not do so because of his ailing mother. Fort said that he was willing to wait for anyone Dr. Burnham recommended so highly.

In the next spring Mrs. Beaumont died and Jeremiah went to Bowling Green to study law, not in Fort's office, however, for the lawyer had returned to Congress. Jeremiah's only friend in the town was Wilkie Barron, another law student, from whose mother Jeremiah rented a room. Fort returned from Washington in 1820 and took the young man under his patronage. From him Jeremiah learned to look on the law not as a collection of dry statutes but as man's agent of truth and justice. Times were hard in Kentucky following the panic of 1819, and the Legislature had passed a law allowing a twelve-month stay of sale for debt. Fort was on the side of the Relief Party, as those who supported the measure were called.

Wilkie Barron first told Jeremiah of a scandal linking Fort's name with that of Rachael Jordan, daughter of a planter who had died heavily in debt. Called in to help settle the estate, Fort was supposed to have seduced the girl and fathered her stillborn child. Grieved by that story of innocence betrayed, Jeremiah decided to have nothing more to do with his benefactor. In a letter he informed Fort, who was away at the time, of his decision. Fort wrote in reply, but before his letter reached Bowling Green Jeremiah had gone to visit Wilkie's uncle, old Thomas Barron, in Saul County. The Jordan place was only a few miles away from his host's. There he met Rachael Jordan, won her confidence, and, after hearing from her own lips the story of her shame, married her. She accepted him on the condition that he kill Fort.

In the meantime he had become involved in local politics. Wilkie Barron and Percival Scrogg, fanatic liberal editor of a Frankfort newspaper, arrived to take part in a disputed election. After a riot at the polls, in which he and Wilkie fought side by side, Jeremiah was dismayed to learn that his friend was working for Fort. Wilkie advised him to put aside personal grudges for the public good.

Jeremiah and Rachael Jordan were married in 1822. At the time Fort was away on private business. Taking over the Jordan plantation, the young husband devoted all his energies to making the place productive. Sometimes he felt that he had his father's score to settle as well as his wife's, that his hard work would

vindicate his bankrupt father against men like Fort, to whom wealth and fame came easily. Ambitious for the future and foreseeing expansion of the settlements, he formed a partnership with Josh Parham, a rich landowner, and with Parham's son Felix surveyed town sites in the unclaimed western lands. The venture in land speculation fell through, however, when Desha, the Relief candidate, was elected governor in 1824. Parham, an Anti-Relief man, swore that he would never spend money opening up land in Kentucky while the Relief Party was in office.

Rachael and Jeremiah were expecting their first child when Fort returned from the East. Rachael, begging her husband to give up his intention of killing Fort, persuaded him that his first duty was to her and the unborn child. A week later Wilkie arrived at the plantation with a handbill in which Fort, announcing his candidacy for the Legislature, disavowed membership in the Relief Party. Urged by Wilkie, Jeremiah also became a candidate for office. The campaign was a bitter one. Unknown to Jeremiah, the Relief Party printed a broadside in which the scandal involving Fort and Rachael was revived. Jeremiah, to his wife's relief, was defeated by Sellars, the candidate he opposed.

Two months later Rachael had a miscarriage. One the same day a handbill was mysteriously delivered to the house. Signed by Fort, it refuted the campaign slanders against him and accused Rachael of having her first child by a mulatto slave. That night Jeremiah reached his decision to kill Fort. As soon as he could leave his wife in a neighbor's care he rode to Frankfort. Disguised, he went at night to the house in which Fort was staying, called him to the door, and stabbed him to death. He then rode home and told Rachael what he had done.

Four days later officers appeared and summoned him to Frankfort for examination in connection with the murder. Believing that there was no evidence against him, he went willingly. But his enemies were already busy manufacturing false clues, and to his surprise he was held for court. By the time of his trial bribery and perjury had done their work. In spite of the efforts of Dr. Burnham and other loyal friends his case was lost when Wilkie appeared to testify against him. Although many believed him innocent, Jeremiah was sentenced to be hanged on August 20, 1826. Meanwhile Rachael had been arrested and brought to Frankfort, where she and her husband shared the same cell. Jeremiah's lawyers appealed the sentence. When they failed to produce one of the handbills defaming Rachael, the appeal was denied.

Two days before the execution date Wilkie Barron and several men broke into the jail and freed the prisoners, who were taken secretly to a refuge ruled over by La Grand' Bosse, a river pirate. There, from one of Wilkie's former henchmen, Jeremiah learned that Scrogg and Wilkie had forged the handbill responsible for Fort's death. In despair, Rachael killed herself. Realizing how he had been duped, Jeremiah tried to return to Frankfort and reveal the truth. Wilkie's man overtook him and cut off his head.

Wilkie went into partnership with the Parhams and became rich. Still politically ambitious, he was elected senator. One night in Washington he shot himself. Among his effects, to be uncovered in an old trunk years later, were some letters and a manuscript in which Jeremiah Beaumont, during his months in prison and in the outlaw camp, had written his story of deceit and betrayal. No one would ever know why Wilkie had kept those incriminating papers. Unable to destroy the truth, he had tried to conceal it. Perhaps at the end, like Jeremiah, he wondered whether the striving, pride, violence, agony, and expiation had all been for nothing.

THE WORLD OF THE THIBAULTS

Type of work: Novel
Author: Roger Martin du Gard (1881- 1958)
Type of plot: Social chronicle
Time of plot: Early twentieth century
Locale: France
First published: 1922-1940

> *Principal characters:*
> M. THIBAULT, the father
> ANTOINE, his older son
> JACQUES, his younger son
> GISE, an orphan girl reared by the Thibaults
> MME. DE FONTANIN, a Protestant woman
> JÉROME DE FONTANIN, her husband
> DANIEL, her son
> JENNY, her daughter
> MEYNESTREL, a socialist leader

Critique:

The story of the Thibaults is a remarkable depiction of French bourgeois family life. The length of the completed work is of little importance when one considers that Martin du Gard has achieved a closely-knit plot and an absorbing story of pre-World War I days, making his novel a history of a place, a people, and a whole society. For managing his vast story within unified bounds the author of *The World of the Thibaults* richly merits the honor and praise he has received. In the United States the novel has appeared in two volumes, *The Thibaults* and *Summer 1914.*

The Story:

M. Thibault was furious when he learned that Jacques had lied to him and had run away with young Daniel de Fontanin. The Abbé Binot, Jacques' teacher, had even more disquieting news. From a copybook which had fallen into the abbé's hands, it was apparent that Jacques, not yet fourteen, had formed an unnatural friendship with Daniel. What was worse, the de Fontanins were Protestants.

Antoine Thibault, already a doctor, went to see Mme. de Fontanin to learn what he could about Daniel and his friendship with Jacques. Antoine found

her a very attractive, sensible woman, who rejected Antoine's hints of improper relationship between the boys.

They questioned Jenny, Daniel's younger sister, who had come down with a fever. To Antoine's practiced eye, Jenny was suffering from meningitis. When neither Antoine nor the other doctors could help Jenny, Mme. de Fontanin called in Pastor Gregory, her minister. He effected a miraculous cure of the girl by faith healing.

Jacques and Daniel got as far as Marseilles. Although Jacques was the younger, he was the moving spirit in the escapade. He had revolted against the smug respectability of his father and the dull Thibault household. M. Thibault was such an eminent social worker that he had no time to understand his own family. But the suspicions of the Thibaults were unfounded; the friendship between Daniel and Jacques was only a romanticized schoolboy crush.

When the runaways were returned by the police, Daniel was scolded and forgiven by his mother. Jacques, on the other hand, was put in a reformatory founded by his father. There, Jacques' spirit was nearly broken by brutal guards and solitary confinement. Only by devious means was Antoine able to get his brother away from his father's stern discipline. He took a separate flat and had Jacques live with him, assuming responsibility for his younger brother's upbringing.

Jérome de Fontanin, Daniel's father, ran away with Noémie, a cousin, and Nicole, Noémie's daughter, came to live with the de Fontanins. Nicole was very attractive and Daniel tried to seduce her. But Nicole had before her the unhappy example of her mother and resisted him.

Under Antoine's care, Jacques slowly recovered his mental health. During the summer vacation he was greatly attracted to Jenny de Fontanin. Just as Jenny was beginning to care for him and to overcome her aversion to physical contact, Jacques disappeared.

For three years the Thibaults thought Jacques was dead. Only Gise, an orphan girl reared by the Thibaults, had hoped that he was still alive. One day she received from England a box of rose buds like those she had sprinkled on Jacques just before his disappearance. Sure that Jacques was alive in England, Gise went to school in England, where she hoped to find him.

Antoine followed a different course. He came by chance on a Swiss magazine which carried a story called *Sorellina* or *Little Sister*. Antoine thought that he could see both the Thibault and de Fontainin families thinly disguised in the story. Disquieted, Antoine engaged a detective agency in Geneva to trace the author.

Antoine's own life was not too happy. On an emergency case one night he met Rachel, an adventuress. They became lovers. Little by little Rachel told him the story of her sordid past, a story which strangely endeared her the more to Antoine.

She had once been the mistress of the ferocious Hirst, a man of fifty, who had been having incestuous relations with his daughter, Clara. Rachel's brother had married Clara and they had gone to Italy on their honeymoon. A few days later Clara had written to her father,

asking him to join them. After his arrival, the young husband learned the true relationship between father and daughter. To avoid a scandal, Hirst had strangled Clara and her husband and had thrown their bodies into a lake.

Rachel said she was through with Hirst. But one day she said she had to make a trip to the Congo to see about some investments. When Antoine saw through the ruse, she admitted she was going back to Hirst. He had sent for her. Antoine sadly accompanied Rachel to Le Havre and helped her embark.

In Geneva, Jacques had become an international socialist and an influential writer, according to a report from the detective agency. Then M. Thibault developed a serious illness. Fearing that his father would die, Antoine went to Geneva and asked Jacques to return, but M. Thibault died without recognizing his errant son. At the funeral Gise saw Jacques again and realized that she still loved him. But Jacques had lost all his affection for her.

Jenny was still afraid of Jacques, and in her frigidity she had even come to hate him. Daniel was busy as a successful artist. Feeling no ties in Paris, Jacques returned to Geneva.

He worked there during that fateful summer of 1914. Under the leadership of Meynestrel, a group of socialists were busy uniting the workers of England, France, and Germany in an effort to stop the impending war by paralyzing strikes. Jacques was frequently sent on secret missions. One such trip was to Paris just before general mobilization was decreed.

By chance Jacques saw Jenny again. The new Jacques, mature and valuable to the pacifist movement, soon converted Jenny to his views. They finally fell in love.

Mme. de Fontanin's husband had died in Vienna, where he was suspected of embezzlement. Thinking to clear his name, she went to Austria in spite of the imminence of war. While she was gone, Jacques became a frequent visitor to the de Fontanin flat. When Mme. de Fontanin returned early one morning, she was shocked to find Jacques and Jenny sleeping together.

Jenny planned to leave for Geneva with Jacques. At the last moment, however, she decided to remain at home. Jacques was free for his humanitarian mission. He and Meynestrel had their own plan for ending the war.

Jacques took off from Switzerland in a light plane piloted by Meynestrel. He had with him several million pamphlets which called on both Germans and French to lay down their arms. But the plane went into a dive over the French lines and Meynestrel was burned to death. Jacques, severely wounded, was captured by the French as a spy. While he was being carried to headquarters on a stretcher, one of the orderlies shot him in the temple.

Gassed severely during the war, Antoine realized that his recovery was impossible. On leave, he visited his old country home near Paris, where he found Mme. de Fontanin a competent hospital administrator and Nicole a good nurse. Jenny was happy, bringing up Jean-Paul, her son and Jacques'. Daniel had come back from the front a changed man, for a shell splinter had unsexed him. Now he spent his time looking after Jean-Paul and helping the nurses.

Back at the hospital in southern France, Antoine received a necklace from Rachel, who had died of yellow fever in Africa. He tried to keep notes on the deteriorating condition of his lungs. He lived until November 18, 1918, but he never knew that the Armistice had been signed before his death.

THE WORLD'S ILLUSION

Type of work: Novel
Author: Jacob Wassermann (1873-1934)
Type of plot: Social criticism
Time of plot: Prior to World War I
Locale: Europe
First published: 1919

Principal characters:
CHRISTIAN WAHNSCHAFFE, son of a wealthy German capitalist
BERNARD CRAMMON, Wahnschaffe's aristocratic friend
EVA SOREL, a dancer
IVAN BECKER, a Russian revolutionist
AMADEUS VOSS, Wahnschaffe's boyhood friend
KAREN ENGELSCHALL, a prostitute befriended by Wahnschaffe

Critique:

The World's Illusion is a representation by the German novelist, Jacob Wassermann, of the dual nature of European society prior to the first World War. The first book of the novel deals with brilliant, upper-class life in European society, of which the protagonist of the novel is an example. The second book deals with the same protagonist, who left the vanity and culture of his world for the horrors of life among the proletariat in the worst of European slums. Thus the author was able to show the decay of European society on its highest and lowest levels.

The Story:

Christian Wahnschaffe was an unusual person, even as a child. In boyhood he was without fear. He would harry an entire pack of mastiffs belonging to his father, ride the wildest horses, and take risks in huntings; but he always came away without harm, as if his life were charmed. As young Wahnschaffe grew older he lost none of his daring. Because his father was a very rich man, Christian lived in the best European society. One of his close friends was Bernard Crammon, a member of the Austrian aristocracy, who traveled with him everywhere.

During a stay in Paris, Crammon saw a young dancer, Eva Sorel, in an obscure theater. The dancer so impressed Crammon that he introduced her into his circle of leisure-class intellectuals, where she met Christian Wahnschaffe. Orphaned at an early age, the first things that Eva could remember were connected with her training as a tight-rope walker with a troupe of traveling players. One day a crippled Spaniard bought the little girl's liberty from the gipsies in order to train her as a dancer, for he recognized the possibilities of her beauty and grace. When she was eighteen the Spaniard sent her to Paris with his sister to make her debut. Shortly afterward she had met Bernard Crammon.

Christian Wahnschaffe fell desperately in love with Eva Sorel, but she refused him as a lover. Although she was charmed by his appearance and his personality, she remained aloof, for she saw in him a man who had not yet learned to appreciate the aesthetic and intellectual life of his time.

Christian had a rival for the love of Eva Sorel, a young English nobleman, Denis Lay. Lay was as handsome as Christian and more talented in the world of the intellect; he was also Christian's equal in the world of physical accomplishments. Lay appealed far more to Eva than did the German. However, there was something about Christian that mysteriously fascinated the girl.

THE WORLD'S ILLUSION by Jacob Wassermann. Translated by Ludwig Lewisohn. By permission of the publishers, Harcourt, Brace & Co., Inc. Copyright, 1920, by Harcourt, Brace & Co., Inc. Renewed, 1948, by Ludwig Lewisohn.

Denis Lay's rivalry lasted but a few months. One night while he entertained Eva Sorel, Crammon, Christian, and a large company aboard his yacht in the Thames, the passengers saw a crowd of striking dock workers gathered on the banks of the river. Lay dared Christian to compete with him in a swimming race to the shore to investigate the crowd. When the Englishman leaped overboard and started for the shore, strong undercurrents soon dragged him under, despite Christian's efforts to save him. The next morning his body was recovered. The incident had a profound effect on Christian.

Some time later, in Paris, Christian met a refugee Russian revolutionary, Ivan Becker. Becker tried to make Christian understand something of the misery everywhere in Europe and the exploitation of the poor by the classes above them. When Christian finally asked Becker what he should do, the Russian replied that everyone in the upper classes asked the same question when confronted by problems of inequality and poverty. But, continued Becker, it was really a question of what the poor man was to do.

One night Becker took Christian to see the wife and four children of a man who had attempted to assassinate the elder Wahnschaffe. Disturbed by the degrading poverty of the household, Christian gave them a large sum of money. Later he learned that it was almost the worst thing he could have done, for the woman wasted the gold in foolish purchases and loans to people who had no intentions of repaying her.

Christian began to be bored with the life of leisure and luxury he had led. It seemed to him that he should do something better with his life. He lost interest in his gem collection and when he discovered that Eva Sorel desired his world-famous diamond, the Ignifer, he sent it to her.

The dancer, meanwhile, had achieved great success. In Petrograd the Grand Duke Cyril, a man of great political influence under the tsar, offered to lay everything he could command at her feet. She refused him and, still fascinated by the memory of Christian, returned to Western Europe. During a holiday she sent for Christian and took him as her lover. The sweetness of the affair was blunted, however, by Christian's new liberalism. He had become friendly with Amadeus Voss, a young man who once had studied for the priesthood, and consequently had become more than ever convinced of the futility of his life. One day Eva was injured when a large stone, thrown by a drunken man at a fair, struck her feet. At her home, while Christian was bathing and binding her swollen feet, he felt that he was kneeling to her spiritually as well as physically. His whole mind rebelled against this discovery, and he left the dancer precipitately.

A few weeks later, with Crammon, Christian went to Hamburg to see a friend off to America. After the ship had sailed, Christian and his friend wandered about the waterfront. Hearing screams in a tavern, they entered. There they found a man mistreating a woman whom they rescued and took to an inn. The following morning Christian returned and told her that he would take care of her. When she said that she was Karen Engelschall, a prostitute, Christian assured her that he only meant to take care of her as a human being. He had already decided to go to Berlin to study medicine and she readily agreed to go there too, since her mother and brother were living in that city.

Christian's father and brother had become much richer, and both held posts in the German diplomatic service. The elder Wahnschaffe wished Christian to take charge of his business, but Christian refused. Deciding to become a poor man and to help humanity, he also sold the land he had inherited from his mother's family. That was the reason for his decision to study medicine. His friends and his family thought him mad, and his father threatened to have him

4231

placed in protective custody in a sanatorium. Even the people Christian had taken into his care, Amadeus Voss and Karen Engelschall, thought he was mad. They had previously had visions of great wealth to be gained through him.

Karen died within a few months of bone tuberculosis. By that time Christian had returned all of his fortune to his family and was almost penniless. Then Karen's brother committed a murder and tried to implicate Christian. With patience Christian played upon the nerves of the brother until he admitted having committed the crime, exonerating Christian. Shortly afterward the elder Wahn-schaffe appeared at the Berlin tenement where his son was living and attempted to persuade him to return to his rightful place in society before the reputation of the entire Wahnschaffe family was utterly ruined. Christian refused, but he agreed to disappear entirely. Nothing more was heard of him. Sometimes rumors sifted back to his former friends and his family that he had been seen among the poorest people in London, New York, or some continental city, and that he was doing his best to make life easier for the unfortunates of this world.

WOYZECK

Type of work: Drama
Author: Georg Büchner (1813-1837)
Type of plot: Psychological realism
Time of plot: Early nineteenth century
Locale: Germany
First presented: 1913; first published: 1879

> Principal characters:
> FRIEDRICH JOHANN FRANZ WOYZECK, a military conscript
> MARIE, his sweetheart
> A DRUM MAJOR, Marie's other lover
> ANDRES, another soldier, Woyzeck's friend
> A CAPTAIN
> A DOCTOR

Critique:

Although this drama of proletarian life was written more than one hundred years ago, it is surprisingly modern in its blending of naturalism and expressionism and in the writer's use of technical devices more common to the twentieth-century stage than to that of the nineteenth. Left incomplete at the end of Büchner's brief but eventful life, the play owes its present form to editors who have arranged the writer's scattered scenes and notes in an acceptable chronological sequence. The play was based upon an actual event, for Johann Christian Woyzeck, a conscript convicted of the murder of his common-law wife, was publicly executed at Leipzig on August 27, 1824. Before his execution a considerable amount of medical testimony dealing with the condemned man's state of mind and body had been assembled. The result was that when Büchner began to write his drama he had at hand what amounted to a psychological case history of his principal character. The playwright presented his chief figure sympathetically against his larger background themes of man's inhumanity and social injustice. The work is remarkable also for the writer's ability to dramatize states of psychopathological tension. The drama provided the story for Alban Berg's experimental modern opera, Wozzeck.

The Story:

Franz Woyzeck was a conscript fusilier, a poor, simple soldier with a peasant's slow mind and a peasant's superstitions. The only happiness he had in his wretched existence came from his humble devotion to his sweetheart Marie and their small son. Because his army pay did not provide for the support of his household, he was forced to earn additional money by performing menial tasks about the camp and in the garrison town where his regiment was stationed.

Having served as a barber's apprentice in his youth, he was often called in to shave his Captain. The officer, a man of speculative, ironic temperament, liked to talk about such topics as time and eternity, matters which were beyond Woyzeck's comprehension. Sometimes the Captain jokingly reproved the poor fellow for his lack of morals, since he had fathered a child without benefit of a wedding ceremony. Woyzeck always declared that if he were a gentleman with a laced coat and a cocked hat he would try to be virtuous, too. Virtue, he thought, was a privilege of the educated and the great, not for miserable creatures like himself.

An eccentric Doctor also paid Woyzeck a few small coins to act as the subject of fantastic medical experiments. The soldier was supposed to live on a diet of peas and to hold his water for stated periods of time. When Woyzeck tried blunderingly to explain his views on nature and life, the Doctor was delighted. He thought that Woyzeck's halting remarks showed an interesting aberration, and he predicted that the man would end in a madhouse.

One day Woyzeck and his friend Andres went into the country to cut wood for the Captain. Woyzeck began to talk wildly about the Freemasons and claimed that they had burrowed under the ground, so that the earth they had hollowed out was rocking under his feet. Their secret signs having been revealed to him in dreams, he was fearful of their vengeance. Andres, usually a matter-of-fact fellow, became rather alarmed when Woyzeck pictured the Last Judgment in the glowing colors of the sunset. Returning home, Woyzeck tried to explain to Marie the vision he had seen in the sky. She was hurt because in his excitement he failed to notice his son. That afternoon a handsome, bearded Drum Major had ogled Marie while she stood at her window and talked to a friend outside. She wondered about Woyzeck and his strange thoughts. Marie was hearty and earthy. She could understand people's emotions better than she could their ideas.

Woyzeck and Marie went to a fair. As they entered one of the exhibits, the Drum Major and a Sergeant came by and followed them into the booth, where the barker was showing a horse that could count and identify objects. When the showman called for a watch, the Sergeant held up his timepiece. To see what was going on, Marie climbed upon a bench and stood next to the Drum Major. That was the beginning of their affair. A short time later Woyzeck found Marie with a new pair of earrings which she said she had found. The simple-minded soldier said that he had never been lucky enough to find anything in pairs. While Woyzeck was on duty or doing extra work, the Drum Major would visit Marie in her room. Full-blooded and passionate, she found herself ready to yield to his advances.

In the meantime Woyzeck had no suspicions of her infidelity. One day, as he was bustling down the street, he met the Captain and the Doctor. The Captain began to talk slyly about beards and hinted that if Woyzeck were to hurry home he would be in time to find hairs from a bearded lover on Marie's lips. Woyzeck became so pale and nervous that the Doctor showed great clinical interest in his reactions. The Captain assured Woyzeck that he meant well by the soldier and Woyzeck went loping home. When he peered steadily into Marie's face, however, he could see no outward signs of her guilt. His scrutiny disturbed and then angered her. She defied him, practically admitting that she had another lover, but she dared Woyzeck to put a hand on her. Unable to understand how anyone so foul could look so beautiful and innocent, he left the house. Not knowing what else to do, he went to the Doctor's courtyard. There the physician made him appear ridiculous in front of a group of medical students.

The next Sunday Woyzeck and Andres were together in the barracks, Woyzeck restless and unhappy because there was a dance at an inn near the town and he knew that Marie and the Drum Major would be there. Andres tried to stop his friend but Woyzeck said that he had to see them for himself. He went to the inn and through an open window watched Marie and her lover dancing. Andres, fearing a disturbance, finally persuaded him to go back to town. Karl, a fool, was among some loafers near the inn door; he said that he smelled blood.

That night Woyzeck, unable to sleep, told Andres that he still heard music and saw the dancing. He also mumbled about his vision of a knife in a store window. The next day Woyzeck encountered the Drum Major at the inn and the two men fought. Woyzeck, the weaker of the two, was badly beaten by his swaggering rival. Mad with jealousy, he went to a pawn shop and bought a knife like the one he had seen in his dream. At the barracks

4234

he gave away most of his possessions. Resisting Andres' attempt to get him to the infirmary. he went to Marie and asked her to go walking with him. On a lonely path near the pond he took out the knife and stabbed her to death.

Then he went back to the inn and danced madly. When a girl named Kaethe noticed bloodstains on his hand, he said that he had cut himself. Questioned further, he screamed that he was no murderer and ran from the inn. Wanting to get rid of the incriminating knife which he had left beside Marie's body, he threw it into the pond. His first throw fell short. Desperate, he waded out to hurl the knife into the deep water, got in over his depth, and drowned.

A group of playing children heard some adults talking about the murder. They ran to Woyzeck's son and told him that his mother was dead.

THE WRECK OF THE GROSVENOR

Type of work: Novel
Author: W. Clark Russell (1844-1911)
Type of plot: Adventure romance
Time of plot: Nineteenth century
Locale: The Atlantic Ocean
First published: 1877

Principal characters:
MR. ROYLE, second mate of the *Grosvenor*
MR. COXON, the captain
MR. DUCKLING, the first mate
MARY ROBERTSON, a survivor from a shipwreck

Critique:

This novel, quite apart from its love story, is in the true romantic tradition. The characterization is credible, and the action well-motivated. In addition, the author underlines a period in maritime history with his arguments for better treatment of the sailor.

The Story:

As the *Grosvenor* was preparing to leave its British port, the wind died and the ship lay anchored in the Downs. The crew aboard grew more and more discontented, until at last the cook stopped Mr. Royle, the second mate, and showed him a biscuit from the ship's store. This biscuit, as well as the other food served to the crew, was crawling with vermin and inedible. When Mr. Royle brought the matter to the attention of Captain Coxon, that officer was indignant; the food was good enough for sailors who, he insisted, had eaten much worse food. Furthermore, he did not want Mr. Royle to fraternize with the crew. It was apparent, however, that the crew was likely to mutiny once the ship was on the high seas, and so the captain and Mr. Duckling, the first mate, went ashore and came back with an entirely new crew.

After the ship had been a few days at sea, the new crew approached Mr. Royle to complain of the rations. The captain had the food brought to his table, where he tasted it without flinching, but he hinted that he would put in at some convenient port and take aboard

new stores. When he made no attempt to change the ship's course, however, the crew became even more resentful. Mr. Royle tried to remain neutral. If he so much as spoke to any of the crew, the captain would consider him mutinous. If he sided with the captain and Mr. Duckling, the crew, in the event of a mutiny, would probably kill him. But his anger mounted and his disgust reached a high point when the captain refused to rescue survivors from a shipwrecked vessel.

Some time later another wrecked vessel was sighted, and the crew insisted that Mr. Royle be permitted to bring the survivors aboard. The survivors were Mr. Robertson, owner of a shipping firm, his daughter Mary, and a man who had gone mad from the terrifying experience of shipwreck at sea. Mr. Royle did everything he could for the Robertsons; the third survivor died. For his part in the rescue Mr. Royle was confined to his cabin and put in irons.

One night the crew mutinied. The captain and Mr. Duckling were killed, and Mr. Royle was set free. He promised to steer as the crew wished, if they in turn would promise not to kill the steward, whom they especially hated because he was in charge of ship stores.

It was the plan of the mutineers to anchor off the coast of the United States, and then, after they had reached shore, to pass themselves off as shipwrecked sailors. But after a while Mr. Royle discovered that the real intention was to scuttle the ship and leave him and the Robertsons aboard to die. With the help of the loyal boatswain, he hoped to foil the scuttling attempt.

Mr. Royle, who had become very fond of Mary Robertson, told her frankly of the situation. They decided to say nothing to her father, who was losing his memory. Mr. Royle planned to steer the ship close to Bermuda instead of the Florida coast. Since none of the crew knew anything about navigation, he was able to set his own course. The boatswain planned to hide himself below decks and kill the man who went below to bore the holes in the ship's bottom.

One dark night Mr. Royle threw a box of nails over the rail and everyone thought that the boatswain had fallen overboard. In reality, he had gone into hiding. When the time for the scuttling drew near, Stevens, the leader of the mutineers, went down to do the work, instead of another member of the crew. Mr. Royle was frightened, for if Stevens were killed the crew would soon discover his death. But the leader came back and ordered the lowered longboat to pull out. As the crew rowed away from the ship, the boatswain appeared to tell that he had merely plugged in the holes as fast as Stevens bored them. When the crew in the longboat saw what had occurred, they attempted to board the vessel. All, except one, were unsuccessful. That sailor was put to work.

When a storm arose, those on board were unable to handle the ship. The ship began to leak and Mr. Royle realized that the water could not be pumped out. During the storm Mr. Robertson died. A Russian steamer passed by, and refused to save them. The mutineer lost his mind and died. Then the longboat, pushed toward them by the storm, collided with the ship. Mr. Royle decided to abandon the *Grosvenor*. Before they left the sinking ship he and Mary Robertson pledged their love to each other.

Mr. Royle, Mary, the boatswain, and the steward pushed off in the longboat. At last they sighted a steamer which answered their signals. After Mr. Royle had gotten Mary Robertson aboard, he collapsed. When he awoke, he found himself in bed, attended by a Scottish doctor. Mary came in with the boatswain. They told him the steward had gone completely mad.

Mary reminded Mr. Royle of his promise of marriage, but he said that he could not marry her before he had made his fortune. She insisted that he would not be a poor man if he were married to her. She said that she loved him for himself, and she knew that he loved her for herself, not for her money. Mr. Royle finally agreed. They were married, and Mary provided handsomely for both the boatswain and the steward for the remainder of their lives.

WUTHERING HEIGHTS

Type of work: Novel
Author: Emily Brontë (1818-1848)
Type of plot: Impressionistic romance
Time of plot: 1750-1802
Locale: The moors of northern England
First published: 1847

> *Principal characters:*
> MR. EARNSHAW, owner of Wuthering Heights
> CATHERINE, his daughter
> HINDLEY, his son
> HEATHCLIFF, a waif
> MR. LINTON, proprietor of Thrushcross Grange
> MRS. LINTON, his wife
> ISABELLA, their daughter
> EDGAR, their son
> FRANCES EARNSHAW, Hindley's wife
> HARETON EARNSHAW, Frances' and Hindley's son
> CATHERINE LINTON, Catherine Earnshaw's and Edgar Linton's daughter
> LINTON HEATHCLIFF, Isabella Linton's and Heathcliff's son
> ELLEN DEAN, housekeeper at Thrushcross Grange
> MR. LOCKWOOD, tenant at Thrushcross Grange and narrator of the story

Critique:

Published under the pseudonym of Ellis Bell, *Wuthering Heights* was considered such a risk by its publishers that Emily Brontë had to defray the cost of publication until a sufficient number of copies had been sold. The combination of lurid and violent scenes in this novel must have been somewhat shocking to mid-nineteenth-century taste. Despite its exaggerated touches, *Wuthering Heights* is an intriguing tale of revenge, and the main figures exist in a more than life-size vitality of their own consuming passions. For her novel Emily Brontë chose a suitable title. The word *wuthering* is a provincial adjective used to describe the atmospheric tumult of stormy weather.

The Story:

In 1801 Mr. Lockwood became a tenant at Thrushcross Grange, an old farm owned by Mr. Heathcliff of Wuthering Heights. In the early days of his tenancy he made two calls on his landlord. On his first visit he met Heathcliff, an abrupt, unsocial man, surrounded by a pack of snarling, barking dogs. When he went to Wuthering Heights a second time, he met the other members of that strange household; a rude, unkempt but handsome young man named Hareton Earnshaw and a pretty young woman who was the widow of Heathcliff's son.

During his visit snow began to fall, covering the moor paths and making travel impossible for a stranger in that bleak countryside. Heathcliff refused to let one of the servants go with him as a guide, but said that if he stayed the night he could share Hareton's bed or that of Joseph, a sour, canting old servant. When Mr. Lockwood tried to borrow Joseph's lantern for the homeward journey, the old fellow set the dogs on him, to the amusement of Hareton and Heathcliff. The visitor was finally rescued by Zillah, the cook, who hid him in an unused chamber of the house.

That night Mr. Lockwood had a strange dream. Thinking that a branch was rattling against the window, he broke the glass in his attempt to unhook the casement. As he reached out to break off the fir branch outside, his fingers closed on a small ice-cold hand and a weeping voice begged to be let in. The unseen presence, who said that her name was Catherine Linton, tried to force a way through the broken casement, and Mr. Lockwood screamed.

Heathcliff appeared in a state of great excitement and savagely ordered Mr. Lockwood out of the room. Then he threw himself upon the bed by the shattered pane and begged the spirit to come in out of the dark and the storm. But the voice was heard no more —only the hiss of swirling snow and the wailing of a cold wind that blew out the smoking candle.

Ellen Dean satisfied part of Mr. Lockwood's curiosity about the happenings of that night and the strange household at Wuthering Heights. She was the housekeeper at Thrushcross Grange, but she had lived at Wuthering Heights during her childhood.

Her story of the Earnshaws, Lintons, and Heathcliffs began years before, when old Mr. Earnshaw was living at Wuthering Heights with his wife and two children, Hindley and Catherine. Once on a trip to Liverpool Mr. Earnshaw had found a starving and homeless orphan, a ragged, dirty, urchin, dark as a gipsy, whom he brought back with him to Wuthering Heights and christened Heathcliff—a name which was to serve the fourteen-year-old boy as both a given and a surname. Gradually the orphan began to usurp the affections of Mr. Earnshaw, whose health was failing. Wuthering Heights became a bedlam of petty jealousies; Hindley was jealous of both Heathcliff and Catherine; old Joseph, the servant, augmented the bickering; and Catherine was much too fond of Heathcliff. At last Hindley was sent away to school. A short time later Mr. Earnshaw died.

When Hindley Earnshaw returned home for his father's funeral, he brought a wife with him. As the new master of Wuthering Heights, he revenged himself on Heathcliff by treating him as a servant. Catherine became a wild and undisciplined hoyden who still continued her affection for Heathcliff.

One night Catherine and Heathcliff tramped over the moors to Thrushcross Grange, where they spied on their neighbors, the Lintons. Catherine, attacked by a watchdog, was taken into the house and stayed there as a guest for five weeks until she was able to walk again. Thus she became intimate with the pleasant family of Thrushcross Grange—Mr. and Mrs. Linton, and their two children, Edgar and Isabella. Afterward the Lintons visited frequently at Wuthering Heights. The combination of ill-treatment on the part of Hindley and arrogance on the part of Edgar and Isabella made Heathcliff jealous and ill-tempered. He vowed revenge on Hindley Earnshaw, whom he hated with all the sullen fury of his savage nature.

The next summer Hindley's consumptive wife, Frances, gave birth to a son, Hareton Earnshaw, and a short time later she died. In his grief Hindley became desperate, ferocious, and degenerate. In the meantime, Catherine Earnshaw and Edgar Linton had become sweethearts. The girl confided to Ellen Dean that she really loved Heathcliff, but she felt it would be degrading for her to marry the penniless orphan. Heathcliff, who overheard this conversation, disappeared the same night, not to return for many years. Edgar and Catherine soon married, taking up their abode at Thrushcross Grange with Ellen Dean as their housekeeper. There the pair lived happily until Heathcliff's return caused trouble between them. When he returned to the moors, Heathcliff, greatly improved in manners and appearance, accepted Hindley's invitation to live at Wuthering Heights—an invitation offered by Hindley because he found in Heathcliff a boon companion at cards and drink, and he hoped to recoup his own dwindling fortune from Heathcliff's pockets.

Isabella Linton began to show a sudden, irresistible attraction to Heathcliff, much to the dismay of Edgar and Catherine. One night Edgar and Heathcliff came to blows. Soon afterward

Heathcliff eloped with Isabella, obviously marrying her only to avenge himself and provoke Edgar. Catherine, an expectant mother, underwent a serious attack of fever. When Isabella and her husband returned to Wuthering Heights, Edgar refused to recognize his sister and forbade Heathcliff to enter his house. Despite this restriction, Heathcliff managed a final tender interview with Catherine. Partly as a result of this meeting, her child, named Catherine Linton, was born prematurely. The mother died a few hours later.

Isabella, in the meantime, had found life with Heathcliff unbearable. Leaving him, she went to London, where a few months later her child, Linton, was born. With the death of Hindley, Heathcliff the guest became the master of Wuthering Heights, for Hindley had mortgaged everything to him. Hareton, the natural heir, was reduced to dependency on his father's enemy.

Twelve years after leaving Heathcliff, Isabella died and her brother took the sickly child to live at Thrushcross Grange. Heathcliff soon heard of the child's arrival and demanded that Linton be sent to Wuthering Heights to live with his father. Young Catherine once visited Wuthering Heights and met her cousin Linton. Her father had tried to keep her in ignorance about the tenants of the place, for Heathcliff had been at pains to let it be known that he wished the two children, Cathy and Linton, to be married. And Heathcliff had his way. About the time that Edgar Linton became seriously ill, Heathcliff persuaded Cathy to visit her little cousin, who was also in extremely bad health. Cathy,

on her arrival, was imprisoned for five days at Wuthering Heights and forced to marry her sickly cousin Linton before she was allowed to go home to see her father. Although she was able to return to Thrushcross Grange before her father's death, there was not enough time for Edgar Linton to alter his will. Thus his land and fortune went indirectly to Heathcliff. Weak, sickly Linton Heathcliff died soon after, leaving Cathy a widow and dependent on Heathcliff.

Mr. Lockwood went back to London in the spring without seeing Wuthering Heights or its people again. Traveling in the region the next autumn, he had a fancy to revisit Wuthering Heights. He found Catherine and Hareton now in possession. From Ellen Dean he heard the story of Heathcliff's death three months before. He had died after four days of deliberate starvation, a broken man disturbed by memories of the beautiful young Catherine Earnshaw. His death freed Catherine Heathcliff and Hareton from his tyranny. Catherine was now teaching the ignorant boy to read and to improve his rude manners.

Mr. Lockwood went to see Heathcliff's grave. It was on the other side of Catherine Earnshaw from her husband. They lay under their three headstones; Catherine's in the middle weather-discolored and half-buried, Edgar's partly moss-grown, Heathcliff's still bare. In the surrounding countryside there was a legend that these people slept unquietly after their stormy, passionate lives. Shepherds and travelers at night claimed that they had seen Catherine and Heathcliff roaming the dark moors as they had done so many years before.

THE YEARLING

Type of work: Novel
Author: Marjorie Kinnan Rawlings (1896-1953)
Type of plot: Regional romance
Time of plot: Late nineteenth century
Locale: The Florida scrub country
First published: 1938

Principal characters:
JODY BAXTER, a young boy
PENNY BAXTER, his father
ORA BAXTER, his mother
FODDER-WING FORRESTER, Jody's crippled friend
OLIVER HUTTO, Penny's friend
GRANDMA HUTTO, his mother
TWINK WEATHERBY, Oliver's sweetheart

Critique:

Marjorie Kinnan Rawling's novel, *The Yearling,* deals with one year in the life of a twelve-year-old boy, the year in which he passed from adolescence into young manhood. As the author has pointed out, the book is a description of childhood—its intense sorrows and transient joys. The book also introduces the reader to a way of life which is new and strange. Because of the author's sympathy and understanding, her pleasant interest in nature and wild life, her deep knowledge of human nature, reading *The Yearling* becomes a highly personal experience.

The Story:

The Baxter family consisted of Penny Baxter, his plump wife Ora, and the boy Jody. They lived in a simple cabin in the Florida scrub, where patient, hardworking Penny eked out a meager living by farming and hunting.

Young Jody still saw life through the eyes of a child and found a boy's pleasure in building a flutter mill at the spring when he should have been hoeing the garden patch.

One spring morning the family discovered that Betsy, their black brood sow, had been killed by a bear. Penny recognized the tracks as those of Old Slewfoot, a giant black bear with one toe missing. Determined to be rid of this offender he cornered the animal in the scrub, but his old gun would not fire and the bear escaped.

Unable to afford a new gun, Penny traded a worthless feist to his neighbors, the Forresters, for a new double-barreled shotgun of fine make. The Forrester family consisted of the old parents, six gigantic, lawless sons, and Fodder-wing, a deformed and crippled boy who was Jody's best friend. Penny was reluctant to dupe his neighbors but his very living depended upon Old Slewfoot's destruction. He eased his conscience by telling the Forrester boys truthfully that the feist could not be trained for hunting. His words convinced the suspicious Forresters that the dog was even more valuable than they had thought and it was they who insisted on the trade.

After the old gun had been repaired, it became Jody's great pride. One day while hunting with his father, he shot a buck which Penny sold at the store in Volusia. After selling the venison, Penny and Jody went to see Grandma Hutto, at whose house they spent the night. In the morning everyone was made glad by the unexpected arrival of Oliver Hutto, Grandma's son, just home from sea. Later that day Oliver went downtown, where he met Lem Forrester. Both of the men were courting a yellow-haired girl, Twink Weatherby. When the two started to fight, all of Lem's brothers joined in against Oliver Hutto. Wiry Penny and small Jody also entered the fight with Oliver, since the odds against him were so heavy. After the fight Oliver was badly battered. Jody had been knocked unconscious. To keep people from talking, Twink Weatherby left town on the river boat the next morning.

A short time later Penny discovered that his hogs had disappeared. He suspected the Forresters of having trapped them in order to get revenge for the shotgun deal, and he and Jody started to track the hogs. In the swamp a rattlesnake bit Penny on the arm. He saved himself by shooting a doe and applying the liver to the bite to draw out the poison. Even in the excitement, Jody had noticed that the doe had a fawn. While Penny staggered homeward, Jody went to the Forresters to ask them to ride for Doc Wilson.

The Forresters, with the exception of Lem, evidently held no grudge over the trading of the dog and the fight in town, and they did all they could for the Baxters. One of the boys brought Doc Wilson to the cabin. Later they rounded up the hogs and returned them, and Buck Forrester stayed on at the Baxter cabin to help with the work.

While Penny was still desperately ill, Jody returned to the place where his father had been bitten, and there he found the helpless young fawn. He was so eager to have it for his own that his parents allowed him to bring it home as a pet. Rations were scarcer than ever at the Baxters during Penny's illness, but Jody was willing to share his own food and milk with the fawn. Fodder-wing gave the fawn its name. He called it Flag.

In September a great storm came, destroying most of the Baxter crops. About a month later Old Slewfoot visited the Baxter land again and killed a fat hog. Penny, who was in bed with chills and fever, was not able to follow the great black bear. Later wolves killed one of the calves, and with the Forresters the Baxters hunted down the whole pack which had been bothering all the neighborhood. During the hunt they found ten bear cubs, left motherless after hunters had killed the mother bear. Two of the Forresters took the cubs to Jacksonville and sold them. Penny's share of the profits was used to buy the necessities which would tide the Baxters over the coming winter.

The Baxters had planned to spend Christmas in Volusia with Grandma Hutto and to attend the town's festivities on Christmas Eve. But a few days before Christmas Old Slewfoot again appeared and killed a calf. Penny swore that he would kill the raider, and after several days of determined hunting he found and shot the five-hundred-pound bear.

The Baxters joined Grandma Hutto at the Christmas party. During the evening Oliver Hutto arrived in town with his wife, Twink. To get revenge, Lem Forrester and his brothers fired Grandma Hutto's house and burned it to the ground. Without Oliver's knowing that the house had been fired by the Forresters, Grandma Hutto, Oliver, and Twink left town the next morning on the river boat. They had decided to go to Boston to live.

Back in their cabin, the Baxters settled down to a quiet winter of fishing and hunting. Flag, the fawn, had grown until he was a yearling. The fawn had never been a favorite of Ma Baxter because she begrudged him the food and milk Jody fed him, and because he was a nuisance around the cabin.

In the spring, while Jody was helping his father plant corn, Flag got into the tobacco field and destroyed about half of the young plants. One day, while trying to pull a stump out of the ground, Penny ruptured himself and afterward spent many days in bed. Then Jody had to do all of the farm work. He watched the corn sprouting through the ground

One morning he found that Flag had eaten most of the tender green shoots. Mrs. Baxter wanted to kill the fawn at once, but Penny suggested that Jody build a fence around the corn to keep Flag out. Accordingly, Jody spent many days replanting the corn and building a high fence around the field. When the new planting of corn came up, Flag leaped the high fence with ease and again nibbled off the green shoots.

Her patience exhausted Mrs. Baxter took Penny's gun and shot the fawn. Unhappy Jody had to shoot his pet again because his mother's aim was so poor. Jody felt that the family had betrayed him. He hated them. He left the clearing and wandered into the scrub. With the vague idea of running away from home to join the Huttos in Boston, he headed for the river and set out in Nellie Ginright's dugout canoe. After several days without food, he was picked up by the river mail boat. He returned home, ashamed and penitent, but a yearling— no longer interested in the flutter mill, which now he considered only a plaything for children.

THE YEARS

Type of work: Novel
Author: Virginia Woolf (1882-1941)
Type of plot: Domestic chronicle
Time of plot: 1880-1937
Locale: London
First published: 1937

Principal characters:
COLONEL ABEL PARGITER
ELEANOR,
EDWARD,
MORRIS,
DELIA,
MILLY,
MARTIN, and
ROSE, his children
CELIA, Morris' wife
NORTH, and
PEGGY, children of Morris and Celia
PATRICK, Delia's husband
SIR DIGBY PARGITER, the colonel's brother
EUGÉNIE, his wife
MAGGIE, and
SARA, their daughters
RENÉ (RENNY), Maggie's husband
LADY KITTY LASSWADE, the Pargiters' cousin
NICHOLAS POMJALOVSKY, Eleanor's friend
CROSBY, a servant

Critique:

The entry in Virginia Woolf's diary for November 2, 1932, contains a reference to the novel eventually published as *The Years*. In the beginning it was to be called *The Pargiters,* an essay-novel into which she planned to pour the total sum of her experience in telling of the experiences of a single family through several generations. The pattern was not to follow that of family chronicles such as John Galsworthy and Hugh Walpole had written; instead it was to jump chamois-like across gaps in time between 1880 and the present. A domestic story, lacking the bold technical brilliance of *To the Lighthouse* and *The Waves,* the work may appear at first reading like a reversion to the method employed in earlier books like *Night and Day.* Nothing could be farther from the truth. *The Years* is more than the story of a middle-class family

in all its frustrations, ambitions, triumphs, joys, tragedies, and defeats. In its episodic pattern it represents an effort to capture and record the process of time passing and to catch in fiction that sudden flash of recognition or the moment of perception which in earlier periods was the function of poetry alone. In the separate divisions of the novel, descriptions of the seasons and the flowing movement of the prose convey that sense of change and recurrence which in her later novels Mrs. Woolf tried to dredge from the depths of human consciousness.

The Story:

On a blustery April afternoon in 1880, Colonel Abel Pargiter sat at the window of his club looking out over Piccadilly. Everyone in the street seemed to have somewhere to go, some end in view. The colonel felt that there was nothing for him. At home, in the shabbily genteel house on Abercorn Terrace, his wife was dying of cancer; he had a family of three sons and four daughters to provide for; he was retired, and he was not rich. He thought of his mistress, Mira, who lived in a side street near Westminster Abbey. He would visit her. When he arrived dusk was already falling, filling the dingy rooms with the secret, furtive atmosphere of lust.

In the same dusk, in the house on Abercorn Terrace, Milly and Delia Pargiter were boiling the water for tea. Because their younger sister Rose was wearing a green-smudged pinafore, Milly tried to be severe with her in grown-up fashion. Twelve-year-old, red-haired Martin came home from school. When the colonel arrived and asked for Eleanor, his oldest daughter, Milly reminded him that it was her day for social service. Eleanor appeared, dropping her books on the table. Since her mother's illness she had become the family's mainstay, the keeper of accounts, the soother of hurts, the arbiter of quarrels. Delia went to sit with her mother. She resented Mrs. Pargiter's illness, the ties of sickness and home; in her imagination she saw herself on the platform at a political meeting, the great Parnell beside her. Morris Pargiter, a young barrister, came home for dinner. The family was at the table when Crosby, the servant, brought word that Mrs. Pargiter had suffered a relapse. She died later that same rainy night.

Rain also fell in Oxford. Edward Pargiter put aside the *Antigone* and daydreamed of his cousin, Kitty Malone, a don's daughter with whom he was in love. His friend Hugh Gibbs came in with talk of horses and women. Another friend, Ashley, appeared; but Ashley was jealous of Gibbs and Edward, unhappy and bored, went off to bed. Kitty Malone, reading history with eccentric Miss Craddock, admired Jo Robson; he reminded her of a young farmhand who had once kissed her under a rick. Mrs. Malone, reading the letter which told of Mrs. Pargiter's death, thought of her cousin as a young girl. Edward, she decided, would not do; young Lord Lasswade would make a more suitable match. Mrs. Pargiter was buried on a day of shadows and sunshine.

It was cool in England in the autumn of 1891. In the north, Kitty, Lady Lasswade, shivered on the terrace where she sat with her husband. In Devonshire, Hugh Gibbs told his wife Milly—she had been a Pargiter—that the leaves on the trees were still too thick for good hunting. At Oxford, Edward Pargiter, now a don, walked in the crisp air and thought of poetry. Morris, the lawyer, recalled his childhood as leaves crisped under his feet on the flagstones of the Law Courts. Martin was a soldier in India. Delia had left home to lead a life of her own, and Rose had gone too. Only Eleanor remained, tied to her aging father and the house on Abercorn Terrace, keeping accounts, doing social service work, going to the Law Courts with Celia, Morris' wife, buying children's presents that the colonel would give to his nieces, Maggie and Sara, when he went to dine with his brother, Sir Digby Pargiter. Sir Digby was in politics; his wife Eugénie was pretty and frivolous. The colonel had dinner with Digby and Eugénie on the day Parnell died.

By midsummer, 1907, Martin was back from India, still Captain Pargiter but no longer in the army. Sara Pargiter thought of her cousins as she lay in bed and read Edward's translation of *Antigone*. Her mother and father had gone out to dinner and Maggie with them; it was Maggie's first grown-up party. Sara's back was crooked, for she had been dropped as a child. She read Edward's book and listened to the music of a dance down the street. Finally she fell asleep.

A year later Sir Digby and Eugénie were both dead, and their house had been sold. Colonel Pargiter had suffered a stroke. Sometimes Eleanor, who still looked after him, reflected on what a terrible thing old age was. Sir Digby and his wife had been fortunate, she thought,

4245

dying in their prime. Rose, forty, mannish, returned from suffragette meetings she had been attending in the north. Meeting at the Abercorn Terrace house, she and Martin recalled the time they had quarreled and Rose had cut her wrist with a knife.

After their parents' death Maggie and Sara went to live in Hyams Place, a crescent of shabby old houses. Maggie and Rose met in a shop and Rose went to have lunch with her cousins on a day in 1910. Delia had married an Irishman. For a brief time some of the family —Eleanor, Martin, Kitty, Rose, and Sara —came together at a suffragette meeting. That night, while Sara was telling Maggie about the meeting, they heard shouting in the street outside. The king was dead.

After her father's death Eleanor went on a holiday in Spain and Greece. She was fifty-five, too old to begin a new life. She went to visit Morris and his wife Celia; they had two children, North and Peggy. Maggie was also married, to a Frenchman. The Abercorn Terrace house was sold in 1913, and Crosby went off to live in lodgings in Richmond. Still loyal to the Pargiters, she looked after Martin's laundry and socks.

Martin, coming from his stockbroker's on a spring day in 1914, ran into Sara at St. Paul's and took her out to lunch. They talked about Rose, who had been jailed after breaking windows during a suffragette demonstration. Later they met Maggie and her baby in Kensington Gardens. That night Martin dined with the Lasswades. Sitting beside a young girl at dinner, he suddenly felt that he was old, his life empty.

The war came. One night in the winter of 1917 Eleanor went to have dinner with Maggie and her husband Renny. There were other guests, Nicholas Pomjalovsky, a Pole, and Sara. In the middle of dinner a German air raid began. Later Nicholas tried to explain his hopes for the new world to come after the war. Eleanor felt that here was the man whom she might have married. Maggie confided that he loved only other men. Eleanor, Sara, and Nicholas walked across London in the cold darkness. Eleanor had forgotten the air raid and the wail of the sirens. They wailed again and guns boomed on a November day in 1918. Crosby was waiting in the queue at a grocer's shop. Someone said that the war was over.

In 1937, Eleanor, now over seventy and just back from a trip to India, went to Delia's party, a gathering of the Pargiter clan, with her niece Peggy, now a doctor in a London hospital. Peggy's brother North, who had sold his farm in Africa, took Sara, who had invited him to dinner at her shabby flat. Maggie and Renny, on their way from the theater, went with them. Delia was old; Patrick, her Irish husband, was handsome but hard of hearing. Peggy, looking at Delia and Patrick, wondered how people married, had children. She talked to Martin, who was never at ease with her; she was his doctor and knew his dread of cancer. Rose came in; she had grown stout and deaf. Milly waddled in her fat beside big, jovial Hugh Gibbs. North thought of animals munching in their stalls. Morris, the barrister, was there, and Edward, the distinguished bachelor-scholar. Kitty Lasswade, now the widow of a governor general, appeared in time for supper. Nicholas tried to make a speech and healths were drunk. The young looked at the old and the old looked at the young. Eleanor wondered if there had been a pattern behind these lives, a theme, like a motif in music. Then it was time to go. Eleanor stood at the window and watched a taxi drive up to a nearby house and a young man and young woman get out. The young man was fitting his latch key to the door. The sun was shining; it was a bright new day.

THE YEMASSEE

Type of work: Novel
Author: William Gilmore Simms (1806-1870)
Type of plot: Historical romance
Time of plot: Early eighteenth century
Locale: South Carolina
First published: 1835

Principal characters:
SANUTEE, a Yemassee chief
MATIWAN, his wife
OCCONESTOGA, his son
GABRIEL HARRISON, a young settler
HECTOR, Gabriel's Negro slave
PARSON MATTHEWS, a minister
BESS MATTHEWS, his daughter

Critique:

The Yemassee tells a fast-moving story of adventure and love during the days of Indian warfare in Colonial South Carolina. Simms had not Cooper's ability to picture nature poetically, but his characterizations of Indians are perhaps more accurate.

The Story:

The English settlers, who at first had to accept aid from the Yemassee Indians when the white men landed on the South Carolina shores, had become quite powerful by 1715. No longer did they have to be careful not to offend the Indians; instead, they continually set up farms on the wrong side of the boundary lines between white and Indian territory. Sanutee, one of the Yemassee chiefs, had become suspicious of the colonists; he was afraid that they would soon take over all the Yemassee land. In order to keep them from occupying Indian territory, he had made treaties with other tribes and with the Spanish, who were willing to help the Indians defeat the English. Sanutee's life was made unhappy by his son, Occonestoga, who had been tempted by liquor to become a close friend of the whites. Sanutee was too proud of his ancestry and his position to call a drunkard his son, and it was only by constant pleas that his wife, Matiwan, was able to keep him from completely disowning Occon-

estoga.

One of the recent settlers was Gabriel Harrison, a strange young man whose commanding presence and jolly manner made him both admired and disliked. Among those who liked him was Bess Matthews, the daughter of the old parson, and Walter Grayson, an honorable young farmer. Parson Matthews disliked Harrison because he was too gay and worldly in his manner, and Walter's brother, Hugh, disliked Harrison because he was also an admirer of Bess. Harrison had brought with him a fine Negro slave named Hector, who was his constant companion, and a strong and faithful dog named Dugdale. With these two companions Harrison wandered about the district.

One day in the forest Harrison came upon Sanutee fighting with a stranger over the carcass of a deer. He arrived in time to save Sanutee's life, but the proud Indian expressed no gratitude. Harrison learned that Sanutee's opponent was a sailor named Dick Chorley, who had recently arrived on the coast. Although Chorley said that he had come to trade, Harrison rightly suspected that he was really a Spanish agent who had come to arm the Indians against the English. Harrison sent Hector to spy on Chorley and Sanutee, who had been joined by Ishiagaska, another Yemassee chief.

Hector, hiding in the brush, overheard Chorley's declaration that he had come to South Carolina to arm the Indians. Displaying the wampum belt of an Indian treaty, he asked the Yemassee tribe to join the tribes who were willing to fight the English. Before Hector could return to tell Harrison what he had learned, the slave was captured and taken aboard Chorley's ship.

Harrison guessed what had become of Hector. He found Chorley in the parson's cabin and by threats forced the seaman to sign an order freeing Hector. His action angered the parson, who refused to suspect Chorley of treason. He denied Harrison the right to wed his daughter Bess.

In the meanwhile the Yemassee chiefs were called to a council and asked to sell more land to the English. Most of the chiefs were willing to sell, but Sanutee, who arrived late at the meeting, made a stirring speech against the sale. Interrupted by his drunken son, the old Yemassee almost killed Occonestoga. When he heard that the chiefs intended to sell the land over his protests, Sanutee left the meeting and went to arouse the people against their chiefs. With the aid of an Indian prophet named Enoree Mattee, he so infuriated the crowd that they repudiated the other chiefs and punished them by having the tribal mark cut from their skins, so that they became outcasts from the tribe. Only Occonestoga escaped this punishment.

Occonestoga hid in the woods. One day he saved Bess Matthews' life by killing a rattlesnake that was about to strike her. For his deed Harrison rewarded the young Yemassee with his friendship. Soon afterward he sent Occonestoga back to the Indian stronghold to learn what the Indians were planning. Occonestoga secretly made his way to his mother, Matiwan, who hid him in her tent. By chance Sanutee discovered the boy and ordered that he be killed after having the tribal mark cut from his skin. In desperation, Matiwan killed her son before the sentence could be carried out, for the tribal mark could not be cut from a dead man.

Harrison, realizing that Sanutee was about to lead the Indians against the whites, did his best to get all the settlers to go to the blockhouse for protection. Parson Matthews insisted that the Indians had never been more friendly, and he refused to leave his cabin. Harrison, while scouting in the woods, was captured by Indians. With the aid of Matiwan, who had heard of his kindness to her dead son, he escaped. In his attempt to save Bess before the Indians could seize her, he was almost recaptured. Hector and his dog Dugdale arrived just in time to save him.

Meanwhile Chorley had led a party of Indians and sailors to the parson's cabin and had captured both Bess and her father. Harrison was able to rescue them and lead them to the blockhouse before the Indian attack began. A furious struggle took place, with even the women aiding in the fight to hold off the Indians. Both the Grayson brothers became friendly with Harrison because of the bravery he had shown in saving their families, and together they fought valiantly to save the community. At last the Indians were forced to withdraw.

Harrison made plans to send many of the settlers to Charleston, where they would be safe until troops could be mustered to defeat the Indians permanently. After winning the parson's permission to marry Bess, consent freely given after his heroic defense of the colony, Harrison astonished the group by announcing that he was in reality Charles Craven, the new governor of the province. He had come to the region in disguise so that he could see for himself the true state of affairs on the frontier. He made Hugh Grayson commander of the garrison forces. When he offered Hector his freedom, the old slave refused to be parted from his kind master.

4248

In Charleston, Craven raised a considerable fighting force and returned to battle with the Yemassee Indians on the banks of the Salkehatchie River. When the Indians attacked the camp of the white men, the governor's troops, firing from ambush, shot them down. Sanutee fell, mortally wounded, and Craven saw Matiwan run upon the field and fall weeping by her husband's body. The last of the Yemassee braves was dead.

YOU CAN'T GO HOME AGAIN

Type of work: Novel
Author: Thomas Wolfe (1900-1938)
Type of plot: Impressionistic realism
Time of plot: 1929-1936
Locale: New York, England, Germany
First published: 1940

Principal characters:
GEORGE WEBBER, a writer
ESTHER JACK, whom he loved
FOXHALL EDWARDS, his editor and best friend
LLOYD McHARG, a famous novelist
ELSE VON KOHLER, also loved by Webber

Critique:

What heights Thomas Wolfe might have attained if his life had not ended so suddenly, no one can predict. Certainly he was one of the most forceful writers of the present century. His ability to present real scenes and real people has seldom been equaled by the most mature writers; yet he was a young man when he gave us Of Time and the River, Look Homeward, Angel, The Web and the Rock, and You Can't Go Home Again. His youth showed itself clearly in his novels, in his over-exuberant desire to help humanity in spite of itself, in his lyric enthusiasm for the American dream. But these are minor sins, if they are sins, completely overshadowed by his great ability to portray believable characters and even more by his mastery of the English language. You Can't Go Home Again was his last novel.

The Story:

As George Webber looked out of his New York apartment window that spring day in 1929, he was filled with happiness. The bitter despair of the previous year had been lost somewhere in the riotous time he had spent in Europe, and now it was good to be back in New York with the feeling that he knew where he was going. His book had been accepted by a great publishing firm, and Foxhall Edwards, the best editor of the house, had been assigned to help him

with the corrections and revisions. George had also resumed his old love affair with Esther Jack, who, married and the mother of a grown daughter, nevertheless returned his love with tenderness and passion. This love, however, was a flaw in George's otherwise great content, for he and Esther seemed to be pulling different ways. She was a famous stage designer who mingled with a sophisticated artistic set. George thought that he could find himself completely only if he lived among and understood the little people of the world.

Before George's book was published, he tried for the first time to go home again. Home was Libya Hill, a small city in the mountains of Old Catawba. When the aunt who had reared George died, he went back to Libya Hill for her funeral. There he learned that he could never really go home again, for home was no longer the quiet town of his boyhood but a growing city of money-crazy speculators who were concerned only with making huge paper fortunes out of real estate.

George found some satisfaction in the small excitement he created because he had written a book which was soon to be published. But even that pleasure was not to last long. For when he returned to New York and the book was published, almost every citizen in Libya Hill wrote him letters filled with threats and curses. George had written of Libya Hill and the people he knew there. His only motive had been to tell the truth as he saw it, but his old friends and relatives in Libya Hill seemed to think that he had spied on them through his boyhood in order to gossip about them in later years. Even the small fame he received in New York, where his book was favorably reviewed by the critics, could not atone for the abusive letters from Libya Hill. He felt he could redeem himself only by working feverishly on his new book.

George moved to Brooklyn, first telling Esther goodbye. This severance from Esther was difficult, but George could not live a lie himself and attempt to write the truth. And in Brooklyn he did learn to know and love the little people —the derelicts, the prostitutes, the petty criminals—and he learned that they, like the so-called good men and women, were all representative of America. His only real friend was Foxhall Edwards, who had become like a father to George. Edwards was a great man, a genius among editors and a genius at understanding and encouraging those who, like George, found it difficult to believe in anything during the depression years. Edwards, too, knew that only through truth could America and the world be saved from destruction; but, unlike George, he believed that the truth cannot be thrust suddenly upon people. He calmly accepted conditions as they existed. George raged at his friend's skepticism.

After four years in Brooklyn, George finished the first draft of his new book. Tired of New York, he thought that he might find in Europe the atmosphere he needed to complete his manuscript. In London he met Lloyd McHarg, the embodiment of all that George wanted to be. George yearned for fame in that period of his life. Because his book had brought him temporary fame, quickly extinguished, he envied McHarg his world reputation as a novelist. George was disillusioned when he learned that McHarg thought fame an empty thing. He had held the world in his hand for a time, but nothing had happened. Now he was living feverishly, looking for something he could not name.

When his manuscript was ready for publication, George returned to New York, made the corrections Edwards suggested, and then sailed again for Europe. He went to Germany, a country he had not visited since 1928. In 1936, he was more saddened by the change in the German people than he had been by anything else in his life. He had always felt a kinship with the Germans, but they were no longer the people he had known before. Persecution and fear tinged every life in that once proud country, and George, sickened, wondered if there were any place in the world where truth and freedom still lived.

There were, however, two bright horizons in his visit to Germany. The first was the fame which greeted him on his arrival there. His first book had been well received, and his second, now published, was a great success. For a time he basked in that glory, but soon he, like McHarg, found fame an elusive thing that brought no real reward. His other great experience was his love for Else von Kohler. That was also an elusive joy, for her roots were deep in Germany, and George knew he must return to America to cry out to his own people that they must live the truth and so save America from the world's ruin.

Before he left Germany, he saw more examples of the horror and tyrannny under which the people existed, and he left with a heavy heart. He realized once more that one can never go home again.

Back in New York, he knew that he must break at last his ties with Foxhall Edwards. He wrote to Edwards, telling him why they could no longer travel the same path. First he reviewed the story of his own life, through which he wove the story of his desire to make the American people awake to the great need for truth so that they might keep their freedom. He told Edwards, too, that in his youth he had wanted fame and love above all else. Having had both, he had learned that they were not enough. Slowly he had learned humility, and he knew that he wanted to speak the truth to the downtrodden, to all humanity. Because George knew he had to try to awaken the slumbering conscience of America, he was saying farewell to his friend. For Edwards believed that if the end of freedom was to be the lot of man, fighting against that end was useless.

Sometimes George feared that the battle was lost, but he would never stop fighting as long as there was hope that America would find herself. He knew at last the real enemy in America. It was selfishness and greed, disguised as a friend of mankind. He felt that if he could only get help from the little people, he could defeat the enemy. Through George, America might go home again.

YOU KNOW ME AL

Type of work: Epistolary novel
Author: Ring Lardner (1885-1933)
Type of plot: Humorous satire
Time of plot: c. 1915
Locale: Chicago
First published: 1916

Principal characters:
JACK KEEFE, a ballplayer
AL BLANCHARD, his correspondent
FLORRIE, Jack's wife
ALLEN, Jack's brother-in-law, also a ballplayer
MARIE, his wife

Critique:

Although Ring Lardner's reputation is based on the high level of achievement in his short stories, *You Know Me Al*, his first novel, is a major document in American humor. Several streams of American comic tradition merge in this work: the comic letter, the wisecrack, the braggart character, the use of sporting vocabulary and fractured English, and the general debunking mood. The letters, all written by Jack to Al, are hilarious for their verbal wit, but Lardner also achieved comedy through his use of character and situation. The novel, more than a loosely organized series of humorous letters, achieves unity through the characterization of Jack Keefe. As he egotistically describes his experiences he inadvertently exposes himself. The bitterness of this portrait is foreign to American humor. Apart from the later works of Mark Twain, its parallels must be sought in Swift or Smollett. Lardner does not appear to hate Jack, however; instead, he despairs for him and perhaps pities him.

The Story:

When Jack Keefe, a pitcher, was brought up from the minor leagues by the Chicago White Sox, he began writing a series of letters to his hometown friend, Al. It was a peculiar friendship, however, for Jack was basically incapable of any of the emotions real friendship requires. He patronized Al and used him.

Jack was a braggart and a chronic self-excuser, and the letters gave him a chance to exercise his ego. Al apparently never saw through Jack.

So sublimely self-confident that he felt every trifling detail of his life was important, Jack wrote full accounts of his adventures. Having neither modesty nor shame, he even included episodes in which he appeared foolish.

When Jack reported to training camp on the West Coast, he immediately annoyed the manager by his overeating, refusal to take orders, laziness. Though a powerful right-handed pitcher, he was an indifferent fielder and careless about base runners. The manager tried to handle Jack with irony, but it was lost on him. Whenever he had a bad day, he alibied that his arm was sore. Any hit made against him was the fault of the fielders, the umpires, or the scorers. Jack also believed that he was irresistible to women. In training camp he met a girl from Detroit named Violet, and he planned to romance her when the White Sox were playing Detroit.

Jack did well enough in spring training to be included on the White Sox roster. In his first starting assignment against the Tigers he played miserably. The manager left him in the game as punishment, and sixteen runs were scored against him. Ty Cobb stole four bases. As usual, Jack complained that his arm was sore. By now the manager was thoroughly disgusted with him, and Jack was sent to San Francisco. He sulked and said he would quit baseball, but he went. Violet called him a busher.

In San Francisco he won eleven straight games and became engaged to a girl named Hazel. Recalled by the White Sox at the end of the season, he pitched well enough to be used in the City Series between the White Sox and the Cubs. Hazel asked him for one hundred dollars to pay her fare to Chicago for their wedding. He sent her thirty, and she married a boxer instead. Jack then attempted to marry Violet, but she married another ballplayer. Jack married Florrie, the sister-in-law of a White Sox left-hander named Allen.

When Florrie refused to spend the winter in Bedford, Jack's home town, they rented an apartment across the hall from the Allens. There were many quarrels between the two families, most of them occasioned by Jack's stinginess. Jack had always been convinced that all left-handers were crazy; his trouble with Allen only served to strengthen his conviction. Allen was taking his wife Marie along to spring training. Florrie wanted to go too, but Jack felt that he could not afford to take her. Since he felt that he was underpaid, he tried to get a raise from the club, even though he had already signed a contract. Charles Comiskey, the owner of the White Sox, had already had contract trouble with Jack and refused to grant him any concessions. Jack then tried to join the Federal League, a third major league that was hiring players away from the American and National Leagues; however, the Federal League would have nothing to do with him because he had signed a contract with the White Sox. Then his team learned about this attempted defection. Hog-fat after gorging himself on food and liquor all winter, he was sold to Milwaukee as a disciplinary measure. Florrie left him. Jack, protesting that he would not go to the minors again, borrowed money from Al to return to Bed-

ford. The White Sox were forced to keep him, however, because of a technicality in the waiver rule.

The manager limited Jack's diet and he got into shape good enough to be given another chance with the White Sox. Florrie and Jack were reconciled because she was pregnant, and she soon presented him with a son. At first Jack worried because the baby appeared to be left-handed. Florrie named the baby Allen after her brother-in-law, but Jack insisted that the baby was named for Al. Though he continued to display the same old bragging and complacency, Jack turned out to be a doting father in his own fashion.

After a successful season he was selected to pitch in the City Series, a cause of fresh strife with Florrie because she wanted to attend the games and he wanted her to stay home with the baby. Jack was not concerned about the money for a baby sitter as much as he was worried about the welfare of his son. When the team bribed Florrie to stay home, she used the money to hire a baby sitter. Jack then decided to leave her, but changed his mind when he learned that she would have custody of the child. After another argument with the Allens, Jack moved his family out of the apartment which they shared and for which Allen paid the rent.

The White Sox wanted Jack to join the world tour the team was making with the Giants, but he did not want to be away from the baby. The real reason for taking him was to keep him in shape, but Jack believed that baseball fans in other countries wanted to see him. They coaxed him to Canada because Christy Mathewson was going that far. Then they told him that President Wilson was afraid Japan would declare war if Jack did not go there to play. Convinced at first, he later began to worry about the dangers of the ocean voyage and backed down, but when he was told that Allen would be taken in his place, his vindictiveness triumphed over his fear. He sailed away boasting of triumphs to come.

YOUMA

Type of work: Novel
Author: Lafcadio Hearn (1850-1904)
Type of plot: Exotic romance
Time of plot: The 1840's
Locale: Martinique
First published: 1890

Principal characters:
YOUMA, a young Negro slave
GABRIEL, another slave, in love with Youma
MAYOTTE, a white child entrusted to Youma's care
MONSIEUR DESRIVIÈRES, Gabriel's master
AIMÉE, wife of M. Desrivières and Mayotte's mother
MADAME PEYRONETTE, Youma's owner and Mayotte's grandmother

Critique:

This book is an understanding story of Negro life in the West Indies, written essentially from the Negro's point of view. Whites enter the story only as they are forces or background figures for the lives of the Negroes who are the principal characters. That this novel should have come from the pen of Lafcadio Hearn is not surprising, for he had spent months in the West Indies and had seen for himself the life and personality of the Negro. Even more important, Hearn had been aware of the Negro and his problems in the United States, particularly in Louisiana. Like much of Hearn's work, *Youma* is filled with pictures of exotic scenery and life. A story of West Indian slavery, the novel is also a vehicle portraying the life, customs, folklore, and lush scenery of a beautiful island.

The Story:

Youma was a pet slave and the godchild of Madame Peyronette. Youma's mother had been the nurse of Madame Peyronette's only daughter, Aimée, and the two children, white and colored, had grown up together almost as sisters. Even when Aimée was sent to a convent to have her manners finished off according to Creole custom, the vacations she spent at home were always in the company of the young Negro slave.

As the girls grew to womanhood, Aimée begged her mother on several occasions to give Youma her freedom, but Madame Peyronette felt that she was guarding Youma by keeping her in slav-

ery. Privately, Madame Peyronette had decided first to find the girl a good husband and then, after she was safely married, to grant her freedom. Before Madame Peyronette could carry out her plan, Aimée married Monsieur Desrivières, son of a wealthy old Creole family. Upon her marriage, Aimée asked that Youma be permitted to serve for her in the new household, a request speedily granted by her mother.

Thirteen months after Aimée's wedding a baby girl was born to her and her husband. The child was named Marie, which the Negroes made into the diminutive Mayotte. Tragedy struck the household a year later when Aimée, who had been caught in a chilling rain while riding in an open carriage, fell ill and died within twenty-four hours. Before she died, Aimée begged Youma to assume the duties of a nurse for little Mayotte. Youma, recalling the kindnesses she had received at the hands of Aimée, vowed to do the best she could for the motherless child.

Monsieur Desrivières went to his sugar plantation at Anse-Marine, in another section of the island, for he could not remain in the same house after his wife's death. Not long after, little Mayotte being in delicate health, Madame Peyronette sent her, in Youma's care, to the plantation. The grandmother thought that the climate at the plantation would be better for Mayotte.

The little girl and Youma loved the life at the plantation; for both it was an experience in people. Little Mayotte was irked at times because she was not permitted to mingle freely with the little colored children. This was not caused by difference in race but by fear that she was in danger of sunstroke while participating in their games. To pass the time, Mayotte and Youma went on walks in shaded places or sat on the verandas while Youma told folktales of her race.

One afternoon Youma warned Mayotte that if she heard so many tales during the day she would see zombies at night. Mayotte laughed and asked for another story. But that night she screamed to Youma that something was in her room. As Youma stepped into the room to calm the child, she felt under her foot a tremendous snake. Keeping the snake imprisoned beneath her foot, Youma called for help as the serpent writhed itself about her legs and body. When Monsieur Desrivières and the servants arrived with a light, they found Youma holding down a large and poisonous reptile. One of the slaves, Gabriel, swung a cutlass and lopped off the snake's head. Fortunately for the girl and the child, Youma had stepped on the snake immediately behind the head, and it had not been able to strike at her with its fangs.

The incident earned for Youma the respect of everyone at the plantation. Gabriel, in particular, showed his admiration by bringing gifts of fruit and spending the hours of early evening listening to her tell stories or sing to little Mayotte. He even made a rustic bench which he placed beside the little pool where Youma took Mayotte to play in the water. Finally Gabriel gave her a pair of earrings; when she put them on, he knew that she was willing to marry him. Gabriel, wishing to marry Youma, was told that Madame Peyronette's permission was necessary, since Youma belonged to her. When asked, Madame Peyronette refused to give permission; she felt that it would be wrong to permit Youma, who had been brought up almost as a white girl, to marry Gabriel, who, although a fine specimen of manhood, was only a field hand.

Gabriel and Youma were grievously disappointed at the denial of their request. When Gabriel, a resourceful fellow, proposed that he and Youma elope and cross the channel to a British-held island where slavery had been abolished, Youma almost succumbed to his temptations, until she remembered her promise to care for Mayotte. With that promise in mind, she refused to desert her charge.

Within a few days of the refusal, Youma and Mayotte were sent back to the city. Not long after, the year being 1848, word spread through the West Indies that a republic had been proclaimed in France and that slavery would soon be abolished in Martinique. Feeling ran high, for there were only twelve thousand whites on the island and more than a hundred and fifty thousand Negroes. The whites, knowing full well of the troubles in Haiti years before, were extremely cautious in dealing with the colored people. Even so, rumors began to spread that the whites were conspiring to retain slavery. An outbreak began over the imprudent whipping of a slave on the very eve of emancipation. Thousands of slaves poured into the city from the country.

Madame Peyronette, Youma, and Mayotte, after taking refuge with another family in a large, well-built stone house near the army barracks, believed that they would be safe from the mob. But when the hordes of slaves poured into the city a crowd gathered in front of the house and finally broke in. Since the whites on the second floor were temporarily out of their reach, the slaves set fire to the house. When some of the whites tried to escape by leaping out of windows, the mob killed them immediately.

Youma, in an effort to save Mayotte and herself, went out on a balcony and identified herself as a slave. Gabriel, who happened to be in the crowd, tried to save them, but the bloodthirsty blacks refused to let the white child be spared. Youma, rather than leave Mayotte to die alone, stood on the balcony with the child until the walls of the house collapsed and killed them both.

YVAIN

Type of work: Poem
Author: Chrétien de Troyes (c. 1150-c. 1190)
Type of plot: Chivalric romance
Time of plot: Sixth century
Locale: Britain
First transcribed: After 1164

Principal characters:

YVAIN, a knight of King Arthur's Round Table
LAUDINE DE LANDUC, whom he married
LUNETE, a damsel in Laudine de Landuc's service
KING ARTHUR
QUEEN GUINEVERE
SIR GAWAIN, Yvain's friend and King Arthur's nephew
SIR KAY, the cynical seneschal
HARPIN OF THE MOUNTAIN, a giant slain by Yvain

Critique:

Yvain, ou le Chevalier au Lion, is the most complicated of the chivalric romances written by Chrétien de Troyes. Episodic in structure, rather conventional in moral theme, it derives from various sources: Ovid's *Metamorphoses* and the *Art of Love,* Vergil's *Aeneid,* and the Arthurian materials presented in the *Historia Regum Britanniae,* by Geoffrey of Monmouth. The remarkable aspect of the work is the fact that the parts make up the whole fabric as a pattern and not as a patchwork, giving the modern reader almost as great a sensation of exhilaration from the tribulations and triumphs of the hero as the work must have given the court of the Countess Marie de Champagne, for whom the poet wrote to rather exact specifications.

The Story:

At the season of Pentecost, King Arthur held his court at Carduel in Wales. After dinner on that feast day a knight named Calogrenant told a tale of adventure which was not altogether to his credit, and for which he was mocked by Sir Kay the Seneschal.

Calogrenant revealed that seven years before he had journeyed beyond the forest of Broceliande. After a night's lodging in the tower of a courteous vavasour he continued on his way until he encountered a giant seventeen feet tall who was guarding some wild bulls in a clearing. The giant told the knight that if he sought some marvel he was to look for a spring in a mysterious wood, for water from the spring poured on a nearby stone would bring down upon him a storm such as few men had ever seen, with bolts of lightning that would blind him and thunder that would shake the earth. All befell as the giant had foretold. After the storm had ceased a knight appeared and challenged Calogrenant to a duel because of the great damage caused in his demesne by wind and rain. The two fought and Calogrenant was overthrown. So shamed was he in that encounter that he had never told the story before.

One of those who listened to his tale was Yvain, a valiant knight who swore to avenge the shame of Calogrenant, his cousin-german. Yvain was also mocked by Sir Kay. While they spoke King Arthur came from his chamber and to him Queen Guinevere told the tale as she had heard it. The king thereupon swore an oath that he must see these wonders for himself and that any of his knights who wished could accompany him on the venture. But Yvain, thinking that the quest should be his alone, left the court secretly and rode over mountains and through valleys until he came to the forest of the magic spring. When he poured a basin of water on the stone, a great storm arose. After the storm the strange knight appeared and he and Yvain battled until their lances splintered and their armor had been pierced in many places. At last Yvain dealt his enemy a blow that shattered his helmet and split his skull, but even then the knight did not fall down at once but galloped off to take refuge in his castle. Yvain, riding in close pursuit of his foe, was trapped when a portcullis fell before him as well as behind him when he rode through the gate. There the maid Lunete found him and saved his life with the gift of a magic ring which made him invisible while the nobleman's vassals searched for the knight who had given their lord his mortal hurt. While he was thus protected, Yvain saw the Lady Laudine de Landuc, the mistress of the castle, a lady so fair that he fell in love with her on the spot. The maid Lunete, seeing how matters stood, concealed Yvain and ministered to him, and between times she spoke to her lady, urging her to put aside her anger and grief and to take a new husband who would be master of her domain and defender of the magic spring. Lunete was so cunning in her speech that her lady finally agreed to do as the damsel suggested. Then Yvain was brought from the chamber where he was hidden. Falling on his knees before the Lady Laudine he begged forgiveness for killing her lord in fair fight. The lady, impressed by Yvain's comeliness and bravery, was soon reconciled, and the two were wed with great rejoicing.

As he had sworn, King Arthur came with his knights to see the magic spring, and Sir Kay again mocked the absent Yvain, who had sworn to avenge his cousin's name. Then the king poured a basin of water on the stone and immediately the rain began to fall and the wind to blow. When the storm had subsided, Yvain appeared to challenge King Arthur's knights, and Sir Kay begged the first encounter. But Yvain quickly unhorsed the braggart seneschal and then revealed himself to King Arthur and the other knights. All were delighted to find Yvain safe and hale. For a week thereafter Yvain and his lady entertained the royal party with feasting and entertainment of all kinds.

At the end of that time, as the king was preparing to depart, Sir Gawain urged Yvain to return to Britain with them and to take part in all tournaments so that none could say that so brave a knight had grown weak and slothful in marriage. The Lady Laudine agreed, but on the promise that Yvain would return to her a year hence. Before he left, she gave him a ring set with a stone that would keep its wearer from all harm as long as he would keep his sweetheart in mind.

So successful was Yvain in all the tournaments that were held throughout the land that he forgot his promise until the Lady Laudine sent a damsel to denounce him as a hypocrite and liar and to demand the return of the ring. Yvain, overcome by remorse at the thought of losing his lady's love, went mad and lived, naked and distracted, like a wild beast in the forest. A hermit living there gave him bread and water and so succored him until one day the noble lady of Noroison and her two damsels found the naked man asleep under a tree. The lady and her maids attended the knight and anointed him with a soothing, magic ointment to restore his wits. On his recovery Yvain pledged himself to the lady's support and to champion her against Count Alier, who was plundering her lands. So fierce was his attack on the marauders that the count yielded himself and gave his oath that he would live in peace from that time on. Afterward, having refused to accept the lady's hand or to take her as his mistress, Yvain rode away in search of new adventures.

As he was wandering through the wood, he came upon a lion and a fire-breathing serpent that held the beast by the tail. Yvain drew his sword and slew the scaly monster. From that time on the grateful lion became the knight's inseparable companion.

At last Yvain returned to the magic spring where all his adventures had begun. There he found the maid Lunete held a prisoner in a nearby chapel by orders of the Lady Laudine. The damsel was to be burned the next day, and she wept that she had no one to defend her against charges brought by a wicked seneschal who had persuaded her mistress that the maid had acted falsely in the sad affair of the Lady Laudine's marriage to Yvain. The knight, without revealing himself, promised to act as her champion before he rode away to find lodgings for the night. At last he came to the castle of Sir Gawain's brother-in-law, only to learn that the baron was threatened with the death of his four sons, prisoners of a dreaded giant, Harpin of the Mountain, unless the father would give his daughter over to the lewd embraces of the ogre's lackeys. In spite of the fact that Yvain had not much time, he rode out and slew the giant, with the help of the lion, because of his friendship for the baron's kinsman, Sir Gawain. Refusing to give his name, he said he wished to be known only as the Knight with the Lion. Then he rode as fast as his horse would carry him to the chapel in the forest, where the pyre had already been prepared on which the maid was to be burned. Although wounded in his encounter with the giant, Yvain fought the seneschal and his two brothers. Again, with the lion's help, he was victorious, and the false knights whom he slew were burned on the funeral pile prepared for Lunete. When confronted by the Lady Laudine he again refused to reveal his identity, so ashamed was he of his inconstancy, but called himself the Knight with the Lion. Lunete had recognized him, however, and she accompanied him for some distance when he rode away. Although she promised to keep his secret, she declared that she would bring about a reconciliation be-

tween him and his lady if it were ever in her power to do so.

Disconsolately, Yvain departed to seek other adventures, but he was unable to travel far because of the wounds he and the lion had suffered in their battles with Harpin of the Mountain and the three false knights. At length he came to a fair castle where the lord's retainers helped him from his horse and attended gently to the lion, which Yvain was carrying on his shield. There they stayed, attended by maidens skilled in surgery, until both the man and the beast were completely healed. Then they continued on their way.

About that same time the lord of Noire Espine died and his older daughter claimed the whole of his estates, saying that she would give no share to her sister. When the younger daughter went to King Arthur's court to plead her case, she learned that her older sister had been there before her and that Sir Gawain had promised to act as her champion. Granted forty days in which to find a champion of her own, the maid set out in search of the famed Knight with the Lion.

Along the way she fell ill, but the quest was taken up by a friend whose search brought her at last to the magic spring while Lunete was saying her prayers in the chapel close by; and the Lady Laudine's damsel was able to point out to the traveler the road Yvain had traveled many days before. So the maid came finally to the castle where the knight and the lion had been nursed back to health. Told that the two had departed only a short time before, she rode after them as fast as she could. Overtaking the knight and his beast companion, she told her story, and Yvain promised to help the younger sister in her need.

Before he could act for the maid, however, he was to engage in still another desperate adventure. Toward nightfall he and the damsel came to the town of Pesme Avanture, where, as they approached the castle, all the people called out to them to turn back; but Yvain paid no heed to their warnings. Entering the castle, the knight found three hundred maidens working at all kinds of embroidery; they were, they told him, hostages for the king of the Isle of Damsels, the ransom he had paid to escape doing battle with two half-devils born to a mortal woman and an imp. Yvain and the damsel were courteously received by the lord of the castle, however, and that night everything was done in their honor. But when Yvain prepared to depart the next morning, the owner of the castle told him that he could not go without fighting the black sons of evil. The prize, if he won, would be the hand of the baron's beautiful daughter and suzerainty of all her father's demesne. Although Yvain tried to refuse the terms of the offer, the lord assured him that no knight who had lodged in the castle could avoid or renounce the battle. Although the lion was shut away from Yvain, the beast managed to scratch his way beneath the threshold of the room where he was confined, and he arrived on the scene of the conflict in time to save sorely wounded Yvain by rending one devil outright and so disconcerting the other that the knight was able to lop off the evil creature's head.

With this victory Yvain released the wretched hostages from their imprisonment. Over the protests of the lord of the castle, he renounced the hand of the daughter and rode away with the damsel to the court of King Arthur.

Great was the joy of the younger sister when the Knight with the Lion arrived in time to champion her cause against her avaricious sister, defended by Sir Gawain. The struggle lasted all day and into the dusk. By that time both knights were exhausted, but neither knew the identity of the other until Yvain at last proposed postponement of the contest until the next day. Then Sir Gawain, recognizing his friend's voice, granted him the victory, while Yvain, in turn, refused this boon and reversed the decision. King Arthur finally solved the problem by granting them equal prowess in arms and conferring upon the younger sister her rights after the older one had incautiously admitted her attempt to dispossess her sister.

As soon as Yvain was cured of his wounds, he set out once more for the magic spring, accompanied only by his faithful lion. Again he poured water on the stone and brought down such a storm that the Lady Laudine feared her castle and the town would be washed away. Meanwhile, the damsel Lunete spoke to her mistress in such winning fashion that the lady, losing all the resentment she held against her husband, promised to restore him to her favor and love. So Yvain and his lady were reconciled after many troubles and trials, to the great happiness of Lunete and all their vassals.

ZADIG

Type of work: Novel
Author: François Marie Arouet de Voltaire (1694-1778)
Type of plot: Social satire
Time of plot: Remote antiquity
Locale: Babylon
First published: 1747

> *Principal characters:*
> ZADIG, a wealthy young man
> MOABDAR, King of Babylon
> ASTARTÉ, his queen
> SÉMIRE, Zadig's first betrothed
> AZORA, Zadig's first wife
> CADOR, Zadig's best friend
> ARIMAZE, "The Envious," Zadig's enemy
> MISSOUF, an Egyptian woman
> SÉTOC, an Arab merchant
> ALMONA, Sétoc's wife
> NABUSSAN, King of Serendib
> ARBOGAD, a happy brigand
> ITOBAD, a rich lord
> OGUL, another lord, a voluptuary

Critique:

Voltaire's most famous satirical tale criticizing the manners, beliefs, and philosophical views of his times is, of course, *Candide*. Yet *Zadig* makes many of the same critical comments and in much the same comic style. The difference is partly one of style and partly one of direction. In *Candide* Voltaire chose a simple, ingenuous youth whose misadventures, ridiculously exaggerated, brought out by a kind of refreshing contrast the difference between innocence and false sophistication. Because of the extreme hyperboles used to describe Candide's adventures, the work is sometimes grandly amusing; but also on this account it is sometimes unconvincing, even as an obviously fanciful tale. *Zadig*, on the other hand, is the story of an educated, sensible young man who escapes from great difficulties by continuing to be calmly sensible. The humor, consequently, is more restrained; it resides more in the subtle inversions of style and thought than in the grosser inversions of plot. Both tales convey Voltaire's naturalistic disdain of the religious and philosophical dogmas of his times and his preference for a rational and compassionate consideration of the problems of society.

The Story:

Zadig, a charming young man with a good education and great wealth, lived in the time of King Moabdar in Babylon. Despite the fact that he was a very sensible young man, or perhaps because of it, he never boasted of his own abilities or tried to find fault in others. He expected that with the advantages he modestly enjoyed he would have no difficulty in being happy. But he was mistaken in this belief.

In rescuing the beautiful Sémire from kidnappers, Zadig was injured by an arrow in his left eye. The great doctor Hermes predicted that he would lose the eye because wounds in the left eye never heal. When Zadig's eye healed, the doctor wrote a book proving that it could not have happened. Unfortunately, Sémire, to whom Zadig had been betrothed, decided that she did not like one-eyed men and, in her ignorance of Zadig's recovery, married Orcan, the young nobleman who had sent the kidnappers to seize her.

Zadig married Azora, the wisest girl in the city, who took a frivolous interest in handsome young men. When she chastened a widow for changing the course of a stream in order to escape from her vow to stay by her husband's tomb as long as the stream flowed there, Zadig arranged to have Azora told that he had died. He then had a friend named Cador make friendly overtures to Azora and, having done so, to complain of a pain in the spleen for which there was but one cure: rubbing the place with the nose of a man dead no more than twenty-four hours. When Azora came to the place where Zadig presumably was buried, he leaped up to keep her from cutting off his nose with a razor. He said that her act proved she was no better than the widow she had criticized. Finally, when Azora became too difficult to live with, he left her.

One day the queen's dog and the king's horse were lost. Zadig was able to describe the missing animals and tell where they were, but when he said that he had never seen them he was imprisoned. It turned out that he had been able to tell from marks on the ground what the animals were like and where they had gone. When he explained this, he was released. He had learned his lesson, however; when he saw an escaping prisoner, he kept quiet. But he was fined for looking out from his window.

A rich and jealous neighbor named Arimaze and called "The Envious" found a broken tablet on which Zadig had written a poem. Half of the tablet could be read as a poem criticizing the king. But just as Zadig was about to be condemned for insulting the monarch, a parrot dropped the other half of the tablet in the king's lap. Both the king and the queen, and especially the queen, began to hold Zadig in high esteem. Zadig was awarded a goblet for having been generous enough to speak well of a minister who had incurred the king's wrath; such an act was new in the king's experience, and he valued Zadig for it.

Zadig became prime minister of Babylon and by sensible decisions won the hearts of the people. He cured a great lord who was too conceited for his own good by having a band, an orchestra, and a choir sing his praises all day long until the lord in desperation called a halt to the chorus of praise. He also settled a religious dispute that had gone on for fifteen hundred years concerning the question whether one should enter the temple of Mithra with the right foot or the left foot. He jumped in with both feet.

Zadig was popular with the ladies of Babylon, but he succumbed only once and did so without pleasure. He was too much in love with Queen Astarté. The wife of Arimaze, enraged because he rebuffed her, allowed her husband to send her garter to the king so that he might be deceived into believing that Zadig and the queen were already lovers. The queen warned Zadig that the king meant to kill him. Zadig escaped to Egypt.

Upon arriving in Egypt, Zadig found an Egyptian beating a woman. When Zadig intervened, the jealous Egyptian assumed that Zadig was a rival lover, and a fight ensued, ending in the Egyptian's death. The woman, Missouf, far from being grateful, screamed that she wished Zadig had been killed instead. When four men seized her, he allowed her to be taken, not realizing that the four men were couriers from Babylon who had mistaken Missouf for the queen, who had also disappeared.

Since Zadig had killed a man, the Egyptians condemned him to be a slave, and he was bought by an Arab merchant named Sétoc. At first the merchant valued Zadig's service more than he did Zadig, but he finally came to see the value of Zadig's intelligence and common sense. The incident which proved Zadig's ability concerned an attempt to prove a Hebrew guilty of not returning a loan made to him by Sétoc. By pretending that he would bring into court the stone on which the loan was transacted, Zadig trapped the Hebrew into a description of the stone, thereby proving that he really was the man to whom the loan had been made.

Zadig next convinced an Arabian widow that she should not leap upon the burning funeral pyre of her husband. He did this by making her realize that there were still attractive young men in the world.

By pointing out that they all admitted the existence of a Superior Being, he settled a dispute between an Egyptian, an Indian, a Chaldean, a Celt, and others concerning the nature of the universe and its operation. He was saved from execution by the priests when Almona, the young widow, pretended that she would allow the priests to make love to her if they signed a pardon; when the priests came to her, they were greeted by judges who condemned them. Sétoc was so much impressed by her cleverness that he married her.

Zadig showed that one can judge an honest man by making candidates for the comptroller's position engage in a dancing contest. Only one candidate resisted the money Zadig had placed in a passageway, and only he danced lightly and with grace, the others being fearful of jostling the money from their pockets.

Having done this service for King Nabussan of Serendib, to whose kingdom Zadig had been sent by Sétoc, Zadig then undertook to show which of the king's hundred wives were faithful. Only one resisted the temptations of money, youth, and power to which Zadig exposed them.

After settling a revolt of the priests against Nabussan, Zadig, guided as always by the sayings of Zarathustra, set forth to find news of Queen Astarté. He met a happy brigand, Arbogad, who reported that King Moabdar had been killed in an uprising, but the robber had no news of the queen. Zadig then met an unhappy fisherman who had lost his money, his wife, and his house during the revolt in Babylon. Since some of the money owed the fisherman was for cream cheese which he had sold to Zadig and Queen Astarté, Zadig, without revealing his identity, gave the fisherman half the money he had.

Zadig then met some women hunting for a basilisk which was to be used to cure Ogul, their lord and master. Among the women Zadig was overjoyed to find Queen Astarté. She told him that Zadig's friend Cador had helped her to escape from the king, that the king had married Missouf, and that she had frightened the king out of his wits by speaking to him from within a statue in the temple in which she was hidden. The revolt in Babylon had resulted from the king's madness, and he had been killed. Queen Astarté had then been captured by the Prince of Hyrcania. She had escaped from him only to be captured by the brigand Arbogad, who sold her to Ogul.

By curing Ogul, Zadig then managed to free Queen Astarté and to win more honor for himself. He told Ogul that a bag contained medicine that would go through his pores only if he punched it hard enough. The resultant exercise cured the lord.

Returning to Babylon, Zadig entered a jousting tournament and a battle of wits in order to win Queen Astarté as his wife. Despite the trickery of Itobad, who stole his armor and pretended to be the victor after Zadig had won the tournament, Zadig managed to win both contests—partly through the encouragement of the angel Jesrad who was disguised as a hermit—and he married Queen Astarté. As king, Zadig was a just and compassionate ruler under whom Babylon became a prosperous and happy empire.

ZAÏRE

Type of work: Drama
Author: François Marie Arouet de Voltaire (1694-1778)
Type of plot: Historical tragedy
Time of plot: During the reign of Osman, Sultan of Jerusalem
Locale: Jerusalem
First presented: 1732

Principal characters:
OROSMANE (OSMAN), Sultan of Jerusalem
LUSIGNAN, a prince in the line of the kings of Jerusalem
ZAÏRE, and
FATIME, slaves of the sultan
NERESTAN, and
CHATILLON, French gentlemen
CORASMIN, and
MELEDOR, officers of the sultan

Critique:

In *Zaïre,* Voltaire the sardonic skeptic is absent; only Voltaire the tragic dramatist remains. In this play the great French writer gives human dimensions to a grand theme of jealousy, and although the drama is not ordinarily regarded as the equal of *Othello,* to which it bears a sometimes startling resemblance, it has merits of its own which are worth considering. *Othello* presents a hero, noble in character, who is made jealous by the lies of Iago, his lieutenant. Othello and Desdemona form two points of a triangle that involves Cassio only by innuendo. In *Zaïre,* on the other hand, the triangle has three strong corners: Orosmane, the proud and noble Turk, is one; his betrothed, Zaïre, is another; and, as a combined but none the less actual protagonist, the Christian God and Zaïre's Christian family is the third. Orosmane's suspicions of Zaïre's brother Nerestan, resulting from his ignorance of Nerestan's relation to Zaïre and from his knowledge of Zaïre's change of heart, is a well-founded, although misplaced, jealousy. Here East meets West in mortal struggle, and the passion reflects itself in the personal lives of the lovers.

The Story:

Fatime and Zaïre were slaves of Orosmane, Sultan of Jerusalem, but their lot was not an unpleasant one. Although Orosmane had the power to treat them as mere chattels and to use them for his pleasure in his seraglio, he treated them with respect and consideration. Nevertheless, Fatime was disturbed to find that Zaïre was not only resigned to her fate but giving the appearance of actually enjoying it. When she asked Zaïre to explain why she no longer wept or looked forward to the return of Nerestan, who had gone to France to seek ransom for them, Zaïre replied that she found it difficult to yearn after a mode of life she had never known. Since childhood she had been confined to the seraglio under the care of Orosmane, and she had grown fond of her life and even of her master.

Fatime then reminded Zaïre that Nerestan, who had conducted himself so nobly in the battle of Damas as part of the Christian army fighting against the Turks, had been captured by Orosmane but, because of his courage, was later released on his word to return with ransom for the Christian prisoners, including Fatime and Zaïre.

Zaïre replied that two years had passed since Nerestan's departure and that perhaps Nerestan had made the promise to return with ransom for ten slaves only because there was no other way for him to escape a similar servitude. She admitted that she had admired Nerestan at the time of his promise, but she had decided to think of the matter no longer.

Zaïre then confessed to Fatime that Orosmane was *her* slave, that he loved her, and that she loved him. She quickly added that this love did not mean that she had consented to become his mistress. The truth was that Orosmane's love for her was so strong and pure that he planned to wed her.

Fatime, delighted to hear that Zaïre would be elevated from the place of a slave to that of sultana, had one misgiving—she wondered whether Zaïre had forgotten that she was a Christian. Zaïre replied that she did not even know who her parents were; she had only Nerestan's surmise, because of the cross she had worn since childhood, that she was a Christian. Since she had been a slave from her childhood it was only natural that her faith reflected the customs of the place where she was reared. With Fatime, Zaïre admitted, the situation was different; Fatime had been captured in adulthood, and had deliberately embraced Christianity before becoming a slave. Although Zaïre regarded herself as a Mussulman, she admitted that she was impressed by the Christian faith; but she assured Fatime that her love for Orosmane was so strong that she no longer considered becoming a Christian.

Orosmane then entered and expressed his love for Zaïre and his intention to marry her. As he professed his love, a servant entered and announced the arrival of Nerestan.

Nerestan entered and told the sultan that he had come with ransom for the prisoners and that he was willing to remain as Orosmane's slave. The sultan, impressed by Nerestan's honor, replied that he would release not merely ten but a hundred prisoners. The only ones who would have to remain were Lusignan, a French nobleman who claimed the hereditary right to rule in Jerusalem, and Zaïre.

Nerestan protested that Orosmane had promised to release the prisoners, and Zaïre in particular, if the ransom money were brought from France. But Orosmane permitted no discussion of his decision. He dismissed Nerestan and ordered Zaïre to prepare to assume her place as his sultana.

After the others had gone, Orosmane remarked to Corasmin, one of his officers, that Nerestan had sighed and fixed his eyes on Zaïre. When Corasmin warned his master against jealousy, the sultan replied that he could not be jealous of Zaïre since she was truth itself.

Chatillon, a French gentleman released at Orosmane's command, praised Nerestan for having arranged the release of the prisoners, but Nerestan refused to be gratified by Chatillon's praise because of Orosmane's refusal to release Zaïre and Lusignan. Chatillon agreed that without Lusignan, the great Christian leader and soldier who had fought so valiantly in defense of Caesarea, there was no joy in his own release.

Nerestan then told Chatillon how, as an infant, Nerestan had been carried from the smoking ruins of the city of Caesarea to the seraglio. Zaïre had been a fellow captive.

Chatillon tried to encourage Nerestan by suggesting that Zaïre might charm Orosmane into releasing Lusignan, but Nerestan knew that Lusignan would not accept liberty under such circumstances.

Zaïre then entered and told Nerestan that she regretted not being able to return to France with him, but her love for Orosmane made that impossible. She assured him that she would use her new status to protect the Christians and to relieve the wretched. As evidence of her intentions she offered Lusignan's freedom, granted at her request by the sultan.

After Lusignan's release Nerestan told him how Nerestan, almost from his birth, had been a slave in Solyma, and how he had been able to escape to fight with Louis against the Turks. Lusignan, greeting Chatillon, an old friend who had been captured with him at Caesarea, reminded the Christian knight that he, Lusignan, had seen his own wife and two

4265

sons die there, and that another son and a daughter had been taken from him. Chatillon remembered that he had baptized the daughter just before the Saracens swept her and her brother away.

When Nerestan remarked that he had been captured at the age of four, the age of Lusignan's son when he was taken, and when Lusignan noticed that Zaïre wore a cross that he had given to his wife as a present, it was revealed that Nerestan and Zaïre were Lusignan's long-lost children. Zaïre, deeply moved by this discovery, vowed to be a Christian from that moment.

Believing them to be friends from the time they were slaves together, Orosmane permitted Zaïre to meet with Nerestan. Unknown to the sultan, however, Zaïre's declaration as a Christian had inspired Nerestan to urge her to give up Orosmane altogether, even after Nerestan learned that Zaïre had hoped to wed the Turk. Zaïre was torn by emotional conflict; she knew Orosmane's virtues and loved him as a person, but she could not tolerate disappointing the hopes and faith of her brother and father, particularly after learning from Nerestan that her father was near death.

When Zaïre asked Orosmane to defer their nuptials, the sultan was amazed; her excuse, that Lusignan was dying, seemed to him insufficient. After Zaïre left in tears, Orosmane raged to Corasmin and revealed his fear that he had cause to be jealous of Nerestan. He resolved not to allow himself to be governed and deceived by Zaïre.

Orosmane confronted Zaïre again and told her that he no longer loved her; but when she wept and protested her love, he repented. Yet, when she left him, he wondered again about her virtue. When guards intercepted a letter sent to Zaïre by Nerestan, Orosmane interpreted the references to secrecy and to faithfulness as signs of a lover's passion, and he accepted Corasmin's suggestion to send the letter on to Zaïre in order that they might observe her behavior. In suppressed fury and jealousy he once more confronted Zaïre and asked her for the name of his rival. Although she insisted that she had no other master, he could no longer believe her.

Orosmane had one last faint hope that the romance was one-sided, instigated by Nerestan, but his slave's report that Zaïre had received the letter with trembling and weeping, and that she had promised to meet Nerestan that night, confirmed his fear that she loved another. Zaïre, trying desperately, in the meantime, to reconcile her duty to her family and Christianity with her love for Orosmane, hoped that he would understand and pity her.

Orosmane intercepted Zaïre at the place of her meeting with Nerestan and, calling out that she had betrayed him, stabbed her to death. When Nerestan arrived and revealed that Zaïre was his sister, the Turk was overcome with grief and remorse. After ordering Corasmin to free all the Christians, he killed himself with his dagger. Nerestan, aware of the depth of Orosmane's remorse and sensing the love that became perverted by jealousy, admitted his respect for Orosmane and lamented the sultan's death.

EL ZARCO

Type of work: Novel
Author: Ignacio Manuel Altamirano (1834-1893)
Type of plot: Romantic tragedy
Time of plot: 1861-1863
Locale: Province of Morelos, Mexico
First published: 1901

Principal characters:
NICOLAS, an Indian blacksmith
EL ZARCO, a bandit
MANUELA, in love with El Zarco
DOÑA ANTONIA, her mother
PILAR, Doña Antonia's godchild, in love with Nicolas
MARTÍN SÁNCHEZ, a rancher, El Zarco's enemy
EL TIGRE, El Zarco's lieutenant

Critique:

Ignacio Manuel Altamirano is the first Mexican who may truly be called a novelist, working with an awareness of and within limitations imposed by a clearly defined literary form. A patriot and a veteran of the War of Reform, he found the materials of his fiction in the life of that turbulent period. *El Zarco* illustrates his expressed intention to present Mexican life and to interpret faithfully the spirit of the people. It is a somber work, historial in background, deeply probing in psychological depth, and suffused with the beauty of the Mexican landscape. Two characters stand out from the background against which they move: Manuela, an impulsive, headstrong girl brought to folly and ruin by infatuation and greed, and Nicolas, an Indian representative of the class in which Altamirano saw a bright promise for the future of his nation. Completed shortly before the writer's death, the novel appeared posthumously eight years later.

The Story:

During the War of Reform, and after, bands of robber outlaws took advantage of the troubled times to overrun those districts of Mexico where the local authorities, in a land still disturbed by civil war, were powerless to make effective reprisals against them. Roaming the countryside in armed bands, the *plateados*, as they were called, waylaid and murdered travelers, kidnapped wealthy estate owners for ransom, and levied tribute on the villages and haciendas. For their amusement they often wantonly burned the canefields and inflicted brutal tortures on their prisoners.

A town terrorized in this fashion was Yautepec, a pleasant village of the *tierra caliente* in the province of Morelos. By day the people maintained lookouts in the church towers to give warning of approaching marauders; at night they barricaded themselves in their houses, so that after sunset the little town in the middle of its circling orange groves resembled a place of the dead. The bandits, some five hundred strong, had their headquarters at Xochimancas, a nearby ruined hacienda from which they made forays to ravage the whole district. Their leader was El Zarco, a man of savage temper and cruel disposition whose bloody exploits caused all respectable and decent people to fear him. The bandits sometimes entered the town and rode boldly through the streets.

On an evening in August, 1861, Doña Antonia sat in the inner courtyard of her house with her daughter Manuela and Pilar, her godchild. The two girls were plaiting flower garlands for their hair. After a time Manuela began to tease Pilar because her friend was making a wreath of orange blossoms, the flower of weddings; Manuela was twining a circlet of roses. When Manuela complained pettishly of her dull life, her mother rebuked her sharply, saying that the girl ought to forget fiestas and dances, and take a husband who would protect her. Doña Antonia's choice was Nicolas, the sober and industrious blacksmith of the estate at Atlihuayan. At this suggestion Manuela began to speak scornfully of the Indian, as she called him, and declared that she would rather have El Zarco as a suitor. She added that Nicolas might be good enough for Pilar, but she herself would never have him. Pilar blushed but said nothing.

Before Doña Antonia could reprove her daughter further, Nicolas, a nightly caller, arrived with the news that the night before the *plateados* had robbed and killed an English family traveling to Acapulco and that a cavalry detachment was being sent from Cuernavaca to pursue the bandits. Alarmed at this latest outrage, Doña Antonia decided that she and Manuela would go to Mexico City until times grew better; they would travel with the troops as their escort for part of the dangerous journey. Nicolas thought her decision a wise one for Manuela's sake.

Later, while Nicolas was on his way back to Atlihuayan, another rider was traveling toward Yautepec. The horseman was El Zarco. In the village he turned down a dark lane that led to a stone wall surrounding Doña Antonia's orange grove. Drawing rein beneath a giant sapota tree, he whistled twice. An answering whistle came from the darkness under the tree where Manuela was waiting for her lover.

El Zarco had met Manuela in Cuernavaca during a brief period when he and his men were aiding the government forces, and the two had been strongly drawn to each other. After he had established himself at Xochimancas, the bandit learned that the girl and her mother had returned to Yautepec. Through his spies in the village he had arranged to see her regularly. El Zarco found her whole-hearted devotion flattering to his vanity. Manuela, refusing to believe the stories of his violence and cruelty, saw him only as a handsome, brave caballero. Now, unwilling to leave Yautepec, she told him of Doña Antonia's plans and asked him to take her away. Before they parted that night they had arranged for him to carry her off to Xochimancas. In parting, El Zarco gave her several small boxes for safekeeping. After his departure she saw that one was bloodstained. The boxes contained a diamond ring, two bracelets, and earrings. Putting them on, she went to a pool in the garden and looked at her reflection by the light of a lantern. She buried the jewels with other gems and money that El Zarco had already entrusted to her.

The next night Manuela fled with El Zarco to his hideout, leaving behind a note in which she told her mother goodbye. Heartbroken, Doña Antonia asked Nicolas to go with her to beg that the cavalry troop from Cuernavaca would hunt down the bandits and rescue Manuela. When the commander refused, Nicolas charged the officer with shirking his duties. The blacksmith was placed under arrest and ordered held for trial.

Pilar, upset by the news of Nicolas' arrest, tried to visit him in prison but was turned back by his guards. Nicolas, hearing her pleas, realized that it was Pilar and not Manuela whom he truly loved. The authorities of Yautepec and the manager of Atlihuayan were all indignant over the treatment Nicolas had received. When the commander set out to take his prisoner to the capital, a large party accompanied the troops to see that the blacksmith received full justice. Through the intercession of the owner of Atlihuayan, Nicolas was finally released. He returned to Yautepec in time to see Doña Antonia on her deathbed, for the poor woman was dying of grief over her daughter's disgrace. After her death

Nicolas continued to ride into the village each evening, but now he went to visit Pilar.

Meanwhile, at Xochimancas, Manuela lived a different and sordid life of lawlessness and violence. Forced to associate with the disreputable women of the *plateados*, ogled and showered with lewd compliments from the men, she was at first terrified by her new surroundings. She realized at last that she had been attracted to El Zarco by infatuation and greed, not love. In particular, she was horrified by the condition of a French prisoner, tortured daily to extort from him a greater ransom. At a fiesta to celebrate one of El Zarco's raids she was forced to dance with El Tigre, a repulsive creature who told her that El Zarco would tire of her eventually and turn her over to one of his lieutenants. El Tigre intended to be the man.

A short time before, El Zarco had killed the father and son of a rancher named Martín Sánchez. Swearing revenge, Sánchez sold his property and bought arms and equipment for twenty men he recruited to track down the bandits. After he had made several successful raids on the outlaws other men were roused from their apathy and fears to join him. In an encounter at La Calavera, in which Nicolas took part, El Zarco was wounded and taken prisoner. With him was Manuela.

In spite of Martín Sánchez' protests, El Zarco cleverly arranged to have his trial held in Cuernavaca. While the prisoners were being taken there, bandits fell on the escorting troops and set El Zarco and Manuela free. Sánchez, determined to end lawlessness in the region, obtained from President Juarez authority to hang without trial any bandit who fell into his hands.

The wedding day of Pilar and Nicolas arrived at last. After the mass had been said they started by coach for Atlihuayan with friends invited to the feast to be held there. On the way they met a troop of horsemen led by Martín Sánchez, who asked the party to drive on without stopping. At that moment Manuela appeared from behind the horsemen and begged help of Nicolas and his bride. El Zarco and El Tigre, she said, had been captured and were to be executed. Martín Sánchez told how he had saved the wedding party from an ambush. Pilar, filled with pity for Manuela, wanted to take that unfortunate creature into the coach, but the distraught girl cried out that she would rather die with El Zarco than see Pilar in her wreath of orange blossoms. Saddened, the wedding party rode on.

Shot down by a firing squad, El Zarco's body was then hung from the branch of a tree. Manuela, seeing her lover dangling there, gave a loud cry and fell to the ground. Blood ran from her mouth. Several men tried to lift her but she was already dead.

ZULEIKA DOBSON

Type of work: Novel
Author: Max Beerbohm (1872-1956)
Type of plot: Romantic satire
Time of plot: Early twentieth century
Locale: Oxford, England
First published: 1911

Principal characters:

ZULEIKA DOBSON, a charmer
THE WARDEN OF JUDAS COLLEGE, her grandfather
THE DUKE OF DORSET, an Edwardian dandy
KATIE BATCH, daughter of his landlady
NOAKS, a poor student

Critique:

Sir Max Beerbohm, caricaturist, critic, novelist, and essayist of distinction, is one of the great wits of the century, a writer and artist whose cleverness is balanced by moral insight and whose irony is matched by gentle humor. *Zuleika Dobson* is his only novel. On one level it is a burlesque of Oxford undergraduate life, on another a quiet thrust at affectation and absurdity wherever they may be found. Set in the university town of Oxford during the reign of King Edward VII, the novel leads the reader a fantastic chase as he follows Zuleika's romantic achievements among impressionable undergraduates. Perhaps Beerbohm's main purpose was to ridicule sentimental novels of the Edwardian period. He does much more. The characters, especially the figure of Zuleika herself, are pointed, memorable, and fascinating. The plot is a wonder of extravagant imagination, the ending unexpected but appropriate. This novel has a place of its own in twentieth-century fiction.

The Story:

Left an orphan, lovely Zuleika Dobson became a governess. Because the older brothers of her charges always fell in love with her, however, she lost one position after another. She moved unhappily from job to job until one enamored elder son taught her a few simple tricks of magic. Then she became an entertainer at children's parties, where she interested older men if not the children.

Before long she received an offer to go on the stage, and during a long European tour she crowned success with success. Paris raved over her. Grand dukes asked her to marry them. The pope issued a bull against her. A Russian prince had her magic devices, such as the demon egg cup, cast in pure gold. Later, traveling in America, she was pursued by a fabulous millionaire. But Zuleika ignored her admirers. She wanted only to find a man impervious to her charms; with him she felt she could be happy.

Between theatrical seasons she went to visit her grandfather, the Warden of Judas College at Oxford. As usual, every man who saw Zuleika fell in love with her. One night her uncle had at dinner the wealthy, proud, handsome Duke of Dorset. Although the duke fell in love at first sight, his pride and good manners kept him from showing his true feelings. During dinner he was only casually attentive and on one occasion actually rude. Zuleika was captivated. Thinking him a man who did not love her, she herself fell in love for the first time in her life. Later that evening the duke discovered that his studs had turned the same colors as Zuleika's earrings, one black, the other pink. Abashed, the duke fled.

The next morning, paying a visit to his rooms, Zuleika was let in by his landlady's daughter Kate. When the duke, unable to restrain himself, confessed his, love, Zuleika was disappointed. On her arrival she had envied Kate the chance to be near him; now she could never feel the same toward him again. The duke, astounded by her strange attitude, tried to induce her to marry him by reciting his titles and listing his estates, houses, and servants. He told her of the ghosts who haunted his ancestral home and of the mysterious bird which always sang on the roof the day before one of his family was to die. His recital failed to impress Zuleika; in fact, she called him a snob.

The duke was chagrined when he realized that Zuleika did not want him as a husband. He was cheered, however, because she expected him to take her to the boat races that afternoon.

On their way to the races the duke and Zuleika met a great many people. The men immediately fell in love with her. The duke, whose good looks had always attracted attention, passed unnoticed. Piqued by his inability to keep her to himself, he threatened to commit suicide. The idea charmed Zuleika; no one had ever killed himself for her. But as the duke climbed the railing of the barge, she changed her mind. Catching his arm, she begged him to wait until the next day. If he would spend the day with her, she would try to make up her mind and answer his proposal.

The duke could not see her that night, however, for he was presiding at a dinner of an ancient Oxford club called the Junta. The club was most exclusive. At one time, for almost two years, the duke had been the only member. Each year he had faithfully nominated and seconded prospective members, only to find each time a blackball in the ballot box. Finally, to keep the club from becoming extinct, he had voted in two more members. That night the club was having guests. The duke, conscious of tradition and *noblesse oblige,* could not miss the dinner.

The Junta had been founded by a man named Greddon, whose lovely mistress was named Nellie O'Mora. At each meeting Nellie was toasted as the most bewitching person who had ever lived, or ever would. Rising to propose the toast, the duke was overcome by confusion. Unwilling to break with tradition or to slight his opinion of Zuleika, he resigned his position as president. His resignation was a wasted gesture. Neither the other members nor the guests could offer the toast, for they too were in love with Zuleika. The duke then confessed that he intended to die for her the next day. Not to be outdone, and wishing to imitate the duke in all things, the others decided to die with him.

Later that night the duke met Zuleika on the street. Overcome by love, he caught her in his arms. When he said that he wanted to live in order to be with her, she chided him for breaking his promise. Still later he returned and stood under her window. She emptied a pitcher of water on him. The drenching convinced the duke he was no longer held by his promise.

As news of the intended suicides spread swiftly through the colleges, the other undergraduates planned also to die for Zuleika. The next morning the duke tried to dissuade them, particularly his friend Noaks, a rough and unattractive boy whom Zuleika had noticed when she first came to Oxford. To keep his friends from dying, the duke was ready to change his own plans. Then a telegram arrived from his old butler. The legendary bird had sung the night before. The duke was now convinced. Die he must.

Everyone went merrily off to the boat races that afternoon. At last the great moment came. Calling out Zuleika's name, the duke jumped from the barge into the river. Immediately hundreds of young men ran, jumped, fell, and tottered into the water, calling her name as they went under.

That night Oxford was empty except for elderly officials and dons. Zuleika had hoped that perhaps one man had not loved her, perhaps one young man was left in Oxford. And Noaks was still in his room. Having turned his ankle, he had been unable to go and die with the others. When she found him hiding, ashamed, in his room, he became engaged to Katie Batch, who before had loved only the duke. Zuleika, seeing Noaks at his window, called to him in delight. Katie appeared, however, and embarrassed Zuleika by telling her that the duke had died only to keep his ducal promise, not for love of Zuleika, because it was Katie he had really loved. Noaks, convinced that Katie did not love him, jumped from the window. The last undergraduate in Oxford had perished.

Discouraged because she could find no man insensible to her charms, Zuleika returned to her grandfather's house. Then, struck by a sudden idea, she ordered a special train to take her to Cambridge. Another university meant, perhaps, another chance.

AUTHOR INDEX

ABÉLARD, PIERRE
Historia calàmitatum, VI—1566
ABOUT, EDMOND FRANÇOIS
King of the Mountains, The, VII—1902
ADAMS, HENRY
Education of Henry Adams, The, IV—1030
ADAMS, JOHN
Defense of the Constitutions, A, IV—862
ADDISON, JOSEPH
Sir Roger de Coverley Papers, The, XIII—3503
AESCHYLUS
House of Atreus, The, VI—1630
Persians, The, XI—2811
Prometheus Bound, XI—3081
Seven Against Thebes, XIII—3429
Suppliants, The, XIV—3661
AESOP
Aesop's Fables, I—36
AINSWORTH, WILLIAM HARRISON
Jack Sheppard, VII—1789
Old St. Paul's, X—2641
Tower of London, The, XIV—3838
Windsor Castle, XV—4161
ALAIN-FOURNIER
Wanderer, The, XV—4070
ALARCON, PEDRO ANTONIO DE
Three-Cornered Hat, The, XIV—3760
ALCOTT, LOUISA MAY
Little Women, VIII—2075
ALDINGTON, RICHARD
Death of a Hero, IV—828
ALDRICH, THOMAS BAILEY
Story of a Bad Boy, The, XIII—3617
ALEGRÍA, CIRO
Broad and Alien Is the World, II—410
ALEMÁN, MATEO
Guzmán de Alfarache, VI—1435
ALLEN, HERVEY
Anthony Adverse, I—147
ALTAMIRANO, IGNACIO MANUEL
Zarco, El, XV—4267
AMADO, JORGE
Violent Land, The, XV—4025
AMICIS, EDMONDO DE
Romance of a Schoolmaster, The, XII—3262
AMMERS-KÜLLER, JOHANNA VAN
Rebel Generation, The, XII—3135
ANDERSEN, HANS CHRISTIAN
Andersen's Fairy Tales, I—116
ANDERSON, MAXWELL
Winterset, XV—4174
ANDERSON, SHERWOOD
Dark Laughter, III—800
Poor White, XI—3010
Winesburg, XV—4165
ANDREYEV, LEONID
Seven Who Were Hanged, The, XIII—3443

ANNUNZIO, GABRIELLE D',
see D'ANNUNZIO
ANOUILH, JEAN
Ring Round the Moon, XII—3225
APULEIUS, LUCIUS
Golden Ass of Lucius Apuleius, The, V—1346
AQUINAS, THOMAS
Summa Theologica, XIII—3652
ARETINO, PIETRO
Courtesan, The, III—714
ARIHARA NO NARIHIRA
Tales of Ise, XIV—3682
ARIOSTO, LUDOVICO
Orlando Furioso, X—2678
Suppositi, I, XIV—3666
ARISTOPHANES
Acharnians, The, I—21
Birds, The, II—338
Clouds, The, III—614
Ecclesiazusae, The, IV—1026
Frogs, The, V—1280
Knights, The, VII—1927
Lysistrata, VIII—2143
Peace, The, X—2761
Plutus, XI—2912
Thesmophoriazusae, The, XIV—3747
Wasps, The, XV—4090
ARISTOTLE
Poetics, The, XI—2923
ARNOLD, MATTHEW
Sohrab and Rustum, XIII—3541
ARTSYBASHEV, MIKHAIL
Sanine, XII—3340
ASCH, SHOLEM
Apostle, The, I—164
Nazarene, The, X—2530
AUDEN, W. H.
Poetry of Auden, The, XI—2926
AUGUSTINE, SAINT
Confessions, III—646
AUSTEN, JANE
Emma, IV—1061
Mansfield Park, VIII—2232
Northanger Abbey, X—2584
Persuasion, XI—2813
Pride and Prejudice, XI—3049
Sense and Sensibility, XIII—3420
AZUELA, MARIANO
Underdogs, The, XIV—3967

BACCHELLI, RICCARDO
Mill on the Po, The, IX—2361
BACON, SIR FRANCIS
Essays, IV—1103
New Atlantis, X—2536
BALE, JOHN
King John, VII—1890

I

II

AUTHOR INDEX

AUTHOR INDEX

AUTHOR INDEX

RIMBAUD, ARTHUR
Season in Hell, A, XIII—3397
ROBERTS, ELIZABETH MADOX
Great Meadow, The, V—1388
Time of Man, The, XIV—3787
ROBERTSON, THOMAS WILLIAM
Caste, II—502
ROBINSON, EDWIN ARLINGTON
Man Against the Sky, The, VIII—2200
Tristram, XIV—3890
ROJAS, FERNANDO DE
Celestina, II—526
ROLLAND, ROMAIN
Jean-Christophe, VII—1803
RÖLVAAG, O. E.
Giants in the Earth, V—1326
Peder Victorious, X—2766
RONSARD, PIERRE DE
Poetry of Ronsard, The, XI—2987
ROSSETTI, CHRISTINA
Poetry of Christina Rossetti, The, XI—2941
ROSSETTI, DANTE GABRIEL
Poetry of Dante Gabriel Rossetti, The,
XI—2944
ROSTAND, EDMOND
Cyrano de Bergerac, III—776
L'Aiglon, VII—1947
ROUSSEAU, JEAN JACQUES
Confessions, III—649
Émile, IV—1053
New Héloïse, The, X—2541
ROWLEY, WILLIAM see MIDDLETON
AND ROWLEY
RUIZ DE ALARCON, JUAN
Truth Suspected, XIV—3907
RUSKIN, JOHN
King of the Golden River, The, VII—1899
RUSSELL, W. CLARK
Wreck of the Grosvenor, The, XV—4236
RYDBERG, VIKTOR
Last Athenian, The, VII—1956

SACHS, HANS
Wandering Scholar from Paradise, The,
XV—4076
SACKVILLE, THOMAS, see NORTON AND
SACKVILLE
SAINTE-BEUVE, CHARLES AUGUSTIN
Volupté, XV—4056
SAINT-EXUPÉRY, ANTOINE DE
Night Flight, X—2566
SAKI
Unbearable Bassington, The, XIV—3940
SALTEN, FELIX
Bambi, I—248
SÁNCHEZ, FLORENCIO
Gringa La, VI—1413
SAND, GEORGE
Consuelo, III—680
Indiana, VII—1735
SANDBURG, CARL
Abraham Lincoln, I—9
People, Yes, The, X—2797
Remembrance Rock, XII—3168
SANTAYANA, GEORGE
Last Puritan, The, VIII—1976
Scepticism and Animal Faith, XII—3368
SANTO KYODEN
Inazuma-byôshi, VII—1726
SAPPHO
Ode to Aphrodite, X—2600
SAROYAN, WILLIAM
Human Comedy, The, VI—1663

SARTRE, JEAN-PAUL
Nausea, X—2527
SASSOON, SIEGFRIED
Memoirs of a Fox-Hunting Man, IX—2314
Memoirs of an Infantry Officer, IX—2323
SCHILLER, JOHANN CHRISTOPH
FRIEDRICH VON
Don Carlos, IV—951
Wallenstein, XV—4067
William Tell, XV—4155
SCHOPENHAUER, ARTHUR
World as Will and Idea, The, XV—4221
SCHREINER, OLIVE
Story of an African Farm, The, XIII—3623
SCOTT, MICHAEL
Tom Cringle's Log, XIV—3822
SCOTT, SIR WALTER
Antiquary, The, I—152
Bride of Lammermoor, The, II—396
Fair Maid of Perth, The, V—1170
Fortunes of Nigel, The, V—1253
Guy Mannering, VI—1429
Heart of Midlothian, The, VI—1490
Ivanhoe, VII—1783
Kenilworth, VII—1880
Lady of the Lake, The, VII—1940
Lay of the Last Minstrel, The, VIII—1991
Marmion, IX—2258
Old Mortality, X—2638
Quentin Durward, XII—3102
Rob Roy, XII—3244
St. Ronan's Well, XII—3322
Talisman, The, XIV—3691
Waverley, XV—4094
Woodstock, XV—4213
SCUDÉRY, MADELEINE DE
Artamène, I—197
SENECA, LUCIUS ANNAEUS
Thyestes, XIV—3782
SHAKESPEARE, WILLIAM
All's Well That Ends Well, I—79
Antony and Cleopatra, I—155
As You Like It, I—205
Comedy of Errors, III—632
Coriolanus, III—686
Cymbeline, III—773
Hamlet, Prince of Denmark, VI—1449
Henry the Eighth, VI—1517
Henry the Fifth, VI—1520
Henry the Fourth, Part One, VI—1522
Henry the Fourth, Part Two, VI—1525
Henry the Sixth, Part One, VI—1528
Henry the Sixth, Part Two, VI—1531
Henry the Sixth, Part Three, VI—1534
Julius Caesar, VII—1855
King John, VII—1893
King Lear, VII—1896
Love's Labour's Lost, VIII—2123
Macbeth, VIII—2150
Measure for Measure, IX—2292
Merchant of Venice, The, IX—2331
Merry Wives of Windsor, The, IX—2334
Midsummer Night's Dream, A, IX—2353
Much Ado about Nothing, IX—2481
Othello, X—2697
Pericles, Prince of Tyre, X—2806
Rape of Lucrece, The, XII—3122
Richard the Second, XII—3208
Richard the Third, XII—3211
Romeo and Juliet, XII—3286
Taming of the Shrew, The, XIV—3699
Tempest, The, XIV—3717
Timon of Athens, XIV—3790
Titus Andronicus, XIV—3800
Troilus and Cressida, XIV—3898
Twelfth Night, XIV—3915
Two Gentlemen of Verona, XIV—3923
Venus and Adonis, XV—3996
Winter's Tale, The, XV—4171

AUTHOR INDEX

SUDERMANN, HERMANN
  Dame Care, III—780
  Song of Songs, The, XIII—3559
SUE, EUGENE
  Mysteries of Paris, The, IX—2495
  Wandering Jew, The, XV—4073
SUETONIUS TRANQUILLUS, GAIUS
  Lives of the Caesars, VIII—2078
SURTEES, ROBERT SMITH
  Handley Cross, VI—1454
  Hillingdon Hall, VI—1560
  Jorrocks' Jaunts and Jollities, VII—1832
  Mr. Facey Romford's Hounds, IX—2394
  Mr. Sponge's Sporting Tour, IX—2405
SWEDENBORG, EMANUEL
  Divine Love and Wisdom, IV—921
SWIFT, JONATHAN
  Gulliver's Travels, VI—1426
SWINBURNE, ALGERNON CHARLES
  Atalanta in Calydon, I—218
SWINNERTON, FRANK
  Nocturne, X—2582
SYNGE, JOHN MILLINGTON
  Deirdre of the Sorrows, IV—867
  Playboy of the Western World, XI—2904

TACITUS, CORNELIUS
  Annals of Tacitus, The, I—137
TAINE, HIPPOLYTE
  Philosophy of Art, XI—2842
TARKINGTON, BOOTH
  Alice Adams, I—60
  Kate Fennigate, VII—1878
  Monsieur Beaucaire, IX—2449
  Seventeen, XIII—3445
TASSO, TORQUATO
  Jerusalem Delivered, VII—1809
TAYLOR, EDWARD
  Poetical Works of Edward Taylor, The,
    XI—2920
TEGNÉR, ESAIAS
  Frithiof's Saga, V—1278
TENNYSON, ALFRED
  Enoch Arden, IV—1072
  Idylls of the King, The, VII—1703
TERENCE
  Andria, I—121
  Brothers, The, II—416
  Eunuch, The, V—1128
  Phormio, XI—2853
  Self-Tormentor, The, XIII—3417
THACKERAY, WILLIAM MAKEPEACE
  Barry Lyndon, II—270
  Henry Esmond, VI—1514
  Newcomes, The, X—2546
  Pendennis, X—2783
  Vanity Fair, XV—3984
  Virginians, The, XV—4037
THEOCRITUS
  Poetry of Theocritus, The, XI—2996
THOMAS, DYLAN
  Collected Poems, 1934-1952, III—622
THOMAS A KEMPIS
  Imitation of Christ, The, VII—1716
THOMPSON, DANIEL PIERCE
  Green Mountain Boys, The, VI—1405
THOREAU, HENRY DAVID
  Walden, XV—4064
THUCYDIDES
  History of the Peloponnesian War, VI—1587
THURBER, JAMES
  My Life and Hard Times, IX—2492
TOLSTOY, COUNT LEO
  Anna Karénina, I—131

Cossacks, The, III—692
Death of Ivan Ilyich, The, IV—833
Kreutzer Sonata, The, VII—1929
Power of Darkness, The, XI—3030
Resurrection, XII—3179
War and Peace, XV—4078
TOMLINSON, H. M.
  Sea and the Jungle, The, XIII—3385
TOURNEUR, CYRIL
  Revenger's Tragedy, The, XII—3191
TOYNBEE, ARNOLD
  Study of History, A, XIII—3649
TROLLOPE, ANTHONY
  Barchester Towers, II—257
  Doctor Thorne, IV—937
  Framley Parsonage, V—1265
  Last Chronicle of Barset, The, VIII—1959
  Orley Farm, X—2686
  Phineas Finn, XI—2845
  Phineas Redux, XI—2848
  Small House at Allington, The, XIII—3523
  Vicar of Bullhampton, The, XV—3998
  Warden, The, XV—4085
TROWBRIDGE, JOHN TOWNSEND
  Cudjo's Cave, III—763
TSAO HSUEH-CHIN
  Dream of the Red Chamber, IV—991
TURGENEV, IVAN
  Fathers and Sons, V—1198
  House of Gentlefolk, A, VI—1633
  Month in the Country, A, IX—2460
  Smoke, XIII—3530
  Virgin Soil, XV—4028
TWAIN, MARK
  Connecticut Yankee at King Arthur's Court, A,
    III—668
  Huckleberry Finn, VI—1654
  Life on the Mississippi, VIII—2046
  Prince and the Pauper, The, XI—3056
  Roughing It, XII—3301
  Tom Sawyer, XIV—3829
TWAIN, MARK and
WARNER, CHARLES DUDLEY
  Gilded Age, The, V—1331

UDALL, NICHOLAS
  Ralph Roister Doister, XII—3114
UNDSET, SIGRID
  Axe, The, I—236
  In the Wilderness, VII—1723
  Kristin Lavransdatter, VII—1932
  Snake Pit, XIII—3533
  Son Avenger, The, XIII—3546
UNKNOWN
  Abraham and Isaac, I—7
  Arabian Nights' Entertainments, The, I—172
  Aucassin and Nicolette, I—221
  Bevis of Hampton, II—320
  Circle of Chalk, The, III—593
  Epic of Gilgamesh, The, IV—1080
  Everyman, V—1153
  Finn Cycle, The, V—1221
  Grettir the Strong, VI—1409
  Guy of Warwick, VI—1432
  Havelok the Dane, VI—1476
  Huon de Bordeaux, VII—1675
  Lazarillo de Tormes, VIII—1994
  Mabinogion, The, VIII—2145
  Mahabharata, The, VIII—2177
  Nibelungenlied, The, X—2549
  Pilgrimage of Charlemagne, The, XI—2873
  Poem of the Cid, XI—2914
  Reynard the Fox, XII—3200
  Robin Hood's Adventures, XII—3247
  Second Shepherds' Play, The, XIII—3403
  Sir Gawain and the Green Knight, XIII—3498
  Song of Roland, The, XIII—3556
  Star of Seville, The, XIII—3604
  Story of Burnt Njal, The, XIII—3626

XV

AUTHOR INDEX